To Julian,

With deep gratitude for all
that you have done – both in the
example & inspiration of your own work,
and in the encouragement & guidance
behind this book!

Very best wishes,

Benedict

Music, Subjectivity, and Schumann

The concept of subjectivity is one of the most popular in recent scholarly accounts of music; it is also one of the obscurest and most ill-defined. Multifaceted and hard to pin down, subjectivity nevertheless serves an important, if not indispensable purpose, underpinning various assertions made about music and its effect on us. We may not be exactly sure what subjectivity is, but much of the reception of Western music over the last two centuries is premised upon it. *Music, Subjectivity, and Schumann* offers a critical examination of the notion of musical subjectivity and the first extended account of its applicability to one of the composers with whom it is most closely associated. Adopting a fluid and multivalent approach to a topic situated at the intersection of musicology, philosophy, literature, and cultural history, it seeks to provide a critical refinement of this idea and to elucidate both its importance and limits.

BENEDICT TAYLOR is Reader in Music at the University of Edinburgh and editor of *Music & Letters*. His publications include *The Melody of Time: Music and Temporality in the Romantic Era* (2015) and, as editor, *Rethinking Mendelssohn* (2020) and *The Cambridge Companion to Music and Romanticism* (2021).

Music, Subjectivity, and Schumann

BENEDICT TAYLOR

University of Edinburgh

CAMBRIDGE
UNIVERSITY PRESS

University Printing House, Cambridge CB2 8BS, United Kingdom

One Liberty Plaza, 20th Floor, New York, NY 10006, USA

477 Williamstown Road, Port Melbourne, VIC 3207, Australia

314–321, 3rd Floor, Plot 3, Splendor Forum, Jasola District Centre,
New Delhi – 110025, India

103 Penang Road, #05–06/07, Visioncrest Commercial, Singapore 238467

Cambridge University Press is part of the University of Cambridge.

It furthers the University's mission by disseminating knowledge in the pursuit of
education, learning, and research at the highest international levels of excellence.

www.cambridge.org
Information on this title: www.cambridge.org/9781009158084
DOI: 10.1017/9781009158091

First published 2022

A catalogue record for this publication is available from the British Library.

Library of Congress Cataloging-in-Publication Data
Names: Taylor, Benedict, 1981– author.
Title: Music, subjectivity, and Schumann / Benedict Taylor.
Description: [1.] | New York : Cambridge University Press, 2022. | Includes bibliographical
references and index.
Identifiers: LCCN 2021055094 (print) | LCCN 2021055095 (ebook) | ISBN 9781009158084
(hardback) | ISBN 9781009158091 (ebook)
Subjects: LCSH: Schumann, Robert, 1810–1856. Criticism and interpretation. | Music – 19th
century – Philosophy and aesthetics. | Music – 19th century – Analysis, appreciation. |
Subjectivity. | Self (Philosophy)
Classification: LCC ML410.S4 T139 2022 (print) | LCC ML410.S4 (ebook) | DDC 780.92–
dc23
LC record available at https://lccn.loc.gov/2021055094
LC ebook record available at https://lccn.loc.gov/2021055095

ISBN 978-1-009-15808-4 Hardback

Contents

Examples

Acknowledgements

This book has slumbered for longer than I probably intended before reaching the light of day. The first ideas go back to a train journey home from Edinburgh in July 2013, a time during which I was just finishing my second book, *The Melody of Time*. Slowly, what might have been a superfluous chapter treating the seemingly opaque idea of subjectivity in relation to time grew into a book in its own right. That such reckless expansion might occur was an eventuality foreseen by me at the time, but I foolishly dismissed it as unlikely to happen; of course, it did in the end, as I knew deep down it always would. I'm still not entirely sure whether this was a good idea, but at least I don't have to go through all the work of writing it again. I recall from these early stages a stimulating discussion with Michael Phillips that convinced me that the subject was worth tackling, though the precise details of what we came up with faded from my memory before I had time to make note of them; then again, the philosophical ambition of those ideas was such that it was probably easier this way. Conversations with Julian Johnson over several breakfasts in Cambridge, Massachusetts in early 2015 also proved inspiring and helped me crystallise the design of the resulting book.

The chapters were finally written between 2016 and 2019, a time in which many things in the world seem to have taken a decided turn for the worse, and several who were with us then are now no more. Still, there are fond memories of people who have contributed to the formation of this book. Daniel Chua offered generous hospitality and stimulating discussion in Hong Kong in August 2016; Dean Sutcliffe similarly provided valuable observations on the historical application of the idea of subjectivity, and Scott Burnham was ever supportive and helpful. A wine-fuelled evening in Edinburgh with Ceri Owen led to an unplanned co-edited special issue of *19th-Century Music*, for which I was opportunely forced to bring together several of my ideas relating to Eichendorff, Schumann, and the problem of subjectivity. The resulting article was intended to form part of the larger book I was then planning to write, though in the end the overlap was slighter than originally assumed, probably to the benefit of both pieces. I am especially grateful for the Institute for Advanced Study Berlin for giving me a much needed respite from six years of emails, administration, and teaching through a fellowship at the *Wissenschaftskolleg* in the leafy haven of Grunewald in 2019–20, which finally allowed me to complete the book. I would like to extend my particular gratitude to Achille Varzi, who generously read the whole manuscript and offered much helpful advice on the philosophical side of things, as well as Karol Berger and Michael Steinberg.

Parts of this work were presented at the International Musicological Society Conference in Tokyo, March 2017, and at colloquia and lectures in Queen's University Belfast, King's College London, Heidelberg, Berlin, and Leipzig, and I would like to thank all those who offered comments and suggestions on these occasions. Finally, Kate Brett has been a constantly supportive and encouraging editor at Cambridge University Press, and without her desire to see this book to print it might have been kept hidden from sight for at least another decade, if not forever.

Abbreviations

Briefwechsel	Clara and Robert Schumann, *Briefwechsel: Kritische Gesamtausgabe*, ed. Eva Weissweiler, 3 vols. (Basel and Frankfurt: Stroemfeld/Roter Stern, 1984–2001).
GS	Robert Schumann, *Gesammelte Schriften über Musik und Musiker*, ed. Martin Kreisig, 2 vols. (Leipzig: Breitkopf & Härtel, 1949).
Neue Folge	Robert Schumann, *Briefe: Neue Folge*, ed. Gustav Jansen, 2nd ed. (Leipzig: Breitkopf & Härtel, 1904).
SB	Clara and Robert Schumann, *Schumann Briefedition*, ed. Michael Heinemann, Thomas Synofzik, et al., 50 vols. (Cologne: Dohr, 2008–[25]).
Tagebücher	Robert Schumann, *Tagebücher*, ed. Georg Eismann and Gerd Nauhaus, 3 vols. (Leipzig: Deutsche Verlag für Musik, 1971–82).

All citations from letters have been given from *SB* where available. In the case of the correspondence between Clara and Robert Schumann, these have been supplemented by the relevant *Briefwechsel* page numbers. Letters not yet released in the ongoing *SB* edition are cited from the earlier *Neue Folge* or other specific source used.

Preamble

Schumann, Subjectivity

Oh, that I were
the viewless spirit of a lovely sound,
A living voice, a breathing harmony,
A bodiless enjoyment – born and dying
with the blest tone that made me![1]

In one of the most famous utterances from Byron's *Manfred*, the eponymous protagonist, standing perilously atop a mountain peak in the Alps and set to throw himself off into oblivion far below, longs to be transformed into the musical strain he hears piping away in the distance. Desperately seeking to escape from himself, to flee from his own guilt-ridden existence, the tormented anti-hero wishes to *become* music – to be at one with its tones, living and dying with the irresistible flow of melody, following its inevitable course from sound into silence. Short of complete annihilation of his being, the only solace he can envisage is that of losing his sense of self through such immersion in the living presence of sound that his spirit may fuse with that of music. In such intense experiences as this, as Byron's tortured protagonist recognises, the emotionally susceptible human subject may hear music so deeply that, as T. S. Eliot put it, 'you are the music, while the music lasts'.[2] Manfred's case exemplifies perhaps the ultimate degree of what in this study will be called musical subjectivity: not conceiving music to be *like* the self but desiring the self to *be* music.

Byron's lines form an apt starting point for this present book. For the work in which they are found inspired Robert Schumann to what, by his own account, was one of his most personal creations, the incidental music he wrote in 1848 to Byron's drama.[3] *Manfred* is also a piece which foregrounds a particularly Romantic notion of subjectivity: not only the nineteenth century's concern with the alienated individual, with the reality of subjective feeling and an inescapably egocentric perspective on the world,

---

[1] Byron, *Manfred*, Act I, Scene 2, ll. 52–56.
[2] T. S. Eliot, 'The Dry Salvages', V, from *Four Quartets*.
[3] See Wilhelm Joseph von Wasielewski, *Robert Schumann: Eine Biographie* (1858; revised fourth edition, Leipzig: Breitkopf and Härtel, 1906), p. 398.

but with the *sound* of subjectivity, with the roles music and voice may play in constructing a sense of living presence, identity, and recognition – the distinction between music and speech, sound and silence, presence and absence, .between the living and the dead.

The nineteenth century, as many writers would have it, is 'the age of subjectivity'. After the universalism, sociability, and appeal to the *sensus communis* of the Enlightenment, Romanticism firmly placed the burden of philosophic truth back onto the individual, onto the thinking, feeling, meaning-making subject who constitutes the world for itself and provides its own criterion of authenticity.[4] In this era of subjective surplus, it was the Germans most of all who gained a reputation for pre-eminence in gazing inward into the depths of the self. 'We prefer to live in the inwardness of emotion and of thinking' proposed their most celebrated thinker of the time: 'our mind, more than that of any other European nation, is in general turned inwards'.[5] It was moreover in music that many German intellectuals and artists found the ideal form of articulation for this sense of subjective inwardness and interior depth – music, of all the arts, being in their estimation the most subjective. And of all composers during this period (and perhaps ever since), it is surely Robert Schumann who has most often been characterised, for better or for worse, through recourse to the notion of subjectivity.

The rhetoric of subjectivity has accompanied the life and music of Schumann throughout the last two centuries. By his own account, the young Schumann felt there was 'more subjectivity than objectivity' in his judgements and work, discerning that his temperament expressed itself more strongly in feeling and imagination than in the power of external observation.[6] Even within his lifetime, critics of radically opposed persuasions would pick up on this perception. For Franz Brendel, Schumann stands as 'subjectivity in its most pointed form'. The composer reveals himself in his music as 'a subject focused entirely on itself, one that lives and breathes exclusively in its own inwardness . . . an individuality that

---

4 See, for instance, Isaiah Berlin, *The Roots of Romanticism*, ed. Henry Hardy (London: Chatto & Windus, 1999); Andrew Bowie, *Aesthetics and Subjectivity: From Kant to Nietzsche* (Manchester: Manchester University Press, 2003); Michael P. Steinberg, *Listening to Reason: Culture, Subjectivity, and Nineteenth-Century Music* (Princeton: Princeton University Press, 2004).

5 Georg Wilhelm Friedrich Hegel, *Philosophy of Mind* (*Encyclopaedia*, Pt III), trans. W. Wallace and A. V. Miller (Oxford: Clarendon Press, 2007), §394, p. 49.

6 Robert Schumann, *Tagebücher*, ed. Georg Eismann and Gerd Nauhaus, 3 vols. (Leipzig: Deutscher Verlag für Musik, 1971–82), vol. I (1827–38), p. 242 ('Sein Temperament . . . aeußert sich mehr als Empfindungs, denn als Anschauungsvermögen, daher mehr Subjektiv.[ist] als Objekt[ivist] in seinen Urtheilen u. Producten; das Gefühl starker, als das Streben').

expresses only itself and its personal emotional states, [depicting] the world only as far as the Self has been touched by it'.[7] His nemesis, Eduard Hanslick, did not begrudge Brendel the general point. Schumann, thought Hanslick, was 'not for the majority but for individuals': his works are 'too interior and strange . . . too deep, too simple'.[8]

Already in his lifetime, then, Schumann emerges in critical reception as an inward-looking, self-absorbed figure, the creator of highly personal music whose veiled secrets and whimsical individuality bespeak the subjectivity of its creator. Far from receding as Schumann's music became ever more firmly established and better comprehended by a growing public in the decades after his death, such portrayals would solidify into a truism. His first biographer, Wilhelm Joseph von Wasielewski, introduced his 1858 study by noting how the music of his former friend and colleague constantly 'points back to the subjective quality of the creating artist'. 'The productions of his mind never became objective, and never broke loose, or freed themselves from his individual self.'[9] These same themes would be taken up and perpetuated by most subsequent writers. August Reissmann, writing in 1865, held that Schumann 'never regarded music otherwise than as the art of representing those things which stirred his soul', just as Hubert Parry, two decades later, proposed that 'the natural bent of his disposition seemed to be to look inwards'.[10] Indeed, in William Henry Hadow's opinion the composer was if anything 'too intensely subjective' – to this extent displaying 'the same strengths and weakness as Byron', claimed Hadow, an artist 'with whom he has often been compared'.[11] This link between Schumann and subjectivity has been perpetuated throughout numerous textbooks and popular histories down to the present day, showing little sign of diminishing even now.

[7] Franz Brendel, 'Robert Schumann with Reference to Mendelssohn-Bartholdy and the Development of Modern Music in General (1845)', trans. Jürgen Thym, in R. Larry Todd (ed.), *Schumann and His World* (Princeton: Princeton University Press, 1994), pp. 334, 323–4.

[8] Eduard Hanslick, *Sämtliche Schriften: Historisch-kritische Ausgabe*, ed. Dietmar Strauß (Vienna: Böhlau, 1993–), vol. I (*Aufsätze und Rezensionen 1844–48*), p. 106 (quoted by Leon Botstein, 'History, Rhetoric, and the Self: Robert Schumann and Music Making in German-Speaking Europe, 1800–1860', in R. Larry Todd (ed.), *Schumann and his World* (Princeton: Princeton University Press, 1994), p. 4).

[9] Wasielewski, *Robert Schumann*, p. viii, translation taken from the English edition, *Life of Robert Schumann*, trans. A. L. Alger (Boston: Oliver Ditson, 1871), p. 8.

[10] August Reissmann, *Robert Schumann: Sein Leben und Seine Werke* (Berlin: Guttentag, 1865), p. 34; C. Hubert H. Parry, *Studies of Great Composers* (London: George Routledge & Sons, 1887), p. 317.

[11] William Henry Hadow, *Studies in Modern Music: Hector Berlioz, Robert Schumann, Richard Wagner* (London: Seeley and Company, 1893), p. 224.

This inclination is epitomised in one of the most celebrated of all characterisations of the composer, Friedrich Nietzsche's famous barb in *Beyond Good and Evil* (1886). Schumann, 'who took himself seriously, and from the start was hard to take', possessed 'a dangerous tendency (doubly dangerous among Germans) to quiet lyricism and intoxication of feeling'. Characterised in passive, self-absorbed terms, Schumann is memorably dismissed as that strange figure, 'half Werther, half Jean Paul, fleeing into the "Saxon Switzerland" of his soul'. 'Is it not good fortune', wonders Nietzsche aloud, 'a relief, a liberation, that precisely this Schumannesque Romanticism has been overcome?'[12] As so often with Nietzsche, outward scorn masks a deeper personal affinity. The Saxon-born philosopher had adored much of Schumann's music as an adolescent and would ultimately share the same unhappy fate as his predecessor, spending the final years of his life insane.

When it comes to loving Schumann, of course, few figures have done so more openly than the twentieth-century French theorist Roland Barthes. And for Barthes, Schumann is similarly characterised by the language of subjectivity – 'the musician of solitary intimacy, of the amorous and imprisoned soul *that speaks to itself*'.[13] As this example underscores, even in a poststructuralist climate where the notion of the subject has been undermined, or when the search for full selfhood appears to result inevitably in failure, Schumann remains the paradigmatic case of subjectivity. Hence Barthes may speak of the composer's early piano cycle *Carnaval* as 'the theatre of the decentring of the subject', while for the Lacanian thinker Slavoj Žižek, 'the very formal structure of Schumann's music expresses the paradox of modern subjectivity: the bar – the impossibility of "becoming oneself", of actualizing one's identity'.[14]

One of the most prominent factors contributing to the perceived subjective quality of Schumann's music lies in how – at least in the popular imagination – his life and work are bound inextricably together. Already in

---

[12] Friedrich Nietzsche, *Jenseits von Gut und Böse*, §245, in *Sämtliche Werke*, ed. Giorgio Colli and Mazzino Montinari, 15 vols. (Berlin and New York: de Gruyter, 1980), vol. V, p. 188. 'Saxon Switzerland' is the name given to a range of high peaks in Saxony that rival the Alps in scenic impact (a feature that would be utilised by Romantic painters such as Caspar David Friedrich in his *Wanderer über dem Nebelmeer* and Carl Gustav Carus in the picture given on this book's cover). Both Schumann and Nietzsche were natives of Saxony.

[13] Roland Barthes, 'Loving Schumann ', in *The Responsibility of Forms: Critical Essays on Music, Art, and Representation*, trans. Richard Howard (Oxford: Blackwell, 1985), p. 293, emphasis mine.

[14] *Ibid.*, p. 296; Slavoj Žižek, 'Robert Schumann: The Romantic Anti-Humanist', in *The Plague of Fantasies* (London: Verso, 1997), p. 205.

Wasielewski's pioneering account of the composer, the author informs his readers that 'Robert Schumann was so rare a nature, that his creative powers, especially at the outset, can be fully understood and correctly judged only by a knowledge of his life and its manifold conditions.'[15] One hundred and forty years later his modern biographer John Daverio would likewise claim that 'art and life are perhaps more closely interwoven in Schumann's music than in that of any other composer of the nineteenth century'.[16] To a greater degree than with almost any other composer, the biographical subject who created it is commonly felt to be present behind Schumann's music. Accounts of the composer's life are dominated as to an equal degree are those of his music by the story of his love for Clara Wieck and how the two heroically overcame her wicked father's scruples to marry – a love story acquiring almost mythic status in music history. Such associations are only aided by the composer's tendency to encode the names of the loves in his life into his music in the form of musical ciphers, dancing letters, and musical sphinxes – to the extent that posterity will discover coded messages enshrining his beloved's name in his music (the ubiquitous 'Clara' theme) even when there is no evidence for this supposition whatsoever.[17] (This interweaving of life and art becomes especially problematic, of course, when we reach the composer's final mental illness, the works of Schumann's later years having long lain under the dubious shadow cast back on them retrospectively by his mental breakdown in the early months of 1854.)

Moreover, the subjective quality of Schumann's music, the sense that the composer is somehow present within his work, is often accompanied by the feeling of a personal relationship with his inner world as listeners. Schumann appears to speak intimately to each and every one of those who love his music. A recent account by cellist and confirmed *Schumannianer* Steven Isserlis may stand as representative of a popular view of this quality. For Isserlis, Schumann 'was perhaps the ultimate romantic, confessional composer . . . much of his music explored his own deeply private world . . . allow[ing] us to eavesdrop on his inner life'.[18]

---

[15] Wasielewski, *Robert Schumann*, pp. vii–viii / *Life of Robert Schumann*, p. 7.

[16] John Daverio, *Robert Schumann: Herald of a "New Poetic Age"* (New York: Oxford University Press, 1997), p. 131; such views are also mentioned, and problematised, at the start of Daverio's volume.

[17] The idea was popularised by Eric Sams in a series of pieces in *The Musical Times* from the late 1960s on; a strong challenge to it was issued by John Daverio, though despite its questionable basis the 'Clara theme' has proved hard to eradicate from popular writing on the composer.

[18] Steven Isserlis, 'In defence of Schumann', *The Guardian*, 1 July 2010. Isserlis appeals to a comparable claim made rather earlier by Sir Thomas Beecham: 'When we listen to other

Similarly, pianist Jonathan Biss, writing in the same newspaper a few years later, contends that Schumann's music 'is not only lofty, but personal. Excruciatingly personal. So much of its shattering emotional power comes from the feeling it conveys that confidences are being shared – that Schumann is disclosing the sorts of truths one often hides even from oneself.'[19] What both musicians are expressing is that peculiar quality many of us also feel when listening to this music, that we are eavesdropping on Schumann's innermost thoughts, on his very self. Or is it in fact on ourselves?

Perhaps owing to this personal quality, this sense of identification on the part of performers and listeners with the subjectivity of the music and that of the composer behind it, and the evident vulnerability of both, Schumann inspires highly protective, personal feelings of affection on the part of his followers. Even if he occasionally appears to fall short, his music is still loved for what we think it is trying to do, for the fragile subject we faintly discern resounding behind the notes, and it will be defended passionately by devoted *Schumannianer* against critical attack. The subjectivity of Schumann's music arises from the sense that there is something deeply personal inside it, something personal to us too; that its idiosyncrasies may be understood by those who hear that 'softer tone' that resounds for them alone, in whose presence, so it seems, they hear something of themselves.

Aims of This Study

From his own time down to the present day, then, Schumann has routinely been associated with all things subjective, with intimacy, interiority, emotionality, idiosyncrasy, with music that says something about our innermost, most private sense of self. For critics, intellectuals, musicians, and public alike, Schumann signifies subjectivity. Set against this cultural background, the present study seeks to explore and interrogate the now-conventional association between Schumann's music and the idea of

composers', holds Beecham, 'we are seldom forgetful that the author of the discourse is addressing himself to a thousand or two others beside ourselves. There is none of this platform manner about Schumann, who has accomplished the miraculous feat of clothing exquisite and delicate fancies in subtle and secret phrases that each one of us feels to have been devised for his own especial understanding.' *A Mingled Chime: Leaves from an Autobiography* (London: Hutchinson and Co., 1944), p. 5.

[19] Jonathan Biss, 'From fact to fantasie: discovering the real Schumann', *The Guardian*, 18 May 2013.

subjectivity. It has three broad aims, which for the sake of convenience may be designated as *critical*, *musical*, and *philosophical*.

1. *Critical*. First is an attempt to define and refine the use of subjectivity as a term applied to music – to clarify its various possible meanings and functions, to delimit its range of applicability and offer justification for its use. As with so many other popular expressions, 'subjectivity' is a central, though at times diffuse and insufficiently clear conceptual term in much musicological discussion. This book consequently aspires to undertake a critical examination of the notion of musical subjectivity, focusing on Schumann as the ideal case study for this task.

2. *Musical*. Conversely, alongside this specific critical urge to elucidate the idea of subjectivity there is a reciprocal desire to draw on the analytical and aesthetic perspectives suggested by this term as a means of interpreting Schumann's music. Of course, I am aware that viewing Schumann through this lens could easily reinforce certain conventional tropes of reception history, and I would like to make clear from the start that the idea of subjectivity is not the only approach to understanding Schumann, nor should the term be applied in a blanket fashion to all his music. The private poet of the piano and solo Lied also wrote symphonies, *Der Paradies und die Peri*, an opera, and numerous pieces for communal music-making or pedagogical purposes. Nor should we dismiss the more public Schumann, that which appears to speak (as it were) in the first-person plural or third person, as being somehow not the 'true' Schumann. Nevertheless, since his day subjectivity has proved a central category for understanding Schumann, and this notion may therefore afford us with a particularly valuable means of exploring and interpreting part of his musical output.

3. *Philosophical*. Ultimately, the exploration of subjectivity in Schumann's music is a pretext for a bigger claim about music and subjectivity through-out the last two centuries in Western culture. Subjectivity, alongside related notions such as the subject and the self, is often viewed as a problem – indeed as a peculiarly contemporary problem characteristic of the modern era. A larger philosophic import is provided by this study's consideration of how music, the medium that historically was singled out as the most subjective of the arts at this time, may constitute an active force in con-structing subjectivity, a way of articulating a culture's sense of what it is to be a human subject. This musical articulation need not simply reinforce existing structures but can create new expressions of subjectivity; in an account where the idea of musical agency is foregrounded, a particular concern is in bringing to light what music might tell us about subjectivity that other communicative forms of expression do not, or at least not in the same way.

To avoid or at least forestall some of the misunderstandings that can be common in musicological discussion, a few words about the methodological premises and intended scope of this book may also be in order. Firstly, a comment on the use of history and its relation to theory. I should make clear from the outset that this account is not intended primarily as an exercise in historical reconstruction, in recovering an earlier understanding of subjectivity apparently held in Schumann's time, but rather as critiquing and enriching our current understanding of Western classical music – Schumann's music in particular, taken as an exemplary instance – and its relation to the idea of subjectivity. Although much of the discussion is rooted in the historical and cultural world of early to mid-nineteenth-century Germany, Schumann's music has remained part of European musical culture up to the present day, and with it a reception history that sees it as a peculiarly potent expression of a modern form of subjectivity, however subtly this conception may have altered since the composer's time. What I am trying to explicate is something broader and more directly relevant to our current concerns.

Hence, while drawing on history, this book is manifestly philosophical and transhistorical rather than antiquarian in both means and ends. Transhistorical is not the same as ahistorical or timeless: rather, it points to the enduring legacy of the past, for better or for worse, in the present, the 'persistence of subjectivity' as a concern over the last two centuries. This is not, therefore, to hold that modern-day discussion of musical subjectivity is identical to that of the early nineteenth century, and I do not claim that my account of subjectivity in Schumann's music is identical to something he or his contemporaries would have recognised – though neither is it wholly unrelated either. My belief (one shared by many others in the fields of philosophy and the history of ideas) is that something akin to subjectivity has been present throughout a long period of human history, even if the forms it takes and the significance attached to them have sometimes changed. Schumann's life and music offers an especially pointed historical manifestation, one whose relevance – as we have seen – still holds for today.

This relation to history and openness to diverse theoretical formulations has further important implications on the models of subjectivity used. With any complex topic such as this, it strikes me as extremely unlikely that any one approach will exhaust the idea's meaning or the different ways in which one may profitably understand it. Rather, one needs a flexible and inclusive range of approaches to the problem, each of which may draw out some important aspects but is inevitably silent on others. Thus, I have tried to avoid the type of enquiry that assumes a currently fashionable theorist is the first and last word on a topic that has been discussed since antiquity; equally, I have been open to a wide range of perspectives from Plato to postmodernism, encompassing along the way German Idealism and Romanticism, psychoanalysis, and analytic philosophy, without, I hope, being unduly biased towards or against one. The turn to postmodern or poststucturalist theories of the subject has, for instance, been especially prominent in musicology over the last decade, and I draw in these pages on familiar figures such as Lacan, Kristeva, Žižek, Derrida, and Lévinas, who in many cases offer useful perspectives on the topic, but not to the neglect of other, no less relevant thinkers before and after.

Finally, I am aware that the surname 'Schumann' in my title could refer to one of at least two composers: either Robert, the subject under investigation here, or Clara (née Wieck). The latter is far from absent from these pages, and in a handful of places her music is discussed, albeit within the wider context of her husband's work. I have written elsewhere on Clara Schumann's music, and the burgeoning interest in her life, career, and, especially, compositional output is one of the most heartening developments in contemporary musicology.[20] But the focal point of the widespread discourse on musical subjectivity over the last two centuries has undeniably been Robert rather than Clara Schumann, and it is accordingly his life and work that is taken as a case study for exploring this theme.

Structure and Outline

Taking its inspiration from its subject matter, this book is arranged as a series of *Fantasiestücke* or *Subjektivitätsszenen* around the subject of Schumann and subjectivity. Save for the opening 'Prosopopoeic Preliminaries' and the corresponding 'Epilogue' (which themselves form a higher-level frame lying outside the main body of the work), these chapters are split into contrasting pairs, reflecting the movement from self to other that seems so deeply bound up with the notion of subjectivity in the modern era. While not wedded to chronological sequence and flitting freely between works, genres, and periods, a degree of linear order is still present across the volume, insofar as the book moves most generally

---

[20] See, for instance, my article 'Clara Wieck's A minor Piano Concerto: Formal Innovation and the Problem of Parametric Disconnect in Early Romantic Music', *Music Theory and Analysis*, 8/2 (2021), 1–28.

from a concentration on Schumann's music of the 1830s and early 1840s towards a greater focus on his later music in the closing chapters. Moreover, the broader philosophical argument unfolds in a cumulative fashion, whereby problems arising in one chapter are often addressed in the chapter that follows – normally to be followed by yet more questions that will similarly require future elaboration. Nonetheless, readers should feel free to tackle the contents of this book in any order they wish: it would be inopportune in a study which foregrounds Schumann's music and Romantic notions of subjectivity to insist upon too strict a sense of linear narrative.

The opening chapter, 'Defining Subjectivity', sets out the terminological and conceptual ideas that provide a basis for the remainder of the book. Problematising the topic of musical subjectivity, it explicates the various meanings that have been given to this awkward notion and through increasing clarification proposes a range of potential meanings. Subjectivity here appears to refer to the experience of music as akin to a living being, an animate consciousness, but such that the experience may be of an apparent immediacy that shades it into a privileged first-person perspective – as if somehow viewing it as part of oneself. The second part of the chapter looks in turn to how subjectivity manifests itself both in music and in history, interrogating the notion of the musical subject through a series of questions that may be summarised as *who, how* and *where, when* and *why*? One of the properties of the idea of subjectivity identified here is that it is not a pregiven entity but a dynamic process that requires our own active participation for its interpretation. And thus, while a number of conceptual questions remain to be answered at the close of this chapter, it is given to the main body of the book to respond to these matters.

Part I, 'Hearing Subjects', turns attention to Schumann, addressing the composer's early grappling with the Romantic problematisation of subject-ivity and personal identity and the notion of the divided subject frequently present in his music of the 1830s and early 1840s. In 'Hearing the Self', I trace the historical development of subjectivity in music up to Schumann's time, relating this to the breakdown of the model of the transcendental subject, the emergence of Romantic irony and whimsical questioning of subjective identity in writers such as Jean Paul and E. T. A. Hoffmann. Against this backdrop we may better understand Schumann's creation of his alter egos Florestan and Eusebius, his love of personas and masks, use of ciphers and sphinxes, and questioning of continuity and coherence in the piano music of the 1830s. In 'Hearing Selves', I delve more deeply into the musical features that make this sense of divided subjectivity palpable. This chapter examines the conflicting voices and sense of irony present in Schumann's *Lieder* of 1840, above all his settings of Heine, alongside the split levels of discourse created in instrumental music through the use of tonal dualism, and the use of metric dissonance to suggest a conception of the self as an agglomeration of diverse bodily rhythms subsisting through overlapping temporal processes.

Part II, 'Hearing Presence', examines in more depth two aspects identified in Chapter 1 that contribute to a sense of subjectivity in music: the feeling of embodied presence or immediacy of self-possession, and the notion of vocality, epitomised here in what I call the 'coming to lyricism' paradigm. Crucial in philosophical accounts of subjectivity since at least the start of the nineteenth century is the notion of self-consciousness or self-recognition. By this token, ascribing subjectivity to music is to hear it not only speaking as an I, but speaking *as if knowing* it is speaking as an I. When does music appear to be aware of itself, and how might this be manifested? Chapter 4, 'Presence of the Self', offers an initial approach to answering this question, examining the healing of the divided self by the emergence of a sense of unifying, embodied subjectivity in some of Schumann's songs and instrumental works, and to what extent we might speak of such moments as constituting a form of musical reflexivity or self-consciousness – a topic which will necessarily spill over into the following chapter. In Chapter 5, 'Presence of the Other', the implicit subject / object split reintroduced into the musical subject by the need for its own self-recognition finds a potential solution in the presence of an other in whom the self may see itself mirrored. Indeed, Schumann's writing and music suggests a blurring of identities and fusion of self and other that resonates strongly with the Romantic mythology of hermaphroditic union, as seen in the 1841 song collection *Liebesfrühling* jointly written with his newly-wed Clara Wieck. Through this mirroring and recognition of self in other, Schumann's music may in certain cases be claimed to achieve a state of self-conscious awareness, to 'hear itself singing'. Yet, as pointed to at the chapter's close, such doubling of self and other always runs the risk of narcissism – the idea that the beloved object is merely a self-image, a fabrication of the subject's desire.

Such negative conclusions are drawn out to greater length in the following pair of chapters that constitute the book's third part, 'Hearing Absence'. Chapter 6, 'Absence of the Other', points to moments in Schumann where the music is marked by the absence of another's voice, be it through the Romantic evocation of distant voices in pieces such as the *Novelletten*'s 'Stimme aus der Ferne', or, more troublingly, the loss of voice in songs like

'Des Sennen Abschied' and 'Die Sennin' – a non-presence often explicitly denoting death, as is the case at the close of *Frauenliebe* or in the Kerner setting 'Aus das Trinkglas eines verstorbenen Freundes'. As is found increasingly in Schumann's later work, the music may pointedly not trace a successful 'coming to lyricism': the emergence of an expected lyrical voice is missing. This tendency is epitomised in the genre of melodrama, where music accompanies a declaimed speech that refuses to attain the subjective presence of lyricism; and in pieces such as *Manfred* and the later Ballads for Declamation such absence of lyrical voice may point not only to the absence of the other but also to the absence of the subject itself. Thus, Chapter 7, 'Absence of the Self', explores the potential loss of self implied by the absence of lyrical voice, highlighted in the missing silent 'inner voice' of the *Humoreske*, which forms an apt exemplification of later twentieth-century accounts of the illusory, 'barred' subject proposed by such thinkers as Lacan, Kristeva, and Žižek, or the empty centre at the heart of the Eichendorff *Liederkreis* that results from the absence of a unified subject position and any sense of narrative continuity.

The absence of a singular first-person voice in music, however, may simply indicate that the music is speaking in the plural, in the third person, or in some more objective manner. These questions are examined in the opening chapter of Part IV, 'Hearing Others'. Looking first at the use of quotation, allusion, and intertextuality in Schumann's music (in this, picking up the question of 'whose voice?' left at the close of Chapter 4), 'Hearing Another's Voice' goes on to explore questions of intersubjectivity and the collective seen in the 'objective' tendency of Schumann's music across the 1840s, the distinction between a divided subject and multiple subjects in the composer's choral, orchestral, and chamber works, before considering the attempted union of self with world, the subjective with the objective, in two of his later songs, 'Abendlied' and 'Nachtlied'. This eighth chapter thus focuses on those examples from Schumann's music that have a generally positive ethos, when self and other can still be distinguished. In the ensuing 'Hearing Oneself as Another', however, this is no longer the case. Here, the lack of self-recognition in music may point to psychological disorder and self-estrangement, this chapter tackling the problematic notions of late style and madness in Schumann's oeuvre. Still, misrecognition, mishearing, and their resulting subjective estrangement are wound throughout Schumann's oeuvre, from the close of the Op. 35 Kerner cycle and the enigmatic piano miniature 'Vogel als Prophet' to the magical mirror scene from *Genoveva*; in extreme form it is manifested in the depiction of madness in the Andersen setting 'Der Spielmann'. Most troublingly, the loss of musical self-recognition is epitomised autobiograph-ically in the theme of the late *Geistervariationen*, with its reworking of an idea found in the slow movement of the Violin Concerto, but one which Schumann misattributed to the spirits of Schubert and Mendelssohn. Yet as I argue at the chapter's close, the psychological state of the music's virtual subjects often bears scant relation to anything that can be shown to apply to the actual biographical subject, Robert Schumann. In recognising signs of insanity in Schumann's music, commentators are often reading their own presuppositions into it; ironically, in the acoustic mirror of Schumann's music they are merely misrecognising themselves.

Thus, finally, in the Epilogue to this book, I turn away from the hypothet-ical subjects heard in music and inward to our own selves, as thinking, feeling, meaning-making subjects, as interpretants of music and our own subjectivity alike. Why are the notions of subjectivity associated with Schumann's music still of relevance today? What is the work that music does that enables it to become one of our most cherished means for hearing ourselves, for self-recognition? And what are the attendant dangers – hermeneutic, aesthetic, but more significantly ethical – in such an endeavour?

Prosopopoeic Preliminaries

First, then, we must learn the truth about the soul divine and human by observing how it acts and is acted upon.

Plato, *Phaedrus*, 245b

1 | Defining Subjectivity

'Defining Subjectivity'. The title invites hubris. How does one attempt to define such an all-pervasive yet hopelessly nebulous notion? Frustratingly polysemous in its application, subjectivity is one of the most popular and yet at the same time obscurest terms in the modern human sciences. Not without justification does one of the most valuable previous musicological accounts of the topic disclaim any direct approach to this question, insofar as subjectivity, in the author's view, escapes definition by its very nature.[1]

The difficulty arises in part as subjectivity appears not to be a single thing. Neither is it, at least by some accounts, reducible to a group of things. Slightly more securely, subjectivity might be argued to be a relation between things. But it is one where its apparent basis – the subject or self – is itself hotly disputed, even denied by some commentators. And then, even after coming to some provisional answer to all these concerns, how do we begin to relate this concept to music, which similarly appears to elude all verbal confinement?

Faced with this situation, one might be forgiven for dismissing the whole topic as yet another musicological example of conceptual diffuseness, humanistic hermeneutics at its idlest and most fuzzy. Yet for all these evident difficulties, still we encounter the term, perhaps even use it, rely on it implicitly or explicitly to underpin various assertions made about music and its effect on us. We may not be exactly sure what subjectivity is – at least when summoned to define it – but much of the reception of Western classical music in the last few centuries seems premised upon it. If only for heuristic purposes, some characterisation – however provisional – is necessary.

One time-honoured way of starting out might be to look to common understandings of the notion, what it has been taken to mean by earlier authors, how it has been used both generally and in a more specialised musical context, in order to refine a better working definition. And already

---

[1] Julian Johnson, 'The Subjects of Music: a Theoretical and Analytical Enquiry into the Construction of Subjectivity in the Musical Structuring of Time' (DPhil diss., University of Sussex, 1994), p. 25.

even the simplest of starting points, the entry for the term in the *Oxford English Dictionary*, reveals quite a diverse range of definitions.[2] Most generally, (1) subjectivity may refer to 'a conscious being' – animate life, consciousness. Thus 'a subjectivity' can function as a mildly more pretentious term in place of 'living being' (human or possibly animal), one possessing consciousness. (An earlier age might have spoken of 'soul'.) Taken further down these lines, the term shades into something akin to *self*-consciousness ('consciousness of one's perceived states'), crucially introducing an awareness of self to this animating consciousness.

More familiar is quite another meaning: (2) subjectivity as a uniquely personal and often idiosyncratic quality, 'the quality or condition of viewing things exclusively through the medium of one's own mind or individuality; the condition of being dominated by or absorbed in one's personal feelings, thoughts, concerns, etc.' Significantly for the concerns of the present study, this may be applied more exclusively to that type of 'art which depends on the expression of the personality or individuality of the artist'. As we saw, Schumann is often considered 'subjective' in this sense, in that listeners seem to hear him 'in' his music, to a greater degree than many other composers. But as we shall presently see, it need not be in this sense that musical subjectivity is often constituted. Two other definitions point to subjectivity as akin to subjectivism ('the philosophical theory according to which all our knowledge is merely subjective and relative, and which denies the possibility of objective knowledge') and a form of philosophical idealism (4: 'the character of existing in the mind only').

This is a good enough starting point, but there are several aspects which might be brought out more clearly. What is latent but underdeveloped in the above account, for instance, is the notion of subjectivity as a form of first-person experience, one irreducible to any other external or objective viewpoint (that fabled 'view from nowhere' in Thomas Nagel's formulation).[3] This aspect is brought into greater relief by Robert C. Solomon's entry for 'subjectivity' in the *Oxford Companion to Philosophy*. For Solomon, subjectivity is something 'pertaining to the subject and his or her particular perspective, feelings, beliefs, desires'. Especially important is the idea of perspectivalism, the realm of experience

---

[2] 'Subjectivity', *Oxford English Dictionary Online* (2009).

[3] Thomas Nagel, *The View from Nowhere* (New York: Oxford University Press, 1986). As Nagel argues in a celebrated earlier paper, 'every subjective phenomenon is essentially connected with a single point of view'. With regard to such experience, 'the idea of moving from [subjective] appearance to [objective] reality seems to make no sense' ('What Is It Like to Be a Bat?', *The Philosophical Review*, 83 (1974), 437, 444).

'typically defined with reference to the first-person standpoint'. Often defined in opposition to objectivity (something only implicit in the third definition above), subjectivity may also pick up the pejorative connotation that it is based on unjustified personal prejudices and a limited standpoint (i.e. the contrary of universal; a negative inflection of the second OED definition).[4]

Also left unstated is the nature of the relationship between subjectivity and other seemingly related concepts, most obviously the subject, but potentially extending further to such disputed notions as the self, ego, transcendental 'I', and so on. More properly one might propose that subjectivity relates to the subject as an activity does to an actor; in some accounts, the activity might indeed constitute the subject. Thus defined, subjectivity may refer to a range of 'self-reflective activity', with the crucial emphasis on the subject's process of mediation between itself and the external world or 'other'.[5] But in some accounts (especially German Idealist philosophers such as Schelling and Hegel), the actual self is just such an activity, not an object, and thus becomes almost indistinguishable from subjectivity. At the broadest level, then, it appears that subjectivity may often be used – sometimes imprecisely – as an umbrella term for matters 'concerning the subject' and is thus general enough to include such notions as subject, self, persona, individual, agency, and self-consciousness.[6]

I should like to set out openly here that no single unitary definition of subjectivity is being proposed within this book. What we might outline from the foregoing discussion, however, is a range of possible uses – some slightly contradictory – that might be of use for considering music. These include subjectivity as referring to a conscious, living being; self-consciousness or similar reflexive awareness of self; a unique first-person

---

[4] Robert C. Solomon, 'Subjectivity', *The Oxford Companion to Philosophy*, ed. Ted Honderich (Oxford: Oxford University Press, 1995), p. 857.

[5] Kim Atkins (ed.), *Self and Subjectivity* (Oxford: Wiley Blackwell, 2005), p. 1.

[6] As Atkins notes, the expression 'the self. . . is more appropriately understood as a colloquial umbrella term that encompasses a range of concepts that relate to self-reflective activity' (which she has earlier identified with subjectivity), such as 'consciousness', 'ego', 'soul', 'subject', 'person', or 'moral agent' (*ibid.*, p. 1). Jerrold Seigel likewise argues that 'however clearly it may be possible to distinguish them', terms like 'self, subject, identity, person . . . are permeable and sometimes merge into each other'. They 'constitute a vocabulary of selfhood, a linguistic register from which we single out one or another depending on the context in which we employ the idea of the self, or the particular purpose we ask it to serve' (*The Idea of the Self: Thought and Experience in Western Europe Since the Seventeenth Century* (Cambridge: Cambridge University Press, 2005), p. 16). Despite my desire to define the topic more precisely, in this book I still follow, to a certain extent, Seigel's accommodating guidelines.

standpoint (based more upon immediate feeling and sense of self); the means of the subject's mediation to external world or self-articulation, and a range of subjective concepts – the self, subject, and so on – with a tendency to emphasise the active, temporal dimensions of existence.

Defining Musical Subjectivity

Unsurprisingly given this leeway, subjectivity may be, and has been, applied to music in many diverse ways. One might, for instance, indicate a personal and idiosyncratic quality to the composer's style, or to the performer's rendering, or to our own flights of hermeneutic fancy as listeners (sometimes most apparent in a negative sense when we encounter an interpretation that jars with our own [OED's definition 2]).[7] Or we might be referring to the amorphous nature of music's existence (the sense that the musical work is largely a mental or intentional construct, lacking tangible objecthood [OED definition (4)]). But to offer an initial clarification of the general sense I am interested in here, *by musical subjectivity, I refer most particularly to a way of understanding music as being in some way like a (human) subject, whether as a virtual living being, an extension of our own consciousness, or something with which we closely identify.* While the music may not really *be* a subject, it is necessary for it to be heard 'as if', or as possessing unmistakable subjective qualities, not simply as our own projection (though ultimately, of course, it is just this).[8] In a further, less demanding sense, though, the subjectivity of music may also be understood as arising from the fact that as an artwork – as a creation of a human subject – it is one of the modes of articulation of such a subject, and as such constitutes 'subjectivity'. (This is a more immediately defensible position, yet in many ways open to much vaguer use insofar as virtually all music is thereby subjective, to the same degree.)

Musical subjectivity in this sense, or something like it, has been around for a long time; the close connexion between the soul (the classical 'proto-subject' as it were) and music was often noted in ancient times, while from

---

[7] See especially Lawrence Kramer, 'Subjectivity', *Interpreting Music* (Berkeley and Los Angeles: University of California Press, 2011), ch. 3, pp. 46–62.

[8] This formulation is an example of the literary-rhetorical concept of 'prosopopœia' ('a rhetorical figure by which an inanimate or abstract thing is represented as a person, or with personal characteristics' [OED]). Most recently Robert Hatten has proposed the term 'virtual' to describe the quality of the agency or subjectivity heard in music; see *A Theory of Virtual Agency for Western Art Music* (Bloomington: Indiana University Press, 2018), pp. 1–2.

the nineteenth century on barely a Romantic thinker misses the chance to equate music with the flow of subjective consciousness. In the mid-twentieth century, the writings of a figure such as Theodor Adorno provide ample illustration for the association between the cultural work done by music and the notion of subjectivity. For modern musicological purposes, however, recent English-language discussion of subjectivity is significantly indebted to a tradition initiated by Edward T. Cone's 1974 study *The Composer's Voice*, which introduces the idea of the musical *persona* (with an accompanying array of assorted agents and protagonists). Cone proposes early on that 'the expressive power of every art depends on the communication of a certain kind of experience, and that each art in its own way projects the illusion of the existence of a personal subject through whose consciousness that experience is made known to the rest of us'.[9] This musical persona is very much like the fictional subject of a poem, the lyric 'I', or the 'I' that we encounter in a first-person novel; significantly, Cone's way into the discussion is through song, moving from the persona (or multiple personae) of the text to the virtual personae of the musical setting, and thence to consideration of instrumental music. For Cone,

any instrumental composition, like the instrumental component of a song, can be interpreted as the symbolic utterance of a virtual persona. This utterance may be a symbolic play, in which a number of virtual agents assume leading roles. It may be a symbolic monologue in which a single agent addresses an audience. It may be a symbolic soliloquy, a private utterance that an audience overhears. Very likely it is a complex structure involving all these modes .... But in every case there is a musical persona that is the experiencing subject of the entire composition, in whose thought the play, or narrative, or reverie, takes place – whose inner life the music communicates by means of symbolic gesture.[10]

As is apparent in the preceding formulation, Cone desires ultimately to reduce a plurality of personae or lesser 'agents' to one overriding synthetic persona: 'in the last analysis all roles are aspects of one controlling persona, which is in turn the projection of one creative human consciousness – that of the composer'.[11] It is repeatedly qualified, however, that this 'composer's

---

[9] Edward T. Cone, *The Composer's Voice* (Berkeley: University of California Press, 1974), p. 3.
[10] *Ibid.*, p. 94.
[11] *Ibid.*, p. 114. This feature is particularly emphasised by Cone in later revisions of his theory applied to the multiple personae of songs: see 'Poet's Love or Composer's Love?', in Steven Paul Scher (ed.), *Music and Text: Critical Inquiries* (Cambridge: Cambridge University Press, 1992), pp. 177–92. Cone's views on this point have been critically engaged with in several articles by Fred Everett Maus, Berthold Hoeckner (see especially 'Poet's Love and Composer's

voice' is not actually identifiable with the real composer of the music; rather, it is an idealised projection (in a footnote early on in his account, Cone points to literary critic Wayne Booth's notion of the 'implied author' of a literary work).[12] The 'Schubert' that we hear in *Winterreise* or the C major Quintet does not really give us access to the voice or consciousness of the Franz Schubert who actually wrote these compositions and died in 1828.[13] Finally, towards the end of his book, Cone also raises another characteristic of one of the most curious aspects of what I call subjectivity: the aspect of personal identification with the music, even the overlapping of our own subjectivity with the composer's fictional one.

> When we listen to music . . . we must follow it as if it were our own thought. We are bound to it – to its tempo, to its progression, to its dynamics. We can recall the past or foresee the future only as they are reflected in our awareness of each moment of the perpetually flowing present. And if that awareness is sufficiently acute, and our attention sufficiently constant, we can succeed in feeling that we have *become* the music, or that the music has become ourselves.[14]

> To listen to music is to yield our inner voice to the composer's domination. Or better: it is to make the composer's voice our own.[15]

Though the word 'subject' appears on several occasions, Cone does not actually use the term 'subjectivity' in his book. Yet the theoretical concerns of his account clearly point to the same thing: a musical subject, persona, agent, or voice, given anthropomorphic qualities and heard as expressing human experiences and emotions. His account has provided a foundation for future discussion of voice, agency, and narrativity, especially in song and opera.[16] Moreover, the concerns of

---

Love', *Music Theory Online*, 7/5 (October 2001)), and most recently Seth Monahan's 'Action and Agency Revisited', *Journal of Music Theory*, 57 (2013), 321–71.

[12] Wayne C. Booth, *The Rhetoric of Fiction* (Chicago: University of Chicago Press, 1961), esp. pp. 70–3, cited by Cone, *The Composer's Voice*, p. 2. Cf. *ibid.*, p. 85: 'the persona's experiences are not the composer's experiences but an imaginative transformation of them; the reactions, emotions, and states of mind suggested by the music are those of the persona, not the composer'.

[13] Carl Dahlhaus has similarly distinguished between the biographical subject Beethoven (who composed, ate, drank, grew deaf, and squabbled with his sister-in-law) and the aesthetic subject 'Beethoven', whom successive generations have heard and empathised with in his music, and to this day may be heard alive and in rude health (*Ludwig van Beethoven: Approaches to His Music*, trans. Mary Whittall (Oxford: Oxford University Press, 1991), p. 31).

[14] Cone, *The Composer's Voice*, p. 156.   [15] *Ibid.*, p. 157.

[16] See, for instance, Lawrence Kramer, *Music and Poetry: The Nineteenth Century and After* (Berkeley and Los Angeles: University of California Press, 1984), and *Franz Schubert: Sexuality, Subjectivity, Song* (Cambridge: Cambridge University Press, 1998); Carolyn Abbate, *Unsung Voices: Opera and Musical Narrative in the Nineteenth Century* (Princeton: Princeton University Press, 1991); the work of Anthony Newcomb, Fred Everett Maus, and Berthold

Cone's work have become widespread in musicology of the last few decades.

Few of the numerous scholarly writings that draw upon ideas of subject-ivity, persona and agency stop to interrogate what these terms mean, however, or how they might be supported.[17] The reason is due less to scholarly indolence than to the fact that many of us feel we instinctively know what these words mean, or at least how we are using them, and believe they serve an important and indispensable purpose, but find that attempting a better definition gets us caught in a conceptual thicket for no good purpose.[18] A handful of significant exceptions foreground the notion of subjectivity and provide clues to what it might mean. Of these, the most detailed subsequent study that explicitly addresses the idea of how subject-ivity is constructed in music (as opposed to the cultural work done by musical subjectivity, the primary focus of several other accounts discussed presently) is given in the work of Naomi Cumming.[19]

In a 1997 article and her posthumously published 2000 monograph, Cumming approaches the question of musical subjectivity from a semiotic angle.[20] The terms 'subject' or 'persona' are introduced by her in recogni-tion of the fact that 'a complex expressivity, emerging through the play of signs at many levels, [can] in many contexts be heard as a quasi-personal utterance by some virtual entity – not the composer or performer, but an

---

Hoeckner. A symposium dedicated to Cone's book was also edited by Maus, ' Edward T. Cone's *The Composer's Voice*: Elaborations and Departures', *College Music Symposium*, 29 (1989), 1–80, with contributions by Marion A. Guck, Charles Fisk, Fred Everett Maus, James Webster, Alicyn Warren, and a response by Edward T. Cone. More recent work on narrativity and voice since the start of the new millennium has departed further from Cone's concerns, but it still stands as a key musicological text in the field.

[17] This matter is highlighted in Seth Monahan's valuable recent discussion of the often-unconscious ascription of various types of agency to music in scholarly writing, 'Action and Agency Revisited'.

[18] I speak from personal experience. Much of the present chapter could be considered an expansion of the brief account of subjectivity I give in *Mendelssohn, Time and Memory: The Romantic Conception of Cyclic Form* (Cambridge: Cambridge University Press, 2011), pp. 26–31, which was kept deliberately concise, partly from necessities of space, but also to avoid opening up more troublesome issues which could never be satisfactorily addressed there.

[19] A further significant work in this context, Robert Hatten's *A Theory of Virtual Agency*, appeared after most of this present book had been completed. Hatten's discussion of how a sense of lower-level agency can be formed in music is valuable and will be returned to later; his broader account of musical subjectivity complements rather than supersedes the accounts of Cone and Cumming presented here.

[20] Naomi Cumming, 'The Subjectivities of "Erbarme dich"', *Music Analysis*, 16 (1997), 5–44; *The Sonic Self: Musical Subjectivity and Signification* (Bloomington: Indiana University Press, 2000). The latter volume places particular emphasis on the subjectivity of the performer, especially in its opening chapters.

"utterer" created by the musical passage in question'.[21] Evident here is how in Cumming's account the musical subject is an *emergent* quality, not a preformed thing or merely the sum of its constituent parts, created from multiple elements in the music that invite interpretation as a subjectivity:

> a musical 'subject' can emerge in time as an integration of various 'subjectivities' in the work. Any attributions to music of qualities that would normally be applied to living beings, such as locality, gesture, or volition, indicate that subjective content has been heard. The sense of a 'subject' emerges from these things, but is not reducible to them.[22]

Also apparent is how for Cumming, the subjectivity really has to be understood as 'in' the music. Following Susanne Langer, the expressive content of the music is not simply our own projection but appears to inhere in the work, making its own demands for recognition, a persona that is in this sense 'other'.[23]

> Musical personae are not the ephemeral masks behind which the composer's face can be discerned, but neither are they the distorted reflection of one engaged in listening. They inhere in the text of the work itself, as it is performed, inviting the listener's engagement in a manner that transforms his or her own subjectivity.[24]

Just like the self, the musically signified persona 'may be imagined as a "super-sign", an emergent entity negotiating the continuous integration of life representations (affects and memories) in time'.[25] This virtual subject is inseparable from the temporal course of the music, not something which stands behind it: it is something which 'demands to be encountered in order to be known, and which cannot be simply paraphrased or summarized'.[26] Here, Cumming comes close to suggesting that our acquaintance with music's persona is akin to a first-person experience. Cumming's account of musical subjectivity is one of the most detailed and rewarding available. While the plethora of overlapping but distinct conceptual terms – subjects, personae, agents – she calls upon barely reduce Cone's already extensive list, her explication of the ways in which music constructs a sense of subjectivity, its characteristic ways of signalling a 'sonic self', provides strong grounds for future development.[27]

---

[21] Cumming, *The Sonic Self*, p. 241.

[22] Cumming, 'The Subjectivities of "Erbarme dich"', 11–12.

[23] Cumming, *The Sonic Self*, pp. 223–4.

[24] Cumming, 'The Subjectivities of "Erbarme dich"', 17.   [25] Cumming, *The Sonic Self*, p. 209.

[26] *Ibid.*, pp. 223–4.

[27] Maus already comments that a codification and evaluation of Cone's 'elaborate technical vocabulary' in *The Composer's Voice* would be helpful ('Introduction', ' Edward T. Cone's *The Composer's Voice*: Elaborations and Departures', *College Music Symposium*, 29 (1989), p. 7).

Quite a different approach is taken by Julian Johnson, who has drawn on the idea of subjectivity productively throughout many publications. The piece that most directly addresses the meaning of the term is his 1994 doctoral dissertation, which, even if dating from an early stage of his output, provides the most convenient summary of the idea for our purposes.[28] For Johnson as we saw, 'subjectivity resists definition. This is because it is not a thing but a structure of relations between other things.' Moreover, he claims, discreetly absorbing the lessons of poststructuralist thought, it is something that 'has a history', being subject to historical and cultural change.[29] Subjectivity possesses a rich plurality of meanings across different discourses, meanings that are not equivalent to each other. And in case this were not challenging enough, 'philosophical theories of subjectivity tend to reveal the inadequacy of a theoretical articulation of the nature of the subject, not least because language is above all others the medium in which subjectivity is articulated to itself'.[30] Indeed, 'the subject has no existence except in the media through which it realizes and externalizes itself'.[31]

Subjectivity emerges as a far more slippery concept in his account, yet partly owing to this insistence on understanding it as a process, as a means of self-articulation whereby the subject realises itself, art may have a vital role to play by not just reflecting but in fact constructing subjectivity. Music, in particular for Johnson, 'challenges and redefines notions of subjectivity'.[32] This is due to its position as a product of human activity – as a real form of subjectivity, of the human subject seeking to articulate itself – and exemplified in the parallel drawn between music and the subject as a structuring of time.

Time is the constitutive dimension of the subject, and it is for this reason that music stands in a privileged relationship to the subject. Music provides not only a revelation of the subject but a site for the subject's creation. It possesses the potential for this function because the defining activity of music is also that of the subject – the structuring of time.[33]

Subjectivity is a structure of relations in time which attempts to preserve a central unity in spite of the negativity of diversity, and which functions for consciousness as a central referent for diversity. Music, by creating abstract structures in time which relate directly to this pattern articulates models of subjectivity.

---

[28] Part of the thesis was published as 'The Status of the Subject in Mahler's Ninth Symphony', *19th-Century Music*, 18 (1994), 108–20.

[29] Johnson, 'The Subjects of Music', p. 25. Michel Foucault and Julia Kristeva, in particular are elegantly assimilated in Johnson's thesis.

[30] *Ibid.*, p. 30.   [31] *Ibid.*, p. 61.   [32] *Ibid.*, p. 30.   [33] *Ibid.*, p. 50.

The variety of different structural organizations of musical time is testimony to the variety of 'models' of the subject.[34]

Indeed, Johnson makes the strong claim that 'the structures of music are those of the subject rather than being analogous to, or resembling those of some subject "in itself".[35] Given Johnson's insistence on subjectivity's resistance to objectification and his concentration with the wider cultural and aesthetic questions that mark its relation with music, we should not look to this source for help with this initial attempt to demarcate the terminological boundaries of the concept. But in emphasising the work music does on behalf of subjectivity, music *as* subjectivity, Johnson's thesis offers numerous promising ways of exploring this topic, several of which will be taken up later.

Lawrence Kramer is another contemporary scholar who has productively employed the concept of subjectivity in a variety of ways to argue for the constitutive role of music in modern culture. Music, for Kramer, 'has acted as a basic formative medium of modern subjectivity'.[36] Along comparable lines to Johnson, he points to 'music as a site of subjective mobility or negotiation', whereby to this day people 'still tune their sense of self to music'.[37] In arguing for this role, Kramer sees instrumental music as particularly significant:

Instrumental music suggests the post-Enlightenment conception of the subject as a mode of depth, an inner space filled with recesses, layers and unfathomed reaches. ... One reason for these identifications is an alliance between the way the subject was conceived and the era's heightened emphasis on the capacity of music to bypass language. Subjective depth was (and is) generally identified with an unsymbolisable uniqueness that stands in excess over anything that the subject can say or that can be said about it.[38]

Especially important in Kramer's account is how music can blur the distinction between self and other, this art form possessing a power

---

[34] *Ibid.*, p. 54.   [35] *Ibid.*, p. 61.   [36] Kramer, *Interpreting Music*, p. 3.

[37] Kramer, 'The Mysteries of Animation: History, Analysis and Musical Subjectivity', *Music Analysis*, 20 (2001), 153. This article is probably the most detailed attempt by this author to address how music conveys a sense of subjectivity in the manner I am concerned with here, though other useful accounts may be found in *Franz Schubert: Sexuality, Subjectivity, Song*, pp. 28–34, and, with greater emphasis on the subjectivity of musical interpretation, *Classical Music and Postmodern Knowledge* (Berkeley and Los Angeles: University of California Press, 1995), pp. 19–25, and 'Subjectivity Unbound: Music, Language, Culture', in Martin Clayton, Trevor Herbert, and Richard Middleton (eds.), *The Cultural Study of Music: A Critical Introduction* (Oxford: Routledge, 2012), pp. 395–406.

[38] Kramer, 'The Mysteries of Animation', 158.

'to implant subjective states in the listener that are paradoxically both native and alien, impossible either to own or disown'.[39] Thus he can conclude that 'the primary action of music in [the modern] era is not to express subjectivity, no matter how expressive of feeling or "musical personality" some of it may be. Its primary action is to invite subjectivity.'[40]

One final important scholarly account of subjectivity from the last two decades is given by Michael P. Steinberg, who, as with the previous two accounts, focuses more on what subjectivity *does* than how we might demonstrate it in music. Steinberg is at pains to distinguish between subjectivity on one hand and the 'self' and 'subject' on the other. He sees the former more as a mode of negotiation, or relation, between self and society or culture, which can be carried out – indeed, is best articulated – in art, especially in music. Subjectivity is 'the subject in motion, the subject in experience and analysis of itself and the world'. Subjectivity does not denote a *property* of the subject but rather the *life* of the subject, 'conceived in such a way as potentially to produce an internal critique of the category of "the subject"', that is, itself.[41] 'The endless work of subjectivity involves the constant renegotiations of the boundaries between self and world', culture and language. It is also a historical category, emerging from post-Enlightenment claims on the subject in relation to the power structures of society. For Steinberg here, the figure of Jean-Jacques Rousseau is especially important in positing music at the core of the modern concern of subjectivity.[42]

Music does the work of subjectivity, is a mode of subjectivity with the power to organise and structure subjectivity (i.e. itself). To exemplify his claim, Steinberg calls upon what he styles 'two fictions of modern music', 'unwarranted ascriptions from a commonsense point of view' in that they 'ascribe capacities of consciousness and agency to music'. First, music can and does *speak* in the first person (his own, oblique response to Edward Cone's famous opening question in *The Composer's Voice*: 'if music is a language, then who is speaking?'), and second, music can *listen* to itself. The latter point relies on another 'fundamental fiction', that music 'has the capacity for memory, a sense of past and future, and a language for their articulation'. This implies nothing less than the idea that music must be understood (at least at times) as being self-conscious. And because music is

---

[39] *Ibid.*, 159.   [40] *Ibid.*, 157.

[41] Steinberg, *Listening to Reason*, p. 5. Also see the related account in the same author's 'Schumann's Homelessness', in R. Larry Todd (ed.), *Schumann and His World* (Princeton: Princeton University Press, 1994), pp. 47–8.

[42] Steinberg, *Listening to Reason*, p. 7.

granted the ability to listen, it implies 'that the subjectivity inscribed in musical utterance is immediately a mode of intersubjectivity.' Departing from Cone, and coming closer to the later writers cited, Steinberg insists the subjectivity we hear in the music is not that of the composer or anyone outside the music but is rather 'of the music itself'. 'Musical subjectivity cannot therefore be absorbed into the subject-positions of the composer or the listener.'[43]

Steinberg's two fictions are extremely discerning formulations and touch on crucial elements of how music might be said to convey a sense of subjectivity. Sadly, for the immediate concerns of this chapter he does not attempt to justify them any further on an analytical, phenomenological, or historical level (they remain simply 'unwarranted ascriptions', heuristic conveniences). They do, however, suggest highly rewarding approaches to defining the qualities of music that make it appear subjective.

The Identity of the Musical Subject

In the preceding accounts, the subjectivity in music has been attributed to various possible subjects – the composer or an idealised compositional persona in Cone, the performer or music in Cumming, the listener in Kramer, the 'music itself' in Steinberg. It may help here, prior to proposing a more detailed summing up of the meanings that may plausibly be assigned to musical subjectivity, to offer our own analysis of possible subjects, a form of response to Cone's famous opening question already alluded to by Steinberg.[44] For if there is a subject present in music, who might it be that we hear?

(1) The Performer. Most straightforwardly, when listening to music we hear a subject who is the performer, or the 'persona' projected by the performer. He or she really is 'there' and producing the sounds.[45] And – in the human voice especially, but also by extension in

---

[43] *Ibid.*, p. 9. See Cone, *The Composer's Voice*, p. 1.

[44] Comparable, though not identical, taxonomies relating to the specific question of agency can also been found in Anthony Newcomb, 'Action and Agency in Mahler's Ninth Symphony, Second Movement', in Jenefer Robinson (ed.), *Music and Meaning* (Ithaca, NY: Cornell University Press, 1997), pp. 133–4, and Monahan, 'Action and Agency Revisited', 327–33.

[45] At least in live performance, recording technology obviously introduces more complexity, but does not really alter the fact that we hear the sounds of a performer who 'was there'. Electronic music certainly clouds this issue. However, it lies outside the boundaries of my concern in this book with the music of the Western classical tradition.

instrumental performance – we undeniably do hear the sound – the audible trace – of another human subject. This is undeniably one sense of subjectivity in music. But this is not the subjectivity I am primarily interested in here. To illustrate this point, we normally hear the same subject 'in' the music – in a specific piece by Tchaikovsky or Brahms, or what have you – irrespective of who is performing. Maybe the performer adopts different sonic 'personas' when approaching Bach and when playing Kodály. And conversely, we might think that Casals and Fournier maintain some sense of their own sonic identity across different repertoires. But this is already departing from the straightforward sense that the subject we hear in music is the human performer and into hermeneutic territory, as is given away by the use of terms like 'persona'. Thus, there is certainly a direct sense in which the performer is one candidate for the identity of the subject in music (one about which Cumming has written with great insight), but also other important senses, as yet unclarified, in which he or she is not.[46]

(2) The Composer – another seemingly straightforward, though in fact highly problematic, candidate. If music communicates a persona or subject, there is an obvious reaction to attribute this to that of the composer. A work of music is the product of human activity and undeniably reflects to some extent the subject who created it. In the Romantic era especially, music was often seen as a form of self-expression, and thus the expressive states that appear to be communicated by music can easily – though questionably – be attributed to those of the creator.[47] This is particularly the case with someone like Schumann, whose music has long been bound up with details of his personality and private life. Of course, although this view has long been attractive and appears ineradicable in popular aesthetics and programme-note journalism, demonstrating such links is extremely problematic. It would be hard to deny that many works seem to reflect the emotional state of the composer at the time of their creation (I think of Mendelssohn's late F minor Quartet), but counterexamples are rife

---

[46] A recent contribution to this discussion of performer agency is Edward Klorman's *Mozart's Music of Friends: Social Interplay in the Chamber Works* (Cambridge: Cambridge University Press, 2016); see esp. ch. 4, 'Analyzing from within the music: toward a theory of multiple agency', pp. 111–55. On the interaction of different agencies see also Rebecca Thumpston, 'The Embodiment of Yearning: Towards a Tripartite Theory of Musical Agency', in Costantino Maeder and Mark Reybrouck (eds.), *Music, Analysis, Experience* (Leuven: Leuven University Press, 2015), pp. 331–48.

[47] This is the concern of Mark Evan Bonds's new study, *The Beethoven Syndrome: Hearing Music as Autobiography* (New York: Oxford University Press, 2020).

(Beethoven's Second Symphony is a classic case). It might seem a banal point to make, but the present existence or non-existence of the actual composer also appears to have no impact on the continued existence of the musical subject. Thus, as was indicated before, the authorial persona in the music is at the very least a partially fictional 'implied author'. Thus, we come to:

(3) The Aesthetic Subject (a virtual persona or imaginary construction). This category may divide into two broad types (which may intermix or divide further): first, the easily accepted idea that (especially with texted or theatrically staged music) we hear music conveying the subject speaking through words or represented on stage. Just as we speak of the subject of a text written in the first person, so it seems easy to accept that in a song music conveys the feelings of the protagonist. Verbal or dramatic representation clarifies the existence of the musical subject (though, as we will see, the subject in language is, in fact, just as much a construction as the musical one). But, as an extension of this, we arrive second at the regulative fiction of the musical persona or aesthetic subject: that music, even without verbal designation or representation, is somehow akin to another consciousness or subject.

(4) The Listener. A fourth possible sense, which is briefly mentioned here but will become important later in this book, is that the subject in the music is actually the listener. In fact, in a straightforward sense, this is the only real consciousness that we directly encounter – our own.[48]

In the current account I am interested primarily in the third category above. This is the most problematic, troublesome, least obvious, most hermeneutic, and perhaps therefore the most fascinating. But all these definitions have some valuable implications, which will be drawn upon at later stages of this study.[49]

---

[48] An intriguing proposal extending this category has been proposed by John Butt in his notion of an 'implied listener'. See ' Do Musical Works Contain an Implied Listener? Towards a Theory of Musical Listening', *Journal of the Royal Musical Association*, 135 (2010), 5–18.

[49] There are some variants or possible admixtures of the above. If we hear or mentally rehearse a piece in our head, the performer is virtually obliterated (or becomes us). Another thought-experiment might be to consider the status of the subject when a composer is performing (and furthermore listening) to music he or she has composed. My proposal is that in some cases the composer/performer would sense that he or she had become the music, which was functioning as an extension of the self.

Propaedeutic Definition of Musical Subjectivity

We might now be in a position to propose a slightly more refined working definition of subjectivity as applied to music, drawing on the work of the scholars cited earlier in the chapter but informed by the wider meanings of the term outlined before. By 'definition' I mean something closer to circumscribing a cluster of related conceptual areas, drawing circles ever more narrowly around what are still quite fuzzy and general notions. It was a point made earlier that subjectivity itself may be an emergent concept, an activity or process rather than an essence waiting to be revealed. In a sense, this entire book could be thought of as a gradual process of defining, explicating, or articulating subjectivity; one that moves from the largely descriptive in the present chapter, which seeks to provide a heuristic framework for the ensuing discussion of Schumann's music, to propose a more normative understanding of the concept by the end of the book.

Subjectivity in music refers to a range of features:

- Most basic is the experience of music as in some sense alive, as a living, animate being. As we saw at the start, this is an elementary definition of subjectivity more generally. This interpretation, while metaphorical, is relatively uncontentious. Music has almost invariably been heard as possessing movement, while the association with metaphors of organic life has been customary since the late eighteenth century. One might often associate this apparent capacity for self-movement with 'agency'.

- This living quality may often appear to be, possess, or be akin to, a *consciousness* – the capacity for perception, thinking, and understanding. Again, this is a basic condition of most philosophical understandings of the soul, self, or subject.[50] How this quality is applicable to music (a point addressed later) is rather less straightforward, but answers might be found in homologies between consciousness and music rooted in their sense of unity amid temporal flux and apparently immaterial nature.

- Furthermore, following Steinberg, this sense of consciousness should have the potential for being heard at times as *self*-consciousness. It is not simply the case that music may appear animate and possess agency, but it is as if the music is aware of itself, can relate to itself and act reflexively. Once more, the criterion of self-awareness is fundamental to philosophical understandings of the self or subject. But how this condition relates to music is yet trickier. Again, we might propose looking to music's temporal nature, particularly as constituted through

---

[50] In *De Anima*, for instance, Aristotle identifies local movement and thinking, understanding, and perceiving as properties of that which possesses soul (*On the Soul*, III/3, 427a).

its apparent ability to reflect on its own course through stylised processes of memory and anticipation.

- More abstractly, there is often a sense of gaining somehow a *first-person perspective* on this self-consciousness – a sense of personal identification with the music where normal boundaries between self and other seem annulled. The apparent immediacy of music's presence and emotional expression permits us to empathise or relate to it as if it is part, or an extension of ourselves. (To put this in linguistic terms, such music may speak as an 'I', but our identification may become such that that it is felt as almost our own 'I'.) How this is done, and why this should be the case, is one of the most fascinating questions to explore.

- Most generally, as with the broader non-musical explanation given earlier, subjectivity may be a useful umbrella term to gather a number of 'subjective' concepts such as *agency, persona, voice, aesthetic presence, subject*, or *living quality*. How these terms might be differentiated still requires clarification.

Yet there are several other, more abstract ways in which music may be said to relate to subjectivity, on quite a different level from the previous examples, which call for acknowledgement here.

- At the broadest level and rather undermining the foregoing attempt at definition, one may (as with Johnson, or indeed Adorno before him) see subjectivity as less something 'in' music, a fictional construct or way of 'hearing as', than what music is, in a real sense, doing. Music *is* subjectivity. This is both valuable and yet for certain purposes excessively general (as all music is thereby subjective, albeit in different ways, which may be productively interrogated).

- Finally, our own relation to music may be constitutive of subjectivity (an extension of the third point above), but in a sense in which it is more accurate to speak not of the *music's* hypothetical subjectivity so much as of *our* subjectivity. Music, as Kramer implies, solicits or invites our own subjectivity as listeners (or indeed performers).

The summary just given outlines some ways in which music may plausibly relate to the idea of subjectivity, understood in a broader, non-musical context. Yet for all the familiarity of the idea in recent musicological writing and musical reception, the idea that there should even be a subject in music at all, in sounds, is far from self-evident. *Why* should music suggest a subject? How does this occur, what justification may we find to support this? What does the subject sound like? A number of such questions arise which require some circling back over ground already traversed, albeit in more detail now. The following section attempts some responses to these problems.

The Sound of Subjectivity: A Preliminary Phenomenology of the Musical Subject

'Accounts of musical subjectivity', writes Lawrence Kramer, 'have often been bedevilled by a nagging sense of futility. The subjective content of music feels unimpeachably real, but the moment one tries to specify it, it risks seeming paper-thin by comparison to the solidity of form, technique and structure, the stuff of analytical understanding.'[51] Kramer is touching on a fundamental concern here. For all the attraction of hearing some form of subjectivity in music, it is not immediately obvious in a more concrete, analytical sense where this subjectivity might be located.[52] Taking our bearings from a question posed by Steinberg ('what does it mean to recognize a first-person voice in music?'), we could equally ask here: *how does music sound when it is speaking in the first person?*[53] Are there any characteristic 'signs' of subjectivity? How else do we read subjectivity into musical sounds?

I would propose there exist a cluster of characteristic markers of musical subjectivity, some more specific and analytically locatable, in particular works or passages, others looser and more diffuse, affinities between our experience of sounds and subjects applicable to a broad range of music.[54] More specifically, one might point to the concepts of *voice* or *vocality* on the one hand, and to the sense of musical *agency*, created especially from a sense of tonally directed motion, on the other. More generally, we may speak of a sense of bodily *presence* felt through music and an apparent affinity with certain attributes of consciousness. Music's expressivity – its status as a preeminent language of the emotions – also readily lends itself to the projection of an underlying subject in whom such affects might be located. Not to be ignored either is the role of language – titles, programmes, tropes in reception history – and other 'extramusical' factors in denoting or suggesting the existence of a musical subject.

---

[51] Kramer, 'The Mysteries of Animation', 174.

[52] Eero Tarasti similarly worries about this question: 'Where are the musical subjects? Are they in the music, the musical enunciate itself? If so, where exactly?' (*A Theory of Musical Semiotics* (Bloomington: Indiana University Press, 1994), p. 108).

[53] Steinberg, 'Schumann's Homelessness', p. 47.

[54] The discussion from here on partly builds on the work of authors cited in the previous sections, especially that of Naomi Cumming, though it will be apparent that my interest in semiotics is less pronounced than hers.

Voice, Vocality, and Lyricism

'Voice', proposed Aristotle long ago, 'is a kind of sound characteristic of what has soul in it; nothing without soul utters voice'.[55] Many centuries later Jean-Jacques Rousseau would observe similarly how 'as soon as vocal signs strike your ear, they proclaim a being similar to yourself; they are, so to speak, the organs of the soul'.[56] The most obvious way in which we hear subjectivity in sound is when another subject gives voice to itself: in a direct sense the sound *is* that of a subject.

Naturally this notion of voice may occur through speech as well as through song, but what is crucial here is not the semantic import of any words but rather the very sound of the voice, its sensuous immediacy and musical quality.[57] As a consequence, the sound of the singing voice is perhaps the primary locus for hearing subjectivity in music. It is hence no surprise that Edward Cone starts out his account of the musical persona with the genre of song, for song not only contains a verbal, grammatical component that helps denote the existence of a subject but further presents the listener with the actual sound of a human subject. The subjectivity here may, of course, be identified directly with that of the performer, but the vocal quality may often be understood in a more metaphorical sense of persona or aesthetic subject.

This is particularly the case when this category is extended to the notion of vocality, those qualities of sonic production and gestures characteristic of the singing voice. Though Aristotle continues his explanation by stating that it is 'only by a metaphor that we speak of the voice of the flute or the lyre', this metaphor is still one that runs extremely deep. Vocal elements in instrumental music readily connote the presence of a subjective voice: not only does the sound originate in the activity of a human subject, but its gestures call to mind the characteristic signs of the human singing voice. Nowhere is this more apparent than with those instruments capable of a sustained *cantabile* line such as the violin, cello, or clarinet, but even in a percussive instrument such as the piano the presence of lyrical elements

---

[55] Aristotle, *On the Soul*, II/8, 420b.

[56] Jean-Jacques Rousseau, *Essay on the Origin of Languages, in which Melody and Musical Imitation Are Treated*, ch. xvi, trans. John T. Scott in *The Collected Writings of Rousseau* (Hanover, NH: University Press of New England, 1998), vol. vii, p. 326.

[57] Moreover, at least in a historical sense, from the mid-eighteenth century and throughout much of the nineteenth, music was often given a historical primacy over spoken language, whereby the articulation of language was either considered as a falling from the immediacy and fullness of music, or song and speech were understood as originating from a common undivided unity (as the example of Rousseau's *Essay* demonstrates).

can establish a putative sense of a subjective voice in the music. Thus, any vocal gesture, even if not produced by the human voice, may allude to the presence of some (fictional) subjectivity; the emergence of a lyrical voice in an instrumental texture might strongly suggest the emergence of a musical subject. Furthermore, once established as a believable metaphor, the notion of a virtual subjective voice may be extended (often through verbal signalling) to types of production which would be inconceivable from a normal human body. From this, we may not only be led to more unusual notions of flowers and birds speaking of an entire landscape calling forth a voice but also to more uncanny senses of disembodiment and absence, of production from inanimate or lifeless objects.[58]

Agency: Tonally Directed Motion, Interaction of Melody, Harmony, and Rhythm

A second factor in the audible manifestation of subjectivity lies in what might be called music's sense of agency – its apparent ability to act towards a defined end – and how this gives rise to a dynamic, living quality. We remember from Cumming that 'any attributions to music of qualities that would normally be applied to living beings, such as locality, gesture, or volition, indicate that subjective content has been heard'.[59] Western music from the common practice era possesses a remarkable capacity to create such an illusion of animation and volition through the power of tonal harmony to instil a sense of logical causation between events and directed motion (the feeling that one harmony follows as a necessary consequence of the preceding, that large-scale cadential articulations are set up as inevitable goals that the music strives towards); the ability of certain types of thematic working to imitate a process of evolving organic life; the control of rhythm, metre, hypermetre, and phrase rhythm to articulate the music's temporal progression into intelligible units whereby its future course may be partially predicted; and not least the art form's indispensible metaphor of movement. It is not that the music appears to be moved by an external source but rather that it appears to be moving itself, to be capable of self-animation. 'In hearing the movement in music', claims Roger Scruton, 'we are hearing life – life conscious of itself'.[60]

---

[58] This idea of music as an art of 'possibly animate things' has recently been taken up by Holly Watkins in *Musical Vitalities: Ventures in a Biotic Aesthetics of Music* (Chicago: Chicago University Press, 2018).

[59] Cumming, 'The Subjectivities of "Erbarme dich"', 11–12.

[60] Roger Scruton, *The Aesthetics of Music* (Oxford: Clarendon Press, 1997), p. 353.

Clearly hearing life in music is a metaphor, an illusion we may (or may not) choose to believe, but it is nevertheless a concept that arose at a point in history particularly relevant for this present study. The years around 1800 witnessed a rise in the idea of art as free creation exhibiting the purposive characteristics of nature and a capacity for organic growth, and a particular predilection for understanding music through metaphors of organic life.[61] From E. T. A. Hoffmann's arboreal explanations of Beethoven to Schopenhauer's identification of music with the striving of the will, the ideology of organicism infiltrates musical aesthetics and reception throughout the next century. Such views reach their apogee (or logical nadir) in formulations such as Heinrich Schenker's notion of *Tonwille*, 'the biological factor in the life of tones', a sense of dynamic will rooted in tonal motion whereby the notes do not merely conform in their succession to the grammatical rules set by external custom but instead follow one another as if from an inner necessity. Implausible though it might sound, Schenker stresses how 'we should get used to the idea that tones have lives of their own, more independent of the artist's pen in their vitality than one would dare to believe'.[62]

Much tonal music, especially in the Classical-Romantic idiom, possesses this quality of apparent agency. Robert Hatten, building on the work of Steve Larson, has recently argued that in cases where musical gestures move against seemingly 'natural' forces or tendencies (e.g. a sense of 'gravity', 'friction', or tonal 'magnetism') a sense of virtual agency may be readily discerned.[63] To this extent, of course, it is hard to differentiate between the sense of subjectivity present in different works or composers: the notion emerges as a rather general one. However, we might view this basic sense of a living quality as a lowest common denominator for the constitution of musical subjectivity: agency, sentience, but not necessarily intelligent, self-conscious life. Once a quality like vocality is added to this base level we move up from a sense of brute animation to something closer

---

[61] The literature on musical organicism is considerable; for an overview see Ian Bent (ed.), *Music Analysis in the Nineteenth Century* (Cambridge: Cambridge University Press, 1994), vol. I, pp. 11–17.

[62] Heinrich Schenker, *Harmony*, ed. Oswald Jonas, trans. Elizabeth Mann Borges (Chicago: University of Chicago Press, 1954), p. xxv.

[63] Hatten, *A Theory of Virtual Agency*, pp. 15–64, drawing on Steve Larson, *Musical Forces: Motion, Metaphor, and Meaning in Music* (Bloomington: Indiana University Press, 2012). See also Monahan, 'Action and Agency Revisited', and Michael Klein, *Music and the Crises of the Modern Subject* (Bloomington: Indiana University Press, 2015), 'Intermezzo: On Agency', pp. 122–6.

to self-consciousness. The highest form of self-consciousness is music that appears to be recognising itself, hearing itself.

The account just given is premised upon music creating the illusion of coherence and causality, where later events may be seen as outcomes of earlier ones, thus giving a sense of purposeful directedness and agency. Some music, however, questions such coherence. As Kramer points out, when this sense of logical continuity and natural self-animation breaks down, the sense of a subject may disintegrate and the music quickly appears artificial, its gestures false.[64] Perhaps this is the same for human as for musical subjects. What is especially fascinating about Schumann's music is to what lengths it problematises such coherence while still managing to suggest a sense of subjectivity.

Bodily Presence and Affinity with Consciousness

'Birds whistle, man alone sings,' observes Rousseau, 'and one cannot hear either a song or an instrumental piece without immediately saying to oneself: another sensitive being is present.'[65] Not only does the sound of a voice indicate subjectivity, but in a more fundamental, visceral sense it points to the physical presence of the subject. More generally, our experience of music may often involve a quality of what could be called 'subjective presence', an almost tangible sense of contact with another being or consciousness, as if we are in the presence of another subject. Scott Burnham has written insightfully in this context of music's 'almost coercive immediacy, its apparent ability to generate and sustain a feeling of presence', an attribute he finds especially prominent in the music of Beethoven.[66]

Significant though this idea may be, it is hard to define precisely how this quality of presence is conveyed. Some suggestions might, however, be proffered. First, despite its erstwhile intangible quality, sound is vibrating matter, utterly material in its physical basis. Music is not merely an abstract, amorphous entity but substantially corporeal, and we sense it through our bodies, not just our ears and minds. Moreover, unlike, say, visual elements, one cannot shut one's ears to sound: music intrudes, whether we like it or not, into our very being. To experience music is to immerse oneself in the corporeal presence of sound. Performing, listening

---

[64] Kramer, 'The Mysteries of Animation', 164–8.
[65] Rousseau, *Essay on the Origin of Languages*, p. 326.
[66] Scott Burnham, *Beethoven Hero* (Princeton: Princeton University Press, 1995), pp. 13, 164–5.

to, or even imagining music can be as much a question of bodily feeling as of auditory cognition, and may invite our own sympathetic physical response.[67] Second, in attending to music, an art in a medium which vanishes even as it appears, we are necessarily attending with greater concern than usual to the experienced present – one made more conscious through the necessity of memory in music's constitution. And as Cone noted, if that awareness is sufficiently acute, 'we can succeed in feeling that we have *become* the music, or that the music has become ourselves'.[68]

But why should this manifest itself in some cases as subjectivity? To respond to this question, we might consider the idea ventured earlier that subjectivity may entail a privileged sense of first-person perspective. Since music, as sound, affects us in a more direct and unmediated manner than the subjects constructed by language or even visual imagery, as an embodied, immersive experience, we may feel this presence as 'really present', as part of our own physical being.[69] This need not be confined to moments of distinct lyrical expression but may be sensed in complete textures, in an accompanimental wash of sound, or when rhythmic cycles in the music seem to parallel the rhythms of the body (consider the effect of the reiterated accompanimental figure in the slow movement of Beethoven's Fourth Symphony, like the gentle throb of a heartbeat). Moreover, music's sense of simply 'being there', existing without any determinate concept or object may offer a strong parallel to a feeling of pure self-consciousness or self-presence.[70] It has often been sensed that

---

[67] See especially Eric Clarke, *Ways of Listening: An Ecological Approach to the Perception of Musical Meaning* (New York: Oxford University Press, 2005).

[68] Cone, *The Composer's Voice*, p. 156. Or in T. S. Eliot's famous words, quoted earlier, music may at times be 'heard so deeply' that 'you are the music, while the music lasts' ('The Dry Salvages', V, from *Four Quartets*).

[69] It is worth underscoring this bodily dimension of musical subjectivity, given the recent musicological appeal to 'the body' and the wider 'material turn' of previous decades, especially as accounts of subjectivity from Schumann's time often emphasise seemingly immaterial notions of interiority over worldly corporeality. Here the model of a 'multidimensional self', set out by Jerrold Seigel, offers a useful corrective. For Seigel, accounts of the self or subject may draw upon three different aspects or dimensions, which he entitles the bodily or material, the relational, and the reflective (*The Idea of the Self*, p. 5). Accounts of subjectivity that address all three are usually richer than those that concentrate on or reduce to one of them, although few theories entirely ignore any of the three.

[70] Marshall Brown, for instance, has argued that the Kantian revolution in consciousness is mirrored in the music of Mozart and his successors ('Mozart and After: The Revolution in Musical Consciousness', *Critical Inquiry*, 7 (1981), 689–706). On the proposition that Kant made the musical into the ground of cognition see Andrew Bowie, *Music, Philosophy, and Modernity* (Cambridge: Cambridge University Press, 2007), p. 86. I discuss these points at greater length in *The Melody of Time: Music and Temporality in the Romantic Era* (New York: Oxford University Press, 2016), pp. 115–23.

there is something peculiarly akin between music and the nature of our subjective consciousness or self. The connexion between music and consciousness is a long-standing one, yet one that has repeatedly proved intractable to define with adequate clarity (as much because the latter is at least as slippery and resistant to definition as subjectivity). We may, however, point to a shared sense of flux and capacity for temporal continuity, an enduring identity across time unattached to any definite physical object – similarities that have led some philosophers to claim that there is an 'ontological affinity between consciousness and sound'.[71]

Expressivity

One of the most powerful of all ways in which music evokes the presence of a human subject is through its expressivity. For much of Western history, music has been known as 'the language of the emotions', for its remarkable capacity to convey human feelings or sentiments. As set out earlier, the identity of the subject who is the source of these feelings is not necessarily clear, but one of the most persuasive responses is to understand the emotional qualities of music (and indeed art more widely) as the expression of an 'imagined utterer'.[72]

Much of the foregoing discussion has been implicitly defensive, trying to provide some grounds for the far-from-commonsense view that there is somehow a subject present in music. Yet viewed from another perspective the regulative fiction of the subject, rather than being a hermeneutic liability, is a protection or buttress against conceptual disintegration, shoring up a host of otherwise unmoored beliefs and values. Does not subjectivity function in some ways as a necessary construct – that by virtue of which we may speak of music's expressiveness, our capacity for feeling empathy or sympathy with it, without calling upon the discredited notion that we are actually feeling the same emotions that the composer felt? If music, for instance, is heard as sad (I emphasise 'the music as sad', not simply that we are sad when listening), and emotions are qualities predicable of human consciousnesses, then positing a (fictional) subject simply clarifies the

---

[71] Laird Addis, *Of Mind and Music* (Ithaca, NY: Cornell University Press, 1999), p. 69. The possible link between the two has received a substantial literature; for a range of accounts see the chapters in David Clarke and Eric Clarke (eds.), *Music and Consciousness: Philosophical, Psychological, and Cultural Perspectives* (Oxford: Oxford University Press, 2011), and Ruth Herbert, David Clarke, and Eric Clarke (eds.), *Music and Consciousness 2: Worlds, Practices, Modalities* (Oxford: Oxford University Press, 2019).

[72] To use the expression of Bruce Vermazen, 'Expression as Expression', *Pacific Philosophical Quarterly*, 67 (1986), 196–223.

fictional but powerful expressive quality perceived.[73] The musical subject here is being used rather like the idea of 'subject' in classical philosophy – as a ground or basis for predicates. It is a construct – imaginary, but useful.

Thus, it is no surprise that the recent 'affective turn' in the humanities and work on music and emotion has sought to advance the persona theory set out by Cone and subsequent writers. Philosophers like Jerrold Levinson, Aaron Ridley, and Jenefer Robinson have productively drawn on the notion of a fictional subject or persona in order to explain the sense that what is heard as emotion in music is not the feelings of the composer or merely a case of resemblance or isomorphism between musical processes and the phenomenology of emotion but may sometimes be best understood as arising from a hypothetical protagonist 'in' (or 'behind') the music.[74] For Robinson, importantly, not all music need be understood as the expression of an imagined persona, but this metaphor is particularly suited to Romantic music.[75]

This point has been recently developed by Michael Spitzer in his large-scale history of music and emotion, which connects the modern idea of the musical persona to nineteenth-century ideas on expression. 'In the nineteenth century,' Spitzer claims, 'musical emotion was individuated in human subjects and bodies'.[76] One of the best examples he finds is Schumann's use of the alter egos Florestan and Eusebius. 'For the Romantics, emotion is character. Whereas ... the modern notion that a fictional agent owns a stable personality was simply foreign to early eighteenth-century psychology, ... the Romantics saw emotion (or passion) as both an emanation of character, and a means of stabilizing character.' Moreover, 'Personifying an inner emotion also meant rendering character visible within the surface physiognomy of the music.'[77]

---

[73] A similar point is made by Hatten in *A Theory of Virtual* Agency; see ch. 6, 'Virtual Subjectivity and Aesthetically Warranted Emotions', pp. 178–201.

[74] Jerrold Levinson, 'Hope in the *Hebrides*', in *Music, Art, and Metaphysics* (Ithaca, NY: Cornell University Press, 1990), pp. 336–75; Aaron Ridley, '*Persona* Sometimes *Grata*: On the Appreciation of Expressive Music', in Kathleen Stock (ed.), *Philosophers on Music: Experience, Meaning, and Work* (Oxford: Oxford University Press, 2007), pp. 130–46; Jenefer Robinson, *Deeper than Reason: Emotion and Its Role in Literature, Music and Art* (Oxford: Oxford University Press, 2005), esp. ch. 11. One of the leading critics of such an approach is Stephen Davies; see 'Contra the Hypothetical Persona in Music', in *Themes in the Philosophy of Music* (Oxford: Oxford University Press, 2003), 152–68.

[75] Robinson, *Deeper than Reason*, p. 321; 307–15; Ridley likewise proposes some music rewards the projection of a virtual persona more than others.

[76] Michael Spitzer, *A History of Emotion in Western Music* (New York: Oxford University Press, 2020), p. 314.

[77] *Ibid.*, p. 311.

If an emotion could be discharged in a flash in a character piece – a musical analogue of Romantic irony's favored genre, the fragment – then changes in musical style meant that, for the first time in history, an emotional script could also be unfolded across a large-scale work. To individuate an emotion is to treat it as the *motion* of a persona in a temporal narrative; in music, this meant a compositional 'subject' moving across the virtual tonal landscape of the work[.]

This is why, out of all the historical styles in his survey, Spitzer considers Romantic music to be best suited to the theory of the musical persona.[78] Significantly, he also notes the value of our contemporary term 'subjectivity', which for him 'amalgamates character and emotion into a single efficacious force'.[79]

Linguistic Association

The preceding discussion is still frustrating in its generality – this, despite the stated attempt at providing a phenomenology of musical subjectivity, an analytical inventory of what specific musical features denote a subject. There *may* be apparent similarities between the sense of self, consciousness, or subjectivity in music, but we rarely have the means to pin this down in anything like a precise sense. Much of this, of course, is due to the difference in denotative ability between music and language. Music's feeling of subjective presence is as potent as it is vague. Could one, for instance, differentiate between first-person singular and first-person plural in music? How does music sound when it is speaking as a 'we' (or, with particular relevance for Schumann, how is this in turn distinguishable from music speaking as multiple selves)? These are problems that will be returned to later in this book, though I should note now that no precise answer will be forthcoming, the task being unavoidably hermeneutic.

It is ironic that this ostensibly most 'subjective' art seems distinctly hazy on such issues. But is this really a problem? For much music does come to us with verbal clues as to its subjective content. We see ample evidence for this in the tactic adopted by Edward T. Cone, whose path into the subject is through song, not just the fact of its vocality, but through the fact that it is a genre of music possessing a text which designates a subject as speaking or singing. Having grounded the apparent validity of his discussion by these means, Cone proceeds to consider the use of persona in instrumental music possessing an explicit or implicit verbal programme, specifically the programmatic symphonies of Berlioz. In both cases, the verbal application of

---

[78] *Ibid.*, p. 315.   [79] *Ibid.*, p. 311.

subjective properties to the work is facilitated by the music already having such labels attached. Similarly, when Schumann designates one character piece 'Chiarina' and another 'Estrella', and we know from biographical information that these names refer to women he knew at this time, our sense of who the subject might be, its identity, is greatly facilitated. (Of course, 'Chiarina' is no more the real historical Clara than 'Eusebius' is Schumann himself in dreamy mode; the identity is once again of a fictional, implied aesthetic subject.) This is not to deny that words are in some cases extrinsic, 'extramusical' (an admittedly problematic category). But so much of our understanding of music is extramusical in this sense. Distinguishing too zealously on this point runs the risk of creating a false dichotomy. At least there is no need to insist on musical purity all the time. Language possesses greater determinacy in denoting subjects than music, and this can be used productively when coming into conjunction with music. And when no such verbal pointers are present, one should not insist on greater precision than is appropriate in this art.

Still, there are some things music appears to do better than words. One such example is its sense of immediacy, as noted before, its apparent ability to work on pre-cognitive, emotive levels of consciousness.[80] And music's indeterminacy need not always be viewed as a problem.

Productive Indeterminacy

The comparative indeterminacy of music's positing of a subject is, in fact, one if its strengths. One of the reasons why music is so potent as a model of human subjectivity derives from the multiple ways in which a sense of subjectivity may be suggested without being delimited. Picking up on this point, Fred Everett Maus has argued that 'musical textures usually invite several discrepant individuations of agents without resolving the issue, and [this] play of different individuations is an important part of musical experience'.[81] As he elsewhere proposes, 'in musical thought, agents and actions sometimes collapse into one another':

This indeterminacy between sounds as agents and as actions is possible because a musical texture does not provide any recognizable objects, apart from the sounds,

---

[80] See, for instance, the argument made by Eric Clarke in 'Lost and Found in Music: Music, Consciousness and Subjectivity', *Musicae Scientiae*, 18 (2014), 354–68, drawing on the work of cognitive psychologist Antonio Damasio, specifically *The Feeling of What Happens: Body, Emotion and the Making of Consciousness* (London: Heinemann, 1999).

[81] Fred Everett Maus, 'Agency in Instrumental Music and Song', *College Music Symposium*, 29 (1989), 37.

that can be agents. If the sound is regarded as action, the listener may also, seeking a perceptible protagonist, attribute those actions to the sounds as agents. In music, Yeats's enigma – how to tell the dancer from the dance – arises continuously and vividly.[82]

Developing such themes, Charles Nussbaum argues similarly that the 'nonconceptual nature' of musical representations 'tends to dissolve epistemic and metaphysical barriers between subject and subject and between subject and object, a result that encourages simulation of virtual musical objects and further enhances emotional involvement'.[83]

Music may be heard as an action or type of agency, as speaking to us through another persona, as immediately expressive of feelings and emotions that are felt as ours, as pure presence, as another consciousness, or even as an extension of or surrogate for one's self. Such a view implicitly qualifies Cone's thesis that all music possesses a univocal subject, speaks in a single unitary voice. Often there is not a single, realistic subject formed by the music, but disparate elements of that which may constitute a subject (like – employing a fruitful homology – modern ideas of the complexity of the human subject). The very indeterminacy of the subject permits the fluid movement between otherwise contradictory perspectives, allowing us to construct an apparently impossible object which is both ourselves and 'other'.[84] Music may suggest a sense of subjectivity sufficient to invite our own subjective response, to allow us to fill its vacant space with subjective attributes, to empathise with it, without circumscribing it. Thus, as Alastair Williams puts it,

Music is an invitation to subjectivity: it participates in the construction of subjectivity by allowing us to inhabit it with our bodies and to experience something beyond the confines of ourselves. Thus when we interact with music we are asked to occupy a subject position, or, put more precisely, we are interpellated by a subject position to which we can respond by means of identification, dialogue, or rejection.[85]

---

[82] Fred Everett Maus, 'Music as Drama', *Music Theory Spectrum*, 10 (1988), 70.

[83] Charles Nussbaum, *Musical Representation: Meaning, Ontology, and Emotion* (Cambridge, MA: Massachusetts Institute of Technology Press, 2007), p. 257.

[84] As Eric Clarke proposes, 'music affords peculiarly direct insight into a limitless variety of subjective experiences of motion and embodiment – real and virtual' (*Ways of Listening*, p. 90). Similarly, for Watkins, 'Music creates a multitude of virtual worlds, or virtual configurations of space and time, that listeners can vicariously experience as alternative forms of embodiment, affect, spirit, thought, or some combination thereof. ... Music both diversifies the self and extends it toward other selves in motion, whether real or imaginary, human or not.' *Musical Vitalities*, p. 4.

[85] Alastair Williams, 'Swaying with Schumann: Subjectivity and Tradition in Wolfgang Rihm's "Fremde Szenen" I–III and Related Scores', *Music & Letters*, 87 (2006), 396.

Some music – even from the nineteenth century, even from Schumann – may not appear to solicit the listener's response in terms of another subject. But this sense is powerful enough in others.

The Arbitrary Subject: Music and Language

A final point, towards which the previous discussion has been moving, is the extent to which the fictional status of the problematic and problematised musical subject differs from that of language. Repeatedly we felt compelled to defend the notion that speaking of subjectivity in music was meaningful. Implicitly, we seemed to labour against the notion that subjectivity in music is somehow artificial, fictional, at root a mere fantasy, whereas if only we could draw on language everything would be fine. The use of verbal texts in songs or programmatic music was even introduced to support the plausibility of positing a subject in music. On the face of it, this would be a defensible position. But this is all overlooking one obvious point. For the subject of language is just as much a fiction as music's. The use of the first-person singular pronoun, even its sound, when I speak it, when I say 'I', is just as arbitrary, just as constructed. (It is still meaningful, at least if this sentence is understood by another reader. So is the subject in music.) We might read *War and Peace* or *The Brothers Karamazov*, *Middlemarch* or *À la recherche du temps perdu*. But there is no real human subject present in any of these books, no more than there is in Beethoven's *Eroica* Symphony or Tchaikovsky's *Pathétique*. Asking where the subject is in music is in this sense no less problematic than that in a novel, or for that matter in a visual image (a portrait, on film). Yes, music seems less clear than language in its capacity to designate who is speaking. But in both cases the 'who' is entirely fictional. All are constructs, conventions we choose to hear, metaphors by which we live, so much so that their constructed nature sometimes escapes us.

Looking at it, the subject of language, albeit more precisely denotative, is just as arbitrary. What we think of as the subject is largely a grammatical construct. And in both language and music, the fact that a sound or an inscription designates, connotes, or is sometimes interpreted as suggesting a subject is a priori arbitrary but a posteriori not.[86] (Perhaps, even, hearing a subject in musical sounds is on occasions mildly less arbitrary, such as

---

[86] See Clark, *Ways of Listening*, p. 40, drawing on Roland Barthes, *Elements of Semiology*, trans. A. Lavers and C. Smith (New York: Hill and Wang, 1968), p. 51.

with the case of vocality, as it is here functioning as an indexical referent, not symbolic.)

Arguments against the reality of the subject, or those that construe it as simply a construction of language or society, are familiar from poststructuralist thought. The grammatical construct who is allegedly thinking and writing, and whose words you (that equally grammatical construct?) are reading now, does not want (with any sense of his illusory agency) to enter this debate here. But it is worth remembering that, no matter how far we wish to go down the poststructuralist path, if the subject is constructed through language and other cultural forms of meaning, music is equally implicated in such constructions of subjectivity. And, while this is a topic that must be left for exploration elsewhere, it may be worth considering whether in some senses music might actually hold out the tantalising possibility of escaping from certain linguistic aporias associated with the subject, or at least doing something different from words. This is not to suggest that we could be modern subjects and have the same self-understanding without language; nor, too, would I venture too much on whether this musical self-understanding is not already partially inculcated, bound up with the linguistic means we use to describe it (as exemplified by this book). But this musical subjectivity is importantly different from verbal subjectivity and cannot therefore be entirely reduced to it. Both music and language provide possible ways of constructing a sense of self.

The Emergence of Subjectivity: The Musical Subject in History

Though hearing a subject in music may seem on the face of it as 'subjective' in the bad sense – that is, an arbitrary interpretation – as we have seen it is, in fact, a cultural belief, in other words, intersubjective, the product of society. As Cumming usefully underlines, 'what is "heard in" the sounds . . . has been heard according to a learned code of recognition'.[87] Thus it does not make sense to claim impressions of subjectivity are merely subjective; rather, they are intersubjective, socially constructed (like language, like other types of meaning). If the subject in music is socially constructed, this necessarily means the idea arose in a specific historical and geographical culture. To this extent, asking why there is a subject in an apparently ahistorical, a priori manner is deceptive; not only is it difficult to answer, but it asks a wrong question. It is much easier to show that music was

---

[87] Cumming, *The Sonic Self*, p. 17.

understood in a number of ways that afforded, supported, even demanded, the notion of subjectivity just traced. Tracing the 'archaeology' or 'genealogy' of music's relation to the idea of subjectivity is actually far simpler than defining subjectivity per se.

The Historical Rise of Subjectivity

While one might think from some discourse that the subject is a timeless entity, subjectivity as a concept has a history. It is indeed noteworthy that the earliest instances for the use of the term recorded in the OED all date from the first part of the nineteenth century (most come from Coleridge, who was deeply steeped in contemporary German Romantic and Idealist thought). There is, in fact, general consensus among scholars that subjectivity, and the related notions of the subject and self upon which the idea draws, are in certain essential respects modern concepts. Though some present-day analytic philosophers of mind are adamant that 'the sense of the self arises almost irresistibly from fundamental features of human experience and is no sense a product of "Western" culture, still less a recent product of it, as some have foolishly supposed', others are more circumspect.[88] Of course, in certain epistemological respects the structures of the mind and self-awareness surely have been relatively constant across the last few millennia of human history, but the importance accorded to the subject or self – even its labelling as such – has undoubtedly changed within this time period.[89] As Robert Pippin observes, it is 'only relatively recently in Western history that we began to think of human beings as something like individual, pretty much self-contained and self-determining centres of a causal agency', a event that is normally located in the period after 1600.[90]

In antiquity it was customary to speak of the 'soul', but not of being 'a self'.[91] Personal identity was not such a concern; for the Homeric heroes, anger, wrath, courage were visitations from the gods, not intrinsic aspects

---

[88] Galen Strawson (ed.), *The Self?* (Oxford: Blackwell, 2005), p. vi.

[89] Charles Taylor notes how making 'self' into a noun, speaking of 'the' self or 'a' self, reflects something important which is peculiar to our modern sense of agency (the Greeks, he observes, had their reflexive 'gnothi seauton' – the celebrated Delphic 'know thyself!' – but not really the sense of 'ho autos', 'the self'). Taylor, *Sources of the Self: The Making of the Modern Identity* (Cambridge, MA: Harvard University Press, 1989), p. 113.

[90] Robert B. Pippin, *The Persistence of Subjectivity: On the Kantian Aftermath* (Cambridge: Cambridge University Press, 2001), p. 7. For a slightly divergent view see Seigel, *The Idea of the Self*, p. 25.

[91] See John Barresi and Raymond Martin, *The Rise and Fall of Soul and Self: An Intellectual History of Personal Identity* (New York: Columbia University Press, 2006); for a briefer introduction, see also the same authors' 'History as Prologue: Western Theories of the Self', in

belonging to their personal selves, just as for Plato love and artistic inspiration were divine beneficence. For Charles Taylor, in his important study of
the self and modern identity, a crucial move inwards is initiated by
Augustine, who distinguishes between the outer and inner man (the *inter-
iore homine*), the space where I am present to myself. Augustine's turn to
the self was thus a turn to a radical reflexivity.[92] But, it is above all from the
seventeenth century onwards that the modern understanding of the subject
is born. With René Descartes's *cogito*, the self is made into the ground for
human knowledge, an unassailable centre for the philosophic enterprise
upon which the rest of the world must hold. And with this epistemological
turn in philosophy and the breakdown of the older 'ontic logos' we witness
a decisive shift to the modern sense of subject, whereby we place within the
subject 'what was previously seen as existing, as it were, between knower/
agent and world, linking them and making them inseparable'.[93] The early
modern 'self' replaces the ancient 'soul'.

In an era of ever-growing social emancipation and enfranchisement
from an earlier condition of absolute rule this was the subject rooted in
personal identity and self-possession, one that, in the words of Thomas
Reid, formed 'the foundation of all rights and obligations, and of all
accountableness'.[94] The result was that 'notion central to the self-
understanding and legitimation of the bourgeois form of life: the free,
rational, independent, reflective, self-determining subject'.[95] Rather than
being defined by anything outside itself, conforming to an external end,
a subject of another, the modern 'bourgeois subject' is subject purely to
itself. The subject is not a pre-given thing: 'a human subject is, rather,
a meaning-*making* subject ... a self-conscious subject'.[96] In fact, given
that it can only be known to itself, from a first-person perspective, it
demands self-exploration: we must explore what we are in order to
establish our own identity – it is given in no other way. 'The domain is
within, that is, *it is only open to a mode of exploration which involves the
first-person stance.*'[97]

However, with such exploration it gradually became clear that this sense
of self was a curious, even fragile thing, one which upon analysis was ever in

---

Shaun Gallagher (ed.), *The Oxford Handbook of the Self* (Oxford: Oxford University Press,
    2011), pp. 33–55.
[92] Taylor, *Sources of the Self*, p. 129.   [93] *Ibid.*, p. 188.
[94] Thomas Reid, *Essays on the Intellectual Powers of Man* (1785) (Cambridge: John Bartlett, 1850),
    p. 112.
[95] Pippin, *The Persistence of Subjectivity*, p. 5.   [96] *Ibid.*, p. 2.
[97] Taylor, *Sources of the Self*, p. 389, emphasis mine.

danger of becoming either little more than fictional, divided within itself, or else infinitely unknowable to itself (what Gilbert Ryle would memorably call the 'systematic elusiveness' of the concept of 'I').[98] John Locke famously sees the self and our sense of personal identity to reside in consciousness. 'Consciousness always accompanies thinking, and makes everyone to be what he calls "self" and thereby distinguishes himself from all other thinking things; in this alone consists personal identity ... Whatever has the consciousness of present and past actions is the same person to whom they both belong.'[99] It follows that we are what we remember, our identity relies on narrative continuity, the stories we construct about ourselves. David Hume took the implications of this theory and drew them out to reach the more drastic conclusion that 'the identity, which we ascribe to the mind of man, is only a fictitious one'.[100] Not all were willing to subscribe to this level of scepticism. Immanuel Kant's philosophical revolution amounted to a subjectivising of our knowledge of the world (albeit as objective epistemological preconditions). For Kant, the self is not a fiction but part of the very structure of consciousness, a transcendental 'I' or ground of apperception. However, since it is that by virtue of which our empirical self is able to perceive at all, this transcendental self cannot in itself be perceived. And anyway, others asked, how could we stand back from our self to see this self? How can a subject be at once completely an object to itself? By what means can we illuminate that obscure inner space of apparently infinite depths?

Thus, around the beginning of the nineteenth century the subject occupied a central yet perilous position in philosophy. Either, taking a sceptical line, it was a fiction, a narrative told (by itself), or it was something that escaped itself at the moment of looking, a transcendental precondition that was forever unknowable. It is within this new notion of the subject, one that is self-conscious, reflexive, a 'meaning-making subject', but one that is apparently ever unknowable to itself, that art may play a particularly vital role. For if the subject is that which is accessible only to itself, it can be approached only by its own forms of articulation, in the narratives it tells, in the way it configures

---

[98] Gilbert Ryle, *The Concept of Mind* [1949] (Harmondsworth: Penguin, 1990), p. 178.

[99] John Locke, *An Essay Concerning Human Understanding*, ed. Peter Nidditch (Oxford: Clarendon Press, 1975), II/27 'Of Identity and Diversity', § 9. 16.

[100] David Hume, *A Treatise of Human Nature*, ed. L.A. Selby-Bigge (Oxford: Clarendon Press, 1951), I/IV/6, 'Of Personal Identity', § 15, p. 259. In keeping with other thinkers of the Scottish Enlightenment such as Adam Smith, Hume has a broader, more pragmatic conception of selfhood than this one-dimensional reflective one, being inclined to see the self as based more fundamentally in bodily passion and practically constituted through social interactions.

temporally distended events into meaningful articulations of time. And this is what art was understood as achieving.

Music as an Articulation of Subjectivity

'Something fundamental changes in the late eighteenth century', claims Taylor. 'The modern subject is no longer defined just by the power of disengaged rational control but by this new power of expressive self-articulation as well – the power which has been ascribed since the Romantic period to the creative imagination.'[101] Subjectivity, following one definition proposed earlier, is less what the subject *is* than how the subject articulates itself – what it *does*. If art constitutes a primary means by which the subject expresses and realises itself, then it is already inherently a form of subjectivity. This is a major reason for the enormous surge in interest in aesthetics around the start of the nineteenth century. For many philosophers, thinkers, and poets after Kant and Schiller, art is the manner in which the self can intuit itself, a reconciling of freedom and necessity, conscious and unconscious, an externalisation of human spirit, a means by which the subject can recognise itself.[102] Such views were supported by the idea of organicism as the dominant mode for understanding art and expressivist views of creativity.[103] And music, above all, was seen as the subjective art *par excellence*, owing to its apparent absence of material substance, its sense of supratemporal identity amidst temporal passing, and not least its long-established ability to act directly on human feelings at a period when the notion of *Gefühl* was seen as a more unmediated, precognitive means of expression that bypassed perceived problems in language.[104]

   Thus, it is a truism of Idealist philosophy and Romantic thought that music is resounding subjectivity, 'the art of reflection or of self-consciousness' that 'takes as its subject-matter the subjective inner life itself'.[105] One of the clearest of all illustrations can be found in Hegel, for whom 'music is spirit, or the soul

---

[101] Taylor, *Sources of the Self*, p. 390, emphasis mine.

[102] Classic formulations may be found in Friedrich Schiller's *Aesthetic Education of Man* and F. W. J. Schelling's *System of Transcendental Idealism*.

[103] See M. H. Abrams, *The Mirror and the Lamp: Romantic Theory and the Critical Tradition* (Oxford: Oxford University Press, 1953); Taylor, *Sources of the Self*, pp. 368–90.

[104] See especially Andrew Bowie, *Aesthetics and Subjectivity*. A classic formulation of this priority of feeling over all reflection is given by Novalis, who famously asserts that 'The borders of feeling are the borders of philosophy' (Novalis, *Fichte Studies*, ed. Jane Kneller (Cambridge: Cambridge University Press, 2003), No. 15, p. 13).

[105] Schelling, *Philosophy of Art*, trans. Douglas W. Stott (Minneapolis: University of Minnesota Press, 1989), p. 162; G. W. F. Hegel, *Aesthetics: Lectures on Fine Art*, trans. T. M. Knox, 2 vols. (Oxford: Clarendon Press, 1975), vol. II, p. 909.

which resounds directly on its own account and feels satisfaction in its perception of itself'. Music, in his belief, is brought into being by the 'complete withdrawal, of both the inner life and its expression, into subjectivity', taking 'the subjective as such for both form and content'.[106] One might look equally to Friedrich Schlegel, to Wackenroder, Novalis, Jean Paul, Wordsworth, Coleridge, and to a whole host of writers and thinkers down to the twentieth century, for other comparable formulations. As I have argued elsewhere, in the years after 1800 music becomes omnipresent as a metaphor for understanding the continuity and flow of experienced time, for explicating the nature of consciousness, and at the broadest level for reconciling the temporally separated events of our lives into a meaningful continuity. Indeed, a strong case can be made that music was seen as the closest thing to the self, to consciousness, to the 'absolute subjectivity' for which all other names were lacking.[107]

If, as Paul Ricoeur holds, the problematic of personal identity 'can be articulated only in the temporal dimension of human existence', then music would appear to possess a privileged capacity to articulate this sense of selfhood.[108] At any rate, many writers and thinkers in the Romantic era believed this to be the case. It was noted before that the connexion between music and subjectivity often appeared tenuous when approached from an ahistorical perspective. But viewed historically, substantiating the link is quite unproblematic, for it is incontrovertible that music was commonly understood in the nineteenth century as a means by which the subject articulated itself, as a form of subjectivity.

In Search of a Subject

This chapter has offered a range of approaches to defining the question of musical subjectivity – what it *is*, what it *has* (i.e. its attributes), what it *does* – reflections that have repeatedly circled back, tracing different paths over this contested subject, in preparation for the main part of this book which follows. In summary fashion now, I would like to offer a handful of theses

---

[106] Hegel, *Aesthetics*, vol. II, pp. 939, 889.

[107] Taylor, *The Melody of Time*, pp. 113–15; the allusion is to Edmund Husserl, *The Phenomenology of Internal Time Consciousness*, trans. James Churchill (The Hague: Martinus Nijhoff, 1964), §36.

[108] Paul Ricoeur, *Oneself as Another*, trans. Kathleen Blamey (Chicago: University of Chicago Press, 1992), p. 114.

or tenets which we may take from the preceding ruminations and may serve as a guide, explanation, or perhaps apologia for the remainder of this study.

The Resistance-Resilience of Subjectivity. No matter how much the notion of the unified subject has been attacked, no matter how many rhetorical claims are made for the death of the subject, subjectivity, as numerous scholars have noted, has proved remarkably resilient as a concept. At the risk of repeating a truism that was already verging on the banal, subjectivity can be many different things for many different people. The resistance to definition of which Johnson speaks is to this extent a valuable property. This is said not as an attempt at obfuscating the question, but rather from a desire to avoid reducing the idea of subjectivity to a fixed category which may be used or equally dismissed as merely ideological, as if it were obvious what is meant by this word, and all the ways in which it has been used have a unitary meaning. Furthermore, rather than this resistance to definition being a problem for the term's application to music, we might choose to see this as liberating. Musical subjectivity, perhaps most of all, resists confinement to language.

Subjectivity is not necessarily an object, or a fixed, stable concept. The nature of musical subjectivity is slippery and can refer to many different, though at some level related qualities. It does not simply refer to a sense of persona, or even multiple personae, but may include a sense of animation and agency, expressivity, presence, personal identification, all of which can flow into each other so fluidly as to give rise to otherwise impossible subjects or subjective experiences. 'Subjectivity', I propose, is ultimately the most fitting term for covering the overall sense of our experience of music (in particular, Western music from the later eighteenth century onwards) as being like a living being, consciousness, self, or subject. Its inclusivity is also useful in implicating the 'work' done by music, its mediation between the composer and style, culture, audience, tradition, between ourselves and something else.

Subjectivity is an act – an aesthetic act. Music does the work of subjectivity. Subjectivity is not a preformed entity, but a process in which we, as subjects are involved. When we engage with music's apparent subjectivity, we are engaging with aspects of our own sense of what it is to be a human, meaning-making subject. The role of art and the aesthetic within the philosophical enterprise since Baumgarten, Kant, and Schiller is fundamentally such an attempt at connecting the subject to world, in other words, 'doing' subjectivity. This might not only be used 'to recover stable and reassuring ideas of selfhood' in a manner familiar from recent critiques of aesthetic ideology but it also holds the potential to be transformative or 'world-disclosive'.[109]

Subjectivity is always intersubjectivity; as a form of mediation it requires interpretation and an interpretant. Subjectivity is mediated through relations with others; effectively, then, it is always intersubjectivity. Whether in the relation of self to society, or listener to music, subjectivity is a process of mediation and (self) understanding. Subjectivity is not at all the same as solipsism: the subject is always a subject *for* someone, for someone else (even if to itself), always bound up with the dialectic of self and other. Taking up an important point from Hegel, subjectivity is how the subject appears, manifests itself, as an object to an other, a mode of understanding premised upon difference. Even when we hear 'ourselves' in music, this is something that is yet 'other'. Only through such alterity is there the possibility of attaining self-recognition, in other words, a fuller sense of subjectivity.

Subjectivity as Emergent. I am aware that many questions concerning this curious idea of subjectivity, ones which might by rights have been expected to have been answered in this preliminary definitional section, remain to be satisfactorily addressed. By good fortune, an apt pretext may be found for their absence here and deferral to a later stage. Since subjectivity arises from our forms of mediation, in fact depends on our ability to propose interpretations which may be accepted or rejected but which are always provisional and can be added to, we might agree with earlier scholars that subjectivity is something that is *emergent* – both not only in the everyday sense that it comes into being over time but also in the more specialised sense that its identity is not fully definable in advance or reducible to its constituent parts (and hence plausibly calls for a narrative account of the specific course taken in its formation). This book is in a manner a mediation on music's mediation (something which equally may be accepted or rejected), in another manner constituting a form of subjectivity. And this quality will manifest itself across this book, emerging piece by piece.

---

[109] Kevin Korsyn, *Decentering Music: A Critique of Contemporary Musical Research* (Oxford: Oxford University Press, 2003), p. 44; on music's subjectivity as, on the contrary, 'world-disclosive' see especially Bowie, *Music, Philosophy, and Modernity.*

PART I

Hearing Subjects

2 | Hearing the Self

Schumann and the Rise of Subjectivity

In terms of the historical emergence of subjectivity, Schumann was certainly fated to live in interesting times. As we have seen, the composer entered the world during a period in which the nature of the self and personal identity was keenly disputed, and the capacity of art to articulate this quality was valorised as never before. Few would argue with Michael Steinberg's assertion that nineteenth-century music is 'a language of subjectivity'.[1] Nevertheless, while this notion of subjectivity is undeniably in important respects a product of the age and culture into which Schumann was born, music's close association with the human subject – its ability to convey significant aspects of what we would now call subjectivity – is not entirely an invention of the early nineteenth century.

Where exactly we should locate the beginnings of musical subjectivity is open to question, but many scholars would hold that the development of a new sense of self-representation in music around 1600 through the new forms of opera and madrigal is related in an important way to an emerging sense of a modern subject.[2] Others have located a potential emergence of musical subjectivity even earlier, in the medieval period (just as a new sense of the individual has been located around the twelfth century in Europe).[3] The notion of music as the language of the passions – the baroque *Affektenlehre* widespread in the seventeenth and

---

[1] Steinberg, *Listening to Reason*, p. xi.

[2] See, for instance, Susan McClary, *Modal Subjectivities: Self-Fashioning in the Italian Madrigal* (Berkeley: University of California Press, 2004), *Desire and Pleasure in Seventeenth-Century Music* (Berkeley: University of California Press, 2012), or Mauro Calcagno, *From Madrigal to Opera: Monteverdi's Staging of the Self* (Berkeley: University of California Press, 2012). McClary has argued that the musical expression of this new sense of modern self may have even occurred prior to its explicit verbal articulations, such as in celebrated philosophical accounts by Descartes and Locke.

[3] See, for example, Judith Peraino, *Giving Voice to Love: Song and Self-Expression from the Troubadours to Guillaume de Machaut* (Oxford: Oxford University Press, 2011). Most recently, Robert Hatten has sought to apply the notion of subjectivity to virtually the entire history of Western music (see *A Theory of Musical Agency*, esp. pp. 139–49, 276–81).

eighteenth centuries – presupposes that music is in some form representative of subjective states, while in recent years scholars have examined the subjectivities potentially set into play by the music of J. S. Bach
and his contemporaries.[4] Certainly by the time of C. P. E. Bach and the
aesthetics of *Empfindsamkeit*, music is considered the exemplary art of
the human soul by virtue of its remarkable capacity to arouse passions
through sympathetic resonance in the listener.[5] And with the music of
the late eighteenth century, above all what is conventionally termed
Viennese Classicism, music's capacity to convey a sense of the modern
subject – one variously negotiating its place within society, enacting the
individual's struggle for freedom, or reflecting the nature of the self
being disputed at this time – is almost an axiom nowadays, avowed in
numerous scholarly accounts.[6] By the time we get to the early nineteenth
century, the ability of music to express some of our deepest and most
cherished notions of selfhood is well-nigh undisputed; modern discussion of the work of Beethoven and Schubert is scarcely conceivable
without some implicit model of musical subjectivity underlining its
interpretation.[7]

On the other hand, there is a danger of historical flattening and
anachronism here, of reducing earlier musical manifestations of potential
subjective qualities to a Romantic conception of subjectivity that still
pervades contemporary assumptions about musical expression and hence
appears universal and historically invariant (this, despite the technological
changes in the making and consumption of music witnessed in the last

---

[4] A good example is John Butt's chapter 'Bach's Passions and the construction of early modern
subjectivities', in *Bach's Dialogue with Modernity: Perspectives on the Passions* (Cambridge:
Cambridge University Press, 2010), pp. 36–96. Jairo Moreno has turned attention to the
representations of the subject that form the epistemological preconditions of music theory in the
early modern era in his *Musical Representations, Subjects, and Objects: The Construction of
Musical Thought in Zarlino, Descartes, Rameau, and Weber* (Bloomington: Indiana University
Press, 2004).

[5] See Daniel K. L. Chua, *Absolute Music and the Construction of Meaning* (Cambridge: Cambridge
University Press, 1999), pp. 114–25.

[6] The idea is linked with the New Musicology of the 1990s and its project to emphasise the socially
situated nature of music and its meanings, alongside the pervasive influence of Adorno on
English-language scholarship in this period. The writings of Susan McClary and Lawrence
Kramer are typical in this regard. A classic early formulation is McClary's 'A Musical Dialectic
from the Enlightenment: Mozart's *Piano Concerto in G major*, K. 453, Movement 2', *Cultural
Critique*, 4 (1986), 129–69.

[7] See, for instance, Scott Burnham, *Beethoven Hero*, Lawrence Kramer, *Franz Schubert: Sexuality,
Subjectivity, Song*, Susan McClary, 'Constructions of Subjectivity in Schubert's Music', in
Philip Brett, Elizabeth Wood, and Gary C. Thomas, *Queering the Pitch: The New Gay and
Lesbian Musicology* (New York: Routledge, 1994), pp. 205–33.

century and postmodern assaults on the notion of the self). W. Dean Sutcliffe has recently warned of the 'challenge when considering agency in eighteenth-century music': that it can too readily be equated with a kind of encompassing Romantic subjectivity that is 'only awkwardly applicable to the musical outputs of the eighteenth century'. For Sutcliffe, current accounts of musical agency 'remain rooted in romantic aesthetics'.[8]

One may, in the preceding instances, try to distinguish those accounts that seek to establish what was demonstrably held by figures in a previous period, largely through examination of surviving verbal testimony, from those that, often from a more presentist perspective, read subjective qualities into the music from this time – the historical from the hermeneutical so to speak. Then again, one of the arguments put forward by proponents of the latter viewpoint is – rather aptly in this context – that music's own 'agency' should be listened to and taken as evidence. It is hard to resolve this predicament (one should certainly be wary of reducing all forms of meaning to verbally expressed formulations); nevertheless, accounts of subjectivity applied to pre-nineteenth-century music continually run the risk of imposing a Romantic model onto an earlier repertoire to which it is historically foreign.[9]

What is new, special, or distinct about the nineteenth century, then, and the articulations of subjectivity found in music from this time? Such a question can be hard to answer, and it is probably unwise and ultimately unnecessary to insist on any dogmatic distinction, convenient though it may be, that would set off previous musical representations of subjectivity from those in the nineteenth century. There are aesthetic and stylistic changes, of course, such as the movement from the baroque doctrine of the unity of affect to the topically diverse, mixed styles of the later eighteenth century, but these do not, in themselves, undermine the attribution of subjective qualities to earlier music. At most, this might point to later music being more complex in the range and nuance of subjective states it can be heard to express (though even this assertion might be disputed by some scholars).[10] More significantly, though, the epistemological and interpretative frameworks available to historical listeners are plausibly different. The primarily physiological basis of the eighteenth-century aesthetic of sensibility often

---

[8] W. Dean Sutcliffe, *Instrumental Music in an Age of Sociability: Haydn, Mozart, and Friends* (Cambridge: Cambridge University Press, 2019), pp. 122, 123. To this extent Sutcliffe's call for adequate historicising of the concept forms the opposite pole to Robert Hatten's universalising impulse in his 2018 theory of musical agency.

[9] An example of a sensitive and nuanced approach along these lines is given by Butt, 'Bach's Passions and the construction of early modern subjectivities'; see especially his conclusion, p. 96.

[10] For a broad backdrop to this question see Spitzer, *A History of Emotion in Western Music*, ch. 6–8.

differs from later Romantic theorising on the manner subjectivity is conveyed by music, while nineteenth-century accounts of music often drew on organic metaphors of life, attributing a type of virtual agency to music that is not really found beforehand to anything like the same extent.[11] It is, moreover, only in the early nineteenth century, Mark Evan Bonds has argued, that listeners readily began to hear the emotions conveyed in music as stemming from the composer – as subjective self-expression – rather than as an objective construct.[12] More speculative are attempts to relate the growing sense of musical subjectivity at this time to the developing historical understanding of the nature of the self, as formulated, for instance, in contemporaneous philosophical discourse.[13] The precise mechanism by which music reflects or parallels contemporary conceptual thought is not always clear, but whether it is necessary to demonstrate this link is again a matter for debate.

What certainly can be affirmed, however, is that the early nineteenth century is the first time that the idea of subjectivity becomes explicitly foregrounded as part of the framework within which music was understood, just as the term itself comes to prominence at this time. Prior to this, accounts of musical subjectivity tend to take their evidence from the music, not from the contemporaneous discussion of music – or at most indirectly from the latter, by reading elements that would nowadays be termed subjective back into it; from this historical point onwards, though, music's subjectivity becomes openly recognised in reception. This is especially true in the German-speaking world, in which both subjectivity and the idea of music as a higher or deeper form of communication becomes dominant at this time to an unprecedented degree.[14] Subjectivity and musical subjectivity alike are privileged discursive concepts of the early nineteenth century.

Along with this open acknowledgement of music's status as an art of subjectivity comes a greater propensity for exploring the problems associated with subjectivity at this time, for questioning the unity of the subject, its ability to know itself – a task which art was deemed pre-eminently suited

---

[11] On the latter point, see especially Michael Spitzer, *Metaphor and Musical Thought* (Chicago: University of Chicago Press, 2004). As Spitzer argues, 'The illusion that music can embody human qualities is irreducible from our musical experience', though we 'have plenty of latitude in how to hear its human aspects' (p. 12).

[12] Bonds, *The Beethoven Syndrome*, which offers a useful, if perhaps overly reductive historical account of subjective expression in musical reception over the last 250 years.

[13] See especially Brown, 'Mozart and After', and Johnson, 'The Subjects of Music', pp. 73–9.

[14] On music's relation to the notion of subjective depth in German culture at the time see Holly Watkins, *Metaphors of Depth in German Musical Thought: From E. T. A. Hoffmann to Arnold Schoenberg* (Cambridge: Cambridge University Press, 2011), pp. 1–50.

to undertake. If, for Julian Johnson, 'what unites classical composers is their suggestion of achieving the formal integration of a coherent subject while in their different ways failing to do so. Classical music is thus not the expression of an integrated subjectivity so much as the search for one, an experimentation, a projection of different possible forms', Romantic composers both consciously acknowledged and took considerably further this process.[15] And Schumann is one of the first musicians who explicitly and most adventurously sought to explore the nature and complexity of modern subjectivity through music.

Carnivalesque Characters: Searching for Subjectivity in Schumann

In a note written around 1830, Robert Schumann muses to himself concerning an acquaintance – a 'youth I've long loved and observed. I would like to portray his soul', he writes, 'but I don't know it completely'.[16] The subject whom Schumann is addressing here in the third person – 'S.' – is none other than himself. Around the same time, Schumann would create his famous alter egos, Florestan and Eusebius, in an attempt to articulate the complex and multiple sense of identity he felt characterised his subjective being. Significantly, too, despite having reckoned his talents as musician and poet to be equal at this stage, from this point on he turned decisively to the composition of music to express his artistic impulses.

It is with the works of his first creative decade – from his first published opus, the 'Abegg' Variations of 1831, to the outpouring of Lieder in 1840 – that Schumann has become celebrated as a supposedly 'subjective' artist, a feature probably aided by the fact that his music from these years consists almost entirely of works in the intimate genres of solo piano piece and song.[17] Of these, Schumann's 1834–5 piano cycle, *Carnaval*, Op. 9, is

---

[15] Johnson, 'The Subjects of Music', p. 78. This feature distinguishes, for instance, readings of Beethoven's late music as manifesting the fissures of the modern subject, familiar from Adorno and his followers – readings imposed on the music, plausibly or otherwise, without recourse to questions of authorial intent or historical attestation – from later cases where composers (such as Schumann) can be explicitly shown to raise such questions of subjectivity in their writing.

[16] Schumann, 'Beylage zu Hottentottiana' (vol. IV, 1829–30), *Tagebücher*, vol. I, p. 242: 'S. ist d. Jüngling, den ich lange liebte u. beobachtete. Seine Seele möcht' ich mahlen, aber ich kenne sie nicht ganz'.

[17] The few exceptions to this generic restriction – most prominently the G minor ('Zwickau') Symphony of 1832/3 – were unfinished and unpublished by the composer in his lifetime. Schumann's Opp. 1–23 correspondingly consists entirely of solo piano music.

perhaps the primary source for attributions of subjectivity to his oeuvre; at any rate, it is one that commentators have commonly fastened onto, and makes a convenient starting point for our present purposes. *Carnaval* presents a parade of character pieces and dances, named variously after characters from the Italian *commedia dell'arte* ('Pierrot', 'Arlequin', 'Pantalon et Colombine'); real persons from Schumann's fictitious 'Davidsbund' circle, either under the fanciful names he had given them ('Eusebius' and 'Florestan' as two sides of Schumann himself, 'Chiarina' as Clara Wieck, 'Estrella' as Ernestine von Fricken), or other composers under their own names ('Chopin', 'Paganini'); evocative or 'characteristic' titles (e.g. 'Papillons') along with suggestions of some latent action ('Reconnaissance', 'Aveu'), and more or less generic names of dances and marches ('Valse noble', 'Valse allemande', 'Marche des "Davidsbündler" contre les Philistins'). In this series of twenty-two miniature pieces, the nature of subjective identity is toyed with, fragmented, destabilised, even perhaps placed in question.

'Scènes mignonnes sur quatre notes' Schumann describes his carnival, for almost every one of the miniature scenes is based on a musical cipher, a series of notes that cryptically encode the name of the Bohemian town 'Asch', from which the composer's then betrothed, Ernestine von Fricken, hailed. In German musical notation, 'Asch' can be spelt through the four pitches A-E♭-C-B (A Es[=S] C H); more concisely, it can also be rendered with the three pitches A♭-C-B (As C H). Schumann will use both forms throughout his cycle, the former in the first half of the collection, the latter primarily in the second part. But in finding that Ernestine's hometown was eminently 'musical', Schumann also delighted in finding these same four notes were present in his own name (SCHA, or E♭-C-B-A) – 'indeed, the only musical letters in it'.[18] Thus in encoding a reference to the town of his beloved, Schumann was also, in a manner, working his own identity anagrammatically into his work.

This feature, cryptically referenced in *Carnaval*'s subtitle (*Scènes mignonnes sur quatre notes*), becomes explicit in the middle of the piece, in an enigmatic section of the score that lies between 'Réplique' and 'Papillons'. Here Schumann sets out, in archaic notation, the three musical ciphers corresponding to his name, SCHA, and the two forms of ASCH. Fittingly, he entitled this section 'Sphinxes' (Ex. 2.1). No one really knows

---

[18] Schumann, letter to Henriette Voigt, 13 September 1834, in Robert Schumann, *Briefe: Neue Folge*, ed. Gustav Jansen, 2nd ed. (Leipzig: Breitkopf & Härtel, 1904), p. 57. Also see his letter to Moscheles, 22 September 1837 (*ibid.*, p. 101).

Ex. 2.1 Schumann: 'Sphinxes', *Carnaval*, Op. 9 No. 9

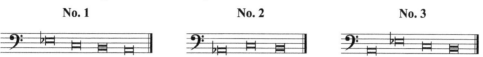

whether these three curious entities were intended to be played; few pianists perform them. They sit silently, sphinx-like, calling attention to a riddle whose full meaning they will not readily disclose.

The three sphinxes appear to offer a clue to the constitution of the music that makes up *Carnaval* – the four (or three) notes on which these 'little scenes' are based. For despite Schumann's different masks, the personas – fictional, fanciful, or real – he jestingly adopts in *Carnaval*, nearly all these subjective revels are underpinned by the same common substance. The sphinxes correspond to the mystery of identity, a substratum present throughout the work. Thus 'Schumann' (or his anagrammatical equivalent 'Asch') would seem to provide an underlying identity to the kaleidoscopic profusion of different characters and scenes. The only trouble is that Schumann himself seems to be absent.

Commentators have generally proved unable to find the composer's own musical cipher appearing directly in any of the pieces. 'SCHA' is not heard in either number corresponding to Schumann's own alter egos: 'Florestan' is based on the four-note ASCH cipher, while 'Eusebius' offers a variant or permutation of it (continuing the loosening procedure seen in the preceding 'Valse noble', which swapped the last two notes around). Even in the piece that follows on from 'Papillons', explicitly entitled 'A.S.C.H. – S.C.H.A. (Lettres dansantes)', only the second sphinx, the three-note cipher for Asch, is actually directly stated. Does this reflect more than the fact that, so compositional genesis would suggest, the musical encoding of 'Asch' was, in fact, the music's primary impulse, and the identification of these notes with Schumann's own name an afterthought which amused him? There certainly seems something playful about Schumann's explicit drawing attention to the 'SCHA' cipher, both as the first of the three sphinxes and in the title of one of the following numbers, and yet his calculated avoidance when it comes to using it in his music. But many writers have gone further, especially in recent decades, in reading this apparent absence as a reflection of a crisis in the constitution of the subject, an emptiness at the core of personal identity. The literary theme of the Carnival is 'the source of all Schumann's piano music', Roland Barthes comments allusively – presumably with the composer's Op.

9 foremost in mind – 'for the Carnival is truly the theatre of this decentring of the subject'.[19] Lawrence Kramer expands on this perspective, in reading *Carnaval* as a symbol of the 'disunity of the socially constructed self' as well as the 'mobility of identity in general'. These character sketches 'challenge the notion that there is a single self behind all the masks'. In this context, what Schumann's sphinxes denote

is not so much a discrete set of references as the anagrammatical process itself, which in this context embodies the carnivalesque extreme of impersonation. The notes assume varied forms throughout the cycle, but they have no primary form, no grounding 'self', an absence underlined by the silence of the S.C. H.A. signature.[20]

For Slavoj Žižek, 'the entire piece thus pivots around "Sphinxes" as its absent, impossible-real point of reference' – in Lacanese, the *objet petit a*, 'the section whose very exclusion guarantees the reality of the remaining elements'.[21] Or adopting a familiar Derridan ploy, we might say the sphinxes form the music's 'supplement', written but not sounded, outside and yet inside the work, redundant and at the same time the key to unlocking it, upon which the rest of the work rests – to this extent like the transcendental basis of the self, a feature underscored by Schumann's decision to erase his own presence, despite the spectral apparition of its empty signifier.

Except that Schumann's cipher *is* actually present in *Carnaval*. Resonant though they may be with popular postmodern concerns, one crucial thing the preceding accounts overlook is that Schumann does – albeit belatedly – join his own party. Briefly, though unmistakably, 'SCHA' is heard in the final piece, the 'March of the Davidsbündler against the Philistines'.

Nearly all the movements of *Carnaval* make their relation to the three- and four-note Sphinxes transparently manifest, incorporating one or other of the ASCH ciphers into their head motives. The exceptions are the two pieces given the names of real composers, 'Chopin' (where it is absent, though inexactly hinted at in the final bars) and 'Paganini' (where it appears unusually in the middle); 'Réplique' (an addendum to the preceding 'Coquette', where it does appear); and the outer numbers – the opening

---

[19] Barthes, 'Loving Schumann', p. 296.

[20] Lawrence Kramer, 'Rethinking Schumann's *Carnaval*: Identity, Meaning, and the Social Order', in *Musical Meaning: Toward a Critical History* (Berkeley and Los Angeles: University of California Press, 2002), pp. 102, 108, 110.

[21] Žižek, 'Robert Schumann: The Romantic Anti-Humanist', p. 207.

'Préambule' and the closing sequence of 'Pause' leading into the 'March of the Davidsbündler' – in which it is present but much less obvious. In these last three examples, we are, in fact, dealing with the same music, part of 'Préambule' which is reprised by Schumann towards the end of his cycle. But this appearance in 'Préambule' is in some ways exceptional. For a start, the following pieces from the first half of the cycle (Nos. 2–7 and 10, discounting No. 9, 'Sphinxes') use only the four-note version A-E♭-C-B, but 'Préambule' takes up the three-note A♭-C-C♭[=B] form found exclusively throughout the second part of the cycle (Nos. 11–12, 14–21). Unusually (to this extent like 'Paganini') the cipher does not appear conspicuously at the start of the number; even more unusually, though (in this unlike 'Paganini'), it is hidden in the bassline, emerging surreptitiously towards the end of the piece (bb. 92–8, Ex. 2.2a).[22] The curtain-raising 'Préambule' remains largely untouched by Schumann's cryptographic conceit.

When this music returns in 'Pause', the same pitches are heard ringing forth the musical name of Ernestine's hometown (bb. 6–12). But when it is reprised yet again within the 'March of the Davidsbündler' (*Vivo*, bb. 99ff), the passage is modified, transposed up a fifth from A flat to E flat major. Initially the cryptic contents seem fated to be lost, but from b. 108 the bassline picks out another pattern – E♭, C, B♮ – joined after a moment's hesitation by an A♮ in b. 111 (Ex. 2.2b). Though half disguised by the quaver rest on the downbeat of b. 111 and fleeting – it never appears again – 'SCHA', the composer's own musical signature, is at least finally present in

Ex. 2.2a Schumann: 'Préambule', *Carnaval*, Op. 9 No. 1, bb. 92–8

---

[22] The four-note 'ASCH' cipher is also first given in the inner, tenor voice in No. 2, 'Pierrot', but migrates into the treble by bb. 5–6. It remains in the treble for all subsequent pieces, albeit subject to melodic variation in Nos. 4 and 5.

Ex. 2.2b Schumann: 'Marche des "Davidsbündler" contre les Philistins', *Carnaval*, Op. 9 No. 22, bb. 107–12

his music. And when this passage returns one final time from b. 201, neither ASCH nor SCHA is to be heard, the bassline, drained of cryptic content, merely circling around G, A♭, and A♮. SCHA is the last cipher that is given in the work; after all the impersonations and motley masks adopted, the composer himself will be the last subject that is heard in *Carnaval*.

Qualities of Subjectivity in Schumann's Early Piano Music

The reading of *Carnaval*'s subjective qualities presented above relies heavily on the relation of the music to verbal labels – the encoding of names in musical notation, the titles given to individual pieces – and how these relate to both the structure of the musical work and notions of subjectivity, the latter generally of a more postmodern hue. The hermeneutic interpretation would be considerably weakened, for instance, if Schumann had not whimsically observed that Asch was an anagram of the musical notes in his own name and called attention to it in the sphinxes and joking title to 'Lettres dansantes' – although pretty much everything in the sounding substance of the music would have remained unchanged. There is, in other words, a sense that such readings are partially intellectual constructions that bear only a tangential relation to what we hear and rely unstably on purported authorial intention as and when it suits. But *Carnaval* could be understood as subjective for many other, often more palpable musical reasons. We might point to the quicksilver and unpredictable alternation of moods, the whimsical interruption of material from other parts of the work or other works, besides the sense that under (nearly) all these diverse masks there lies a common element that somehow binds them together, even – especially – if that common element is itself rather slight.

For instance, 'Préambule' sets out as if a chain of dances, preceded by a curtain-raiser (the *Quasi maestoso* introduction). A quick waltz at b. 24 leads to a more graceful variant at b. 47, but the expected reprise of the latter's rounded binary form switches suddenly into a new and quite different *Animato* passage at b. 71. At b. 80, though, the characteristic thematic figure of the first two waltzes reasserts itself, even as the *animato* section continues; this segues into a fourth section (*Vivo*, b. 87) which draws on both the waltz and animato material in a climactic build-up to the final coda section (*Presto*, b. 114). The ostensibly straightforward generic structure soon breaks down into an unpredictable succession of moods and sections, the music switching suddenly back and forth from one idea to another, even while these are often underpinned by transformations of common thematic material. Similarly, at a larger level across the whole work, Schumann switches unpredictably between different mood pieces and characters, leaves individual numbers open ended and incomplete ('Eusebius' ends on a tonic $^6_4$; 'Florestan' on a dominant ninth), brings back earlier music (this 'Préambule' itself in 'Pause' and 'Marche', the preceding 'Valse allemande' to frame 'Paganini', which thus forms a type of trio or 'intermezzo', as Schumann designates it, within this larger design), and even refers to earlier pieces (the 'Thème du XVIIème siècle' or 'Grossvatertanz' in the finale, which starts off as if an allusion to Beethoven). Most intriguing in this respect is Schumann's fleeting allusion to his own *Papillons*, Op. 2, in 'Florestan' (bb. 8–10), which grows into a longer quotation (bb. 18–22, questioningly marked 'Papillon?' by the composer), and quixotically results (through a subjective chain of association?) in a quite different number entitled 'Papillons' three pieces later.

These constant, playful juxtapositions and sudden reversions of mood and character push against expected norms of musical continuity, question a sense of unified identity in the flow of ideas. And yet somehow these disparate, highly contrasting sections seem to belong together (at least for those audiences who respond favourably to Schumann's music).[23]

---

[23] Schumann's contemporary listeners did not always follow. The composer himself acknowledged this aspect, conceding in a review of a 1840 performance by Liszt of ten of the pieces from *Carnaval* that 'the musical moods change too quickly to be followed by a large audience' (Robert Schumann, *Gesammelte Schriften über Musik und Musiker* [GS], ed. Martin Kreisig, 2 vols. (Leipzig: Breitkopf & Härtel, 1949), 'Franz Liszt: II', vol. I, p. 484).

This may be achieved in part through the sense that common themes or motives are being shared across them; yet this in itself hardly seems a sufficient explanation. In *Carnaval*, for instance, the Sphinxes consist of three or four notes, which scarcely determine the different forms taken by each character piece. Though creating an inner connexion between the majority of the numbers, they merely inform the opening phrase of each piece.[24] Schumann's music appears to be exploring how far discontinuity can be taken, how much the idea of identity can be questioned, while still somehow cohering into something that makes sense. And to understand it, to follow it, one seemingly has to be attuned to the subjective, capricious, whimsical turns of the mind of its creator.

These qualities might productively be extended more broadly to the rest of Schumann's early piano music in considering the sense of subjectivity often heard in them. Schumann's Op. 9 may not be entirely representative of his work from this period, in that its carnivalesque cavalcade of characters and images threatens to overwhelm the sense of individual subjectivity at the centre – it presents 'masks' rather than 'faces', as the composer later put it – but still many of the most important qualities that mark his music as 'subjective' are already set out within its anarchic play of identities.[25] Developing some of the ideas already set out above, we might locate the sense of subjectivity found in much of Schumann's music from the 1830s in a cluster of interrelated features. These could be summarised as: freedom from generic formal structures and apparently content-based designs; suggestive titles and allusive or quixotic gestures; a fantasy-like principle of the succession and juxtaposition of moods; idiosyncrasy; a strong sense of inwardness and interiority; and latent affinities and half-hidden connexions between parts.

Formal freedom. Many of Schumann's works from this time, and certainly those for which he has most often been celebrated, are not in standard pre-existing formal structures but present collections, cycles, or

---

[24] An alternative, slightly less sceptical account of the importance of unity in the cycle is given by Peter Kaminsky in his 'Principles of Formal Structure in Schumann's Early Piano Cycles', *Music Theory Spectrum*, 11 (1989), 211–16.

[25] Writing to Clara Wieck a few years later, Schumann protests: 'concerning my *Davidsbündlertänze* you are wide of the mark; I think that they are *quite different* from *Carnaval* and relate to it as faces to masks' ('sie sind <u>ganz anders</u> als der Carnaval und verhalten sich zu diesem wie Gesichter zu Masken'). Letter of 18 March 1838, in Clara and Robert Schumann, *Schumann Briefedition* [*SB*], ed. Michael Heinemann, Thomas Synofzik, et al., 50 vols. (Cologne: Dohr, 2008–[25]), Series I, vol. 4, p. 266 / Robert and Clara Schumann, *Briefwechsel: Kritische Gesamtausgabe*, ed. Eva Weissweiler, 3 vols. (Basel and Frankfurt: Stroemfeld/Roter Stern, 1984–2001), vol. I, p. 127.

chains of smaller dances, variations, or character pieces. Even if the small-scale structure of these constituent parts is normally straightforward, growing from a basis in rounded binary dance forms (as seen in *Papillons* and *Carnaval*) that are increasingly concatenated into larger nested ternary and rondo-like structures (*Kreisleriana*, *Novelletten*, the opening section of *Faschingsschwank aus Wien*), the succession of such parts is normally non-generic, paratactic, and unpredictable in advance. The fact that there is often little sense of generic form for the listener to refer to increases the sense that it is the 'subjective' contents of the music (or even the whim of the composer) that is determining the succession of ideas. Of course, Schumann also wrote three piano sonatas from this time (Opp. 11, 22, and the *Concert sans Orchestre*, Op. 14), which, while departing from expectations in some respects, nevertheless do significantly reference 'clas-sical' forms, so this aspect of his music should not be exaggerated. Then again, the same reception history that has characterised Schumann as a 'subjective' composer has favoured the formally individual *Fantasie* Op. 17 at the expense of these works, so one can see how this one-sided perception has arisen.

Titles, allusions, quirkiness. Particularly in Schumann's earlier works, this freedom from generic formal schemes is often combined with suggest-ive titles and whimsical references or allusions, both verbal and musical. Such features may variously suggest concealed layers of meaning and intention, pointing to the subjective agency of the work's creator; convey a sense of self-consciousness to the musical discourse; or even question (and thereby foreground) the supposed subjective voice adopted. The use of ciphers or quixotic forms of *Augenmusik*, seen in *Carnaval*'s 'Sphinxes' and used in the 'Abegg' Variations before, draws attention to a projected hidden meaning, foregrounding the creator's subjective agency, while quotations and allusions to other pieces similarly break open the music's usual mode of discourse, suggesting a self-conscious quality to the music and thereby something of a virtual subject. The question of authorship – the identity of the controlling hidden presence – is playfully problematised. Most evident here is Schumann's adoption of his alter egos Florestan and Eusebius, already heard as characters in *Carnaval*, as the pseudonymous composers of several of his following works. The two are named as the authors of the individual dances in the *Davidsbündlertänze*, Op. 6 (1837), their initials being printed at the end of their respective (sometimes joint) contributions; the F sharp minor Piano Sonata, Op. 11 (1832–5), was publicly 'dedicated to Clara by Florestan and Eusebius'; and these dual personas were also at one stage conceived as co-authors of the *Symphonic Etudes*, Op. 13 (1834–5).

Fantasy principle in succession of moods, idiosyncrasy. Speaking of Schubert's music, Schumann observes that 'there is no music that is so psychologically curious in the course and connection of its ideas, and in the ostensible logic of its discontinuities; how few have been able to express as well as he a unique individuality from an abundance of such varying tone-pictures'.[26] As commentators have noted, Schumann's description might just as well be applied to his own music.[27] In works like *Carnaval* or the *Davidsbündlertänze*, the verbal indications in the score point to fictional authorial voices that to some extent justify the non-generic structure and unpredictable shifts in mood; in other works (such as the *Fantasiestücke*, Op. 12, 1837), some poetic import is at least communicated in the individual titles to pieces (though these, in turn, can often raise more questions than they answer). Without explicit designation of subjective authorship or explanation in poetic titles, though, the succession of expressive states becomes yet more enigmatic – 'who' wrote them? what motivates them? – and in this sense even more liable to be heard as rooted solely in the subjective idiosyncrasy of the composer. Already a work like *Kreisleriana*, Op. 16 (1838), marks a greater abstraction from the *Davidsbündlertänze* in its alternation of contrasting moods; some allusion to E. T. A. Hoffmann's fictional musician Johannes Kreisler is indicated by the title, but exactly how it connects, and to which of Hoffmann's Kreisler works, has long been disputed. In the *Novelletten*, Op. 21 (1838), Schumann gives no clue as to any underlying narrative, despite seemingly alluding to the existence of one (or several) in the work's playful title. Most clearly in the *Humoreske*, Op. 20 (1839), the succession of moods (or humours) follows no preconceived generic formal design or given narrative but obeys a fantasia-like principle, in which the unfolding of the music appears to be determined solely by the composer's own idiosyncratic connexion of subjective psychological states.

For Beate Perrey, 'the term "Phantasieren" must be seen as one of Schumann's primary compositional concepts. The frequency of the word in Schumann's writings is striking, as is its appearance as the title of compositions.'[28] And the importance of this fantasy-like quality was

[26] Schumann, letter to Friedrich Wieck, 6 November 1829, *SB* I.2:36.

[27] See, for instance, Nicholas Marston, 'Schumann's Heroes: Schubert, Beethoven, Bach', in Beate Perrey (ed.), *The Cambridge Companion to Schumann* (Cambridge: Cambridge University Press, 2007), p. 50.

[28] Beate Perrey, *Schumann's Dichterliebe and Early Romantic Poetics: Fragmentation of Desire* (Cambridge: Cambridge University Press, 2002), p. 58.

already perceived by Carl Koßmaly in his pioneering 1844 account of Schumann's piano music. In the *Humoreske*, for instance, Koßmaly found 'the great variety of content and form, the continual and quick, although always natural and unforced succession of the most varied images, imaginary ideas and sentiments, fantastic and dreamlike phenomena swell and fade into one another'.[29] Such an abstracted succession of moods, unsupported by either generic formal schemes or by a poetic narrative, places an acute stress on the perceived logic of the musical flow: the question of continuity and discontinuity, of musical and psychological coherence, is seemingly determined by the whims of the composer, his (or her) intuitive feeling of 'what is right'. To understand this idiosyncratic connexion of subjective states, the performer and listener have to be on the same sympathetic wavelength.

A perceptive account of this fantasy principle was outlined two decades before by Carl Maria von Weber, in his unfinished (and rather 'Kreisleresque') novel *Tonkünstlers Leben* (1809–20). For Weber (as for A. B. Marx later), only geniuses should attempt the formal freedom of the fantasy:

An apparently disconnected flight of imagination, that seems to be a *Phantasiestück* rather than a movement obeying the normal rules of musical composition, if it is to be worth anything, can be attempted only by quite outstanding geniuses – men who create a world which is only apparently chaotic and really has an inner coherence that is absolutely sincere in feeling, if only one can tune one's own feelings to the same pitch.

To understand it, then, one must be closely attuned to the innermost world of the creator:

In music ... there is already so much that is vague in expression and so much remains for the individual listener to supply from his own feelings, that such a sympathy is at best possible only to individual spirits who are in complete harmony with each other – I mean that sympathetic understanding of precisely *this* emotional development taking place in precisely *this* manner, finding precisely *these* contrasts necessary and *this* sense true.[30]

---

[29] Carl Koßmaly, 'On Robert Schumann's Piano Compositions (1844)', trans. Susan Gillespie, in R. Larry Todd (ed.), *Schumann and his World* (Princeton: Princeton University Press, 1994), p. 312. Speaking of the *Fantasiestücke*, Op. 12, John MacAuslan similarly observes that 'in Schumann's work, vivid images succeed one another like dreams, without the solidity of objects or the clarity of logical connections'. Thus 'a listener is invited to re-create threads from which they seem to hang'. *Schumann's Music and E. T. A. Hoffmann's Fiction* (Cambridge: Cambridge University Press, 2016), pp. 91, 235.

[30] Carl Maria von Weber, *Writings on Music*, trans. Martin Cooper, ed. John Warrack (Cambridge: Cambridge University Press, 1981), p. 362. The Fantasia forms the culmination of Marx's theory of forms in the *Kompositionslehre* (1837–47). On the rise of the fantasia principle and the historical association, alongside the notion of 'humour', with the creator's own subjectivity in this period see also Bonds, *The Beethoven Syndrome*, pp. 58–77.

It follows that only a few will understand the *Phantasiestück*; and the danger of incomprehension remains an ever-present possibility. Pointedly, in his 1844 review Koßmaly had criticised some of Schumann's early works as striving too much for originality and individuality, the composer erecting a barrier around himself – effectively being too idiosyncratic, too subjective. Such was the Op. 17 *Fantasie*, whose 'eccentricity, arbitrariness, vagueness, and the nonclarity of its contours can hardly be surpassed'. He is like one, who, in the conceit of making himself unapproachable, 'egotistically and stubbornly shuts himself off from the world', thought Koßmaly. 'His work may have been too pithy, dense, and laden with meaning, so that it is difficult to get through it, as if one were lost in a thick, overgrown forest, the path barred from moment to moment by mighty tree trunks or knotty roots, powerful vines and sharp thorns.'[31] Only a few make the journey. But those who do often find something special waiting for them.

Innigkeit: Intimacy, Inwardness, Interiority. 'At first you have to get through some tangled thickets – but then what divine song will open up before you.'[32] Schumann is writing here of Jean Paul, but the same could be said of his own early music. 'Flower, Fruit and Thorn Pieces', reads the initial title of one of Jean Paul's novels, and similarly, deep within Schumann's thicket of thorns there lies an enchanted, interior realm – his *Blumenstück*, as it were. Numerous listeners have related to the intimate tone adopted in certain seemingly characteristic passages of Schumann's music, its sense of possessing a hidden and highly personal interior dimension, in a composer for whom the word *innig* (intimate) was a favourite performance direction. In simplest form this quality is imparted through a gentle lyricism, warmth of feeling, and apparent sincerity of utterance that typifies the Op. 15 *Kinderszenen* especially ('Träumerei' or 'Der Dichter Spricht') – attributes admittedly not unique to Schumann, but nevertheless in which he was unsurpassed. In a piece like the fourteenth of the *Davidsbündlertänze*, however, we may observe a refashioning of such *Innigkeit* that is more personal to the composer. The first four bars of this piece present an appealing little tune, marked 'tenderly and singing', in a simple song-like texture with the melody in the upper voice. From bar 5, though, the melodic line retreats into an inner voice, the rising quaver accompaniment crossing over to occupy the treble register (Ex. 2.3). In fact, from the start the melodic voice has been implicitly shadowed at the lower octave within the

---

[31] *Ibid.*, p. 310.

[32] 'erst muß man durch einiges Dickigt und Struppicht hindurch – dann aber welches Göttersang wird sich Dir aufthun'; Schumann, letter to Clara Wieck, 11 February 1838, *Briefwechsel* I:98 (*SB* I.4:225, which gives 'Götterherz' for 'Göttersang').

Ex. 2.3 Schumann: *Davidsbündlertänze*, Op. 6, No. 14, opening

accompanimental arpeggios, in an inexact form that has already created piquant passing dissonances (the ab^3 heard against the a♮^{2} in b. 2); the two voices – one outer, explicit, on the music's surface; one latent, hidden within – have here exchanged places, opening up an unanticipated sense of depth. The effect of this withdrawal into the inner voice is one of internalisation (and perhaps also of a heightened sense of contentment), of bringing the melody deeper into the body of the music – in short, of interiority.[33]

And this inward feeling can also intimate an inner world of apparently inexpressible depths, a private realm whose disclosure verges on the confessional. One of the most pregnant instances of this latter quality is to be found in the *Fantasie* in C, Op. 17 (1836–8). Here, twice within the opening movement, the initially turbulent, passionate material subsides into a gentler, more imitate variant that serves as a type of secondary theme (albeit in the deeply unclassical keys of the subdominant and flattened mediant respectively). But its final stages unravel before reaching the expected cadential close, marked by halting *ritardandi* and quasi-speech-like gestures. These faltering utterances seem aimed to lead up to the final few bars marked *Adagio*, a passage that promises to reveal the secret that has been so

[33] The idea of 'the body' of Schumann's music, famously raised by Roland Barthes (see 'Rasch', in *The Responsibility of Forms: Critical Essays on Music, Art, and Representation*, trans. Richard Howard (Oxford: Blackwell, 1985), pp. 299–312), has been explored further by Stephen Rodgers in '"This Body That Beats": Roland Barthes and Robert Schumann's *Kreisleriana*', *Indiana Theory Review*, 18 (1997), 75–91, esp. 84.

circumspectly held back until now. But just as the melodic phrase arches up in an expressive appoggiatura (an apparent allusion to Beethoven's *An die ferne Geliebte*), it breaks off on an exquisitely aching dissonance, a suspension over a chromatically altered, diminished seventh harmony (Ex. 2.4). After the two fermatas, the melodic line attempts the expected resolution to f²; but *pianissimo*, belatedly, and most crucially the underlying harmonies have dropped out.

From this unresolved, almost painfully candid moment, the strident *fortissimo* octaves that form the start of the following section brusquely erupt; a more sweeping non sequitur from the preceding music could hardly be imagined.[34] That lone, unsupported f, teetering on the verge of audibility, forms a liminal threshold between the outer and inner subject; the music breaks off while seemingly on the point of uttering something so intimate, so fragile, that it cannot be continued, that its tones prove unable to be sounded. Perhaps the ultimate degree of this type of interiority is music that really is not sounded. In the *Humoreske*'s famous 'innere Stimme' (see Ex. 7.3), the inner voice is the melody that remains silent. But listeners should still notice when it is absent.

Latent thematic substrate as underlying 'subject'. As will be discussed in a subsequent chapter, the silent inner voice of the *Humoreske* may form a convenient metaphor for the unknowable, transcendental ground of the self or the absence that (some thinkers would claim) haunts the heart of self-presence. And one further aspect of Schumann's piano music from these years suggests an apt analogy with the unfathomable unity of the self. This is the recurring sense of commonality half hidden under the surface of the music – how often in Schumann's piano collections of this time the diverse manifestations seem to possess a latent underlying thematic affinity,

Ex. 2.4 Schumann: *Fantasie* in C, Op. 17, i, end of exposition, bb. 77–83

[34] The c♯⁷ diminished seventh chord could conceivably resolve to a D triad, though the minor mode would be rather more likely, and the preceding melodic resolution to f² in the right hand forms a jarring false relation with the f♯ in the following D major harmony.

sometimes sporadic to be sure, but nevertheless impossible to ignore. In some cases this common thematic substrate clearly derives from a variation procedure and is more or less intentional: such is the case with the 'Abegg' Variations, the *Impromptus on a Theme by Clara Wieck*, Op. 5 (1833), several of the *Davidsbündlertänze* (likewise based on a 'motto from C. W.'), and the *Symphonic Etudes* (effectively a set of variations on a theme by Schumann's prospective father-in-law, Baron Ignaz Ferdinand von Fricken). *Carnaval*, as we have seen, offers an ingenious play on this idea. But in other cycles and collections too, the listener is often struck by some element or elements common to several of the constituent pieces, and analysts have sought to uncover the secret bonds that seem to underlie them. *Kinderszenen* is a case in point, taken by Rudolf Réti as a classic case study of thematic process, while subcutaneous links can also be sensed clearly in *Kreisleriana*.[35] It is not always clear whether these apparent connexions were consciously sought by the composer (as is the case in *Carnaval*), or arose unconsciously, perhaps from his method of composing from improvising at the piano; it hardly matters either, as long as this quality is perceived on some level by the listener. Hence while the music may appear highly differentiated on the surface, to flit between one mood and other with little apparent connexion (as in the fantasy aesthetic just outlined), there can still be a sense of underlying coherence that fitfully manifests itself; the different subjective states of mind share a common underlying substratum. (On a creative level, such commonalities could similarly be construed as revealing the subjectivity of the actual composer operational across, and thus linking, these diverse products of his imagination, conscious or otherwise.) And indeed, the very fact that these perceived connexions can in some cases be so slight, so fleeting, so insubstantial when one tries to pin them down, and yet no less tangible when experiencing the music, itself seems to suggest something of the mystery of personal identity, that assumed coherence that underlies the problematised modern notion of the subject.

Subjectivity in the Concerto

The piano music of the 1830s provides a good starting point for discussion of subjectivity in Schumann's music, since not only is this the body of work

---

[35] Rudolf Réti, 'Schumann's *Kinderszenen*: A "Theme with Variations"', in *The Thematic Process in Music* (New York: Macmillan, 1951), pp. 31–55. Also see Hans Joachim Köhler, 'Schumann, der Autodiktat: Zum genetischen Zusammenhang von variativem Prinzip und poetischer Idee', in Gerd Nauhaus (ed.), *Schumann-Studien*, 3–4 (Cologne: Studio, 1994), pp. 188–98.

on which the attribution of subjectivity to the composer is often based, but the solo piano repertoire is in its own right also commonly associated with this quality. However, two other genres could equally be construed as important for the musical transmission or construction of subjectivity. One, also closely identified with Schumann, is the Lied. Having focussed almost entirely on piano works for the best part of a decade, in early 1840 Schumann turned to the composition of song, producing a remarkable number – over 120 – within the following twelve months. The solo song is a quintessential vehicle of subjectivity, owing in part to the intimate forces used, in which the voice of a human subject is actually heard, and in part to the presence of a poetic text, in which the subject of verbal language, the lyric 'I' of Romantic poetry, clarifies, reinforces, or occasionally works against the sense of subjectivity constructed by the music. Both in this and in the interaction between accompaniment and vocal line, the composer can suggest complex shadings of subjectivity, the tension between conscious thought and subconscious desire, the workings of memory and ironies of self-deception. For these reasons, accounts of subjectivity in song have proved prolific in recent scholarship. Many of these aspects will be discussed further in the following chapter, where we will examine in more detail the problem of the self-divided subject.

The other genre of major significance, which will be covered at slightly greater length now, is the concerto. The solo concerto, as developed over the eighteenth century, stylises the interplay between soloist and orchestra in generic form. It can be thus heard as offering a metaphor or musical enactment of the relation between the individual and collective, self and society, and has been the focus for numerous hermeneutic readings along these lines, most notably perhaps Susan McClary's provoking readings of Bach's Fifth Brandenburg Concerto (where the humble harpsichord continuo appears to overthrow the established social order to become a soloist in its own right) and Mozart's K. 453 (whose 'social discourse', McClary contends, reflects the tensions between 'social harmony and individual freedom' inherent in the Enlightenment project).[36] In the solo piano piece or song we are presented with what often seems to be an intimate

---

[36] Susan McClary, 'The Blasphemy of Talking Politics During a Bach Year', in Susan McClary and Richard Leppert (eds.), *Music and Society: The Politics of Composition, Performance, and Reception* (Cambridge: Cambridge University Press, 1987), pp. 13–62, and 'A Musical Dialectic from the Enlightenment', at 159. See further Joseph Kerman, 'Mozart's Piano Concertos and Their Audience', in *Write All These Down: Essays on Music* (Berkeley: University of California Press, 1994), pp. 322–34. This hermeneutic approach to the concerto has become widespread in the last few decades: see, for instance, Julian Horton's recent *Brahms' Piano Concerto No. 2, Op. 83: Analytical and Contextual Studies* (Leuven: Peeters, 2017), ch. 10.

glimpse of the self, of the solitary subject communing with itself, corresponding to the idea of subjectivity as an individual, private quality; but as we saw in Chapter 1, another understanding of subjectivity was as a relational category, arising between subjects and between the self and the world. It is this more relational, 'intersubjective' version of subjectivity that the concerto, as a genre, seems pre-eminently disposed to articulate.

Schumann's three concertos are especially revealing in this context as to the distinctive subjectivity conveyed by his music. Most prominent of these is the Piano Concerto in A minor, Op. 54 (1841–5), Schumann's first completed work in the genre and undoubtedly the most beloved of his concertos, if not of his orchestral works, in general. If the mark of the classical concerto is of productive opposition in its dualism of soloist and orchestra – an example of subjectivity that reveals the individual negotiating amongst others within its social surroundings – Schumann's work evokes a quite different conception, one of integration and oneness, a Romantic dream of unanimity between self and world. It is notable throughout how closely soloist and orchestra are integrated, with little to no opposition between the two: it is as if the latter is effectively an extension of the self – the world feels and sighs and dreams alongside the soloist.

Much of this stems from the reduction of distinctive generic markers of classical concerto form, such as the replacement of the double exposition by a single, unitary exposition in the first movement, and the de-emphasis of the customary textural opposition of tutti and soloist throughout. While the tutti passage at the end of the exposition (bb. 134–55) undeniably refers back to the second ritornello of the classical concerto model (or 'R2'), its contrast with the preceding music is minimised, and as a consequence it sounds more akin to a closing passage in a sonata-form exposition – in part owing to the absence of the customary preparatory trills in the solo part, in part because the orchestra takes over the motivic idea suggested by the soloist in the bars leading up to it, and to some extent as the provisional imperfect authentic cadence (IAC) at this point undermines any strong sense of cadential articulation or break in proceedings. Unanimity of purpose and blending of solo and orchestral voices is characteristic throughout the movement.[37] The opening theme, for instance, is formed as a large-scale period, but its presentation is shared between orchestra and piano, the soloist responding with the consequent phrase to the orchestral antecedent (a similar, though

---

[37] 'The piano is most subtly interwoven with the orchestra – one cannot conceive of one without the other' commented Clara on the original form of the first movement (entry from August 1841, *Tagebücher*, vol. II, p. 180).

appropriately looser process is followed in the initial presentation phrase of the secondary group, initiated here by the soloist). The format is akin to a style of presentation more typically found in a piano trio, say, underscoring the chamber music feel: not confrontation, but intimate dialogue, a feature particularly prominent in the second movement *Intermezzo*. The ensuring transition passage blends piano with orchestra, their respective voices intermingling – now merging, now answering and following each other's lead. Even the final cadenza, though present, is written out and distinctly non-virtuosic in its reflective lyricism.

Schumann's opening movement started life in 1841 as a single-movement *Fantasie*, and the characteristic traits of the fantasy genre are seen not only in the seemingly rhapsodic interweaving of texture and moods but also in the process of thematic transformation that underpins this. The secondary theme, for instance, starts as a major-key transformation of the A minor first subject, elaborating on this idea extensively in its continuation, while the nocturne-like episode at the centre of the movement, an *Andante espressivo* in the remote key of A flat major, further transforms this material into an intimate romantic colloquy in which the piano and clarinet murmur fragments of the theme softly back and forth to each other. The coda presents one final variant of this idea, now transformed into a $^2/_4$ march, while the exposition's closing section derives from material already presented in the transition. Just as in Schumann's solo piano music of the preceding decade, thematic commonality suggests a common substance, a consistent subject persisting under the music's varied moods. This sense of a single overriding subjectivity is underscored by the recall of the concerto's opening material at the close of the slow movement: the characteristic descending third motive given in the woodwind, in major- then minor-mode forms, conjuring up the first movement's secondary and primary themes respectively – to which the soloist twice responds with a gesture that unmistakably alludes to the concerto's very opening flourish (Ex. 2.5). The effect is of a memory, as if the music is able to reflect on its past, suggestive not only of a consistent subject underlying the concerto's different parts but of a self-conscious subject – Michael Steinberg's second 'fundamental fiction' of modern music. This brief, though telling recall of the musical past leads directly into the finale, whose main theme offers one further metamorphosis of the idea heard at the concerto's opening; the preceding reminiscence is the moment of self-conscious recognition of affinities that lie under the material of all three movements.

There are, of course, good reasons other than the desire to express a dreamy Romantic subjectivity why the concerto should take this form. In Op. 54, as Claudia Macdonald has argued, Schumann was taking pains to integrate soloist and orchestra in order to avoid what he saw as the debased virtuoso concerto model, in which the orchestra was little more than a backing for the pianist's individual display; his choice of a unitary exposition and the reduction of the concerto first-movement ritornello form to a purely sonata structure is likewise part of a much wider tendency in music at this time.[38] But still, these compositional choices have distinct implications for the model of subjectivity conveyed by the music. Throughout the work the orchestra and soloist share material as if complementary actors, with little to no sense of friction between them. So much so, that the two may appear little more than two sides of the same consciousness. There is no real division between the individual and the world. We could well recall here that for Franz Brendel writing in 1845 – the year the concerto was finished – Schumann's music revealed 'a subject focused entirely on itself, one that lives and breathes exclusively in its own inwardness', not connected directly with circumstances of the external world but which 'appropriates them through fantasy. It is an individuality that expresses only itself and its personal emotional states … depict[ing] the world only as far as the Self has been touched by it.'[39] Rather than intersubjectivity, a relationship with others, Schumann's concerto suggests the self-communion of a single, all-embracing subjectivity – a pantheistic unity of man and nature, or even a Romantic Idealism that tends towards solipsism, whereby the world is merely a projection of the subject; that (in the words of Johann Gottlieb Fichte) 'the not-self is itself a product of the self-determining self, and nothing at all absolute, or posited outside the self'.[40]

The Piano Concerto is, admittedly, the most pointed form of such integration in the composer's oeuvre. Schumann's following work in the genre, the Cello Concerto, Op. 129 (1850), makes more distinction between tutti and solo passages (probably reflecting questions of instrumental balance), though the first movement still unfolds in a unitary exposition with material shared intimately across the two: the motto-like wind chords that punctuate the opening, for instance, are immediately taken up by the soloist as the basis of the primary theme.[41] The Violin Concerto in D minor

[38] Claudia Macdonald, *Robert Schumann and the Piano Concerto* (New York: Routledge, 2005); on the latter point see especially Stephan D. Lindeman, *Structural Novelty and Tradition in the Early Romantic Piano Concerto* (Stuyvesant, NY: Pendragon Press, 1999).

[39] Brendel, 'Robert Schumann with Reference to Mendelssohn-Bartholdy and the Development of Modern Music in General', pp. 323–4.

[40] J. G. Fichte, *Science of Knowledge*, trans. Peter Heath and John Lachs (Cambridge: Cambridge University Press, 1982), p. 195.

[41] On the chamber music quality of the concerto see further the recent account by Peter H. Smith, 'Schumann's A-minor Mood: Late-Style Dialectics in the First Movement of the Cello Concerto', *Journal of Music Theory*, 60 (2016), 69–72.

Ex. 2.5 Schumann: Piano Concerto in A minor, Op. 54, ii, link into finale, bb. 103–8

(1853), however, reverts more obviously to a more dualistic conception. Uniquely for Schumann, the opening movement offers a classical double exposition with the opposition between soloist- and orchestra-dominated sections prominent, while at the same time mapping onto an underlying sonata framework of unusual clarity. But for one of its most beautiful moments we hear again the sense of subjective reverie and oneness with the world that characterised the nocturne episode of the Piano Concerto's development section – only deepened now and perhaps a touch more troubled, as if the self is becoming lost inside its own inner world.

The movement's second subject is already marked by a curiously looping thematic construction; cut short in the orchestral exposition (bb. 31–41), the theme is elaborated at greater length in the solo exposition, with the arrival at a $\frac{6}{4}$ in b. 106 initiating an extensive recycling of its earlier stages over an active dominant that spins the theme out to forty bars. In the development section the same theme returns, corresponding to the rotational order observed throughout this movement, though now unusually transformed into the tonic minor (b. 177; much of the development is strangely based around V/i). From the familiar repetitions of the theme's opening motive there emerges a new, more lyrical answering phrase in the clarinet (b. 183, Ex. 2.6), to which the soloist, in turn, expressively responds, the original motive fading into the background as an accompanimental line in the orchestral violins as the music softens to the major.

Ex. 2.6 Schumann: Violin Concerto in D minor (1853), i, development section, bb. 183–203

Ex. 2.6 (cont.)

In the following bars, the material is gently passed between clarinet, violin, and oboe, the music repeatedly circling towards related major keys (F, C) and back to tonic minor, dwelling on the idea at ever greater length, just as the impending formal duties of retransition slip ever further into the background (the latter will slowly emerge from b. 203 after the music, having come to a virtual standstill, awkwardly finds its way back to D via some chromatic slipping).[42] While there is an intimate interplay between soloist and the individual voices of clarinet and oboe, at the same time there is once again a sense that all three are part of the same larger consciousness, living and breathing together. For the first time in the piece, there is a sense of connexion, of unanimity between the subject and the world. And yet in reaching inwards into this pool of calm at its heart, the subject may seem to be momentarily losing itself in its own reverie – wrapped up in its own interiority, as if oblivious to any world outside its own.

---

[42] Joseph Kerman speaks aptly of 'entropy' and tonal and rhythmic 'stagnation' at this point. For him, this is 'a dark and disturbing passage', and yet the most impressive in the whole piece. 'The Concertos', in Beate Perrey (ed.), *The Cambridge Companion to Schumann* (Cambridge: Cambridge University Press, 2007), p. 191.

*

Sphinxes are enigmatic creatures; known for guarding temples and shrines, they also have a propensity for setting riddles. Those who cannot solve their mystery are mercilessly devoured. Famously, Oedipus solved the riddle of the sphinx that had stationed itself outside Thebes, the answer to whose question was 'man'. But this did not ultimately help him escape his own preordained fate, whose cause lay in something unknown to him – his own true identity. The irony, as Adriana Cavarero points out, is that Oedipus knew what 'man' was in general, but not himself, his own identity as an individual subject.[43] 'The most difficult thing is to portray oneself, and γνῶθι σεαυτόν [know thyself] is a weighty saying', held the young Robert Schumann.[44] In his Op. 9, on the other hand, the riddle set by the sphinxes remains obscure (and for better or worse, no hermeneutist has yet been slaughtered for proposing a dubious answer). But, if there is a solution to this puzzle by a composer who had earlier admitted 'what I actually am is not yet clear to me', it would surely involve the problem of subjective identity – the SCHA cipher that forms a silent presence behind the music of *Carnaval*, anagrammatically informing the multitude of masks donned, but which only itself emerges covertly near the end.[45] The answer to the sphinxes' riddle would seem, not to be 'man' in general, but the specific individual, Schumann (or his stylised musical persona, 'Schumann'), whose subjectivity animates the revelry of impersonations, appropriating the characters and events of the external world through his own creative fantasy. The riddle of this music is the riddle of subjectivity – a subjectivity so pronounced that it posits others figures and events as extensions of itself.

This chapter has offered a brief sketch of the historical situation in which the subjectivity of Schumann's music emerged and a preliminary account of the ways in which his early music from the 1830s might be heard as subjective, in line with elements of its reception from his own day to the present. Subjective qualities may be identified in numerous idiosyncratic traits: in the multiple personas adopted in several of his piano pieces from this time; in the use of ciphers, eccentric titles, and allusions, imparting a secretive yet apparently meaningful subtext to the music; in the non-generic formal structures and resulting fantasia-like succession of psychological states; and in the often inchoate sense of a common thematic thread

---

[43] Adriana Cavarero, *Relating Narratives: Storytelling and Selfhood*, trans. Paul Kottman (London and New York: Routledge, 2000), pp. 7–15.

[44] Schumann, *Tage des Jünglinglebens*, 14 January 1827, *Tagebücher*, vol. I, p. 30 ('es ist das Schwierigste, sich selbst darzustellen, u. das γνῶθι σεαυτόν ist ein gewichtes Wort').

[45] *Ibid.* ('Was ich eigentlich bin, weiß ich selbst noch nicht klar').

or substrate underlying and thus somehow linking the diverse moods and musical phenomena. Three genres, in particular have appeared to be particularly suited to conveying this sense of subjectivity: the solo piano piece, which occupied Schumann almost exclusively in the 1830s; the solo song (considered here in passing), to which he suddenly turned in 1840; and the solo concerto, whose archetypal instance, the Piano Concerto, started life in 1841. We ended, however, with a much later work, indeed one of the composer's last pieces, the Violin Concerto, and hints of darker matters (that here need not be taken as having any biographical import, though in the past often have been interpreted in this manner).

For Roland Barthes, Schumann was 'truly the musician of solitary intimacy', and in much of the early piano music Schumann seems to reveal a private, self-absorbed subject, apparently overheard whilst in intimate soliloquy.[46] Notably, however, a similar subjective sensibility can still be found in the supposedly intersubjective, public genre of the concerto, in which the world inhabited by the orchestra often seems to be so intimately linked with that of the soloist as essentially to form an extension of it. Underlying the sense of integration in the concerto was the question of whether this constituted intersubjective dialogue or was not perhaps a form of self-communion – Barthes's 'amorous and imprisoned soul that speaks to itself' – highlighting a potential tendency towards solipsism found in Romantic conceptions of the subject.[47] This touches on a point that will recur throughout his book: the problem of subjective identity in music, the difficulty in identifying when the other voices heard are really other or one's own (a question that is not necessarily resolved through the presence of a verbal text, as will be seen shortly). This is certainly one side of a characteristic Romantic subjectivity: the longing for an all-embracing whole, in which self and world are connected. Another, no less important aspect, however, has also been implicit behind much of the foregoing discussion, namely the converse situation in which the self is divided, the subject split within itself.

In 1830, Schumann had claimed he wanted to know his own soul but lamented that he didn't know it completely. The third-person perspective taken by the composer here implicitly adopts a distance from himself, in which his self becomes both subject and object to itself. In doing this, though, he has tacitly introduced a split in his self: indeed, this is nothing less than an instantiation of the classic dilemma of self-apperception that haunted philosophical accounts of the subject in the modern era, above all

[46] Barthes, 'Loving Schumann', p. 293.   [47] *Ibid.*

in Idealist and Romantic thought. Yet for Schumann, the divided sense of self was, in fact, often something liberating, something that could be explored, played with, and above all given creative expression through art. In *Carnaval*, we recall, not only was Schumann symbolically present in his SCHA cipher, gazing out in the first of the three sphinxes and surreptitiously woven into the closing number of the work, but also more appreciably in the two pieces named after his alter egos, Eusebius and Florestan. Chapter 3 takes further the question of subjectivity in Schumann's music by exploring in more depth an issue already hinted at in the preceding pages: the problem of the self-divided subject.

3 | Hearing Selves

Fragmentary Selves

'Eusebius', the fifth number of *Carnaval*, ostensibly offers a portrayal of the dreamy, introverted side of its composer's character. Set at a gentle *Adagio*, it is marked throughout by cross-rhythms arising from the use of different metric patterns between the right and left hands: seven notes against the notated duple metre in the outer a sections; paired groupings of five and three notes in the b section, whose left hand complicates matters further by switching to triplets for its final two bars (bb. 11–12, Ex. 3.1). The intended effect may be of a floating, paradoxically almost unmeasured quality to the rhythmic motion, and perhaps the complex notation should be understood as primarily pointing to a written-out *rubato* quality; on the other hand, to realise this at all accurately, the performer has to split his or her attention across two almost incommensurable temporal levels simultaneously, aptly enough enacting a split in their own consciousness. Moreover, the piece is in a sense incomplete; it starts from a tonic first inversion, the four-bar opening idea effectively forming an expanded cadential progression, and its ending, on a tonic $^6_4$, is left cadentially open. The incompletion of this ending is furthermore itself unnecessary. As with nearly all the other pieces in the opus, 'Eusebius' suggests a rounded binary design, in this case with written-out repeats (aa | ba ba). The piece would thus be expected to close with the repetition of the second part (bb. 17–24), offered now in suitably sonorous amplification, the melodic line given in octaves *mezzo forte* with rolled chordal accompaniment and the full resonance of the sustaining pedal. What is more, the cadence at b. 24 is the one time in the piece that the opening four-bar idea (a) actually achieves cadential closure. On each of the three previous occasions the phrase has been heard (bb. 4, 8, 16), the bass had remained on the dominant, forming an unfinished $^6_4$ inversion of the final tonic, but at b. 24 the bass line finally descends to E♭, creating a satisfying sense of formal completion. Schumann's decision to repeat this second half again at b. 25 not only creates a formally superfluous second repetition (aa | ba ba <u>ba</u>) but brings back the incomplete form of the cadence heard at b. 16,

Ex. 3.1 Schumann: 'Eusebius', *Carnaval*, Op. 9 No. 5

Root-position tonic

Ex. 3.1 (cont.)

thus wilfully undermining the closure already achieved, even as the music softly fades away.

While such metrical tensions and cadential undermining barely ruffle the overriding placid tone of 'Eusebius', the following piece, 'Florestan', takes such fragmentation and internal division rather further. If, as Charles Rosen describes, the $^6_4$ at the end of 'Eusebius' suggests 'a closure at once complete and incomplete, leaving the harmony of a final tonic chord but taking away the bass root, as if only the overtones of the tonic note were sustained', no pretence is made in 'Florestan' of anything but incompletion of the most discordant variety.[1] Starting from a dissonant V^9 of G minor, the piece breaks off on frantic reiterations of the diminished seventh harmony contained within its opening sonority, an intensification rather than any resolution of the discordant initial state. Furthermore, this alter ego is riven by his own internal splits: the intrusion of external music, namely the celebrated double reminiscence of Schumann's own earlier *Papillons*, Op. 2 (bb. 8–10, 18–22), besides a latent tonal duality between the ostensible tonic G minor and the relative major, B flat. Indeed, for all its harking on the dominant minor ninth of G minor, the tonic itself barely figures in the piece (a root position harmony is reached only at b. 36, in the centre of the design, and this obliquely from B♭); instead of which, B flat major, on whose dominant the *Papillons* quotation is poised, figures much more strongly throughout.

---

[1] Charles Rosen, *The Romantic Generation* (London: HarperCollins, 1996), p. 655.

Ex. 3.2 Schumann: end of 'Florestan' leading into 'Coquette', *Carnaval*, Op. 9 Nos. 6 & 7

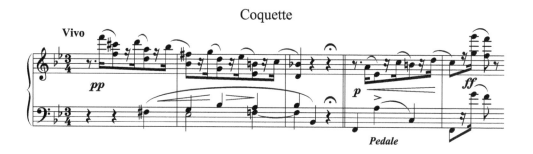

The jarring dissonance at the end of 'Florestan' is resolved only by the ensuing 'Coquette', whose insouciant opening phrase forms a cadence to B flat major, thus reemphasising the alternative key suggested in 'Florestan' (Ex. 3.2). All would seem to be well now; even if Schumann's two alter egos are themselves unable to find satisfactory closure, they might be rescued by this mysterious female figure. Yet the following 'Réplique' immediately takes up the cadential gesture of 'Coquette' – opening with the preceding closing phrase, both a 'response' and 'replication' – but finds itself by its end back in G minor (Florestan's primary key once again). Just as in 'Eusebius', an entirely redundant repetition has ironically destabilised the stability just attained. It is at this stage in the work that the Sphinxes are (or are not) heard.

What are we to make of this? A possible answer might be sought in the title of the following piece, 'Papillons' (butterflies). As suggested before, the reference to *Papillons* in 'Florestan' leads, as if by verbal association, to a piece named 'Papillons', though these butterflies have nothing apart from their title in common with Op. 2. The earlier work, though, is one that by Schumann's own account possesses a connexion with the final two chapters of Jean Paul's novel *Flegeljahre* (1804–5) – a masked ball featuring the confusion of identities between the brothers Walt and Vult, followed by their separation.[2] In *Papillons*, it seems that Schumann was playing with the association between butterflies and souls (the Greek *psyché* can refer to both), in this taking up a theme in *Flegeljahre*, which further plays on the link between these two meanings of psyche and masks ('Larve' means mask as well as larva in German; the masked ball is explicitly designated a 'Larventanz' by Jean Paul).[3] Thus in his Op. 2, Schumann was not thinking of butterflies so much as of a 'little psyche emerging from a cocoon'.[4] Just as in Jean Paul's novel, in which the twins Walt and Vult form alter egos, divided aspects of what is effectively a single subject, so in *Carnaval* the constant exchange of masks might imply the metamorphosis of subjective identity, the emergence of the psyche from a larval stage to first maturity. And yet, as with Jean Paul, there is little sense that we reach an all-encompassing unity at the end. Vult may leave his brother, aware that he is now a superfluous figure in the love between Walt and Wina, but it is hardly the case that these two distinctly dissimilar figures are integrated with each other by the close of the novel.

The same would appear to be the case in the *Larventanz* of Schumann's *Carnaval*. Throughout this curious sequence from 'Eusebius' to 'Sphinxes', apparent attempts at closure and integration are continually broken open, and it is the two imaginary sides of the composer's own personality that are the primary culprits. The idea of personifying two sides of one's psyche into individual characters might be to rationalise opposing tensions in the self into internally coherent tendencies. Yet in *Carnaval*, neither of Schumann's alter egos are stable but instead appear further divided in themselves – between metrical layers, between tonal centres – and internally disintegrated. As Lawrence Kramer points out, the two supposed sides of the composer's personality, Florestan and Eusebius, 'far from encapsulating and stabilizing Schumann's identity', hardly cohere themselves. 'In affirming the nonunitary self, Schumann gives his "own" self an exemplary volatility.' This does not necessarily mean that 'there are no selves, only impersonations', as Kramer has it; but it does suggest that the complexity of subjective identity, its constitution from a multiplicity of opposing drives

---

[2] Jean Paul, *Flegeljahre: Eine Biographie*, vol. IV, ch. 63–4 (in Werke, ed. Norbert Miller and Gustav Lohmann, 6 vols. (Munich: Carl Hanser Verlag, 1959–63), vol. II). On the programmatic subtext of Op. 2 see Eric Frederick Jensen, 'Explicating Jean Paul: Robert Schumann's Program for *Papillons*, op. 2', *19th-Century Music*, 22 (1998), 127–43.

[3] Jean Paul, *Flegeljahre*, pp. 1047 (Larven-Tanz), 1054, 1056 (Larventanz).

[4] Adolf Schubring, 'Schumann und der Großvater', *Neue Zeitschrift für Musik*, 53 (1860), 29–30, cited in R. Larry Todd, 'On Quotation in Schumann's Music', in R. Larry Todd (ed.), *Schumann and His World* (Princeton: Princeton University Press, 1994), p. 85.

and tendencies, resists easy unification.[5] It is this refusal to reduce the self to a simple unity, the willingness to explore its internal tensions and contradictions, that, more than anything else, characterises the subjectivity of Schumann's music.

Responding to the Divided Subject

The notion that the subject is divided, that the self is composed of multiple elements that might not coalesce into a unity, and hence that it may never fully be able to know itself, is one that held considerable resonance in Schumann's day. As suggested at the close of Chapter 2, the dilemma of self-apperception – the apparent impossibility of the subject ever becoming fully transparent to itself, of grasping itself as object without thereby introducing a split in itself – was one of the most fraught philosophical issues of the late eighteenth and early nineteenth centuries. The history of German philosophy in the decades after Kant can well be understood as a search for a solution to this problem: either through the 'absolute I', the 'I = I' sought as a grounding principle in the Idealism of Fichte, Schelling, and even Hegel, or the insistence that this quest for self-reflection is necessarily ever incomplete, as found in Romantic authors such as Friedrich Schlegel or in Novalis's *Fichte-Studien*. It would surely be going too far to suggest that Schumann's interest in exploring the multiple aspects of the self relates directly to such abstruse philosophical problems that preoccupied the minds of an earlier generation, but similar concerns permeated much of the literature and thought of the early nineteenth century, including the work of several authors Schumann was passionately devoted to. As argued in Chapter 1, the fact that the self, though proving recalcitrant to philosophical enquiry, was conceived as being manifest only through its forms of articulation meant that artistic creation could be viewed as a form of self-discovery. For numerous writers and artists who can broadly be characterised as 'Romantic', the recognition of the complexity of the subject provided a justification for exploring and even embracing the conflicts and irrational elements of selfhood that had troubled Enlightenment thought.

Foremost among such Romantic thinkers were two of Schumann's favourite authors, Jean Paul and E. T. A. Hoffmann. As is well known, the novelist Jean Paul Richter (1763–1825) was Schumann's literary

---

[5] Kramer, 'Rethinking Schumann's *Carnaval*', pp. 112, 109, 112.

touchstone and probably his greatest artistic influence from adolescence onwards. 'I often wondered where I would be if I had not known Jean Paul: but yet he seems at least on one side to be entwined with me' wrote the young Schumann in 1828.[6] Indeed, in John Daverio's view, Schumann's discovery of Jean Paul amounted to 'a kind of self-discovery.'[7] Numerous aspects of the author's work appealed to Schumann – the rambling digressions and formal arabesques, his blend of humour and sentimentality, the whimsical allusions and playful self-references – but it was also the manner in which Jean Paul explored the psychology of his characters, in particular, the multiple and often contradictory tendencies of the human subject, that captivated him. 'In all his works Jean Paul reflects himself, but each time in *two* characters: he is Albano and Schoppe, Siebenkäs and Leibgeber, Vult and Walt, Gustav and Fenk, Flamin and Viktor. Only the one Jean Paul is capable of uniting two such different characters within himself.' There are 'always stark contrasts, if not also extremes, united in his work and in himself – and yet it is he alone'.[8] Not coincidentally, Jean Paul is the author usually accredited with introducing the term *Doppelgänger* into mainstream discourse.

E. T. A. Hoffmann (1776–1822) was another author of crucial significance for Schumann whose work famously plays with notions of the split self, with *Doppelgänger* and the conflict between the separate worlds his protagonists inhabit – a writer at once fantastic, visionary, grotesque, and frequently disturbing. Most obviously Schumann's *Kreisleriana* Op. 16 takes its title from Hoffmann's collection of the same name which treats the fictional musician Johannes Kreisler, a deeply conflicted artist torn between the ideal of his music and the mendacity of the world around him, and the protagonist of one strand of the novel *Kater Murr*, whose fragmentary biography is interleaved between the autobiography of a self-satisfied tomcat. In both works we encounter alter egos, doubles, and the blurring of subjective identity: in *Kreisleriana*, for instance, Kreisler finds a kindred soul in the Baron Wallborn (who is probably little more than a fictional self-projection), and ultimately blends with the authorial persona of Hoffmann himself at the close of the collection. But the

---

[6] Schumann, undated note from 1828, *Tagebücher*, vol. I, p. 82.

[7] Daverio, *Robert Schumann*, pp. 37–8. The most extended account of Jean Paul's influence on Schumann's music is given by Erika Reiman, *Schumann's Piano Cycles and the Novels of Jean Paul* (Rochester, NY: University of Rochester Press, 2004). Eric Frederick Jensen provides a survey of Jean Paulian traits in the composer's music in *Schumann (The Master Musicians)* (Oxford: Oxford University Press, 2012), p. 79.

[8] Schumann, *Tagebücher*, vol. I, p. 82.

Fantasiestücke Op. 12 and *Nachtstücke* Op. 23 probably refer to Hoffmann's works too.[9] In Hoffmann the young Schumann not only found an artist who as author, critic, composer, and performer combined musical and literary activities in exemplary fashion, but one who explored the uncomfortable split between different levels of experience and readily plumbed the irrational and often darker aspects of the human psyche.[10]

Schumann's interest in the divided self seems to have predated his reading of Jean Paul and Hoffmann – revealingly, as early as 1826 he had started penning a drama entitled 'Der Doppelgänger' – but the encounter with these authors evidently reinforced a theme that held considerable significance for him.[11] Partly under the influence of such figures, partly no doubt as a consequence of an adolescent search for his own identity at a crucial formative age, in his late teens and early twenties Schumann pondered at length his subjective identity and the difficulty of knowing his true nature. His diaries from these years are, as Beate Perrey puts it, 'clearly the reflections of a self-obsessed young man', showing Schumann repeatedly asking himself who he was and reflecting on the difficulties of describing one's inner nature.[12] Such externalisation, as we saw, also enabled him to adopt a third-person perspective on himself; yet in doing so, he inevitably introduced a split in his self through its division into subject and object, a move whose drawbacks were not lost on him. Writing on his twenty-first birthday, 8 June 1831, Schumann notes one of the more troubling corollaries of this conceptual separation, that of self-estrangement: 'It seems to me sometimes as if my objective self wanted to separate itself completely from my subjective

---

[9] The most extended account of Schumann's artistic relation to Hoffmann is given by MacAuslan, *Schumann's Music and E. T. A. Hoffmann's Fiction*. See also Daverio, *Robert Schumann*, pp. 71–5, Rosen, *The Romantic Generation*, pp. 669–83, and Julian Johnson, 'Narrative Strategies in Hoffmann and Schumann', in Rudinger Görner (ed.), *Resounding Concerns* (Munich: Iudicium, 2003), pp. 55–70. The volume *Schumann und seine Dichter*, ed. Matthias Wendt (Mainz: Schott, 1993), contains shorter accounts of the influence of both Jean Paul and Hoffmann on Schumann: see Kurt Wölfel, 'Schumanns Jean-Paul-Periode', and Susanne Hoy-Draheim, 'Robert Schumann und E. T. A. Hoffmann', pp. 25–32 and 61–70.

[10] Thus, for Johnson, 'Schumann inscribes in his music a divided or even multiple subjectivity similar to that which Hoffmann achieves through the use of parallel narratives, carnivalesque disguise, recurrent Doppelgänger and a blurring of the fantastical and the everyday.' 'Narrative Strategies in Hoffmann and Schumann', p. 70.

[11] See Aigi Heero, *Robert Schumanns Jugendlyrik* (Sinzig: Studio Verlag, 2003), pp. 88–9. The Doppelgänger theme would recur throughout the next decade; lodging with the Wiecks in the early 1830s, Robert would often use the Doppelgänger motive in the games he played with the young Clara, and it continues as a theme in their correspondence over that decade.

[12] Beate Perrey, 'Schumann's lives, and afterlives: an introduction', in Beate Perrey (ed.), *The Cambridge Companion to Schumann* (Cambridge: Cambridge University Press, 2007), p. 10.

self, or as if I stood between my appearance and my being, between form and shadow.'[13]

It is around this time that Schumann happens on the creation of his two celebrated alter egos. On 1 July 1831 he observes: 'Completely new persons enter the diary from today – two of my best friends, whom I've nonetheless never before seen – they are Florestan and Eusebius.'[14] Florestan seems to have emerged first, commonly taken to represent the extrovert and assertive side of Schumann's personality; Eusebius, in contrast, reflects the more pensive, sensitive, and introverted aspects of his creator. These two figures would be joined by Meister Raro (a more mature, integrative persona, attributed variously to a superego element in Schumann, his teacher Friedrich Wieck, or to an amalgamation of the names Clara and Robert), besides the other external characters in the fictional 'League of David' (*Davidsbund*), some of whom we encountered in *Carnaval*. The literary precedent for this conceit is clear; nonetheless, the function of Schumann's pseudonymous alter egos is disputed among biographers. For Peter Ostwald, typically, they form a manner of maintaining balance between dangerous psychical tensions in the composer that would eventually lead to his insanity. John Worthen, on the other hand, disagrees with the idea that they might have been 'ways of recording his divided self'; in context, holds Worthen, Schumann uses his twin personas as a method of self-examination, 'a strategy for him to look at the world and at himself more clearly'.[15] One would probably not go too far wrong to follow John Daverio in pointing to how Schumann's 'best friends . . . represent a poetic solution to the problem of the split self', without needing to impute any deeper mental malaise at this point. Whether or not there was a connexion, Florestan and Eusebius can be adequately explained by the literary context in which Schumann was steeped at the time, without recourse to the spectre of madness.[16]

At first this exploration of the compound nature of subjective identity occurred though literary means, privately in diary entries and publicly through Schumann's journalism, starting with the famous review by Florestan and Eusebius of Chopin's Variations on 'Là ci darem la mano' later in 1831, but

---

[13] Schumann, diary entry, 8 June 1831, *Tagebücher*, vol. I, p. 339 ('Mir ist's manchmal, als wolle sich mein objektiver Mensch vom subjektiven ganz trennen oder als ständ' ich zwischen meiner Erscheinung u. meinem Syn, zwischen Gestalt und Schatten').

[14] Schumann, diary entry, 1 July 1831, *ibid.*, p. 344.

[15] Peter Ostwald, *Schumann: The Inner Voices of a Musical Genius*, revised edition (Boston: Northeastern University Press, 2010), pp. 74–9; John Worthen, *Robert Schumann: Life and Death of a Musician* (New Haven: Yale University Press, 2007), p. 61.

[16] Daverio, *Robert Schumann*, p. 75. A cogent account of Schumann's multiplication of the self here is given by Perrey, 'Schumann's lives, and afterlives', pp. 13–16.

within a few years Schumann would turn to musical expressions of the divided subject too. In piano works like *Carnaval* and the *Davidsbündlertänze* this is something he largely treats playfully, adopting his quasi-autobiographical personas as musical characters or the pseudonymous composers of the music. With time, however, the musical subjects become less explicitly auto-biographical: in *Kreisleriana*, for instance, the figure of Hoffmann's imaginary Kapellmeister replaces Schumann's own alter egos, resulting in a more detached, third-person representation of the self-divided subject. With the turn to song in 1840, the virtual subject or 'lyric I' can no longer be taken to refer primarily to Schumann himself (although this has not stopped over a century and a half of reception history from doing all but this).[17] Indeed, by the early 1840s, the Florestan and Eusebius personas effectively drop out of Schumann's life, not only from his music but also from his music criticism.[18] One may, of course, still choose to identify the virtual subjects of Schumann's music with aspects of the composer's psyche and the playful pseudonyms, he at one stage adopted to express this, but we need to note that in only a few cases is this designated by the composer, and these instances date from the 1830s. A sense of divided subjectivity in Schumann's music need not refer directly to that of its creator: it would be prudent for us to maintain a critical separation between autobiography and art.

Musical Selves: the Phenomenology of the Divided Subject

In Chapter 2 we explored some of the ways in which a sense of subjectivity could be conveyed in music. Ostensibly these implicated a single, coherent subject, though in several cases this was manifested through discontinuities and fragmentation, already suggesting a greater complexity to the assump-tion that the subject in music is generally singular and unified. More specifically now, the inquiry could be extended to consider how music might expressly convey a division or split in the virtual subject projected.

Some possible means have been suggested in the opening examples from *Carnaval*. Aptly, the pieces named after Schumann's two alter egos, 'Eusebius' and 'Florestan', highlight various ways of creating a sense of an internally conflicted or divided subject. These included the use of

---

[17] '*My songs*', the young Schumann had admittedly once written, 'are given to the authentic impression of my self' – but this statement is from over a decade earlier and refers in several cases to settings of poems he had also penned. Schumann, entry from August 1828, *Tagebücher*, vol. I, p. 112.

[18] See Jensen, *Robert Schumann*, p. 108.

conflicting rhythmical and metrical layers (metric dissonance); the alternation or interleaving of different types of material (textural stratification and interleaving), which extended to the recall or quotation of other music; and the opposition of different tonal centres (tonal dualism), allied with fragmentation and harmonic incompletion. One further important category not really covered in *Carnival* (it was barely suggested in the reference to *Papillons* within 'Florestan') stems from the conjunction of music and language, namely the potential tension between the subject expressed in a verbal text and that conveyed in the music, a feature manifest above all in song. The following sections explore these categories in more detail.

Metric Dissonance

One of the hardest aspects of the divided subject to represent through artistic means would seem to be the presence of distinct aspects of the self or multiple 'selves' existing simultaneously. In music, however, this impression can be accomplished fairly simply through the polyphony of separate melodic lines or rhythmic layers. When more than one distinct melodic voice is present, as in traditional counterpoint, the effect might be suggestive of multiple individuals rather than a single, divided individual (this is a point that will be returned to in Chapter 8), but the superimposition of different rhythmic patterns or metres may more readily imply a single subject consisting of multiple parts. Something of this quality was seen in 'Eusebius', with its division into two simultaneous but non-congruent layers of rhythmic motion. The 'self' here can be understood as formed from multiple, overlapping rhythms: not necessarily a tormented or internally warring subject, but a higher-level aggregate of diverse ongoing processes, perhaps even a fiction or regulative concept that holds these disparate elements together.

This is an idea with some pedigree: it is arguably implicit in empiricist accounts of the self given by Locke and especially Hume (though they rejected the more sceptical implications of this position), while elements can certainly be found in the divided self of the Romantics, but it becomes particularly prominent after Schumann's lifetime. A pithy philosophical expression is found in the late writings of Friedrich Nietzsche, who rejected the classical notion of a single, unitary subject and instead proposed that the subject might better be understood as a multiplicity. For Nietzsche, 'The assumption of the single subject is perhaps unnecessary; perhaps it is just as permissible to assume a multiplicity of subjects on whose interplay and struggle our thinking and our consciousness in general is based.'

'The subject' is thus merely 'the fiction that many similar states in us are the effect of one substratum ... the term for our belief in a unity underlying all the different impulses of the highest feeling of reality.'[19] Such ideas have been taken up in more recent years by those working in the fields of cognitive psychology and the philosophy of mind, perhaps most famously Daniel Dennett, who views the 'self' as an illusory construct, formed from multiple streams or 'centres of narrative gravity'.[20]

Such a musical depiction of the multilayered self may appear comparatively benign when the different elements coexist peacefully as in 'Eusebius', but when the disparity between the opposing layers is accentuated, the same technique can also point to darker and more troubled aspects of the psyche. In an influential study from 1999 Harald Krebs has extensively explored the concept of 'metric dissonance' in Schumann's music, whereby two or more opposing metres are simultaneously projected by the music. Writing in the persona of Schumann's Florestan (thus himself instantiating a divided authorial voice), Krebs observes that

the conception of meter as a set of interacting layers of motion ... suggests a link between music and our lives. Our heartbeat is an uninterrupted pulse that spans our entire life. That pulse is overlaid with other more or less regular layers, some of them less continuous than our pulse, many of them much slower – for example, our breaths, our footfalls, our recurrent daily activities, and so on.[21]

In some cases, Krebs suggests, the listener, unable to come to a convincing metrical interpretation of a passage, 'will likely find themselves hovering deliciously and dreamily between metres' (not surprisingly, he attributes these moments to Schumann's Eusebian persona).[22] But more often, dissonance between metric layers may be understood as reflecting internal psychical conflicts within the subject: 'the metrical layers within a particular dissonance are apt symbols for normality, for order, for the objective self ... whereas antimetrical layers suggest the abnormal, the irregular and

---

[19] Friedrich Nietzsche, notes from 1885 and 1887, *Nachgelassene Fragmente* 1885 (40[42]) and 1887 (10[19]), translation by Walter Kaufmann and R. J. Hollingdale from *The Will to Power* (New York: Vintage, 1967), p. 270 and pp. 268–9.

[20] See, for instance, Daniel Dennett, *Consciousness Explained* (Harmondsworth: Penguin Books, 1991), and 'The Self as a Center of Narrative Gravity', in Frank S. Kessel, Pamela M. Cole, and Dale L. Johnson (eds.), *Self and Consciousness: Multiple Perspectives* (Hillsdale, NJ: Lawrence Erlbaum, 1992), pp. 103–15; also the pieces collected in Douglas R. Hofstadter and Daniel C. Dennett (eds.), *The Mind's I: Fantasies and Reflections on Self and Soul* (New York: Basic Books, 1981).

[21] Harald Krebs, *Fantasy Pieces: Metrical Dissonance in the Music of Robert Schumann* (New York: Oxford University Press, 1999), p. 23.

[22] *Ibid.*, p. 173. Krebs briefly touches on Op. 9's 'Eusebius' elsewhere (pp. 53, 143).

the disorderly, the subjective self'.[23] These might be attributed simply to the imagined aesthetic subject in the music, but Krebs also proposes a possible link with the tensions and conflicts in Schumann's own life. Krebs, again speaking through Eusebius, goes on to associate some instances of metrical dissonance in Schumann's music with the idea of insanity, pointing out that Moritz Hauptmann had associated metre – metrical consonance – with health: 'what better means than metrical dissonance to represent ill health – a mind gone awry – than metrical dissonance?'[24] In his subsequent work Krebs has extended his theory to cover the notion of hypermetric dissonance – competing patterns at the level of hypermetre. As it happens, metric dissonance is much less prevalent in Schumann's later music, though there is a greater use of hypermetric conflict there, which may similarly be used to convey subjective alienation.[25]

Metrical dissonance is especially characteristic of Schumann's piano works of the 1830s, the period in which he was most preoccupied with the notion of the divided subject. Aptly enough, the *Davidsbündlertänze* – a work purportedly co-authored by Schumann's alter egos Florestan and Eusebius – contains numerous examples of rhythmic and metric displacement. As Charles Rosen has elucidated here, the effect of psychological disconcertion is not merely something posited in an imaginary subject but really felt by the listener to this music: 'our sense of rhythm is neither fooled nor bewildered but troubled, and little by little this creates an emotional disturbance.'[26] But perhaps the clearest expression of the reciprocity between metrical dissonance and the divided

---

[23] *Ibid.*, p. 172. Erika Reiman has also taken up Krebs's notion of metrical dissonance to propose a distant analogy between the rhythmic structure of Schumann's music and the Fichtean notion of the ego parodied in Jean Paul's *Clavis Fichtiana*. See her reading of the second of the *Intermezzi*, Op. 4 (*Schumann's Piano Cycles and the Novels of Jean Paul*, pp. 54–5), which builds on Krebs's own analysis of the piece (*Fantasy Pieces*, pp. 192–9).

[24] Krebs, *Fantasy Pieces*, p. 173; the example of 'Schöne Wiege', Op. 24 No. 5, is given earlier (p. 161; the impressionable Eusebius is partly repeating Krebs's formulation there). Hauptmann's remark equating metre and health is cited on p. 4. As he acknowledges (p. 20), Krebs is partly developing the link between metric displacement and the composer's madness proposed earlier by Dieter Schnebel, 'Rückungen–Ver-rückungen: Psychoanalytische und musikanalytische Betrachtungen zu Schumanns Leben und Werk', in Heinz-Klaus Metzger and Rainer Riehn (eds.), *Musik-Konzepte: Robert Schumann I* (Munich: edition text+kritik, 1981), pp. 4–89. Some readers may question the turn to biographical explanations at this point.

[25] Harald Krebs, 'The Expressive Role of Rhythm and Meter in Schumann's Late Lieder', *Gamut*, 2 (2009), 267–98, and 'Meter and Expression in Robert Schumann's Op. 90', in Roe-Min Kok and Laura Tunbridge (eds.), *Rethinking Schumann* (New York: Oxford University Press, 2011), pp. 183–205; also see the following chapter in the same volume by William Benjamin, 'Hypermetric Dissonance in the Later Works of Robert Schumann', pp. 206–34.

[26] Rosen, *The Romantic Generation*, p. 227, who offers a useful account of displacement in this work (pp. 224–8).

Ex. 3.3a Schumann: *Kreisleriana*, Op. 16, No. 1 (1838 version), opening

Ex. 3.3b Schumann: *Kreisleriana*, Op. 16, No. 1, opening, bass shifted half a bar forward

fictional subject is to be found in *Kreisleriana*. The very opening of the first piece (*Äusserst bewegt*) violently asserts a 'displacement dissonance' between two misaligned metric patterns – the unstable triplet arpeggiations in the right hand against the syncopated left-hand octaves (Ex. 3.3a). In Rosen's apt description, 'the bass never coincides with a strong beat until the eighth bar, and the extraordinary passage work, which seems to start in the middle of a process already initiated before the piece begins, has a raging violence not often met with'.[27] As Krebs observes, this passage 'projects potentially congruent harmonic planes that have been shifted out of alignment'; bring the left-hand octaves back to the start of the bar to coincide with the notated downbeat and the underlying harmonic structure is largely clarified (at least until b. 4, where the A is actually too early; see Ex. 3.3b).[28] Yet even in this

---

[27] *Ibid.*, p. 669.   [28] Krebs, *Fantasy Pieces*, p. 150.

case the accented b♭s in the right hand would create dissonant appoggia-turas with the implied harmony of the first bar: first a dominant minor ninth, then as ♭6̂ to the tonic arpeggiation in the second half of the bar (which does not resolve directly to the neighbouring a). In fact, the right-hand triplets are themselves hardly metrically secure; starting on a semiquaver anacrusis (thus giving a slight initial emphasis to the final triplet beat), the melodic contour implies a grouping starting on the second triplet in each set, while the accents bring out the first triplet of the notated metre. With Schumann's slurring and at a lively tempo the effect is of an urgent end-weightedness – the melodic line surging up impulsively to the highest pitch in each group, before falling back to renew its ascent once more.

More uncanny is the dislocation between right and left hands in the final piece of the set (*Schnell und spielend*). At first nothing seems especially remiss (a slight twinge may be felt in b. 5, the bass's unexpected final quaver anticipating the following bar), but after the double bar the onsets of the bass octaves become progres-sively dislocated from the metric structure still clearly articulated in the right hand (Ex. 3.4). Unlike the metric dissonance in No. 1, there is no sense that two perfectly logical structures have simply become misaligned: in No. 8 the bass has become an irregular, irrational voice, 'coming in too late or too early for the harmony, emphasizing the weakest beats with no justification from the melody, at odds in fact with the rest of the texture'.[29] The effect is decidedly disconcert-ing, and as Rosen goes on to note, 'each time the opening section comes back, the bass returns in a different, more and more unex-pected way'.[30] In this example, the bass clearly should form an integral part of the texture – it belongs to the overall melodic-contrapuntal conception of the passage (or *Satzmodell* to use the useful German expression) – but it has become estranged from the other elements, a part of the subject that will not be integrated with the rest and obstinately insists on its alterity.

---

[29] Again quoting Rosen, *The Romantic Generation*, p. 680, who formulates this point nicely. A similar effect is made in the composer's setting of Eichendorff's 'Zwielicht' (Op. 39 No. 10), discussed later.

[30] *Ibid.*, p. 681. Also see the same author's discussion of the 'false' counterpoint suggested by Schumann's sporadic accentuation of inner voices: 'in terms of voice leading, they come from nowhere, and they lead to nothing' (p. 683 – a distant echo perhaps of the start of Hoffmann's *Kreisleriana*).

Ex. 3.4 Schumann: *Kreisleriana*, Op. 16, No. 8, opening

Textural Interleaving

Another way in which Schumann may suggest a division in the subjective persona – this time not as temporal simultaneity but through succession – is by the interleaving and intercutting of different thematic or textural strands.

The juxtaposition and alternation of two or more parallel streams within a piece or movement may suggest the ongoing presence of distinct subjective attributes or personas contained within a larger, complex subject. Something similar has been theorised by John Daverio as Schumann's 'interleaving' or '*Kater Murr*' technique, named after the interleaved narrative structure of Hoffmann's Kreisler novel, an important component in what Daverio reads as Schumann's systematic exploration of structures built from fragmentary parts.[31] Of course, the mere alternation of different musical materials need not imply multiple sides of a divided subject; it may point to multiple narratives or multiple characters that are somehow, obscurely, interrelated (just as in Hoffmann's novel), or listeners may indeed reject the positing of a virtual subject altogether. But in some cases, it may seem plausible to interpret the different elements as belonging to a single, internally divided subject.

A clear example is provided again in the *Davidsbündlertänze*, whose eighteen separate dances interleave pieces contributed by 'Florestan' and 'Eusebius' – the purest musical expression of Schumann's stylised division into his two alter egos. The opening number is ascribed to both personas, but thereafter Eusebius generally alternates with Florestan (though having just been heard in No. 3, Florestan impatiently breaks in again with No. 4 – 'Ungeduldig' – before allowing Eusebius to speak).[32] The general principle of expressive alternation – impetuous, often agitated numbers succeeding tranquil, reflective ones – is clear. It is moot whether the listener would know that the two voices belong to a single subject if Schumann had not designated in the first edition the pseudonymous authorship of each piece, but in adding this information he provided a crucial guide to interpreting the work's subjective identities. And in some cases, the two personas appear to run against each other as differing voices within the same number, in such a way as to suggest through more exclusively musical means their latent connexion. This is particularly the case in the penultimate dance (the celebrated 'Wie aus der Ferne'). 'F. and E.' are given as co-authors, but the dreamy opening, with its nostalgic evocation of distance, surely belongs to the Eusebius side of the two.[33]

---

[31] John Daverio, 'Schumann's Systems of Musical Fragments and *Witz*', in *Nineteenth-Century Music and the German Romantic Ideology* (New York: Schirmer, 1993), pp. 61–4.

[32] Not surprisingly, No. 4 is marked by impulsive syncopations throughout, a straightforward example of metrical displacement dissonance, as discussed in the previous section.

[33] Since the preceding No. 16 does not indicate the contributing author and runs straight on into No. 17 after its trio (thus proving incomplete as a structure), it is possible that the 'F and E' at the end of No. 17 refers to both pieces together. Ostensibly No. 16 would appear to be the product of Florestan, and 17, until near its end, of Eusebius. Formal fragmentation again helps the sense that the two subjective personas are interdependent and to some extent incomplete on their own.

At length, its repeated dwelling on the salient pitch G♮ leads by association to the emergence of an intra-opus memory – the recall of No. 2 (also originally penned by 'E.'), in which this pitch formed an expressive appoggiatura to the F♯ that has been present as a pedal throughout No. 17. This time, however, the melancholy of the remembered theme grows into increasing agitation, and the piece ends with some violence in the character of Florestan. Little by little the subjective voice has mutated from Eusebius's to that of his twin, without a clear separation being present. The two personas would appear to belong to one psyche.

The expressive and formal principle of alternation seen in the *Davidsbündlertänze* leads to the design seen in *Kreisleriana*, where there is no longer a semi-autobiographical resonance with Schumann himself but instead an enigmatic allusion to Hoffmann – the divided personality of his fictional composer Johannes Kreisler, or even the split narrative structure of the novel containing the latter's fragmentary biography. In Schumann's Op. 16, not only do the eight separate pieces predominantly alternate troubled and calmer moods but such contrasts are frequently present within numbers, often in such a way as to point to underlying connexions between individual pieces. The central section of No. 3 ('Etwas langsamer', bb. 33–84, scales rising and descending as if in mirror image) surely sounds like a distant allusion to the thematic substance of the preceding number, a gentler echo within a more turbulent piece, and similar material moreover re-emerges later in the work (e.g. bb. 25ff of No. 8). The sense of doubling is underscored by the almost uncanny similarity between the third and final numbers: both are in G minor, and feature a rising melodic idea in trochaic rhythm underscored by low bass octaves (compare Ex. 3.5 with Ex. 3.4 above). What makes the relation all the more unsettling is that the distorted reworking in No. 8 is made with those irregular, distorted bass onsets and hints of mysterious extra voices.

Ex. 3.5 Schumann: *Kreisleriana*, Op. 16, No. 3, opening

This sinister revenant returns twice, and the work ends with its sounds tapering away into silence. The precise identity of the voices or subjects in this work is left under-defined, but the strange doublings and echoes, alongside the interleaved strands of the discourse, suggest some form of division or refraction of the subject into a multiplicity, just as the internally conflicted Kreisler encounters alter egos and *Doppelgänger* throughout Hoffmann's twin accounts.

Tonal Pairing

The pervasive sense of doubling in *Kreisleriana* is underpinned by a further feature that often contributes to the sense of a split in the music's underlying basis: the pairing of keys, in this instance the work's basis around a G minor / B flat major axis. Six of the eight numbers are based in one of these two keys, and even one of the two which is not (No. 7) ends there (moving over its course from C minor to B flat major). Only the opening piece, in D minor, proves an exception, and B flat major is still present within it for its trio. Tonal pairing is a feature frequently discussed in relation to Romantic music, and in Schumann's music in particular.[34] What the concept is taken to mean is often flexible, but generally the term indicates that a piece of music is oriented around a central pair of keys rather than a single key centre (as in a 'monotonal' conception), almost invariably ones a third apart and contrasting in mode (typically relative major and minor, occasionally minor and its submediant major). Whether the relation between the two should be understood as rooted in opposition, or instead the keys treated as complementary sides of the same larger 'double-tonic

---

[34] The concept of tonal pairing, along with the related notions of the double-tonic complex and directional tonality, extends from the work of Robert Bailey (see 'An Analytical Study of the Sketches and Drafts', in *Richard Wagner: Prelude and Transfiguration from 'Tristan und Isolde'* (*Norton Critical Score*), ed. Robert Bailey (New York: W. W. Norton, 1985), esp. pp. 115–21, and the essays in William Kinderman and Harald Krebs (eds.), *The Second Practice of Nineteenth-Century Tonality* (Lincoln, NE: University of Nebraska Press, 1996)), and is used more informally by Charles Rosen in his account of Romantic harmonic practice. It has been applied extensively to Schumann's music by Peter H. Smith: see, for instance, 'Tonal Pairing and Monotonality in Instrumental Forms of Beethoven, Schubert, Schumann, and Brahms', *Music Theory Spectrum*, 35 (2013), 77–102, and 'Associative Harmony, Tonal Pairing, and Middleground Structure in Schumann's Sonata Expositions: The Role of the Mediant in the First Movements of the Piano Quintet, Piano Quartet, and *Rhenish* Symphony', in Roe-Min Kok and Laura Tunbridge (eds.), *Rethinking Schumann* (New York: Oxford University Press, 2011), pp. 235–64. David Kopp also offers a useful reconsideration of the broader phenomenon in his chapter 'Intermediate States of Key in Schumann' in the latter volume (*Rethinking Schumann*, pp. 300–25).

complex', is not always consistent. It might be most profitable to view the two tonics as forming two sides of the same coin, opposed in a sense, intimately linked in another; whether one chooses to point up the difference or the commonality depends on the specific compositional context (or the analyst's agenda). Such pairing may further be linked with the notion of 'directional tonality', where a piece or movement ends in a different key from that in which it started.

Tonal pairing is a common enough feature in music from Schumann's time and need not in itself indicate any specific subjective attributes. But the split between two key centres may certainly help to articulate a split in an underlying subjective persona suggested through other musical means, creating as it were paired 'centres of narrative gravity'. Benjamin Wadsworth has similarly proposed that Schumann's use of directional tonality based on the pairing of two keys can 'create the effect of two opposing mental states (or dramatic agents) within one person's mind'.[35] Shifting focus from one key to another across the course of a piece may convey a change in subjective state, whether one of progressive self-realisation or, conversely, of self-alienation.[36] When the individual piece is itself tonally unresolved (as with *Carnaval*'s 'Florestan') there may be an even stronger sense that the two keys represent fragmentary parts of the same larger subject.

Tonal pairing is prominent within several of Schumann's piano cycles and has received a fair degree of scholarly attention. It is especially evident in *Kreisleriana* and the *Humoreske*, both of which are based around a G minor / B flat major double tonic, while elements can be observed in *Carnaval* (notably in the sequence from 'Florestan' via 'Coquette' to 'Réplique', which again implicates G minor and B flat major) and in the *Davidsbündlertänze* (in which the opposition between G major and B minor takes on a certain significance both within and across numbers).[37] It can also be found in several of Schumann's songs from

[35] Benjamin K. Wadsworth, 'Directional Tonality in Schumann's Early Works', *Music Theory Online*, 18/4 (2012), §4.

[36] Reiman links Gérard Génette's idea of narrative 'focalisation' to tonality in music (see *Schumann's Piano Cycles and the Novels of Jean Paul*, pp. 29, 84); this approach might be usefully extended to dual tonic structures.

[37] Daverio comments on the tonal pairing in Opp. 16 and 21 (*Robert Schumann*, pp. 168, 178), while Rosen highlights the interchangeable nature of G minor and B flat in Op. 16 (*The Romantic Generation*, pp. 673–4). A more substantial consideration of pairing in Op. 16 No. 4 is given by Kopp, 'Intermediate States of Key in Schumann', pp. 315–22. On the *Carnaval* sequence, see also Wadsworth, 'Directional Tonality in Schumann's Early Works', §17–19, and on the *Davidsbündlertänze* Kaminsky, 'Principles of Formal Structure in Schumann's Early

1840, in which the two contrasting keys may often suggest different levels of consciousness. But even the instrumental works in classical genres from the following years include striking examples of tonal pairing. One of the first and most remarkable of these is the First String Quartet, Op. 41 No. 1, dating from 1842.[38]

Though designated as being in 'A minor', Schumann's Op. 41 No. 1 is split between two keys throughout, but in such a way that for most of its course, neither really interact with each other. The work starts with an A minor *Andante espressivo*, marked 'Introduzione' by the composer, whose contrapuntal gestures and plaintive tone call up the ethos of late Beethoven; but this formally complete, cadentially closed section is followed by a sonata-form movement in F major (*Allegro*) that makes no reference to the introduction's key or thematic content and ends securely in F major, as if the introduction had no bearing on the piece.[39] A minor reasserts itself in the second movement scherzo; F major, in turn, is used for the following *Adagio*. The finale reverts to the ostensible tonic A minor, though ultimately closes in A major. Towards its end, however, there is an extended passage of F major that seems to form the only direct contact between the two tonal centres, and thus potentially takes on a crucial significance. Yet what this manifestation of F major achieves is not altogether clear: the passage occupies a formally ambiguous position within the movement's structure, and whether it can be said to resolve the tonal split running throughout the work is moot.

Within each of the first three movements F major and A minor are kept apart from each other; there is little sense that F is exploited as chord VI within A minor, or conversely of A minor being salient as iii within F. The only point in common between the two is an indirect one: their relation to

Piano Cycles', 217–24. Examples of tonal pairing within individual numbers can be found in quite a few other works, such as *Papillons* and the *Intermezzi* Op. 4.

[38] The A minor Violin Sonata, Op. 105, provides another instance from a decade later: see Linda Correll Roesner, 'The Chamber Music', in Beate Perrey (ed.), *The Cambridge Companion to Schumann* (Cambridge: Cambridge University Press, 2007), pp. 133–6, and Peter H. Smith, 'Harmonies Heard from Afar: Tonal Pairing, Formal Design, and Cyclical Integration in Schumann's A minor Violin Sonata, op. 105', *Theory and Practice*, 34 (2009), 47–86, and 'Tonal Pairing and Monotonality', 89–93.

[39] The A minor *Introduzione* appears to have been written after the rest of the quartet was completed, which might suggest that Schumann's original conception was of a piece using 'directional tonality', starting in F but ending in A (see Julie Hedges Brown, '"A Higher Echo of the Past": Schumann's 1842 Chamber Music and the Rethinking of Classical Form', Ph.D. diss., Yale University (2000), p. 244). Roesner has argued, however, that Schumann's initial reference to the work – 'Quartett in *A Moll* angefangen, Satz in *F Dur* und *A moll*' – implies the dual tonal design of the first movement to have been intended from the start ('The Chamber Music', p. 125).

a third key, C major, used as the secondary tonal area in every movement, and even this feature is not really exploited by Schumann. Where the two come into direct juxtaposition is in the finale. F major is briefly suggested in the exposition (bb. 31–4), within a larger C major secondary area that has arrived on the heels of the A minor opening theme. In itself, this key may not seem that significant (many other keys are touched upon within the course of this section), but in its own small way it is an important step, as hitherto the rival tonal centres had been confined to different movements. The same passage is heard again at b. 152 in the development section, but from this point on the entire secondary group of the exposition returns intact, now transposed down a fifth.[40] While not initially heard as a large-scale repetition, the rotational parallelism surely becomes clear to the listener around the reappearance of the closing theme (b. 192): an entire block of music, corresponding to the latter two thirds of the exposition (bb. 23–76), is restated in the submediant, F major (bb. 152–205). At b. 206, however, this F major harmony resolves through an Italian sixth to the dominant of A minor, and from b. 214 the recapitulation of the first theme ensues. Its continuation into secondary (or more accurately closing) material is interrupted at b. 254 by a yet more unexpected event: a soft *Moderato* passage in A major featuring a transformation of the running quavers of the secondary material over a musette-like drone. This forms the decisive breakthrough into the tonic major: from here on, the remainder of the exposition's secondary / closing material reappears transformed into A major, in which key the quartet ends. F major is heard no more.

Some commentators have described Schumann's unusual procedure here as constituting a reverse recapitulation, one that, as Julie Hedges Brown puts it, 'simultaneously resolves the question of key in both the finale and quartet as a whole'. In her view, 'by folding F major into A minor as a large-scale upbeat, the recapitulation resolves a tonal ambiguity of the entire quartet', in which 'F major has challenged A minor as a second tonic'.[41] Regardless of Sonata Theory's recent strictures on the concept, this reading is not without problems: if secondary material appears in a non-tonic key before the return of the primary theme in the tonic, what reason do we have not to view this as simply forming a continuation of the development?[42] Admittedly, on

[40] The F major statement of the S material at b. 152 thus, in fact, corresponds rotationally to the first appearance of this idea in the exposition (b. 23), where it was given in C major before eight bars later being restated a fifth lower in F.

[41] Brown, 'A Higher Echo of the Past', pp. 249, 237.

[42] It is effectively dogma in James Hepokoski and Warren Darcy's 'Sonata Theory' that reverse recapitulations do not exist: see Hepokoski and Darcy, *Elements of Sonata Theory: Norms,*

listening to the piece there is an unmistakable sense that at some stage the F major passage becomes so literal a restatement as to appear reprise-like, albeit in the 'wrong' (or alternative) key. And although most of the secondary material returns again in the tonic after the first theme recapitulation, the rotational parallelism is much less exact there and is furthermore interrupted by the curious musette passage. But either way, it is not obvious exactly how the return in F major of secondary material originally heard in C major can be taken to repair the quartet's ongoing split between F major and A minor. For Linda Correll Roesner, conversely, 'the F major recapitulation, resolving nothing, continues to contribute to the tonal dichotomy of the quartet as a whole.'[43] Which view one adopts may come down to individual preference, but I would suggest that accounts that seek tonal resolution do so primarily from assuming the applicability of a standard narrative paradigm whereby anomalous elements must always be resolved into an overarching unity, rather than responding to the individual properties of the quartet. It may be more persuasive simply to acknowledge that A minor and F major coexist throughout the piece as parallel though largely separate tonal planes, and only in the latter stages of the finale come into any form of conjunction. F is ultimately subordinate to A but is not thereby dissolved. Tonal duality need not be reduced into a unity.

For Hans Keller, Schumann's title, 'String Quartet in A minor', is 'really a polite misnomer .... The man who, in 1833, was afraid of losing his mind is not unafraid in 1842 of losing his tonality.'[44] Interpretatively, Schumann's split tonal structure suggests analogies with the divided musical subject, similar to that seen in his earlier piano cycles such as *Kreisleriana*.[45] Yet such division need not be seen as internally conflicted:

Types, and Deformations in the Late-Eighteenth-Century Sonata (New York: Oxford University Press, 2006), pp. 353–5. A sonata-theory interpretation of this finale, predictably eschewing the reverse recapitulation in favour of a 'type 2' sonata reading, is in fact, given by Peter H. Smith, 'Schumann's Continuous Expositions and the Classical Tradition', *Journal of Music Theory*, 58 (2014), 32–6.

[43] Roesner, 'The Chamber Music', p. 127. Roesner sees the absence of resolution here as related to a higher-level interaction between the centres of F and A that runs over the three Op. 41 quartets.

[44] Hans Keller, 'The Classical Romantics: Schumann and Mendelssohn', in H. H. Schönzeler (ed.), *Of German Music: A Symposium* (London: Oswald Wolff, 1976), p. 216.

[45] Some of Schumann's earlier comments seem to indicate that he saw the quartet genre as to some extent a 'conversation among four people' (e.g. 'Erster Quartettmorgen' (1838), *GS*, vol. I p. 335; see further Daverio, *Robert Schumann*, p. 248). Schumann's rather traditionalist remarks from 1838 need not be taken as applicable to his own work written several years later, but we should acknowledge that this interpretation of a divided subjectivity is not necessarily the author's view – even if it is consistent with his earlier practice.

Op. 41 No. 1 surely points to the expressive and formal richness derived from a split tonal perspective, in which the juxtaposition of A minor and F major sections is less a formal problem to be worked out than an alternative and more variegated means of structuring an instrumental work.

Music and Text: Multiple or Divided Personas in the Lied

The preceding examples suggest various ways of invoking a split in a work's subjective quality that can be achieved through musical means, without the aid of a verbal text to designate the subject involved. But a further and extremely powerful means of indicating a divided or multiple subject can be realised through music's conjunction with words. In its most basic form, the musical subject can be simply identified with the grammatical subject in the text – the denotative precision of language clarifying the more inchoate subjective elements suggested by the music. But the conjunction of verbal and musical markers of subjectivity holds the potential not just of reinforcing but of conflicting with one another, a division that opens up numerous possibilities for indicating a split in the subject's consciousness. For instance, the subject in the text may appear to say or think one thing, but the music indicates he or she is actually feeling another. This may obviously arise in a range of different musical genres – in stage works, for instance, there is also the added level of the action seen on stage – but the classic exemplification in Schumann's music is the solo Lied.

It seems that Schumann's song aesthetic, as much as it can be reconstructed as a coherent position, supported the idea that both voice and piano accompaniment should form interlinked though distinct voices, in which, as Jon Finson puts it, 'the sound and sense of the verse, of the melody, and of the accompaniment run sometimes congruently, sometimes separately but in parallel, sometimes divergently', thus being capable of conveying 'a multilayered psychological process'.[46] Such an approach fits well with more recent theorising on the virtual subjects or personas heard in a compound utterance such as a song. Taking bearings from Edward T. Cone's influential discussion of the musical persona, in the last few decades scholars have examined not only the sense of subjectivity projected

---

[46] Jon Finson, *Robert Schumann: The Book of Songs* (Cambridge, MA: Harvard University Press, 2007), pp. 6–7.

by a song but furthermore the conflict between different personas or 'agents' within it.[47] One of the most promising formulations along these lines has been Berthold Hoeckner's conception of the Lied as a 'multi-voiced utterance', an idea developed specifically in relation to Schumann's contributions to the genre. In an article on the Heine *Liederkreis*, Op. 24, Hoeckner develops 'the notion of a plural voice' or 'multiple persona' in Schumann's music, finding an interpretative tool in Novalis's idea of the subject as consisting of multiple selves or voices.[48] Applying this to Cone's ideas on the identity of the voice we hear in a song, Hoeckner finds a potential tripartite division of the subject or persona: into the 'lyric I' of the verbal text (the poetic persona) and two musical ones, those of the vocal line and of the piano accompaniment (the vocal and instrumental personas). Through such means a musical setting of a poetic text may convey great complexity in the internal divisions and conflicts between different parts of a single subject: the contrast between conscious and subconscious parts of the psyche, between hope and reality, past and present, or dreams and delusion.

Such qualities can be found throughout Schumann's song output, from the *Liederjahr* of 1840 to the settings made a decade later. Most famous, though, are surely the composer's settings of Heinrich Heine from that initial year of 1840 – first and foremost the Op. 24 *Liederkreis* and especially *Dichterliebe*, Op. 48 – in which the bitter irony and divisions of Heine's texts are complemented and sometimes countered by Schumann's own musical forms of self-division.[49]

One of the simplest illustrations of this musical-poetic interaction, where a distinction in the subjective persona communicated by the text is mirrored in Schumann's music, might seem to be the stratification of different speakers found in songs like 'Ich wandelte unter den Bäumen' (Op. 24 No. 3) or again in 'Am leuchtenden Sommermorgen' (Op. 48 No. 12), in which the protagonist is answered by the voice of another, apparently non-human, subject – a little bird (*Vöglein*) in the former, flowers in the latter. In each piece, the change in subjective voice is marked musically by an unexpected harmonic shift to a remote tonal realm (B to

---

[47] Cone, *The Composer's Voice*; see my discussion in Chapter 1.

[48] Hoeckner, 'Poet's Love and Composer's Love', 1.3, 1.4. Hoeckner is responding to an essay by Cone, 'Poet's Love or Composer's Love?', in which Cone modifies his earlier theory.

[49] One of the truisms once regularly encountered in accounts of these songs was that Schumann failed to understand Heine's irony in his settings. We know, however, that Schumann was well aware of Heine's 'burning sarcasm': when he goes against the ironic implications of the text it would be better to conclude there is a different agenda at work, which may itself deepen or bring out a further irony. See further on this point Finson, *Robert Schumann: The Book of Songs*, p. 52.

G and B flat to G respectively), slower tempo (*Langsamer*), and a hushed, *pianissimo* dynamic. Ostensibly, of course, these voices are presented as belonging to distinct subjects, separate from the 'lyric I' of the poem; but are we really to believe that diminutive birds and garden flowers speak to the protagonist in human language about his lost love? As Robert Hatten recognises in a perceptive analysis of the latter song, the flowers may be a projection of part of the subject's own psyche, 'personified and ventrilo-quistically envoiced in the troubled consciousness of a lover who is psych-ically split – one side feeling a justified grievance, the other an overpowering love'. The different agential voices and implied actorial roles 'are all interiorized as parts of a singular subjectivity.'[50] Such a reading does not contradict the text here – it is already implicit in Heine's poem – but is developed further in Schumann's setting, which provides 'what only music can offer – a sense of immediacy juxtaposed with a displacement from reality'. Thus, through music, 'Schumann creates a psychologically more complex and multi-dimensional subjectivity.'[51]

In this instance the tonal split in the music works alongside the split in the subject persona, a technique familiar from the preceding section, but here reinforced by the textual designation of a protagonist or protagonists. In other cases, though, a sense of tonal pairing can create a more complex interaction with the poetic text, bringing out elements only implicit in the latter. Probably the most famous and oft-discussed example of tonal pairing in Schumann's entire oeuvre is that found in the opening song of *Dichterliebe*, 'Im wunderschönen Monat Mai', which oscillates throughout between the dominant of F sharp minor and A major.[52] Heine's text is written entirely in the past tense: 'In the wondrously beautiful month of May, as all the buds blossomed, there in my heart love arose; In the wondrously beautiful month of May, as all the birds sang, there I confessed to her, my yearning and my longing.' There is no immediate tension or discord in this text: the events are typically, even stereotypically romantic (springtime, blossom and birdsong, burgeoning love), and osten-sibly happy (though the talk of 'yearning and longing' perhaps sounds a warning note). It is only in the context of the larger cycle that we might surmise that this love affair did not end happily. This recounts a time in the

---

[50] Hatten, *A Theory of Musical Agency*, p. 159.   [51] *Ibid.*, p. 163.
[52] See, for instance, the discussions in Rosen, *The Romantic Generation*, pp. 41–8, David Neumeyer, 'Organic Structure and the Song Cycle: Another Look at Schumann's *Dichterliebe*', *Music Theory Spectrum*, 4 (1982), 103–4, Nathan John Martin, 'Schumann's Fragment', *Indiana Theory Review*, 28 (2010), 99–106, and especially Kopp, 'Intermediate States of Key in Schumann', pp. 303–13.

past: it is a memory of the past, but possibly one from the standpoint of a more melancholy present, in which any romance is long over.

Schumann's opening, a repeated Phrygian approach to the dominant of F sharp minor, leaves us in no doubt that sadness hangs over the entire scene, to this extent bringing out a reading only intimated in Heine's text; and his ending, on the dominant seventh of the same key, leaves the outcome both uncertain and yet unmistakably pessimistic (Ex. 3.6). Yet between the unresolved $C\sharp^7$ of the piano's refrain that bookends the song and reappears between the two verses, the actual vocal setting is continually drawn towards A major, the relative of the F sharp minor implied by the opening, continuing in an upward movement towards its own subdominant. In fact, the first completed cadence in the piece is to A major (b. 6; there are no fewer than four in the course of the song), while there is not a single cadence to F sharp minor anywhere.

The ostensible F sharp minor tonic is continually pointed to but never actually appears; a more suitable expression of the longing for the unobtainable love object would be hard to imagine.[53] Instead, A major is set up as an alternative tonic, the resulting split between the two tonal centres creating a conflict between the tendencies of the piano accompaniment and that of the voice, corresponding to that disparity between the ostensible message of Heine's text and its meaning within the wider context of the cycle.

For Barbara Turchin, this opening song of *Dichterliebe* serves to adumbrate 'the distinction in expressive function between vocal line and piano accompaniment'.

The voice, the bearer of words and explicit meaning, discloses thoughts and reveals events on a more conscious level (analogous to the explicit statement of a tonality) while the piano unveils a deeper, emotional reality that frequently cuts through the surface of the spoken word (like the implication of a tonality which ultimately undermines one explicitly stated).[54]

Namely, Turchin proposes that '*Im wunderschönen Monat Mai* opens the cycle with *recollections* of love's first bloom; Heine's verses speak in the *past* tense. Schumann's melancholy, tonally ambiguous setting of this poem intimates that what once was, is no longer.'[55] And yet it is more complex

---

[53] Lacanian psychoanalysis would call this the *petit objet a* – the object of desire, on which the entire edifice is based, which would make the subject whole and repair its internal split, but which can never be attained. This perspective is given a more extended discussion in Chapter 7.

[54] Barbara Turchin, 'Schumann's Song Cycles: The Cycle within the Song', *19th-Century Music*, 8 (1985), 234.

[55] *Ibid.*, 234–5.

Ex. 3.6 Schumann: 'Im wunderschönen Monat Mai' (Heine), *Dichterliebe*, Op. 48 No. 1

Ex. 3.6 (cont.)

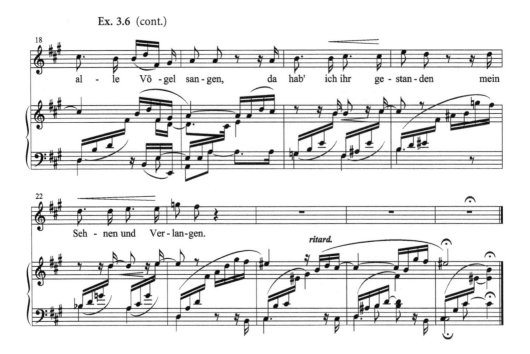

than this, since Schumann's setting is not simply in the minor mode – a 'sad' setting of a 'happy' poem, conveying its ironic disjunction – but oscillates throughout between two keys. The effect is a distinction between temporal levels of piano and voice; grief and remembered happiness. We start from the melancholy present, but such is the immediacy of music that the memories of the happier month of May continually flood back to assume a life and presence of their own, before being in turn punctured by reality with the return of the piano interlude. The text (Hoeckner's 'poetic' persona) is written in the past tense but ostensibly happy; the instrumental persona, ever moping around its unresolved dominant seventh of F sharp minor, inhabits a forlorn present; while the vocal persona, continually bringing the music round to A major and beyond, relives the past of that golden springtime that through it is made fleetingly present.[56] Music here can suggest a division in temporal levels within the consciousness of the subject quite apart from the grammatical tense employed by the poet.

---

[56] As Naomi Cumming earlier proposed, 'Allowing that past states can be made emotionally immediate in the vocal gesture, events that are reported as past may become affectively present, creating a shift in temporal perspective' ('The Subjectivities of "Erbarme dich"', 19).

Another complex split between temporal levels and levels of consciousness is found in the thirteenth song of the cycle, 'Ich hab' im Traum
geweinet' ('I wept in my dream'). Heine's three verses chart at least three
levels of progressive development, underscored by their highly repetitive
formulation:

- movement from a worse to a better state in the dream the poet has of his
  beloved (that she was dead; that she abandoned him; that she still loved
  him);
- reverse chronological movement from a hypothetical future (she is not,
  presumably, dead at the present moment) back through a more recent
  and then to a more distant past;
- the intensification of sorrow in the protagonist (on waking, first his
  solitary tear still flowed ('floss'); the second time he still wept long and
  bitterly; finally the flood of tears still stream ('strömt'), now in the
  present tense).

What is most striking here is how the recollection of the beloved's
kindness, of the lost period of their love, is more distressing than the thought
of her death. (A similar, oft-noted irony is found in the fourth song, 'Wenn
ich in deine Augen seh'', in which the remembered line of the beloved's
avowal of love ('"Ich liebe dich"') receives a considerably more anguished
musical setting than the subject's bitter tears that follow.)[57] This memory
evidently forms some deep wound, one that the subject might prefer to
forget, and which is accessed through reaching back into the ordinarily
hidden parts of the psyche – effectively recovering lost former selves – in
sleep. Schumann's setting at first separates vocal and instrumental personas
almost completely: the initial unaccompanied vocal line is answered by the
sombre funereal figuration in the piano. Numb with pain, the subject's
deeper emotions are held in check; one might indeed not associate the
piano part with any subjective agency at all. But as the memories awake, as
the subject retreats further back into the past, the subconscious parts of the
psyche, seemingly dormant, are stirred. For the first time, at the start of the
third verse the accompaniment, rather than echoing, takes the initiative, pre-
empting and flowing into the opening vocal line (bb. 22–4). And now the
punctuating funereal pattern is missing, the inexorable chromatic ascent of
the piano underpinning the dramatic intensification of the final verse – the
crux of the poem – in which the bittersweet memory of the beloved's former

---

[57] See on this point Rufus Hallmark, 'The Sketches for "Dichterliebe"', *19th-Century Music*,
1 (1977), 116; Perrey, *Schumann's Dichterliebe and Early Romantic Poetics*, pp. 181–8.

kindness returns with full vigour. The memory activated, the poet finds himself in the present, still weeping. The voice breaks off in pain, confronted with this unbridgeable chasm between the past and the bitterness of the present. Fragments of the opening accompanimental figure attempt to reassert the objective self-control of the beginning; and yet nothing is resolved.[58] Schumann's musical setting complements the multilayered complexity of Heine's poem yet deepens the portrayal of the psychological processes involved in moving between the present and recalled past.

In other cases in *Dichterliebe*, the return of the past can have an ironic, disjunctive effect on the present, especially when it appears to arise from a subconscious realm, almost expressly contrary to the conscious volition of the protagonist. In No. 15, 'Aus alte Märchen', the poet proceeds to describe at length the wondrous land disclosed in the 'old fairy tales', a land of happiness and enchantment, in which he could be free from his suffering, could he but reach there. But, of course, he cannot. 'That land of delight, I often see in dreams, yet with the morning sun it melts away like vain foam', he wistfully concludes, the hope of the preceding seven stanzas evaporating in the two final lines. Schumann's setting slows for the penultimate verse (the melody given in augmentation), then dissipates with the close of the poem, at which point the song seems to have come to an inconclusive end; but in an unexpected postlude we hear once more the distant sounds of the enchanted opening music, now *pianissimo*, as if it is still out there, somewhere beyond reach. The bubble has burst, the illusion is punctured, but still the *alte Märchen-Weise* returns, as if gently mocking the rational awareness that comes with the light of day. The ironic effect is created entirely by Schumann. That this is achieved through music is apt, though, as Heine's wording makes it clear that this magical land is related through sound – 'da singt es und da klingt es / Von einem Zauberland' (there [in fairy tales] is sung and sounded / of a magical land).

This unforeseen recall of past dreams in the penultimate number sets the listener up for the final song, 'Die alten bösen Lieder' ('The old, spiteful songs'). Heine's text, proceeding through an array of increasingly hyperbolic images, conveys the poet's urge to rid himself of the past – 'the old, spiteful songs, the bad and bitter dreams' – proposing to send them down the Rhine in an enormous coffin and sink them in the sea, along with his love and his sorrow. The poem signals a rejection of the poet's past,

---

[58] Borrowing from Perrey's description of this passage (*Schumann's Dichterliebe and Early Romantic Poetics*, p. 148). See also Kofi Agawu's concise analysis in 'Structural "Highpoints" in Schumann's *Dichterliebe*', *Music Analysis*, 3 (1984), 170–1.

a rejection of his creations of the past – by implication the very same 'Lieder' we have been hearing in this cycle. But famously, Schumann does exactly the opposite. In his extended postlude to this song, which becomes in effect an epilogue to the whole cycle, he brings back the beautiful postlude to the twelfth song, 'Am leuchtenden Sommermorgen', to round off the work, transforming the preceding C sharp minor into a forgiving D flat major. The moment in which the poetry calls for the past to be buried is the one moment in the cycle when the music's own past unambiguously returns.[59] Obviously there is a wry irony here: the old songs containing his love and pain have not sunk into the depths, but float back to the surface, just as the bubble burst in 'Aus alte Märchen' reforms at the close of that song.[60] But there is also a split opened here between the music's instrumental and vocal/poetic personas: the latter call for closure, the former revisit the past. It is as if at a deeper level the subject does not really believe what it tries to convince itself of: the conscious, rational part of the psyche (the super ego, perhaps) wants to make a break with the past, renouncing its pain, though with this perforce renouncing love and poetry; the emotions, the subconscious side of the psyche, know better, that this cannot be the case, ending like the Op. 24 *Liederkreis* with an affirmation of the poet's ability to transmute the agony of disappointed love into art.

*

Schumann's settings of Heine exemplify to a pointed degree the ability of music to underscore or bring out divided aspects of the subject or 'lyric I' of a poem. The means by which this is achieved may be familiar from those already seen in his instrumental works, such as the split between two tonal levels; in other cases, this quality might arise from the differentiation between different 'personas' – the piano accompaniment, the singing voice, the subject of the poetic text; often it may result from some combination of these. But in some instances, too, this subject may not only appear split, but further able to reflect on these separate elements as belonging to itself. Alongside division comes the possibility of integration. Indeed, as with the classic paradox of self-apperception, it is only through such self-division that

---

[59] There are other possible links between songs in the cycle (indeed the opening of No. 12 reworks the initial Phrygian cadence of No. 1 into an augmented sixth progression), but nothing as overt as this literal recapitulation.

[60] As has often been observed, the potential circularity of Schumann's cycle – the D flat major at the close of No. 16 easily linking up enharmonically to the C$\sharp^7$ heard at the opening of No. 1 – would bring out this cyclical aspect further, just as there will always be another May, and another tale of lost love.

the subject might come to know itself. Division of the self into subject and object is a precondition for deeper subjective self-awareness. For Perrey, correspondingly, the split articulated in Schumann's Lieder actually reflects this reflexive search of the ego for itself. 'Schumann's Romantic "I that seeks itself" found full expression in the Lied', she claims. 'Schumann's Lied speaks the "language of the soul" – a soul which has found its imaginary alter ego. ... the singing voice thus becomes the haunting vision of another, second "I" which promises fulfilment.'[61] But it need not be merely the singing voice that points to this possibility of self-realisation.

The recall of the closing melody from 'Am leuchtenden Sommermorgen' at the end of *Dichterliebe* is a case in point. In that earlier song this was the music that had followed the flowers' reproach to the protagonist not to be angry with their sister (understood as referring figuratively to the poet's lost beloved). Whether the melody that there emerged should be taken to refer to the flowers' speech, or rather to the initial subjective persona of the protagonist, is not defined, but since those flowers were a prosopopœic stand-in for one side of the poet's divided consciousness, either way, we could conclude that this new idea arises from some part of the subject – perhaps the deeper, subconscious recesses of the 'instrumental persona' – and perhaps hints at a sense of forgiveness or at least reconciliation (of the protagonist with his lost beloved; between different parts of his own divided psyche). We recall from the opening chapter how the appearance of vocal gestures may allude to the presence of some virtual subjectivity, the emergence of a lyrical voice in an instrumental texture readily suggesting the emergence of a musical subject. The emergence in this postlude of this tender melodic thread from the slightly aimless descending arpeggios that had hitherto formed the accompanimental texture in this song (an unassuming instance of 'displacement dissonance') gestures at some higher state of subjective consciousness attained within the formerly inchoate instrumental persona.[62] Moreover, it is one that at the close of the cycle is created from the recall of the subject's own past, one that is bound up with the self-reflexivity signalled throughout this final song. On the one hand, the end of *Dichterliebe* manifests an ironic split in the subject between 'vocal' and 'instrumental' personae; but on the other, it marks the emergence of lyricism combined with reflexivity that seems to suggest a sense of subjective self-actualisation

[61] Perrey, *Schumann's Dichterliebe and Early Romantic Poetics*, pp. 56 (referring to a formulation by Friedrich Schlegel) and 54.

[62] Krebs indeed points to the metric dissonance of similar figuration in song 10 of the cycle (*Fantasy Pieces*, pp. 162–3).

in the latter, one that is 'musical' rather than 'literary', rooted in the immediacy of feeling rather than through the analytic mediation of words.

Such gestures towards reconciliation can be found elsewhere in Schumann's oeuvre, in instrumental pieces as well as songs. We saw in Chapter 2 how the composer's concertos were typically marked by a unanimity between soloist and orchestra that questioned the customary interpretative division into an intersubjective relationship between self and world in favour of a larger composite subjectivity. Yet divisions in the subject can still be present, and through the same means explored in this present chapter. A case in point is the late *Fantasie* for Violin and Orchestra, Op. 131 (1853), in which the fundamental opposition occurs not between soloist and orchestra but rather tonally, between the opening A minor introduction and the C major sonata structure that ensues, reworking a procedure seen earlier in the A minor Quartet.[63] Yet in the *Fantasie*, deliberate steps are made towards the integration of this tonal and expressive split. First the introductory material returns within the brief development section, again in A minor, recalling the initial split without by this resolving it; then, finally in the coda, this same material re-emerges, only now presented alongside the sonata material and integrated into a C major context, with which the piece is able to come to a confident close. The music's structural division is reflected on and integrated, through a stylised process of self-consciousness imparted by the recall of the past.

What both these examples show are possible ways in which the musical subject, once divided, might in turn, attain a sense of integration. In both cases this is achieved through reflexive gestures, the recall of the music's own past, combined especially in *Dichterliebe* with a sense of lyrical fruition. Chapter 4 turns to those ways in which the musical subject, notwithstanding its ever-present potential to self-divide, may nevertheless be or become at one with itself.

---

[63] This tonal split is in itself a fairly generic feature of the fantasy genre. Beethoven's Cello Sonata Op. 102 No. 1 – a work that unmistakably alludes to the fantasia aesthetic – offers a notable precedent.

PART II

Hearing Presence

4 | Presence of the Self

Presence

There is a moment midway through the Larghetto of Schumann's 'Spring' Symphony where the primary theme returns in the cellos, enveloped in a gentle wash of orchestral sonority. Around murmuring demisemiquavers in the inner strings Schumann's orchestra spins a gentle web of off-beat pulsations. Delicate pizzicato in the first violins mark the second note of each semiquaver pair, subtly tracing a metrically displaced version of the cellos' melody, just as the double basses do against the bassline heard in the second bassoon, while these same beats are picked out again in the woodwind accompaniment. But the latter is split between registers – flutes and oboes above, clarinets and first bassoon below – into contrasting groupings of four semiquaver beats, giving a subtle registral emphasis to two alternate metric layers of $^2/_8$ within the $^3/_8$ time signature (Ex. 4.1). Part of the reason for the warm haze that surrounds the re-emerging theme comes from the blurred effect of this accompanimental figuration, formed by the over-lapping of distinct rhythmic cycles ongoing simultaneously.

Already on its first hearing, this melody had been heard with syncopations in inner voices, while the metric displacement of the later woodwind accompaniment is foreshadowed in the hemiolas that unobtrusively feature in the original melodic line. And as this theme returns across this movement, its lyrical voice becomes increasingly enveloped within a larger sonorous mass woven of diverse textural elements. On its third statement, now reprised back in the tonic E flat, the violins decorate the principal line in oboe and horn with filigree demisemiquavers, creating a delicate metric blurring with the demi-semiquaver triplets in the violas, while the cellos offer a hint of syncopation in their slurred reworking of the bassline below them. 'Abend' – evening – was the title originally conceived by the composer for this movement, and the music here seems to have given way to reverie. There is a feeling of repose, a calm infused by a sense of blissful fullness, self-plenitude, even self-possession, to the music in

Ex. 4.1 Schumann: Symphony No. 1 ('Spring'), Op. 38, ii, bb. 40–6

these moments. It is as if the musical subject has for once found a stable sense of being, the ability to be at home with itself.

We have seen in Chapter 3 how Schumann is able to use harmonic ambiguity, metrical displacement, and a multifariously stranded texture to suggest a multiplicity or division in the music's apparent experiencing subject. Yet what the example above has revealed is how a feeling of unifying self-presence may equally be created in his music, one in which many of the same techniques are drawn upon to more constructive ends. Just as the self in Schumann's music may often appear to be split, so too may it at times come together into a greater whole.

This quality of lyric dreaming, of amorphous, floating consciousness which pervades the slow movement of the First Symphony is one that has frequently been allied with a sense of self, a presence or fullness of being arguably akin to pure self-consciousness. Marshall Brown has spoken of the state of dreamy reverie in music as the product of a revolution in the understanding of consciousness around the end of the eighteenth century, one given memorable description in the fifth walk from Rousseau's *Rêveries du promeneur solitaire* and theorised, holds Brown, in Kant's *Critique of Pure Reason*. For Brown, the origins of Romantic music are found in development of this sense of 'pure, undifferentiated self-consciousness', in which the music appears lost in a sense of purely internal time generated from the self. 'Nothing is heard or seen in this state except an ongoing rhythmic pulse, flickering in intensity and lacking any more definite shape. Time is felt but not measured.'[1] Expanding on the philosophical underpinnings of this topic, Andrew Bowie has argued that for the Romantic generation the basis for the self was found in preconceptual feeling, the representation of the 'I' being in Kant's phrase 'nothing more than the feeling of an existence without the least concept', which for subsequent thinkers like Friedrich Schlegel and Schleiermacher was often interpreted as making the musical the basis for the self.[2] Indeed, as I have shown in an earlier study, throughout the nineteenth century music becomes a pervasive metaphor for philosophers seeking to understand the self's temporal constitution and immaterial sense of presence, its experience seen as perhaps the closest thing to self-apperception.[3]

Yet here in Schumann the sense of self-possession, of pure auto-affection, is more complex than one of simple unitary being. The self is felt as a collective whole, formed from the overlapping of different pulsations or processes. One need not completely dissolve the idea of the self into a fiction in order to see the congruence with more deconstructionist readings of the nature of the subject such as that found in the later Nietzsche, for whom, as we saw, the self is merely the conscious superstructure of a multiplicity of bodily drives and forces, a conceptual synthesis whose unity is a governing illusion.[4] Rather than emphasising the division (as Chapter 3 has done), one might instead focus on the ability of the self to manifest itself as a collective unity. Although Nietzsche's assertions are characteristically unsupported (and indeed not entirely consistent), recent work in cognitive psychology, phenomenology, and the philosophy of mind provides some plausible grounds for conceiving the self and consciousness as a synthetic operation formed of numerous processes and bodily rhythms, not all of which need be metrically aligned.[5]

---

[1] Brown, 'Mozart and After', 690.

[2] Bowie, *Aesthetics and Subjectivity*, pp. 23, 34–8. The passage cited may be found in a footnote to §46 of Kant's *Prolegomena to Any Future Metaphysics* (see Immanuel Kant, *Werke*, 12 vols. (Frankfurt: Suhrkamp, 1977), vol. V, p. 205).

[3] Taylor, *The Melody of Time*, pp. 65–129.

[4] See, for instance, Nietzsche, *Nachgelassene Fragmente* 1885 37[4] and 40[42].

[5] See Shaun Gallagher, *The Inordinance of Time* (Evanston, IL: Northwestern University Press, 1998), also Dan Zahavi, *Self-Awareness and Alterity: A Phenomenological Investigation* (Evanston, IL: Northwestern University Press, 1999).

As we saw, Harald Krebs has offered suggestive remarks on the link between music and the rhythms of human life afforded through musical metre's interacting layers of motion. Though more concerned with metric dissonance as an expression of psychological turmoil, of a subject divided from itself, Krebs does suggest this technique's capacity to evoke 'a suspended, dreamlike, hovering state' on occasion in Schumann, pointing to the ninth of the *Albumblätter*, Op. 124, 'Impromptu' (1838), as a pertinent example.[6] A similar argument could be applied to the present piece. With its syncopated accompaniment and interlayered rhythmic pulsations forming a soft sonorous envelope, Schumann's Larghetto forms a musical correlate to Rousseau's solitary dreamer lying in his boat, rocked gently by the waves and conscious merely of the rhythms of his self and the immediacy of bodily feeling.[7] We experience the music at these points as we experience aspects of our precognitive selves. Directly felt rather than thought, we attend to it with a meditative concentration on the apparent immediacy of self-presence.

But amidst the focus on accompanimental figuration, sonority, and metric interplay, one important aspect of the music has been neglected up to this point – the melody that emerges from Schumann's background texture. We recall from Chapter 1 that for thinkers since antiquity the appearance of vocality was the strongest sonic sign of a subjective presence, the type of sound 'characteristic of what has soul in it'.[8] Besides its persuasive sense of presence, the slow movement of the 'Spring' Symphony also points to another aspect identified earlier of how subjectivity may be manifested in music: lyricism.

Earlier it was proposed that the emergence of a lyrical voice from a more variegated texture could often be interpreted as the emergence of a musical subject (an idea foreshadowed in Naomi Cumming's suggestive designation of the subject as an emergent 'super-sign').[9] Such a process is

---

[6] Krebs, *Fantasy* Pieces, p. 172.

[7] Another apt musical example for such meditative self-absorption might be given by the outer sections of the slow movement of Schubert's C major Quintet, D. 956. Numerous psychoanalytic implications could clearly be drawn from the retreat into some such infantile cradling or womb-like condition. In Lacanian terms, the subject appears to be brought back to some precognitive state before the separation from the mother and imposition of the symbolic order. Not for nothing does Julia Kristeva associate the pre-symbolic order of the maternal 'chora' with the 'musical' (see *Revolution in Poetic Language*, in *The Kristeva Reader*, trans. Toril Moi (Oxford: Blackwell, 1986), p. 93) – a point we will return to in Chapter 7.

[8] Aristotle, *On the Soul*, II/8, 420b.

[9] 'The "persona" may be understood as comprised of lower-level signs, a kind of provisional reconciliation of their multiplicity into a single impression (no matter how ephemeral). It is . . . an effect of the combination of other semiotic elements in time – a complete character, with

characteristic of Schumann's practice throughout his oeuvre. One thinks of that typical Schumann texture, found especially in his piano writing, with its rustling arpeggios cloaking the fitful emergence and vanishing of fragmentary voices, enough to suggest a subjective voice, but rarely sustaining a melodic line for long enough to suggest a single continuous voice throughout. Like the surfacing of inchoate snatches of thoughts and sensations in a daydreaming mind, the subject is discontinuous to its own consciousness but may potentially always be present.

A good example may be found in the fifth variation that was published posthumously as a supplement to the *Symphonic Etudes*, Op. 13 (Ex. 4.2). In this appealing miniature (penned no doubt by Eusebius), persistent metric displacement and registral disjunction hide an emergent line growing initially from a simple descending scale from b^3 in b. 1 down to c^2 in b. 4. The underlying harmonic structure and phrase syntax is utterly straightforward; interest is imparted by the manner in which Schumann's disjunctive surface proves increasingly amenable to a lyricism that spreads throughout the voices of the texture alongside the normalisation of its metric structure.

The opening melodic line (highlighted by Schumann in quavers above the stave) is initially disguised by entering on the second semiquaver of the bar: though the bass syncopations might lend support to the metric reinterpretation of this pitch as the downbeat, the use of register and harmony obviate any such implication. For a start, theories of metre normally highlight a psychological tendency to hear the first onset in a piece (all other things being equal) as a downbeat, and the fact that this initial beat is both registrally accentuated by being allocated a higher pitch (the highest in the piece) and harmonically consonant (degree $\hat{3}$ over a low tonic root), while the melodic line starts on a $\hat{6}$ appoggiatura over $\hat{5}$ in the bass arpeggiation, weakens any hearing of this nascent voice as the music's primary focus. There is consequently something deliciously off-kilter to the hesitant line emerging from within the texture here, a quality which only becomes clarified or normalised as the phrase progresses. The acceleration in harmonic rhythm across the four-bar antecedent already strengthens the sense of notated metre by b. 3, but melodically it is on the final crotchet beat of b. 6 that the melodic line shifts back into congruence with the rest of the texture by its reworking as a dotted-quaver / semiquaver pair starting now on the notated beat. (The straight quaver pulse continues in the voice's

apparent agency and definite affective tone, heard to emerge from other signs.' Cumming, *The Sonic Self*, p. 208.

Ex. 4.2 Schumann: *Symphonic Etudes*, Op. 13, *Anhang*: Variation V

Ex. **4.2** (cont.)

doubling an octave below, strengthening the emergent sense of melodic line even while imparting a slight rhythmic blurring or heterophonic reverberation.)

Schumann's metric interplay continues after the double bar: bars 9–10 present straight semiquaver groups for the first time in the piece, though the accent on the fourth beat in each bar underscores the end-weighted harmonic construction that postpones the local tonic arrival to this final beat; in the following two bars the evolving scalic motive is inverted into an ascending inner chromatic line. Here, more than ever, the metric uncertainty of the opening has given way to a relatively normal piano texture. Syncopations in b. 12 provide a transition to the metric ambiguities of the reprise. The final four bars return to the opening material, though now the melodic line that emerges firmly on the final beat of b. 14 is doubled in rhythmically exact values. Of the previous metric ambiguity nothing remains in the rather conventional final bar.

What is noteworthy in this étude is how Schumann is able to make the music amenable to a lyricism which initially seemed completely absent: from a widely spaced, almost pointillist arpeggiated texture that seemed to lack any musical subject, conjunct melodic lines gradually emerge, first as simple scalic figures, and then increasingly as independent melodic voices whose lyricism spreads throughout the texture. At first metrically unsure, their status is gradually clarified over each half to arrive at a clear melodic formulation by the end. A musical subject has emerged.

Coming to Lyricism (I): The Voice of the Singing Subject

This strategy – the emergence of a lyrical voice which may be understood to instantiate the emergence of subjectivity – is one that is of great significance within Schumann's music. Schumann's procedure in this last piece articulates a (comparatively primitive) form of a paradigm I will be calling *coming to lyricism*. In this idea, I am building on the work of Julian Johnson, who has written with great perspicuity on the technique of 'calling forth a voice' in Mahler's music, the assertion, collapse, and rebuilding of voice functioning as 'a defining structural process' throughout the composer's symphonies. 'To call forth a voice, to invoke or summon a voice', Johnson explains, 'is to call a presence out of absence. The voice realizes a presence through the physicality of sound, a presence that is at once perceptible and sensuous yet intangible and incorporeal.'[10] 'Coming to lyricism' not only denotes the emergence of a lyrical voice within a texture, often as the expressive goal of an entire piece, but further points to a link with the emergence of subjectivity within the music. This process may be arduous, it may even result in failure; but in all cases there is a sense of a conscious voice emergent within the work – a sense not only of subjective presence but even in some cases a self-conscious presence, a virtual agency that appears to recognise itself. In Schumann, the process of coming to lyricism is one of the most apparent and powerful means of the music's coming to subjecthood.

Such procedures already glimpsed in the *Symphonic Etudes* are echoed or extended in numerous other works of the composer. Particularly instructive for present purposes are those examples given in songs, where a verbal text provides an explicit highlighting of this subject. A fruitful starting comparison (albeit one that in some ways offers a negative perspective on this trope) might be given by the Kerner setting 'Sehnsucht nach der Waldgegend', Op. 35 No. 5 – a song about the absence of song, in which the protagonist expresses his feeling of a loss or diminution of self resulting from his exile from his native woodlands, one that is manifested by his perceived inability to attain a state of lyricism.[11] 'Would that I had never left you' exclaims the alienated protagonist, for 'here in these wide plains everything to me is drear and silent', and 'song stirs itself only but

---

[10] Julian Johnson, *Mahler's Voices: Expression and Irony in the Songs and Symphonies* (New York: Oxford University Press, 2009), pp. 48, 71.

[11] I am assuming the protagonist of Kerner's poem is male given the subject matter and cultural conventions of the period, but there is no reason for the song not to be sung by a woman.

seldom'. The apparent paradox here is that in professing the loss of voice, the subject momentarily attains a condition of melodic fulfilment.

Although we are in truth far from the beloved forests, the opening already suggests (in Schumannesque topical terms) an imaginary wood-land location – the rustling leaves of the accompanimental figuration, in which fragments of a possible melodic line appear picked almost at random out of the piano part; metrically unemphasised and variable in location, they bear little relation to the deflated vocal line around them (Ex. 4.3).[12] As the protagonist becomes ever more drawn into the forest realm inhabited by his imagination, however, the despondent G minor brightens to the relative major, and the initially slow pace of text-setting quickens to one bar per tetrameter line in place of two. Stirred by his memories, by the songs that once sprung from his breast, the second verse proceeds in a remoter and yet brighter F major ($\flat$VII); now the indeterminate rustling has given way to a more straightforward accompanimental texture, the piano part shadows the vocal line in typically Schumannesque heterophonic reverber-ation, and a clear melody is at last unmistakably present. Having come inconclusively to a half-close on V/F in b. 11, the same melodic idea is resumed in the third stanza, but now, as if overcome by the greater vivacity of the memories the accompaniment accelerates into semiquaver arpeg-gios. The instrumental voice that covertly supported the fragile emergence of lyricism in the vocal line in the second verse is no longer needed, it seems: the forest's secret has been imparted to the conscious singing subject, and the waters of its silver springs may bubble freely. But once again, the stanza is unable to attain any more decisive tonal closure than its predecessor, and after another imperfect progression to its dominant, F major is gradually lost in favour of minor keys, and along with it the simple mode of tuneful melody with which it had been associated. Memory's imaginative recreation fails, and the vision slips away. The fifth and final verse returns to the music of the opening: the vocal part trails off, unfinished, on B flat harmony, and it is left to the piano to bring the music back to G minor, the final bars dissipating into imitative mur-murings. The question that remains unclear at the end of the song is whether the subject has been actually able to recognise the fact that the lyricism he so ardently sought was at one point actually attained before being lost. It would appear that he most probably does not.

---

[12] The association of such an accompanimental texture with trees or woods is long standing in Schumann literature; see, for instance, Eric Sams, *The Songs of Robert Schumann* (London: Faber and Faber, 1993), pp. 15–16, 172.

Ex. 4.3 Schumann: 'Sehnsucht nach der Waldgegend' (Kerner), *Zwölf Gedichte von Justinus Kerner*, Op. 35 No. 5

Ex. 4.3 (cont.)

While 'Sehnsucht nach der Waldgegend' registers the successful emergence of a lyrical voice, the drive to full subjecthood is ultimately a failure in this song. There is an apparent breakdown in the musical subject's own capacity for recognition. When, then, does the musical subject appear aware of its own lyricism? To put the point almost tautologically, when does the emergent subject (denoted by the growth of a lyrical voice) seem to be aware of its own emerging lyrical voice (i.e. subjecthood?).[13] One possible example of just such lyrical consciousness is given by the Byron setting 'Aus den hebraischen Gesängen', the fifteenth song of *Myrthen*, Op. 25 (Ex. 4.4).

Schumann's remarkable conception stages the emergence of subjectivity explicitly as a result of song. Again, the opening of the poem speaks of despondency; of a loss or diminution of self. Schumann's opening music is perhaps the most expressive he had written up to this point, at least in the genre of song. ('Zwielicht' from the Op. 39 *Liederkreis* is foreshadowed in more than just the E minor tonality.) Sinuous chromaticised lines cascade down the piano stave, their accented offbeat onset creating a degree of metric uncertainty, and their initial pitches, held over, form expressive suspensions with half-diminished sevenths resolving merely to their fully diminished brethren. Shared imitatively between the pianist's hands, each pair of entries moreover rises by one step on repetition to ratchet up the tension further. Having worked round predominant areas of E and A minor in turn, the B $^6_5$ chord in b. 5 seems set to issue a return to the tonic, but in a departure from harmonic custom the following series of seventh chords slip down *against* the cycle of fifths they imply (B^7–F♯^{7}–C♯^{7}), only then returning the same way to the tonic. The final bar of the introduction is elided precipitously with the singer's entry, his declamatory opening phrase outlining a familiar baroque gesture of anguish, the diminished fourth. Most extreme of all is the subsequent Schubertian wrench from a diminished seventh functioning as vii^7 of B minor to an A minor $^6_4$ in bb. 12–13, harmonic grammar flagrantly contravened in the service of expressive immediacy. This is a protagonist whose heart bears an unusually heavy burden.

Music is consciously sought by this troubled subject as a way to release the darkness in his soul. 'Take! from the wall the lute, only it alone may I yet hear, with agile hand enchant me with its tones, which beguile the heart.'[14]

---

[13] Cf. the 'odd question' Cone poses: 'does a vocal persona know he is singing?' (*The Composer's Voice*, p. 30).

[14] A slightly free rendering by the translator, Karl Julius Körner, of Byron's 'My soul is dark – Oh! quickly string / The harp I yet can brook to hear; / And let thy gentle fingers fling / Its melting murmurs o'er mine ear.'

Ex. 4.4 Schumann: 'Aus den hebräischen Gesängen' (Byron), *Myrthen*, Op. 25 No. 15

Ex. 4.4: (cont.)

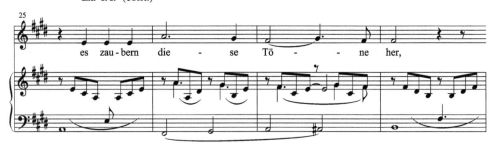

And as the singer's voice dies away there now enters a soft passage in the piano, newly in the tonic major, from which we gradually become aware that a simple but sweetly comforting melodic line is being picked out from among the variegated broken chords (standing no doubt for the lute or harp mentioned). At what point the protagonist becomes aware of the melody is unclear; Graham Johnson, for one, has remarked how 'the singer is so taken up with his plea for relief that he fails to notice that his prayers have already been answered by the music *which he himself sings*' – but that he does recognise it at some point seems undeniable, for after four bars the singer takes up the melody insinuated by the accompanimental arpeggios.[15] The contrast with the declamatory, wide-ranging vocal line of the first quatrain, with its leaps of a ninth, constantly recurring diminished fourths, and prose-like text-setting, could not be greater. In attaining the condition of lyrical melody, the subject experiences a magnifying of being; Byron's poem – and even more its vivid instantiation in Schumann's song – attests to the power of music to re-tune or harmonise the soul.

This emergence of lyricism, and with it the promise of spiritual replenishment, does not, however, attain closure. The darkness returns in b. 38 with the sweeping waves of the opening E minor in a literal repetition of the song's first seven bars. It might seem at this stage that the protagonist has given way to his earlier despair. But this is not going to be another song about failure. The text makes it clear that the singer at this juncture asks for the tones to be 'deep and wild . . . and swept away from joy' ('But bid the strain be wild and deep, / nor let thy notes of joy be first' as Byron has it), and now a dramatic interrupted cadence deflects the music to C major. The following music works through the spiritual anguish yet

[15] Graham Johnson, notes to *The Songs of Robert Schumann*, vol. 7, Hyperion CDJ33107 (2002), p. 68.

again (the momentary recall of the introductory material in bb. 53–7 with the fear 'yes, singer, I must weep') and is, in turn, calmed by the returning instrumental melody (as requested, not too joyful, now in the minor), which again is taken up subsequently in the vocal line as if symbiotically attached to the sounds issuing from the harp. 'For my heart must be broken or healed in song' concludes the singer, and a final E major chord sounding softly in the bass makes it clear that some repose has indeed been found.

'Aus den hebraischen Gesängen' is a pertinent example of a successful coming to lyricism, one that is thematicised in the text of the song and instantiated in Schumann's setting. Music has here healed the soul; its power to alter mood, to attune the self to its surroundings, is successfully realised and, what is more significant, explicitly recognised by the protagonist of Schumann's song. On the other hand, it is not obvious that the lyrical voice heard, which the subject then takes up, is his own. Unlike Kerner's forest exile in 'Sehnsucht nach der Waldgegend', the subject of Schumann's Byron setting can hear the melody that he calls forth, indeed will take it up, but it is nevertheless one that is not originally produced by him.[16]

The problem identified in these two previous examples hinges around the question of self-consciousness. As we saw in the opening chapters, subjectivity may be defined not only through a sense of agency, or, more strongly, a sense of consciousness, but most of all, by the capacity for *self-consciousness*. If the subject of Op. 35 No. 5 demonstrates an unconscious (and faltering) process of coming to lyricism, and that of Op. 25 No. 15 reveals a more successful coming to lyricism, one that is conscious, where might we glimpse a subject that is conscious of its *own* coming to lyricism, in other words conscious of its own emergent self? We might recall once more Roland Barthes's famous designation of Schumann as 'the musician of solitary intimacy, of the amorous and imprisoned soul that speaks to itself'.[17] If Schumann speaks to himself in his music, can he hear himself speaking? Or rather (to remove this question from the possibility of any

---

[16] In the Old Testament context on which Byron draws, Saul is calling forth a song from David's harp. The words of Schumann's song leave the identity of the player slightly ambiguous; the protagonist commands the lute off from the wall ('Auf! von der Wand die Laute'), which could conceivably be a directive to himself, but later the reference to 'singer' strongly implies the presence of another subject who initiates the coming to lyricism (unless we assume a schizoid protagonist, split from himself).

[17] Barthes, 'Loving Schumann', p. 293.

poststructuralist attack on the notion of self-presence in language), when Schumann's musical subject *sings* to himself, can he *hear himself singing*?[18]

One such candidate for a reflexive coming to lyricism can be found in a later song from the Kerner *Liederreihe*, 'Stille Liebe', Op. 35 No. 8 (Ex. 4.5). At first glance, this is another instance of a song about the absence of song, specifically of the vocal protagonist's self-perceived inability to come to song. The first verse is in a wishful subjunctive: 'If I could praise you in songs, I would sing you the longest song.' 'Yet', it transpires in the second verse, 'what has always grieved me, is that I can only silently carry you in my breast'. Once again, the words (what we could think of as the conscious thoughts of the protagonist, to follow an established convention) seem to express failure, while the simple and quietly appealing tune associated with them appears some-what at variance with such sentiments. Its modest scope, admittedly, does not make it the *longest* song conceivable, but it nevertheless possesses an artless charm that belies the apparent profession of mute-ness. But as the third verse now reveals, such assumptions would be misplaced. For even though 'pervaded by bitter sorrow that no song is worthy of you', the poet now reveals 'this pain overcame me, and I sang this little song' ('dass ich sang dies kleine Lied'). We suddenly become aware that the subject *can* hear himself singing: he knows he is singing, and singing *this* song. We as listeners, of course, do not know during the first two verses that this recognition will occur. But does the protagonist, even at the start, know that he is singing 'this little song'? Or is this something of which he gradually becomes aware as the song progresses, recognised retrospectively as having occurred in the past ('that I *sang* this little song')? This is an open question in Kerner's poem. But Schumann's setting does suggest something of the

---

[18] This is referring specifically to Derrida's influential critique of Husserl in *Voice and Phenomenon* (1967). Derrida's intricate argument purportedly shows that certain passages of Husserl relating to the perception of the present, taken from a range of writings across the author's life, are inconsistent, and that the subject can never attain the fabled absolute self-presence of 'hearing oneself speaking'. Grounded as ever in the structures of post-Saussurean linguistics and recourse to this author's familiar tropes (what I call for convenience the category of the 'always already'), this line of attack has no purchase on a temporal system that does not divide into signifier and signified, such as music. However, this should not cause unbounded relief; music has enough problems dealing with the notion of the temporal present (an argument perspicaciously noted by Paul de Man in an engaging critique of Derrida's *Of Grammatology*: 'The Rhetoric of Blindness: Jacques Derrida's Reading of Rousseau', in *Blindness and Insight: Essays in the Rhetoric of Contemporary Criticism* (Minneapolis: University of Minnesota Press, 1983), pp. 102–41).

Ex. 4.5 Schumann: 'Stille Liebe' (Kerner), *Zwölf Gedichte von Justinus Kerner*, Op. 35
No. 8

Ex. 4.5 (cont.)

latter, a musical coming to self-consciousness performed by the sing-ing subject.

The musical signs of a movement to another state of consciousness, in which the fictional musical subject appears able to hear a voice previously considered inaudible within its supposed sonic frame of reference (the movement from noumenal to phenomenal voices, from apparently non-diegetic to diegetic sound), have been much discussed in recent literature. Carolyn Abbate, perhaps the most influential initiator of this line of enquiry, has commented on such sites of musical disjunction, of aural rupture, where the switch from one state to another arises.[19] If one had to locate a liminal moment where such dawning self-consciousness might occur in Schumann's song, one would have to point to the transition from the second verse into the third, more specifically, around the accentuated C flat chord in b. 29.

Kerner's three stanzas are set by Schumann in strophic form, though this straightforward thematic design is notably modified by the imposition of a ternary tonal scheme (E♭–G♭–E♭), creating a sense of return at the start of the third verse that contributes significantly to the sense of self-recognition at this point. Each of the song's three verses is surrounded by a shy descending motive in the piano – a falling triad presented simply in octaves, followed by an expressive half-diminished seventh partially resolving to its fully diminished sibling, the offbeat opening and frequent pauses imparting a decidedly hesitant quality. Heard twice at the song's opening, describing E flat and C minor triads, the passage darkens on its return following the first verse: now E flat minor leads to a C flat harmony, and the second verse emerges in an unexpected G flat major. The movement to the flattened third scale degree serves to shift the music into an interior level, aptly conveying the silent image of the beloved carried deep inside the subject alongside a sense of tonal estrangement from the tonic E flat, coinciding with the self's perceived loss of subjective voice at this moment.

It is with the return of this passage at the close of the second verse that the subject's coming to reflexive awareness appears to be dramatised. Uniquely here the passage is extended into three statements of the descending figure: the first statement proceeds from the G♭ where the second verse had left us, moving down a third in turn to a second iteration of the figure on E flat minor. Effectively we have rejoined the first stage of the progression that was heard in the interlude between verses one and two, and the subsequent initiation of a third statement beginning on C♭ confirms the parallelism. But this first inversion C flat chord marks a crucial juncture. This event is accentuated both dynamically by the *sforzando* marking (the only instance in the piece after the opening bar) and temporally by being held for the longest measured duration, seven semiquaver beats (all other instances of the figure are merely a crotchet long, although the first is given a fermata).

---

[19] Abbate, *Unsung Voices*.

If the music had continued as it had in the previous connecting passage, it would have retraced the progression to G♭ and we would remain alienated from the tonic. Instead, the harmonies slip just a semitone to a [D, F, A♭, C] half-diminished seventh – the same harmony that had been given in b. 4 where this progression had led to E♭ – and a brief chromatic link leads to the entry of the third verse, now back in the tonic.

Although there is an unassuming softness to the return here, the sense of novelty, even wonderment, at the regaining of the tonic is patent. The music is back in the key of the first verse, but as if, following the alienation of the second verse, the subject can now recognise itself for the first time. '*This* is the song that I sang': the musical staging of the point of tonal return coincides with the textural staging of the dawning of self-consciousness, of the subject's reflexive ability to hear himself singing the song that he unknowingly sang before. For the first two verses the piano had echoed the vocal line off the beat in a manner familiar from other diffident lovers (compare it with 'Morgens steh' ich auf', the opening song of the Op. 24 *Liederkreis*). Now quintuplets enliven the texture, incorporating the notes of the vocal line within it; at first submerged as the fourth of each group, at 'ich sang dies kleine Lied' they emerge to greater prominence on the first and final notes of the five, the f and b♭ of 'kleine Lied' being picked out high above the singer's voice in ringing reverberation. At this crucial moment of signification, the 'little song' becomes distinctly audible.

This is no song about the loss of voice; at worst, it is a song about the perceived inadequacy of the protagonist's voice. Even this might be considered dissimulation, however. The lover knows he is singing, and knows he is singing *this* song. But does he know that it is quite nice? Or is this just false modesty? One might think of another highly reflexive song which makes a similarly dubious declaration: 'Nimm sie hin denn, diese Lieder', the final song of Beethoven's *An die ferne Geliebte*, which asserts its predecessors have been 'ohne Kunstgepräng' – without artful ostentation. As other scholars have pointed out, nothing could be further from the truth here.[20] When a reflexive song, a song about its own emergence, claims to be without ostentation, we might see this as a particularly urgent invitation to interrogate its self-conscious credentials. And as will be seen presently, Beethoven's cycle will be important in other ways for this discussion.

---

[20] An idea developed by Nicholas Marston in a perceptive essay covering several of the themes above: 'Voicing Beethoven's Distant Beloved', in Scott Burnham and Michael Steinberg (eds.), *Beethoven and His World* (Princeton: Princeton University Press, 2000), pp. 124–47.

Musical Self-Consciousness

The preceding three songs have traced the problem of self-recognition crucial to many understandings of subjectivity. In Op. 35 No. 5 the subject is singing, but cannot *hear himself* singing, and thus the process of coming to subject-hood fails (for if the protagonist had heard the song he sings in verses 2 and 3, he would not truthfully be able to lament his absence of voice); in Op. 25 No. 15 the subject can hear *someone else* singing (or playing a songlike melodic line), and this results in a healing of his self, but yet it is not his own voice that he hears; finally in Op. 35 No. 8 the subject appears to be – or at least become – aware of his or her own singing. Yet the fact that in a song a protagonist can sing without being (verbally) aware of his song (the case in the first example) suggests the straightforward assumption that the appearance of lyricism automatically implies a *self-conscious* subject is questionable. We might also wonder to what extent we can speak of self-consciousness in music without recourse to the language associated with it (as in a song text, for instance), namely in instrumental music.

Our first example – the slow movement of the First Symphony – was introduced to illustrate the feeling of pure self-presence in music. A lyrical melody – the distinctive marker of subjectivity – was also distinguished, suggesting through a familiar shared cultural code a quality akin to con-sciousness. But could we somehow point to this as being *self-consciousness*, a subject which knows it is present to self? Or – as some readers may begin to wonder – have we simply reached the limits of meaningful talk on music? Is the rest simply silly hermeneutics?

I fear that such an approach could easily turn into the latter, and in some cases most probably does. But undeniable facts of our cultural understand-ing of music suggest the possibility of a more positive outcome than complete dismissal of this topic. The fact is, we *do* talk about some instrumental music as manifesting a self-conscious quality: this category can function as meaningful discourse, it assumes an intersubjective validity based in a common cultural understanding. To take a classic example, much of Haydn's instrumental music has been interpreted as highly self-conscious, playing ironically with listener expectations and generic norms. When we say this, we do not simply mean that Haydn, the real-life composer, was self-conscious when he wrote it (a proposition that is trivially true of pretty much all music one presumes). It is the music that is meant, self-consciousness being an imaginative property projected onto it (despite the fact that the idea of a subjective persona is perhaps less present in Haydn's work than that of Beethoven, say, and it is none the worse for that). Likewise, to take an example often associated with this composer, when *Tristram Shandy* is described as a novel that demonstrates an ironic self-awareness, this does not merely imply that Laurence Sterne was ironically self-aware writing it (though again, no doubt he was). And (as I observed in Chapter 1) there is no more a real subject in the pages of a novel than there is in the notes of a score or its aural rendering. The self-conscious subject of Heine's poetry provides a comparable example – one closer to Schumann's world.

So, unless we wish to reject the notion of subject and self-consciousness created through language (and that would leave us in an interesting state!), the argument that self-consciousness in music is a meaningless category, because there is after all no *real* subject there, simply doesn't hold. Nevertheless, as was argued in that earlier consideration, the subject of music is rather less precise, less tangible, its traces more ambiguous and subject to interpretation. Perhaps the desire to draw up concrete rules for demonstrating such musical self-consciousness is misplaced – the musical subject will ever be fuzzier than the grammatical subject, and more conditional upon an intersubjective consensus of interpretation (hence the ever-present potential for hermeneutic abuse) – but the idea is not always nonsensical, and some critical reflection on how this condition is achieved, on the signs by which it may often appear to be manifested, is a valid activity.

In approaching the problem of how self-consciousness reveals itself in music, we have once again started with song. This has been valuable for several reasons: as identified earlier, vocality has long been the exemplary signifier of subjectivity, while the presence of a verbal text makes the identification of self-consciousness more straightforward (although the interaction between verbal and musical expression can also make the issue more complex, as was the case in Schumann's Heine settings). The question remained as to how one can show self-consciousness unless through language. Can music suggest a virtual self-consciousness without recourse to words?

In animals lacking the capacity for language-use – human infants, non-human primates – a sense of self is typically ascertained through testing the ability of the subject to recognise itself in a mirror. While I am mindful of the potential absurdity of the comparison, we might nevertheless try to extend this general approach to music. It is not clear how music might *see* itself, but more metaphorically, we could find occasions where music appears to *hear* itself. In other words, we must establish that 'music listens'. We see how crucial and aptly chosen Steinberg's 'second fiction' is.

How does music hear itself? The question hovers over a philosophical abyss already broached in the previous two chapters. Self-consciousness – the reflexive consciousness of the self *as* self – presupposes some division of the self into subject and object, the subject standing as its own object to itself. To hear itself, the music would seem to need to reveal a division into subject and object, hearer and heard. Rather than healing the divided self, we appear to have returned to the split subject of earlier chapters.

There is already a potential way of overcoming this division, outlined earlier, through the immediacy of feeling, that same sense of self-possession that was identified in the First Symphony's Larghetto. In many ways this proposed solution is a case of cutting the Gordian knot: it might be persuasive to argue that we experience music with an apparent immediacy suggestive of the precognitive feeling of ourselves; but there is nothing in the music that we could point to that suggests it is fictionally self-aware, that it is not only present-to-self but *knows* it is present-to-self – without introducing a subject/object split. This facet is undeniably highly significant in the idea of subjectivity as the work done by music in constructing our own sense of self, and one that will be returned to in later chapters, but it does not fully solve the issue of how we justify calling the hypothetical *musical subject* self-conscious.

Another solution beckons, however, and possible inspiration can be found in early nineteenth-century German thought. The self must necessarily divide into subject and object, but this can either be at the same moment or part of a process that is temporally distended. In the first case, the subject is inescapably divided from itself. We might think of that now-familiar Schumannesque principle of the heterophonic accompaniment or the 'ungenaues Unisono' remarked upon by Reinhold Brinkmann, the slight desynchronisation of voices that reveals a subject which at any one moment is never fully present to itself but ever divided into subject and object, can *hear itself* because its audible trace is *separated* from itself.[21] Such strictures on the impossibility of absolute self-presence are, of course, common in post-war French thought, from the Sartre of *Being and Nothing* through to the late Merleau-Ponty, from Lévinas to Lacan and Derrida. But in the second instance, a deeper identity across time may be implied. Self-consciousness

---

[21] See Reinhold Brinkmann, *Schumann und Eichendorff: Studien zum Liederkreis Opus 39* (Munich: edition text+kritik, 1997), pp. 60–8, taking up an idea of Adorno. Yonatan Malin has pertinently remarked on how such 'reverberant doublings of a single voice' in Schumann create 'an expansion and deepening of inwardness, a resonant space within the self' ('Schumann: Doubling and Reverberation', in *Songs in Motion: Rhythm and Meter in the German Lied* (New York: Oxford University Press, 2010), pp. 124, 123).

here is an act, a temporal process, the imprinting of a cohering unity onto the distended temporal events across time as philosophers after Fichte held and is given exemplary instantiation in the very nature of music.[22] In this case, music appears to be reflecting on itself by reflecting on its temporally distended course: it is, in short, *remembering* itself.

For Steinberg, 'music's self-consciousness resides in the fiction that the music listens – to itself, its past, its desires'. Music, he reasonably concludes, must therefore be perceived to have 'the capacity for memory, a sense of past and future, and a language for their articulation'.[23] In an earlier study of musical self-consciousness I have pointed to the potential of cyclic instrumental works – that is, pieces that recall material from an earlier movement in a later one – to convey just such a sense of remembering themselves, of reflecting on their own journey, often as a decisive culminating gesture or the crucial means by which they may attain this *telos*.[24] Likewise, the ability of music to stage a stylised sense of remembering, and the techniques by which this may be achieved, has been detailed in a number of studies.[25] Hence we might propose that those instrumental pieces in which the musical past returns in such a way as to suggest a process of remembering may strongly imply a sense of reflexive awareness on the part of the music qua imaginary subject, in other words, a degree of self-consciousness, and one without necessarily bringing us back to a split in the subject. Such cyclic self-reflections are found liberally throughout Schumann's music; one might think of the recollection of the opening movement preceding the finales of the Piano and Cello Concertos (examples which hark back to an established Beethovenian precedent), the integration of the off-tonic introduction at the close of the Violin *Fantasie*, Op. 131, examined at the close of Chapter 3, or the culminating reworking

---

[22] The idea is pervasive in Schelling and Hegel; see again Bowie, *Aesthetics and Subjectivity*, Taylor, *The Melody of Time*, ch. 2. Even a twentieth-century analytic philosopher like Ryle broadly concurs in arguing that introspection – searching for the elusive 'I', which thereby becomes self-divided – is often simply retrospection (*The Concept of Mind*, pp. 159–60).

[23] Steinberg, *Listening to Reason*, p. 9.

[24] See 'Musical History and Self-Consciousness in Mendelssohn's Octet, Op. 20', *19th-Century Music*, 32 (2008), 131–59, extended as chapter 2 of Mendelssohn, *Time and Memory*, which offers a fuller theorisation of cyclic form in the first chapter.

[25] See my 'Schubert and the Construction of Memory: The Quartet in A minor, D. 804 ('Rosamunde')', *Journal of the Royal Musical Association*, 139 (2014), 41–88, as well as accounts by Elaine Sisman ('Memory and Invention at the Threshold of Beethoven's Late Style', in Scott Burnham and Michael Steinberg (eds.), *Beethoven and His World* (Princeton: Princeton University Press, 2000), pp. 51–87), and Kristina Muxfeldt ('Music Recollected in Tranquillity: Postures of Memory in Beethoven' in *Vanishing Sensibilities: Essays in Reception and Historical Restoration – Schubert, Beethoven, Schumann* (New York: Oxford University Press, 2011), pp. 118–47).

of the music's past in the coda to the Piano Quintet, Op. 44. Even better, when a lyrical subject emerges from an instrumental piece, and this is heard as a result of a thematic process whereby the melody is revealed by a stylised staging of remembrance to have been underlying the preceding music, we might find a fitting musical analogue for a coming to lyricism which is at the same time a coming to self-consciousness, one in which this self-realisation serves as the goal of the music.

Coming to Lyricism (II): Reflexive Consciousness in Schumann's Instrumental Music and the *An die ferne Geliebte* Paradigm

We are now in a position to extend the idea of coming to lyricism and self-consciousness to instrumental music. And surely the most famous case of an instrumental work dramatising the emergence of a song theme in Schumann's oeuvre is the *Fantasie* in C, Op. 17 (1836–8). At the end of the first movement, a soft, songlike theme emerges from the ruins; set off from the preceding music in its intimate, secretive tone, it yet appears to be a result of the foregoing movement (Ex. 4.6). And indeed, as several scholars have shown, this idea marks the final stage in a process of thematic transformation that has taken place from the very opening bars, from the scalic descent heard there over dominant ninth harmonies through numerous metamorphoses to its ultimate realisation in this songful theme at the close.[26] This is a coming to lyricism which is simultaneously a disclosure of essence, a retrospective revelation of self-identity. It appears 'as at once the source and the solution of everything in the music up to that final page', the musical articulation of that 'softer note, that resounds for him who secretly listens' of which Friedrich Schlegel's text, affixed as an epigram by the composer, speaks.[27] Moreover, Schumann's original version of the *Fantasie*, where this same theme returned at the close of the final movement, underscores the idea's status as an idea arrived at through a process of recollection.

Of course, it is popularly supposed that the theme here *really is* a song theme – namely the final song of *An die ferne Geliebte* just mentioned,

---

[26] The process of thematic actualisation is traced in several important studies: see especially Nicholas Marston, *Schumann: Fantasie, Op. 17* (Cambridge: Cambridge University Press, 1992), pp. 63–7, Charles Rosen, *The Romantic Generation*, pp. 103–12, Berthold Hoeckner, 'Schumann and Romantic Distance', *Journal of the American Musicological Society*, 50 (1997), 109–26.

[27] Rosen, *The Romantic Generation*, p. 103; the epigram is from Schlegel's poem 'Die Gebüsche'.

Ex. 4.6 Schumann: *Fantasie* in C, Op. 17, i, end

'Nimm sie hin denn, diese Lieder.' Coming to lyricism as the emergence of subjective voice is unmistakably clear when it is the melody of a real song that emerges. But here, if that song is one by Beethoven, one might be forgiven for questioning quite what such lyrical actualisation might imply. If Schumann's *Fantasie* articulates the coming to self-consciousness of a musical subject, the subject would seem, slightly worryingly, to be that of Beethoven, not Schumann (or a fictional 'Schumann' persona). Does it matter whether it is Robert Schumann's own voice or Ludwig van Beethoven's that we hear? (Some postmodern-inclined deconstruction of the autonomous subject into a product of language, culture, and history might seem invited at this point; perhaps the 'truth' of Schumann's work is in revealing inadvertently how the supposedly most intimate and inviolable mineness of the subject is actually a fiction.)[28]

Whether this really is a reference to Beethoven's song cycle is, however, keenly debated; despite the close links of this work to Beethoven, nowhere

---

[28] I will return to this point later in Chapter 8.

does Schumann profess that this passage is an allusion, and we have no evidence that anyone even spotted this seemingly self-evident quotation until over half a century after the composer's death, all of which might cast some reasonably lukewarm water over the assumption that this theme really is meant as a quotation.[29] I do not propose to answer this question definitively (and the unquestioning assumption that this is a conscious allusion will no doubt continue as one of those ineradicable truisms of programme-note journalism), but I am not sure this issue really matters. As Rosen discerns, the point is the theme sounds like Schumann, and such is the way in which the composer has integrated its materials into the preceding movement that when it arrives, it appears as the logical outcome of all that has gone before; 'one cannot take the full measure of Schumann's accomplishment in this work without observing that the quotation from *An die ferne Geliebte* sounds as if Schumann had written it'.[30] What is important for this current discussion is the fact that theme is lyrical, song-like, and emerges out of the thematic working as the music's goal.

But the possible allusion to Beethoven does introduce an important and yet more intricate level of reflexivity into the process of coming to self-consciousness here. 'Take then these songs': as Nicholas Marston has shown, the final song in Beethoven's cycle is a piece that explicitly fore-grounds the notion of musical reflexivity, of recognising one's own singing voice, and the endpoint of a process of thematic modification, one which will result in the cyclic recall of the music of the opening song at its close as the crown of this new temporal self-consciousness.[31] This is the same conceit that was traced in Schumann's 'Stille Liebe' (another song in E flat major), and one which a number of the other works we considered approach.[32] The elusive allusion to Beethoven's song at this point in

---

[29] As Anthony Newcomb has shown, the first printed source for this idea is the revised second edition of Hermann Abert's *Robert Schumann* (Berlin: Harmonie Verlagsgesellschaft für Literatur und Kunst, 1910), p. 64. See Newcomb, 'Schumann's Music and the Marketplace: From Butterflies to *Hausmusik*', in R. Larry Todd (ed.), *Nineteenth-Century Piano Music* (New York: Schirmer, 1990), p. 295; further, Marston, *Schumann: Fantasie, Op. 17*, pp. 36–7, and Todd, 'On Quotation in Schumann's Music', p. 93.

[30] Rosen, *The Romantic Generation*, p. 103.

[31] Marston, 'Voicing Beethoven's Distant Beloved'.

[32] Eric Sams has even proposed that the second half of Schumann's melody (bb. 10–12) alludes to the comparable point in the first song of *An die ferne Geliebte*, 'Auf dem Hügel sitz ich spähend', bb. 5–7 (*The Songs of Robert Schumann*, p. 174). The harmonic progression is not identical, and I feel this link would never be noticed if the two were not in the same key and there were not such established precedent for *ferne Geliebte* allusion-spotting in Schumann, but admittedly there is some similarity. Jon Finson (*Robert Schumann: The Book of Songs*, pp. 77–8) perceives a likeness but no actual allusion.

Schumann's *Fantasie* is perhaps not fortuitous; it is certainly hermeneutically resonant.

Thus, not just the emergence of a song theme, but the emergence of *this
particular* song theme may stand through a broad connotative network
(one unavoidably bound up with verbal meanings and presumed historical
intentions) for the emergence of a radical reflexivity when occurring in an
instrumental piece. I will refer to this as the *ferne Geliebte* paradigm: the
coming to lyricism that is a self-consciousness of lyricism. And as we know,
this certainly does occur elsewhere in Schumann's oeuvre.

Schumann, as is apparent to anyone familiar with even a small part of his
oeuvre, was prone to reusing set thematic ideas across different works (the
so-called Clara theme is perhaps the most famous instance), and he seems
to have been especially keen on this alleged 'ferne Geliebte' theme. Not all
appearances of this idea in his music need denote a self-conscious coming
to lyricism, of course. One such example, dating from a few years later, is
given by the finale of the F major String Quartet, Op. 41 No. 2 (1842), but
here the theme, functioning simply as the movement's second subject, does
not appear as a structural goal of the music and thus any wider hermeneutic
extrapolation on this point seems obscure. More significant, however,
indeed the most famous instance of this theme's use after the *Fantasie* is
its appearance in the finale of the Symphony No. 2 in C, Op. 61 (1845–6),
and here it undoubtedly plays a crucial instigative role in the work's
progression to lyrical fulfilment.

The Second Symphony has often been interpreted as charting
a darkness-to-light trajectory, a psychological journey from suffering to
renewed health.[33] Despite their being in the major, there is a vein of
nervous tension running throughout the first two movements that critics
have eagerly aligned with the composer's own report of the spiritual
malaise he felt at the time he was writing them, and the hyper-
expressivity of the Adagio (long considered a highpoint of Schumann's
symphonic writing) certainly appears to plumb unusual interior depths.
Running alongside this trope of reception history is the work's status as
a highly organised cyclic structure, in which a small group of themes are
developed within and across movements in a sophisticated process of

---

[33] The reformulation of this interpretation for modern times can be attributed largely to the
influential article by Anthony Newcomb, 'Once More "Between Absolute and Programme
Music": Schumann's Second Symphony', *19th-Century Music*, 7 (1984), 233–50, who
underscores the reception tradition of the symphony as implicating a strong sense of
subjectivity in its series of psychological 'soul states' and the personification of thematic entities
'as characters in a narrative' (237).

'organic' evolution. In fact, the two paradigms – one expressive, one formal – can easily be used to support each other, the thematic process interpreted as enacting the psychological progression to spiritual fulfilment.

In an oft-cited letter, the composer divulges that he wrote the symphony while 'still half sick; it seems to me that one must hear this. Only in the last movement did I begin to feel like myself', while similarly to another friend he confessed 'it is a dark piece throughout – only in the last part do a few friendly rays burst forth'.[34] I do not wish to exaggerate the extent to which the metric tensions and close thematic logic of the opening movements should be taken to imply psychological disturbance (one might simply admire the skill with which Schumann has constructed this work, the controlled dynamism directing the first movement development and coda, the harmonic flexibility of the unremittingly brilliant scherzo, the motivic fluidity of the Adagio espressivo). But there seems little doubt that the finale's role is to initiate and ultimately sustain some more positive affirmation after the turbulence of the preceding music. And here, the *ferne Geliebte* theme, arrived at again through an extensive process of thematic variation and actualisation, is once again key to the final overcoming.

Schumann's movement starts out joyfully with an opening flourish and springing dotted march theme; in lieu of a second subject the main theme of the slow movement returns, but now it is livelier, speeded up in a major-key form, and incorporated into the finale's texture of ongoing motivic elaboration. The subsequent return of the opening theme in the tonic suggests a sonata rondo design, and the music continues into an extensive development, including the inversion of the adagio theme. But then comes a barrier: the clouds gather, and almost without warning the music comes to a halt on the tonic minor. We have reached an unforeseen expressive impasse or formal *aporia* in the movement's design: there follows stasis, a general pause.[35]

From this uncertain silence a lyrical theme now emerges; unassuming, climbing smoothly in a 'graceful melodic curve' and reminiscent perhaps of a chorale, this is above all a *vocal* theme (Ex. 4.7a).[36] Though 'new', it is in fact foreshadowed in several earlier themes that had appeared across the

---

[34] Schumann, letter of 2 April 1849 to D. G. Otten (*Briefe: Neue Folge*, p. 300), and letter of 3 March 1847 to Wilhelm Taubert (*SB* II.17:716).

[35] Harmonically there is a parallelism here with the first movement, which had unusually returned to the tonic minor at the climax of the development before dominant preparation of the recapitulation. The form of Schumann's finale foreshadows several aspects of that to Brahms's First Symphony (where another 'vocal' theme famously emerges in a pointedly instrumental context, indeed one that again appears to allude to Beethoven).

[36] The characterisation is Daverio's (*Robert Schumann*, p. 320).

Ex. 4.7a Schumann: Symphony No. 2, Op. 61, finale, new lyrical theme following development section impasse

Ex. 4.7b Schumann: Symphony No. 2, Op. 61, finale, *An die ferne Geliebte* theme at start of coda

course of the symphony: its even conjunct motion has been strongly present since the work's introduction, while the $\hat{6}$–$\hat{7}$–$\hat{8}$ opening formula and chorale-like tone was particularly apparent in the second trio. It is also closely related to an idea that has emerged to greater prominence in the preceding development section of the finale, whose purpose, as Daverio has suggested, resides in its gradual evolution of this lyrical idea.[37] And by no means least significantly, it also evinces a distinct similarity with the final song from *An die ferne Geliebte* (an affinity barely disguised by the octave transferral of its second half; the two are even in the same key, E flat).

With this new event the music is at last able to issue in an extended retransitional passage on the dominant that seems, through its repeated statements of the primary theme and opening flourish, to herald the movement's long-awaited recapitulation. Instead, though, the music breaks off once again, and a now familiar shape is heard: through a minor modification and transposition the new vocal idea has grown unmistakably into the songlike *ferne Geliebte* theme (Ex. 4.7b).[38]

---

[37] *Ibid.*, p. 320.

[38] Again, Newcomb has suggested the erstwhile allusion to Beethoven's theme was not reported until decades after Schumann's death ('Once More "Between Absolute and Programme Music"', 246 n. 26).

What had at first connoted the collective voice of the congregational song is now heard in the more subjective guise of the solo Lied. Its appearance here is also the conclusive sign that the expected form of the movement has been completely overthrown and needs drastic reconceptualisation. We are entering a coda apotheosis; the three thematic rotations of a putative sonata rondo have given way to two rotations of a hybrid exposition / developmental-recapitulation design with a culminating coda.

In this final section, the symphony is crowned by the recall of its opening, the fanfares which had been heard over the embryonic murmuring scalic figures that had given rise to so much of the work's material. At the culmination of this cyclic process the symphony's own past is now explicitly recalled in a triumphant assertion of the work's coming to self-consciousness, born of music's apparent capacity to reflect on its own earlier course. And the catalyst for this musical recall has been the *ferne Geliebte* theme – the melody that we suggested was marked with the imprint of reflexivity from its use in Beethoven's cycle and was used to similar ends in Schumann's Op. 17 almost a decade before. In Schumann's work it has been the gradual emergence of this *ferne Geliebte* theme – the coming to lyricism of this idea across the work – that has brought about the symphony's breakthrough to its final and ultimately joyous state. The march-like optimism of the finale's opening, even the positivity of the reworked Adagio theme as its second subject, have not sufficed to bring the work to a successful conclusion; but a lyrical melody, emerging from a long process of thematic evolution, has instead achieved this goal. And with this comes the recovery of subjecthood – coinciding with the moment that, as Schumann reported, he had begun to feel like himself again.

In his one subsequent symphony Schumann would return to many of these same concerns. The finale of the 'Rhenish' Symphony (No. 3) starts with a jaunty E flat melody which on closer inspection turns out to be yet another reworking of our *ferne Geliebte* theme; after the awestruck solemnity of the fourth movement (the 'Scene in the Cathedral' at Cologne), it is once again this particular melodic idea that lifts the music into brighter (if here rather less sublime) regions. And in the coda to the work, set off from the finale's two preceding thematic rotations as a quasi-independent apotheosis, a cyclic network of themes recalls the symphony's past in a reflexive display of self-reflection and self-constitution. Admittedly, a private subjectivity seems less in evidence in this work; it is more the collective, a music which speaks as a 'we', that is referenced here (an aspect already skirted in the chorale-like passages of the Second Symphony). But that is a matter for another chapter.

*

The current chapter has set out a fuller elucidation of the phenomenology of self-presence in music; an exposition of the important notion of 'coming to lyricism' as bound up with the path to subjecthood (the lyrical voice being a customary marker of subjectivity); and an initial problematisation of the question of self-consciousness, made with reference to the 'coming to lyricism' paradigm just identified. It was argued that coming to lyricism might in some cases be heard to enact a musical coming to self-consciousness, a self-revelation of the musical subject (such self-consciousness having been identified earlier as being perhaps subjectivity in its highest manifestation). But as we saw, the problem of self-consciousness hinges on the question of self-recognition, which in turn implicated the notion of division – the subject's recognition of another object as the self – as an other which is yet at the same time the self. A completely autonomous, self-constituting, and self-recognising subject has long proved a philosophical stumbling block. Even in the *Fantasie* and C major Symphony, it was through another's voice that Schumann's subject appeared to find itself. Hence alterity or division, no sooner having been seemingly laid to rest, re-emerges in another form, in the familiar play of recognition between self as other and other as self. This question of musical self-consciousness is not yet fully played out by the answers offered here. And thus, this initial response to the problem of musical self-consciousness is just part of a larger dialectical trajectory, which will need to be resumed in the following chapter.

5 | Presence of the Other

Duets, Real or Imagined

The *Andante cantabile* of Schumann's Piano Quartet, Op. 47 (1842), is for its greater part given over to a lyrical theme characteristic of the composer's most unabashed flowering of romantic sentiment (Ex. 5.1). Given at the start to the cello, the melody is heard in the warm middle register of the (male) human voice, unmistakably vocal, the very sound of the musical self. Initially the mood is very much of the daydreaming subject encountered already in the slow movement of the First Symphony; Marshall Brown actually references this quartet movement as a pertinent example of the state of self-conscious reverie that was considered in Chapter 4.[1] But as the cello approaches the end of the melodic phrase we become aware of a new voice that has entered: the violin has taken up the melody, overlapping its extended two-crotchet upbeat with the cadential progression of the cello. As the music continues, the cello responds to its new partner by quasi-imitation a fourth lower, the two melodic lines intertwining gracefully around each other. What had started out as a solitary reverie has now unmistakably turned into a romantic duet. One subject has become two: the self has been joined by another.

If the cello is readily associated with the male voice, the higher-pitched violin is clearly ordained to play the female partner in the musical romance that unfolds here. (For a composer for whom life and art seemed so often interlinked, not least in popular reception, such musical gendering may easily be conflated with an autobiographical scenario involving Robert and Clara, one which can rapidly descend into mawkishness.) Yet it is the feminine violin that has taken the lead and has in fact done so right from the start of the movement. The four opening bars present a cadential approach to the tonic B flat decorated by a chromaticised melodic flourish in the violin that overlaps with the entry of the cello theme in bar 3; it is only with the end of the cello's phrase that the listener realises this initial

---

[1] Brown, 'Mozart and After', 695.

Ex. 5.1 Schumann: Piano Quartet in E flat, Op. 47, iii, opening

figure, related in contour to the principal theme, is essentially the tail segment of its melody. Perhaps this other voice – the voice of the other –

Ex. 5.1 (Cont.)

has been gently calling the tune all along; at the very least, there is a strange symbiosis between the two musical personae.

As the movement progresses, the duetting continues between piano and viola, albeit now with a syncopated variant of the theme. Already the subjects of this music have become more blurred; formerly distinct, they are heard now as something more akin to the inner reverberation of the self, in the manner seen in earlier examples from Schumann. This process is taken further in the movement's ensuing central section (bb. 48–72). Contrasting in its chordal, homophonic writing syncopated across the notated barlines and hushed dynamic, this section takes up the tone of subjective interiority familiar from late Beethoven (a conspicuous influence throughout this quartet). Even more clearly we have returned to a more purely singular subject. There is only the sense of a musical self now; the other voice has disappeared.

On the return to the music of the A section, the main theme in viola is decorated with filigree semiquavers in the violin tracing a delicate embroidery around the melody. Whereas the presentation in the opening section between cello and violin seemed undeniably to constitute a true duet, however, here on the reprise the effect is of an ornamented single subject amidst a web of gentle pulsations, akin to the reprise of the primary theme in the slow movement of the symphony. And even when the violin and viola share the theme from b. 88 (now modified to imitation at the second, with a strong subdominant emphasis that suggests imminent formal closure) there is no longer the same romantic feeling; the lyrical continuity resulting previously from the overlapping of melodic phrases is absent too. Possibly one of the reasons for this perception is bound up with the earlier close sonorous identification of the cello's singing voice with the music's primary subject (the voice of a quasi-authorial 'Schumann' as it were), for when the cello subsequently returns with the theme it had played at the movement's start there is a clear sense of return to the initial subjective persona, alongside a similar sense of formal rounding off. Now, however, its song goes unanswered: its vocal partner is missing.

But, with the cadential arrival, at b. 118 a new, surprising sonority greets our ears: a low B♭ in the cello undergirds the movement's final thirteen bars. Pitched a tone lower than its lowest normal note, the cello's C string has been re-tuned during the initial stages of the reprise in order to accommodate this sound. A mundane explanation may, of course, be at hand for this unusual step: the movement is in B flat, and Schumann might simply have wanted a low tonic pedal in the strings to support the piano's new canonic idea presented in the treble above (a figure prophetic, as it will turn out, of the beginning of the finale). But still, the decision is quixotic and invites hermeneutic interpretation. In playing a note that, as Brown observes, 'ordinarily does not exist', the musical subject has suddenly revealed new and unexpected depths. By finding this 'ethereal fundamental' the self has opened out into unsuspected regions, initiating a decisive movement from reverie to action (the finale, prefigured at this precise point in the other instruments).[2] In the cello's re-tuning, the musical subject has effectively re-tuned its own self in light of its experiences across the movement. It is with this return to the voice of the self, following the encounter with the voice of the romantic other, that the music has been able to attain this deepened condition of selfhood.

---

[2] *Ibid.*, 695. Brown interprets the moment as one of clarification, 'as if a preconscious state were yielding to a conscious one'.

In this example from the Piano Quartet, Schumann's music seems to slip at ease between its imputing of a single lyrical subject and at least two distinct subjects heard interacting in musical dialogue. Such fluidity of subjective voice is indeed typical of his chamber music: a similar ambiguity may be glimpsed, for instance, in the slow movement of the Piano Trio No. 1, Op. 63 (1847). Here, following a rhapsodic arioso in the violin that comes to a temporary rest on a dominant-functioning $^6_4$ (b. 10), the newly entering cello takes over the instrumental line from the same pitch (e^1) and for several bars plays the primary line above the violin, relegating the latter to a subdued lower voice barely distinguishable from its partial doubling in the inner parts of the piano. The effect is of the continuity formed by a single voice, with minimal change in tone colour as the violin is succeeded by the cello. Only gradually – hinted first in the violin's brief registral overreaching at b. 16 – do we become conscious that the initial line and the soliloquising solitary subject had been joined at this point by a second voice. With this dawning awareness, too, the music moves away from the troubled searching of the opening *Langsam, mit inniger Empfindung* and into a more animated and lyrically forthcoming passage in the submediant major (*Bewegter*, b. 20) in which all three instruments respond to each other as if at last liberated from earlier inhibitions.[3]

Or take the slow movement of the Second Piano Trio, Op. 80 (composed likewise in 1847), in which imitative murmurings in cello and piano support a romantic melody of Schumannesque sweetness and *Innigkeit* in the violin, a conception calling to mind the subjective plenitude associated earlier with the feeling of pure self-possession, from which the cello gradually becomes an ever-more equal partner, entwining itself lovingly around the violin's sighing phrases. The fact that the melody played seems already to refer to one that had appeared unexpectedly in the development section of the first movement – a theme which itself appeared to allude to an earlier song, 'Intermezzo' ('Your beauteous image / I hold in the depths of my heart'), Op. 39 No. 2 – and will presently grow into this same theme, strongly supports these romantic associations. Such examples chart not merely a coming to lyricism that signifies the emergence of a musical subject, but the emergence of a *second* voice, of an other, out of the self – one that seems deeply bound up with this subject and yet qualitatively different from the divided or multiple subject familiar from earlier chapters.

---

[3] Especially significant at this point appears to be the piano's movement from *una corda* to *tutte corde*.

But such readings are hermeneutically fragile. In the preceding cases are we really hearing a duet, or are we not perhaps hearing an imaginary duet – the fantasy of the solitary self, dreaming to itself of an ideal love object in which it sees itself mirrored? Has the alterity of the encounter with the other voice really initiated the coming to selfhood of the musical subject, in this manner tracing a typical idealist movement of self-consciousness through the mutual recognition of self and other, or are we merely witnessing a narcissistic subject prone to ventriloquism? Of course, there are true vocal duets, where there indisputably are two people or protagonists involved, and Schumann wrote several fine examples of these. But what is more interesting for this current investigation into musical subjectivity – and the specific concern of this chapter – are those moments when one subject becomes two, when two subjects conversely appear to become one, and when a single subject implies the presence of an other, the image of the beloved, within itself.

Robert, Clara, and the Myth of Romantic Hermaphroditism

In a much-cited letter Robert wrote to Clara in June 1839, he looks forward to their eventual marriage, one that not only is a physical or legal union but a fusion of heart and mind, a creative and spiritual interpenetration. 'We will also publish many things in *both our names*' Schumann writes; 'posterity should regard us as one heart and one soul and not find out what is by you and what is by me'.[4] This idea of the two being of 'one heart and one soul' occupied Schumann's thoughts greatly during this period: only the next month, speaking of a composition Clara had sent him, he comes to a similar conclusion concerning their spiritual and creative oneness: 'In your Romance I heard once again now that we must become man and wife. You complete me as a musician, as I do you. Each of your ideas comes from my soul, just as I have to thank you for all my music.'[5]

---

[4] Letter 13 June 1839 ('Wir geben dann auch Manches unter *unsern beiden Namen* heraus; die Nachwelt soll uns ganz wie ein Herz und eine Seele betrachten und nicht erfahren, was von Dir, was von mir ist'), *SB* I.5:544 / *Briefwechsel*, vol. II, p. 571, emphasis in original.

[5] Letter 10 July 1839 ('An Deiner Romanze hab' ich nun abermals von Neuem gehört, daß wir Mann und Frau werden müssen. Du vervollständigst mich als Componisten, wie ich Dich. Jeder Deiner Gedanken kömmt aus meiner Seele, wie ich ja meine ganze Musik Dir zu verdanken habe.' *SB* I.6:139 / *Briefwechsel*, vol. II, p. 629). Schumann also returns to this theme in yet another letter from this time: 'Und dann heißt es Du und ich, und Dein und Mein, und Klara und Robert sind eines, ein Herz und eine Seele' (Letter 18 July 1839, *SB* I.6:173–4 / *Briefwechsel*, vol. II, p. 651).

We have seen in earlier chapters Schumann playing with the divided, fractious subject, seeing aspects of the self as effectively an other to itself. An alternative and more radical step, however, might be to embrace alterity. If the self is ever fated to be split, at least when attempting to know itself (as evinced in the problem of undivided self-consciousness discussed in Chapter 4), the path to full self-possession might well be through reaching out to the other. By fusing the self with an other, the individual subject might overcome the seemingly irreparable divisions in its own constitution. In engaging with this idea, Schumann is tapping into a theme that had assumed major import-ance in early German Romanticism: the myth of lost hermaphroditic unity.

In Plato's *Symposium* the character of Aristophanes famously tells a story of humankind's primal hermaphroditic nature in order to explain the nature of love, the topic under discussion. Once – so his somewhat tongue-in-cheek account goes – humans were double, with four legs, four arms, and two sets of sexual organs, fused at their ribcage with two faces that could see both directions at once. But hubris befell these beings. Such creatures – termed hermaphrodites, after the mythic son of Hermes and Aphrodite, who fused with a nymph with whom he was enamoured and became both male and female – were too powerful and threatened the order of the gods. Zeus, fearful of their capacity, ordered Apollo to split the primal hermaphrodites in two (and in doing so, turned their heads around to face the current way), thus drastically weakening them. Now divided, humans wander the earth searching for their lost other half to make themselves complete once more. Such is the cause of love – 'the name given for our desire and pursuit of wholeness.'[6]

Aristophanes' story forms a key mythic illustration of a subject that is already split and seeks completion by fusing with an other. In this view, the individual subject is inherently only half of a larger originary unity, and thus positively needs another object, the beloved, for completion. Variants of this idea, most commonly associated with a heterosexual fusion of male and female, can be found throughout history – in Cabbalistic interpretations of the Old Testament, in the Hermetic writings of Paracelsus, Boehme, and Swedenborg – and readily align with Gnostic or Neoplatonic myths of a primal wholeness, followed by a division into multiplicity which is de facto a fall into evil, and the attempted regaining of this originary unity.[7] But the notion of hermaphroditism (or androgyny as it is sometimes termed) becomes especially prevalent in Romanticism, where it assumes a status

[6] Plato, *Symposium*, 189d–193e, quotation from 193a.
[7] See M. H. Abrams's classic study, *Natural Supernaturalism: Tradition and Revolution in Romantic Literature* (New York: Norton, 1971), esp. pp. 154–63.

approaching a grounding tenet.[8] For Romantics, the hermaphrodite symbolises the overcoming of painful divisions that beset the modern subject, the union of subject and object, self and other, male and female, an idea particularly prominent in writers such as Novalis and Friedrich Schlegel (already associated by some commentators with Schumann's Romantic aesthetics).[9] In Schlegel's view, humanity is fundamentally hermaphroditic and aspires once more to the progressive union of the sexes. Marriage should not be a legal contract but rather, ideally, the overcoming of distinctions and difference, in which two become one (an idea transmitting a socially emancipatory message that strongly resonated with more politically engaged Romantics).[10] For Novalis, responding to the latent solipsism of Fichte's philosophy (in which alterity is entirely dependent on the self, a construct resulting from its own primary act of self-positing), the point of 'absolute indifference' in which difference is paradoxically both maintained and overcome can only be attained in the hermaphroditic union of the self with the other in which this self is reflected.[11] As A. J. L. Busst, in his classic study of Romantic androgyny, explains, 'at the same time as the hermaphrodite symbolizes the union of the sexes, it represents in addition the self-sufficient narcissist union with the self'. 'The beloved not only reflects the self, but in fact *is* the self. The union of a couple, then, is not the fusion of two distinct entities, but the revelation of an underlying unity.'[12]

---

[8] Albert Béguin, in *L'Âme romantique et le rêve: Essai sur le romantisme allemand et la poésie française* (Marseille: Cahiers du Sud, 1937), identifies androgyny as the foundational myth of the Romantic era; see Catriona MacLeod, *Embodying Ambiguity: Androgyny and Aesthetics from Winckelmann to Keller* (Detroit: Wayne State University Press, 1998), for a good account of this topic. The terms 'hermaphrodite' and 'androgyne' are essentially interchangeable in the literature, though in the following account I prefer to use the former to refer to the Platonic archetype of a union of two individuals into one (an ideal, after the mythic figure Hermaphroditos), whereas the latter will designate a single individual with characteristics of both, neither, or indeterminate gender.

[9] See especially Sara Friedrichsmeyer, *The Androgyne in Early German Romanticism: Friedrich Schlegel, Novalis, and the Metaphysics of Love* (Bern: Peter Lang, 1983). John Daverio, for one, has suggested close parallels between Schumann's outlook and those of the above authors ('Schumann's Systems of Musical Fragments and Witz').

[10] Such ideas may be found, for instance, in Schlegel's 1795 essay 'Über die Diotima', and the (once scandalous, but now rather tame) novel *Lucinde* (1799).

[11] See especially the author's *Fichte-Studien* (1795–6); the image of love as an overflowing or interpenetration of self into other recurs throughout Novalis's writing: it may be found conspicuously, for example, in the relationship between Heinrich and Mathilde at the end of book one of *Heinrich von Ofendingen*. On this topic see also Mary R. Strand, *I/You: Paradoxical Constructions of Self and Other in Early German Romanticism* (New York: Peter Lang, 1998), esp. pp. 7–21.

[12] A. J. L. Busst, 'The Image of the Androgyne in the Nineteenth Century', in Ian Fletcher (ed.), *Romantic Mythologies* (London: Routledge and Kegan Paul, 1967), pp. 62, 63.

As seen earlier, Schumann had already attempted to divide his own personality into two through the imaginary personas of Florestan and Eusebius. But conversely, in the similarly fictional figure of Raro – formed from the last two letters of the name Clara and the first two of Robert – he had also taken imaginative steps towards the fusion of two separate individuals into a single persona that united both. Significantly, this was a fusion of himself with the person who would become the object of his love. Clara – or her *imago*, her internalised, idealised image – provided a love-object, an outlet or in some ways perhaps a safety valve for Schumann in the years up to 1840.[13] This interest in a genuine external subject, we might speculate, may well have helped Schumann steer clear of a dangerous Romantic solipsism, avoiding becoming too wrapped up in his own psyche by identifying his ego with and demanding recognition from something really existing in the outside world.

In 'Widmung' ('Dedication'), the opening song of the Op. 25 collection *Myrthen* given to Clara as a bridal gift on the day of their wedding, 12 September 1840, Robert sets a poem by Friedrich Rückert singing the praise of the beloved, framed revealingly by the lines 'Du meine Seele, du mein Herz . . . Mein guter Geist, mein bess'res Ich' ('You my soul, you my heart . . . My good spirit, my better self'). From his letters, it is clear that Schumann viewed his relation with Clara as a both a union of soulmates and as a means to fill a disturbing void in his own psyche, in which opposing tendencies were threatening to pull his personality apart. 'Within Schumann's mental life' Anne Burton comments, 'the ever-present image of Clara served such an integrating function.'[14] Already it seems during a particularly depressive episode in October 1833, in which Schumann claims he had feared taking his life, the doctor had calmed him down with the advice: 'Medicine is no help here; find yourself a woman, she will cure you at once.' Tellingly, this story is related in 1838 by Robert to Clara herself – the woman whom he now hoped would provide this remedy

---

[13] The term 'imago' (simply the Latin for 'image') was introduced into psychoanalytical language by Carl Gustav Jung but has since been modified by Lacan and post-Lacanian psychologists such as Kristeva, often being associated with the image of the self in the early mirror stage of psychic development or a semi-narcissistic projection of the self onto an external love object. Confusingly, for Schumann 'Raro' could also stand for Friedrich Wieck. The identification of the hermaphroditic union of self and beloved with a surrogate father figure might appear distinctly peculiar, though one could note that the *imago* in Jungian psychoanalysis is generally associated with an internalised parental super-ego.

[14] Anna Burton, 'Robert Schumann and Clara Wieck: A Creative Partnership', *Music & Letters*, 69 (1988), 212.

for him.[15] But this tendency is perhaps most evident in some poetic verses he wrote to Clara later that year which, as Burton observes, 'frankly assign to Clara the task of integrating his warring self-divisions'. These tiny poems tell of Robert's frustrations of waiting, before subsequently idealising Clara and her power to uplift his spirits as the composer 'pins his hopes for happiness completely on his "Klärchen".' Yet fear and anger return: unable to integrate the figures of Florestan and Eusebius, a despairing Schumann calls upon Clara to do so for him. Calming down once more, he finally 'reveals that his soul mirrors hers; she may look inside him and find herself'.[16]

Oft gönnt' ich einen Blick Dir mir in's Innere	*Oft have I let you look inside myself*
Und sah, wie Du beglückt an Deinem Blick.	*And saw how you delight in your gaze.*
Nicht wahr, was Du gesehn in diesem Innern,	*Is it not true, that what you saw inside,*
Es warf etwas von Deinem Selbst zurück.	*Threw back something of your self?*[17]

Schumann's need for finding himself reflected in and fusing his identity with Clara was not just confined to his occasional poetic writing, though: it permeated his musical output. Putting to one side for the moment the disputed notion of a musical theme supposedly formed from a cipher of Clara's name (a topic that will be returned to in Chapter 8), this is seen most clearly in the pair's shared use of material

---

[15] Schumann, letter to Clara of 11 February 1838 ('"Medizin hülfe hier nichts; suchen Sie Sich eine Frau, die curirt sie gleich."' *SB* I.4:222 / *Briefwechsel*, I:96). A few years earlier Schumann had apparently fastened on Ernestine von Fricken for fulfilling this role: 'She, I thought, is the one: she will save you. I wanted to cling with all my might to a female being' – or so he justifies his earlier relationship in the same letter to Clara ('die, dachte ich, ist es; die wird Dich retten. Ich wollte mich mit aller Gewalt an ein weibliches Wesen anklammern.' *Ibid.*, 223 / 96).

[16] Burton, 'Robert Schumann and Clara Wieck', 224, 222–3. I can't help observing that the closing stages of *Davidsbündlertänze* – a work written jointly by Schumann's two personae, 'F' and 'E' – possess something of this same quality. In the penultimate No. 17 the recall of the melancholic second piece of the cycle leads into an increasingly angry and frenetic close in a dark, Neapolitan-inflected B minor (as discussed earlier, Eusebius presumably being succeeded by Florestan in this jointly authored number). Miraculously, however, the C major of the 'entirely superfluous' final number rescues the opus as a whole, returning to and ultimately liquidating the motivic substance of Clara's opening theme that served as a source for much of the work. Schumann told Clara that he had conceived his *Davidsbündlertänze* as telling of a *Polterabend* (eve-of-wedding celebration), and the way in which the final C major redeems the split between Florestan and Eusebius matches the verse he wrote a year later uncannily well (see Schumann's letter of 7 February 1838, *SB* I.4:215 / *Briefwechsel*, I:93).

[17] 'Kleine Verse an Klara von R. S.', 14 and 15 November, *SB* I.5:126. The earlier *Briefwechsel* tentatively follows Berthold Litzmann in dating these verses to a letter sent on 1 December 1838 (see *Briefwechsel*, I: 314; Litzmann, *Clara Schumann: Ein Künstlerleben nach Tagebüchern und Briefen*, 3 vols. (Leipzig Breitkopf & Härtel, 1902), vol. I, p. 257).

from each other's compositions. As Eric Jensen claims, 'nearly every major composition created by Schumann during his courtship of Clara contains references to her work. He was thus able musically to join himself and Clara in a marriage of sorts.'[18] Most openly, the two are musically associated in Robert's *Impromptus on a Theme by Clara Wieck*, Op. 5, and in his portrait of the young Clara, 'Chiarina', from *Carnaval* – though both examples are relatively early works, before the romance between the two had in fact started.[19] But subsequent instances of borrowing or creative interweaving can be found in Schumann's works of the later 1830s – in the *Concert sans orchestre* (the second-movement theme being based on an unpublished *Andantino* by Clara), the Sonata Op. 11 (whose introduction stems from the fourth of Clara's *Quatre Pièces caractèristiques*, Op. 5), the *Davidsbündlertänze* (based on a 'Motto by C. W.' taken from a mazurka in Clara's *Soirées musicales* Op. 6), and the *Novelletten*, named obliquely after Clara, with its famous 'Stimme aus der Ferne' derived from the 'Notturno' of Clara's *Soirées musicales* (which may or may not be further alluded to in the opening theme of the *Fantasie*, Op. 17). The relation was also reciprocal: Robert returned the favour by helping orchestrate Clara's A minor Piano Concerto of 1833–5, and several years later Clara would write her own *Variations on a Theme by Robert Schumann*. As implied in the letter of 2 July 1839 cited above, the fact that both of them had in several cases been able to come up with near-identical musical ideas suggested to the composer that external distinctions between the two in time and space fell away. Art may both provide a symbolic means of fusing self and other, and, Schumann seems to feel, may actually be a product of a deep and mysterious symbiosis between his and Clara Wieck's souls.

As we saw, in 1839, as he was eyeing up marriage, Schumann spoke of the future couple publishing pieces together as 'one heart and one soul'. And indeed, he was as good as his word: within a few months of their marriage the two had embarked upon a unique joint opus, the *Zwölf Gedichte aus F. Rückerts Liebesfrühling*, published in 1841 as Robert's opus 37 and Clara's opus 12. In this collection, the most notable instance of creative collaboration between the pair, the theme of blurred gender distinctions and hermaphroditic union is conspicuously foregrounded in several places in the text and reflected still further in the musical setting and arrangement.

---

[18] Jensen, *Schumann*, p. 149, who provides several examples of such practice in the following pages (pp. 149–61).

[19] *Carnaval* also contains a 'Valse Allemande' that is derived from Clara's *Valses romantiques*, Op. 4.

Androgyny and Symbolic Union in *Liebesfrühling*

Liebesfrühling consists of twelve songs, drawn from over three hundred poems in Rückert's collection of that name. Though the title page of the first edition bore simply the designation 'by Robert and Clara Schumann' with no indication as to the identity of the author of individual numbers, three songs were in fact written by Clara (Nos. 2, 4, and 11), with the remaining nine being contributed by Robert. Urged on by her new husband, Clara had turned her hand to song composition in December 1840; while none of these attempts related to the eventual Rückert collection, Robert was nevertheless spurred on to complete his own nine Rückert settings in the first weeks of January 1841, and subsequently encouraged Clara to set some of this poet's verse. After some setbacks and delays, Clara offered four of these settings to Robert for his birthday in June. Robert reciprocated by presenting the published score of the joint opus as a surprise birthday gift to Clara on 13 September, the day after the couple's first wedding anniversary.[20]

Schumann wrote to his publisher that the songs were related to each other as question and answer, and previous commentators have explored the collection as being structured as a series of responses between male and female protagonists, drawing out possible indeterminacy or ambiguity in the implied gender of the narrative voice in certain songs.[21] However, the hermaphroditic subtext of the cycle goes well beyond this: in fact, the whole work is suffused with verbal and musical blurring of gender and distinctions between self and other, resulting in a spiritual union of male and female personas at its close.

The opening song, Robert's 'Der Himmel hat eine Träne geweint', is replete with highly gendered symbolism. Heaven wept a tear, that intended

---

[20] See Rufus Hallmark, 'The Rückert Lieder of Robert and Clara Schumann', *19th-Century Music*, 14 (1990), 4–13, for further details on this work's genesis.

[21] Schumann, letter to Breitkopf & Härtel, 23 June 1841 (*Briefe: Neue Folge*, p. 431). See especially Melinda Boyd, 'Gendered Voices: The "Liebesfrühling" Lieder of Robert and Clara Schumann', *19th-Century Music*, 23 (1999), 145–62, who observes how 'the gender identity of the poetic voice is often ambiguous' in this collection, and moreover an element which both Robert and Clara recognised and exploited in their settings (146). The question of gender or androgyny is comparatively unexplored in Schumann's output, certainly in relation to existing scholarship on some of his contemporaries (see, for instance, the studies by Jean-Jacques Nattiez, *Wagner Androgyne*, trans. Stewart Spencer (Princeton: Princeton University Press, 1993), esp. pp. 111–27, and Jeffery Kallberg, *Chopin at the Boundaries: Sex, History, and Musical Genre* (Cambridge, MA: Harvard University Press, 1996), pp. 78–86). One of the few accounts beyond Boyd's article is given by Claudine Jacques in her examination of the later dramatic works ('Gender Transitivity in Three Dramatic Works by Robert Schumann: the *Szenen aus Goethes* Faust (WoO 3), *Genoveva* Op. 81, *Das Paradies und die Peri* Op. 50', PhD diss., McGill University, 2011).

to lose itself in the sea. But the mussel came and enclosed it: 'you shall now be my pearl. You shall not fear the waves, for I shall carry you calmly though them.' Earlier commentators have interpreted the meaning of these lines autobiographically: the loving Robert will support his new wife's fragile attempts at composition; together they will produce precious musical offspring.[22] Schumann's setting of the mussel's speech brings out this sense of privileged interiority, slipping unexpectedly to the flattened mediant Cb from the dominant Eb and enclosing the lines within a fourfold plagal oscillation, before a linear descent in the bass (eb^1–bb) guides the music back over shoals of diminished sevenths to the safety of E flat harmony for the entry of the second verse (Ex. 5.2).

But, as Melinda Boyd observes, there is a peculiar gender reversal present here.[23] Traditionally the heavens are denoted as masculine, fertilising the feminine earth with its life-giving rain. Greek myth, for instance, tells of Ouranos' coupling with Gaia as a mystical sexual union between heaven and the earth; more graphically, one might also recall Zeus, everresourceful when it came to mortal affairs, impregnating Danaë with a shower from heaven. Even in the German the definite articles point to this: the sperm-like tear is admittedly feminine (die Träne), but it falls from the masculine heaven (der Himmel), while the mussel is clearly only ever going to be feminine (die Muschel). From this perspective, an androgynous Schumann appears to be the womb-like mussel enclosing Clara's fragile seed. At the very least, the masculine element in this poem appears to be strangely passive, utterly reliant on the feminine for its sustenance.

At the close of the song a new theme emerges in the piano accompaniment as postlude; an undisguised allusion to the popular Neapolitan aria 'Caro mio ben', this is the unexpected offspring of the song, the 'pearl' produced by the union.[24] Clara had learned she was pregnant for the first time a few weeks before Schumann wrote this song, and it is undoubtedly tempting to read an

---

[22] See Graham Johnson, notes to *The Songs of Robert Schumann*, vol. 4, Hyperion CDJ33104 (2000), p. 52. Many writers also interpret the mussel more generally as the male poet offering his loving protection to his female beloved (see Sams, *The Songs of Robert Schumann*, p. 179, Astra Desmond, *Schumann Songs* (London: BBC, 1972), p. 42).

[23] See Boyd, 'Gendered Voices', 154–6, whose article provides a more detailed account of the often-ambiguous gender symbolism throughout the cycle than I can give here. Though relying in part upon Sams's discredited positing of a 'Clara motive', Boyd's conclusion resonates strongly with my current concerns: that the "implicit" or gender-neutral songs appear to acknowledge – or perhaps even yearn for – a more reciprocal, flexible, and less binaristic relationship' between the sexes, concluding thereby that 'the ambiguity of Rückert's poetry proved ideally suited to Robert's concept of "one heart and one soul"' (158).

[24] The song, by Giordani, dates from the 1780s, although which Giordani actually wrote it – Giuseppe senior, Tommaso, or Giuseppe junior – is unclear.

Ex. 5.2 Schumann: 'Der Himmel hat eine Träne geweint' (Rückert), *Liebesfrühling*, Op. 37 No. 1

Ex. 5.2 (Cont.)

autobiographical reference to the events of the couple's life here. This meta-phorical association between procreation and artistic creation will also recur in several places in the cycle, most clearly in the fifth song, while the theme of fluidity, whether rain, rivers, or streaming forth, likewise runs throughout the collection, along with its associated male gendering and latent sexual subtext. In the second song, Clara's 'Er ist gekommen', the male lover has come in storm and rain; for the fifth, 'Ich habe in mich gesogen', the reproductive force of spring has awakened songs in the poet's breast, which stream out over the female beloved; while in No. 9, 'Rose, Meer und Sonne', the beloved is like the all-encircling sea, into whose womb all rivers flow (a theme returned to in the paired tenth song, 'O Sonn', o Meer, o Rose!').

The confusion between subjects found in this opening song – between male and female elements, between passive and active partners – is con-tinued in 'Er ist gekommen': did he take possession of her heart, the singer asks, or not rather she of his? Indeed, the entire opus is permeated throughout by numerous doublings and mirrorings. The final 'So wahr die Sonne scheinet' clearly transforms the melody of the opening song, framing the whole collection through such thematic linking, while 'O Sonn', o Meer, o Rose!' reworks the material of the preceding 'Rose, Meer und Sonne' just as its title and symbolism chiastically reflect it. Duets forming the sixth, seventh, and twelfth songs split the opus into

two near-symmetrical halves, each consisting of six songs and ending with
a duet (the latter starting with one too), while care has clearly been given to
the tonal succession of songs. Both halves are effectively bookended by
songs in A flat (the key of Nos. 1, 3, 6, 7, and 11, and the goal of No. 2) –
with the curious anomaly that having returned to this ostensible tonic in
the penultimate 'Warum willst du and're fragen' the final song is raised up
a level to E flat.[25] In fact, this sense of deliberate near (but not total)
symmetry relates to the larger process across the collection's twelve
songs, and this may be understood as a musical enactment of the progressive coming together of the two lovers into a higher union.

The first five songs alternate between settings by Robert (1, 3, & 5) and
Clara (2 & 4), their respective songs corresponding moreover to what are
plausibly contrasting male and female subject positions (even if, as we have
seen, in several the gender of the subject appears deliberately obscured or
distinctions between self and other partially collapsed). In the work's central
two positions, however, we find the first duets in the collection. No. 6, 'Liebste,
was kann denn uns scheiden?', is admittedly barely a duet; the woman has
little to do but dutifully offer monosyllabic agreement with her male partner's
assertions and to double his final phrase in thirds, and the number could
almost be given as a solo song for a male singer. But this is the first stage in
a larger movement towards the ever-greater integration between the two. And
(from an inevitably male-centric perspective) the attestation by the other of
the subject's expression, her mirroring back of his own words to him, might be
thought of as fulfilling a crucial role in his own journey to full selfhood.

Already in the seventh song, 'Schön ist das Fest des Lenzes', the two are
coming together in something approaching more equal status (Ex. 5.3).
Formed for the most part as a canon between the two protagonists, this
round-dance offers a celebration of nature's season of fertility, where again
the man leads and the woman takes a distinct secondary part ('following at
the wifely distance of a bar' as Johnson wryly puts it).[26] The two are finally
singing as individual subjects and singing the same material, but yet there is
a temporal displacement between their voices that only comes into synchrony in short passages towards the end. Only in the very last song will the
two come together in the same time, and in harmonious accord.

---

[25] On tonal considerations and the possible genesis of the collection's ordering see further
Hallmark, 'The Rückert Lieder of Robert and Clara Schumann', 8–11.

[26] Johnson, *The Songs of Robert Schumann*, vol. 4, p. 65. This imitative treatment is continued in
the following 'Flügel', in which from bar 20 the vocal line chases after the piano accompaniment
without ever quite catching it, just like the youth that the protagonist laments has flown away
from him.

Ex. 5.3 Schumann: 'Schön ist das Fest des Lebens' (Rückert), *Liebesfrühling*, Op. 37 No. 7, opening

This concluding number is, at last, really a duet, balanced equally between the two voices (Ex. 5.4); indeed, it is almost too much of one, the replication of parts, for some critics, appearing exaggerated in its utter simplicity. But this is surely the point. Throughout the collection the doubling of the melodic voice a third apart has suggested the harmonious union of two subjects (it can be seen clearly in the duet passages in the sixth song and close of the seventh), and the almost constant paralleling of the two vocal lines in thirds for the initial stages of this duet offers persuasive grounds for such an interpretation.[27] Yet, no less significantly, this model breaks down at the end of the first verse, and this will be for the crucial moment that the subjects make their mutual declaration of love. Reaching over the soprano's upper voice, in b. 12 the tenor part soars to an eb^1 and the two voices mirror each other in contrary motion; it may not seem much, but the contrast with the utter simplicity of the previous six poetic lines is striking and surely deliberate. The chiastic structure of the text here – 'Du liebst mich wie ich dich, dich lieb' ich wie du mich' – is further reflected in the prominent twofold voice-exchange (ab–c, f–ab) at this moment; indeed, as Rufus Hallmark has revealed, the words for the final repetition of this phrase at the end of the song were rearranged by Schumann so as to be sung against

---

[27] Only the horn-call-like fifths at the opening offer any exception to the persistent use of thirds (or tenths), imparting perhaps a suitably open-air character. The association of parallel movement in thirds with the concordance of two human subjects is longstanding; Sams codifies it as 'comradeship or togetherness' (*The Songs of Robert Schumann*, p. 21), while Jon Finson has picked up on this idea in Op. 25's 'Widmung', speaking of the accompanimental arpeggiations 'running symbolically in parallel motion – two voices acting as one' (*Robert Schumann: The Book of Songs*, p. 23).

Ex. 5.4 Schumann: 'So wahr die Sonne scheinet' (Rückert), *Liebesfrühling*, Op. 37 No. 12, first verse

each other, 'du liebst mich wie ich dich' sounding simultaneously against 'dich lieb' ich wie du mich' in the two voices.[28] In other words, by the end of the work the protagonists are not simply singing in parallel, but their lines merge into a composite entity, forming a chiasm, intersecting and reflecting

---

[28] Hallmark, 'The Rückert Lieder of Robert and Clara Schumann', 20: this modification is present in the autograph and original edition but was wrongly corrected in the later *Gesamtausgabe*.

each other. Schumann's musical images of reciprocity – his mirroring of vocal lines, contrapuntal voice-exchange and intercrossing – match the blurring and eventual identification of 'I' and 'you' in Rückert's text. Upon declaring their love and mutual recognition, the distinction between self and other has become annulled; two subjects have become one, and the cycle's male and female protagonists fused as one heart and one soul.

The Birth of the Self from the Image of the Other

In the example of *Liebesfrühling* the ambiguities between subjects have led to an ultimate union that might be contextualised as hermaphroditic in its overcoming of distinctions between masculine and feminine and self and other. But likewise, taken individually, the goal of each subject has been the recognition of itself in and by the other; the route to full subjecthood has been through the union with the other. This is true above all of the female figure, whose role in the three duets has grown to become ever more an equal partner by the end of the collection.

For some Romantics as we saw, the hermaphroditic union stood for the ideal of marriage as a fusion of equals, and in figures such as Blake and the Shelleys this understanding could be made to function in the cause of women's emancipation.[29] In practice, however, this end was rarely achieved in the early nineteenth century, and women for the most part still played a subsidiary role. Robert, in his relationship with Clara, was far from domineering, and as we saw in many ways looked up to her as his 'good spirit' or 'better self'. But it is still clear that upon marriage he expected her to fulfil her socially determined role as a wife and mother and only then as an artist (despite the fact that Clara was by far the more famous of the two at the time and a primary source of their income). Moreover, it is not clear that Clara herself would have desired full emancipation in the modern sense.[30] Despite Schumann's poetic ideals, there was still a worldly imbalance in this union of heart and soul.

---

[29] See, for instance, Patrick Bizzaro, 'The Symbol of the Androgyne in Blake's *The Four Zoas* and Shelley's *Prometheus Unbound*: Marital Status among the Romantic Poets', in JoAnna Stephens Mink and Janet Doubler Ward, *Joinings and Disjoinings: The Significance of Marital Status in Literature* (Bowling Green: Bowling Green University Press, 1991), pp. 36–51.

[30] As Nancy Reich has claimed, Clara 'was not a feminist and it is doubtful that she sympathized with the views of those women who were just beginning the struggle for equal rights in nineteenth-century Germany' (Nancy B. Reich, *Clara Schumann: The Artist and the Woman* (Ithaca NY: Cornell University Press, 1985), p. 275).

Probably the most celebrated, albeit controversial, example of such idealised but uneven conjugal union in Schumann's oeuvre is the song cycle *Frauenliebe und Leben*, written in the summer of 1840 just as the final obstacles to his marriage with Clara appeared to be falling away.[31] A cycle of eight songs to words by the (male) poet Adelbert von Chamisso providing a female's perspective on her marriage to a man she venerates as being far above her, *Frauenliebe* has understandably attracted its fair share of feminist criticism. Ruth Solie, for instance, has famously charged the work as offering 'the impersonation of a woman by the voices of male culture, a spurious autobiographical act', although later writers, in taking up this theme, have offered more sympathetic interpretations.[32] Even while no one denies the artistic quality of the music or the cycle's continued presence as a cornerstone of the Lied repertory, there remains for some listeners an uncomfortable aspect to these songs.

While conceding that the female protagonist of this cycle is generally depicted in passive, dependent terms vis-à-vis the male figure, and that such a relation was all-too-typical of women's position throughout Europe in this era, we should nevertheless acknowledge that such associations between man as the active subject and woman as the passive object were hardly inviolate, not least for Schumann himself. As Elissa Guralnick notes, 'Schumann's letters to Clara sometimes reflect the same devotional quality' as the protagonist of *Frauenliebe*, citing for illustration a passage from a letter of 1 December 1838 ('you're really the one from whom I receive all life, on whom I am completely dependent'), while Burton similarly observes how 'frequent references to Clara as a deity or priestess signify unmistakable superego attributes'.[33] A more flexible understanding of gender relations was already witnessed in the subjects' tendency towards androgyny and poetic symbolism of *Liebesfrühling*. In other words, the female protagonist of Schumann's Op. 42 not only reflects aspects of its

---

[31] The songs date from July, the month in which the courts ruled in Robert's favour against Friedrich Wieck's opposition.

[32] Ruth Solie, 'Whose Life? The Gendered Self in Schumann's *Frauenliebe* Songs', in *Music and Text: Critical Inquiries*, ed. Steven Paul Scher (Cambridge: Cambridge University Press, 1992), p. 220. Kristina Muxfeldt has countered Solie's charge in her contention that 'implicit in any sincere impersonation is always also a sympathetic identification with one's subject' ('*Frauenliebe und Leben* Now and Then', *19th-Century Music*, 25 (2001), 27–48, republished in *Vanishing Sensibilities*, p. 104). Rufus Hallmark has sought to contextualise the issue historically in his study *Frauenliebe und Leben: Chamisso's Poems and Schumann's Songs* (Cambridge: Cambridge University Press, 2014).

[33] Elissa S. Guralnick, '"Ah Clara, I Am Not Worthy of Your Love": Rereading "Frauenliebe und Leben", the Poetry and the Music', *Music & Letters*, 87 (2006), 590; Burton, 'Robert Schumann and Clara Wieck', 224.

male composer's own personality but may be taken in some respects to stand for any subject, male or female. Placing the problematic gender associations to one side, then, *Frauenliebe* offers an ideal illustration of the path to selfhood as being found through the romantic encounter with the other, seen above all in the emergence of the protagonist's subjective voice out of the image of the beloved in the opening song.

There is a curiously hesitant quality to the beginning of Schumann's cycle. 'Seit ich ihn gesehen' starts with a reiterated I–IV–V^7–I progression in the accompaniment in a slightly faltering, half-remembered sarabande rhythm, out of whose repetition the protagonist's voice emerges in the second bar with a doubling of the upper line (Ex. 5.5). The piano is

Ex. 5.5 Schumann: 'Seit ich ihn gesehen' (Chamisso), *Frauenliebe und Leben*, Op. 42 No. 1, first verse

very much the leading voice, from which the singer takes her bearings. Every note in the vocal line's first four bars is sounded first or concurrently in the piano, and the effect is of the subject's voice growing quasi-*parlante* out of the pre-existing accompanimental idea, entirely dependent upon it for its identity (a feature particularly apparent in the piano's linking gesture over the second two beats of b. 4). Jon Finson comments on the opening's 'somewhat irregular phrase structure and shifting metrical placement, as if both singer and accompanist have been thrown off-balance', and the initial three-bar melodic phrases impart a mildly unstable quality that is only partially compensated for by their sequential continuity.[34] Only on the last beat of b. 6 does a first hint of melodic independence arise with the singer's bb^1 – coincidentally or otherwise occurring on the word 'ich' – a note not present in the piano part until the following downbeat. Around this point, too, the music changes. One can scarcely talk of a distinct melody in the preceding bars. The vocal line at the start had been merely a doubling of the piano's upper voice, which itself had clearly arisen out of the harmonic progression, and while the continuation had grown mildly more lyrical, the sequential construction ensured it remained within the ambit of the underlying harmonic schema. But from the end of b. 7 the music blossoms forth into a true melodic idea, breaking free of the repeated harmonic model and the constraints of the limping sarabande rhythm into a conjunct, cantabile line. With this the subject is ready to venture out on her own. And now, finally, for the repetition of this phrase (b. 9), the vocal part takes wing and soars free of the piano accompaniment that has supported it thus far.[35] 'As if in waking dreams his image hovers before me' run the lines: it is as if the image of the other has given birth to the subject. Emancipated from the accompanimental doubling which drops out at this moment, the subject has emerged as a distinct musical voice – a coming-to-lyricism out of the image of the other.

This emergence of full subjective voice is the crucial moment in the opening song (and of course, as most listeners know, this is the same passage that will be so movingly absent in the postlude to the final song). One may see this, à la Emmanuel Lévinas, as a profound comment on how the self is constituted from the encounter with the face of the other, through a radical alterity which is always already there in the

---

[34] Finson, *Robert Schumann: The Book of Songs*, p. 37.

[35] Most of the pitches of the vocal line are in fact doubled an octave lower in the piano, but this is submerged in an inner voice and virtually never heard (a feature which will become hermeneutically significant much later at the close of the cycle). The movement here to more regular two-bar phrase units also contributes to the increased fluency sensed at this point.

world.[36] On the other hand, such concerns are especially noteworthy in light of the gender transitivity identified previously in Op. 37: just as in 'Der Himmel hat eine Träne geweint', where the male artist had nurtured the fragile female's seed, the procreative force has been allocated to the man. An androgynous male has brought forth the beloved, the female protagonist, from himself, whose gestation was marked by the reiterated cycling of the opening bars. (For a critic alert to the narcissist, male-centric subtext here, this conceit is possibly little more than a male fantasy of hermaphroditic self-sufficiency and reproductive auto-ability, like Adam bringing forth Eve from his own body.[37]) Either way, the path to the musical subject's attainment of a sense of self, denoted by the emergence of an independent lyrical voice, has been through the image of the beloved.

As if bearing out this reading, in the subsequent songs there is generally much more independence between the vocal line and piano accompaniment. This is evident already in No. 2, 'Er, der Herrlichste von Allen', where the piano part is largely reduced to chordal accompaniment and for its brief moments of melodic interest now follows the voice's lead (seen in the dotted rhythm of 'Holde Lippen', imitated in b. 6 in the bass) or offers a dialogic interplay with the vocal line in the interludes following the second and sixth verses. The one major exception to this rule is the fourth song, 'Du Ring an meinem Finger', where the almost constant doubling between singer and accompaniment is clearly marked as relating to the union with the beloved, symbolised by the ring she now wears. Briefly, but no less significantly, this doubling ceases in the song for the passage speaking of the woman's previous solitary state: 'The peaceful, beautiful dream of childhood was over [*ausgeträumet*] for me, I found myself alone, lost in an empty, endless space.' Caught between a cosseted childhood and a womanhood dependent in that period upon matrimonial union, the protagonist is rescued from her loneliness by the piano, which, in offering gentle support for the final words, draws her back to their mutual coupling.[38] Indeed, the use of interplay between voices to stand for union between the female subject and male beloved is clear in the

---

[36] The idea runs throughout much of Lévinas's work; its fullest elucidation is probably given in *Totality and Infinity: An Essay on Exteriority*, trans. Alphonso Lingis (The Hague: Martinus Nijhoff, 1969).

[37] The biblical Adam was commonly associated with hermaphroditism in earlier writings on the topic; see Busst, 'The Image of the Androgyne', pp. 7–8.

[38] More briefly, the obvious doubling of the vocal line drops out at one further point in this song, in bb. 25–6 ('I want to serve him, to live for him'), though the notes do not completely disappear as before but are contained within the accompaniment's harmonies.

postlude to the second song, where the intertwining of musical motives in the final four bars symbolises their romantic attachment – the crucial development in the story between the close of No. 2 (where she observes him as if still at a distance) and the start of No. 3, 'Ich kann's nicht fassen, nicht glauben' (where all of a sudden it transpires he has promised himself to her).[39]

Dein Bildnis wunderselig

The examples above from *Liebesfrühling* and *Frauenliebe* have repeatedly called up a cluster of related images and themes: doubling, reflection, the movement to fusion with the other that is at the same time a deepening or fullest consummation of self. As was found – implicitly in the opening account of the Piano Quartet, more explicitly in the theme of hermaphroditic union present within Schumann's own writings and the jointly authored Op. 37 songs – this is not merely a case of a femininely characterised subject finding completion in a male ideal (as seen in the preceding illustration of *Frauenliebe*), but may work either way, above and beyond gender distinctions. Their discussion points to the constitutive role played by the other in the notion of musical subjectivity. We might return then to the issue of how the other is necessary for the subject's journey to full self-consciousness, foregrounding the question left open at the close of Chapter 4.

Earlier it was pointed out that the attainment of full subjecthood, the knowledge of the self *as* self, faced difficulties when trying to overcome the seemingly inevitable split in the subject. A sense of immediate self-presence or subjective plenitude could be conveyed by music (as heard in the Larghetto of the First Symphony), while the emergence of a singing voice was held to imply strongly the emergence of a conscious musical subject (the 'coming to lyricism' paradigm), but it was difficult to show this subject was self-conscious, aware of itself, without thereby reintroducing a subject/object split. One option proffered was to make this quest temporal, as seen in a stylised process of musical memory whereby the subject appears to remember its own earlier self, demonstrated there across the course of the Second Symphony (though still, there remained a question mark in that piece over whose voice was actually heard). Rather than dividing the self into subject and object, the present chapter has suggested the grounds for an alternative

---

[39] The celebrated 'wedding march' coda of No. 5, 'Helft mir, ihr Schwestern', strongly supports this interpretive strategy whereby the postlude to one song may appear to narrate or enact events properly happening *after* the end of the preceding and *before* the start of the ensuing song.

solution: the fusion of the self with an other, with an object which reflects the self back to itself, through which the subject may recognise itself.

This, of course, is a move with enormous precedent and contemporary relevance for considering Schumann, being a key tenet of German Idealist philosophy (described most famously in the earlier stages of Hegel's *Phenomenology*), while a more highly flowered version, steeped in occult and mystical symbolism, was contained in the Romantic notions of herm-aphroditic union espoused by writers such as Novalis. It is a theme that has been implicit throughout all the preceding examples, from the fleeting appearance of a duet in the slow movement of the Piano Quartet that led to a deepened sense of self at the close, through to the emergence of the subject out of the image of the other in 'Seit ich ihn gesehen'. It will be found even more strongly, however, in two songs that Schumann wrote in the first half of 1840, his famous 'year of song'.

A perfect musical instantiation of this theme is the 'Lied der Suleika', Op. 25 No. 9, a piece dating from February 1840 and forming part of the set that Robert would give to Clara as a bridal gift.

Wie mit innigstem Behagen,	*How with innermost contentment,*
Lied, empfind' ich deinen Sinn!	*Song, I sense your meaning!*
Liebevoll du scheinst zu sagen:	*Lovingly you appear to say:*
Daß ich ihm zur Seite bin;	*That I am at his side;*
Daß er ewig mein gedenket,	*That he eternally thinks of me,*
Seiner Liebe Seligkeit	*The blissfulness of his love*
Immerdar der Fernen schenket,	*Ever bestows to her far away,*
Die ein Leben ihm geweiht.	*Who dedicates her life to him.*
Ja, mein Herz es ist der Spiegel,	*Yes, my heart is the mirror,*
Freund, worin du dich erblickst;	*Friend, in which you behold yourself;*
Diese Brust, wo deine Siegel	*This breast, where your seal*
Kuß auf Kuß hereingedrückt.	*Kiss upon kiss is imprinted.*
Süßes Dichten, lautre Wahrheit	*Sweet verses, pure truth*
Fesselt mich in Sympathie!	*Binds me in sympathy!*
Rein verkörpert Liebesklarheit,	*Love's clarity immaculately embodied,*
Im Gewand der Poesie!	*In the garb of poetry!*

The most prominent feature of Schumann's setting is the extreme overlap present between the vocal line and its almost constant doubling in the piano accompaniment. Few commentators fail to remark upon this property; some, like Stephen Walsh, are not entirely impressed by the apparent redundancy (the result, it is claimed, could almost be a piano piece).[40] As

---

[40] Stephen Walsh, *The Lieder of Schumann* (London: Cassell, 1971), p. 16.

Jon Finson has shown, however, Schumann's conscious adopting of a middle line between a Schubertian and Northern German song aesthetic is generally reflected in his tendency not to present the entire vocal part of a song in the piano; and thus when he does so, as here in 'Suleika's Song', the decision is surely salient: this doubling unmistakably signifies something.[41] 'If we ask why Schumann has written the music in this way', proposes Graham Johnson, 'the key word "mirror" comes to mind.'[42] The constant mirroring and shadowing of the vocal line in the piano reflects the precise 'meaning of the song' spoken of in its text: the presence of the other – and this despite his physical absence – attained through the subject's singing of this song. Indeed, we might say that Schumann's setting does not merely reflect, but instantiates this reflexivity, letting us hear how the voices of the beloved and absent lover may intertwine through the work of art they consciously share. But the mirrorings and reflections do not stop there.

In 'Lied der Suleika', Schumann was setting a poem published by Goethe in his *West-östlicher Divan*, written in the female persona of 'Suleika'. The composer was not to know what is common knowledge now: that in fact these 'Suleika' poems were substantially the creation of Marianne von Willemer, a much younger married woman with whom Goethe conducted a remarkable and largely epistolary romance. Goethe included her poetic creations – sometimes lightly modified, at other times as the basis for his own more extensive elaboration – under the name 'Suleika' as the feminine counterpart to his own 'Hatem' poems in his *Divan* collection, thus creating a fictional romantic interchange between two separated lovers that reflected a real one more acutely than anyone at the time could have guessed ('pure truth . . . in the garb of poetry', as the final verse aptly runs). The unsuspected parallels with Robert's own fusion of heart and soul with Clara's in their artistic collaboration in *Liebesfrühling* are obvious.

The crucial lines come at the start of the third verse: 'Ja, mein Herz, es ist der Spiegel, Freund, worin du dich erblickst' ('Yes! My heart is the mirror, friend, in which you behold yourself', Ex. 5.6).[43] The self is a mirror of the beloved; and in this identification between two human subjects their physical separation is overcome, a hermaphroditic fusion paralleled in Goethe's poetic amalgamation with Marianne von Willemer and matched

---

[41] Finson, *Robert Schumann: The Book of Songs*, pp. 5–7.

[42] Johnson, *The Songs of Robert Schumann*, vol. 7, p. 55.

[43] This third verse appears to be the creation of Goethe; the theme of mirrors and reflection is prominent in the preceding poem from the *Buch Suleika*, 'Abglanz', with its focus on 'Doppelschein', to which Suleika's poem responds (*Poetische Werke: Vollständige Ausgabe*, 10 vols. (Phaidon Verlag: Essen, 1999), vol. II, p. 83).

Ex. 5.6 Schumann: 'Lied der Suleika' (von Willemer/Goethe), *Myrthen*, Op. 25 No. 9, third verse

in the virtually constant reflection of voice in accompaniment.[44] The musical mirroring is indeed astoundingly close, far more than the typical Schumannesque heterophonic accompanimental blurring: even ornamental turn figures are included in the piano part, with merely occasional moments when the two voices are slightly out of synchrony, one fractionally foreshadowing or lagging behind the other. It conveys the impression of two voices coming together in near unanimity, as if the sympathetic resonance between the song in which the absent lover expresses himself and the subject's own feelings, between his image and her heart, is near identical.[45] In the continual returning of the music of the opening verse

[44] Indeed, the number of mirrorings is remarkable: these are texts adopting a female perspective ostensibly written by a man but actually penned by a woman and then extended by this man, that speak of the mirroring of the other in the self, in whose heart the Other recognises himself. And they were set by a composer given to drawing on his betrothed's music for his own compositions, who himself had written barely a year before that she could see herself mirrored in his heart, and barely a year later would be collaborating with her on a joint work published under both their names.

[45] With what one should identify the voice and the accompaniment here is open to interpretation. In the context of the *Divan*, the 'song' mentioned in this 'Lied der Suleika' is presumably the preceding 'Abglanz' from Hatem, but in the immediate context of Schumann's setting we might

(the repetition at the end of the first stanza allowing a five-part ABABA design) Schumann moreover creates a form in which the constant movement away from and back to the opening melody seems to reflect the movement away from and return to self, the reflection of other in self (one in which the third verse, with its mirroring of the beloved in the subject's heart, occupies the centre or heart of the setting). The ultimate union of lover and beloved is given in the postlude: as in the second song from *Frauenliebe*, 'entwined counterpoint in contrary motion roves over the two staves and indicates a conversation of male and female voices as well as a colloquy of mirror images'.[46]

To put this feature into relief, we might compare this song of Suleika with another setting Schumann made – unbeknown – of Marianne von Willemer's verse, the 'Liebeslied', Op. 51 No. 5 (published in 1850).[47] Here, the subject longs 'to open my heart to you', but the other is absent: 'How sadly the world looks at me! In my mind my friend alone dwells . . . I long to embrace him, and cannot.' Instead of constant doubling between voice and piano, we have merely occasional duplicated pitches hidden within the accompanimental figuration – 'rustling semiquavers in vaguely disjointed patterns, which are all about aspiration and a vain search for happiness' – that only here and there shadow the singer's part in distorted reverberation.[48] Wisps of a lyrical line do emerge, fitfully, in the piano, but rather than doubling the voice they respond to it during its silences; this is a duet where the two subjects are separated from each other in time as they are in space. The contrast with the Op. 25 Suleika setting is especially revealing.

Of course, the other, the beloved, is also physically absent in 'Lied der Suleika', but here, crucially, this song is explicitly conceived as the means for bringing them together, creating a union in which the distance in time and space is overcome – an articulation of musical reflexivity familiar from the examples by Beethoven and Schumann discussed earlier. Art reflects or may even constitute this task of subjective self-knowledge, bridging the

well take it as referring reflexively to itself. Thus, the female subject sings a vocal line which is actually her male beloved's song and finds her own feelings (expressed in the piano accompaniment) to be almost totally in sympathy, hence the virtual unanimity between the two. A particularly delightful touch is the moments when the piano part overlaps the vocal line upon repetition of a chromatic rising figure in verses 1, 3, and 5 (ascending a fifth rather than descending a fourth for 'scheinst zu sagen' and 'wo deine Siegel'), as if the singer's heart is skipping a beat in joy.

[46] Johnson, *The Songs of Robert Schumann*, vol. 7, p. 55.

[47] Again, a collaboration between von Willemer and Goethe (the title is Schumann's). It was published cryptically in the 'Ciphers' section of the lengthy supplementary 'Noten und Abhandlungen' Goethe appended to the *Divan*.

[48] The apt characterisation is Johnson's (*The Songs of Robert Schumann*, vol. 4, p. 13).

distance between lover and beloved, providing them with an object in which they may recognise themselves.[49] This theme will be taken up again in another song from later May of that year, the Eichendorff setting 'Intermezzo', Op. 39 No. 2, which mixes the idea of the beloved's image with a musical reflexivity in which the musical subject finally becomes a self-conscious subject through hearing himself singing.

Dein Bildnis wunderselig	*Your wondrously blissful image*
Hab ich im Herzensgrund,	*I hold in the depths of my heart,*
Das sieht so frisch und fröhlich	*It looks so freshly and joyfully*
Mich an zu jeder Stund'.	*At me every hour.*
Mein Herz still in sich singet	*My heart sings softly to itself*
Ein altes schönes Lied,	*An old and beautiful song,*
Das in die Luft sich schwinget	*That soars into the air*
Und zu dir eilig zieht.	*and hastens to you.*

Schumann's vocal line emerges out of the syncopated pulsations in the accompaniment; presented in mid-air over $^6_4$ harmony, the metric and harmonic structure is first clarified through the left hand's tonic downbeat in b. 2 (Ex. 5.7). Initially the song seems to consist of a single vocal line with chordal accompaniment, but in b. 3 the piano's right hand answers the singer's falling fifth span e^2–$a\sharp^1$ with the rising fifth b^1–$f\sharp^2$, creating a new fledgling line which by b. 6 forms no longer merely a response to the vocal part but participates in the melodic unfolding, anticipating the expanded octave ascent in the voice by a semiquaver. From here on, with the disappearance at this point of the reiterated low A that had underscored the downbeats and underlying tonic prolongation of the preceding four bars, the sense of notated metre virtually vanishes. Verse two is given over to total syncopation in the piano accompaniment, with only the vocal line offering any sense of the real metre. From this state of complete metric flux the powerful bass octaves at b. 18 decisively reinstate the downbeat, coinciding with the point of return to the opening music and repetition of Eichendorff's first stanza, imparting a larger ternary form to the song as a whole. And now the bassline descends, briefly forming a new voice obliquely mirroring the vocal line above before driving the music through a strong cycle-of-fifths progression back to the tonic.

---

[49] An idea familiar in German Idealist and Romantic aesthetics; one of the best examples may be provided in Schelling's *System of Transcendental Idealism*, whose close holds up art as 'the only true and eternal organ and document of philosophy'. See my earlier discussion in *The Melody of Time*, pp. 120–2.

Ex. 5.7 Schumann: 'Intermezzo' (Eichendorff), *Liederkreis*, Op. 39 No. 2

Ex. 5.7 (Cont.)

This reprise of the opening verse is the crux of the setting. It is as if the image of the beloved, referred to in the text at this point, has obtained a deeper resonance inside the self: not merely the mirroring of other in the self, but now its recognition as well. But more than this, the repetition of the opening verse here informs us that it is *this* song, the very song being sung, that is the *altes schönes Lied* of the poem – and furthermore that the subject at last knows this, can finally *hear himself singing*. In the palpitations of the second verse, as the metric structure dissipates into pure, unmeasured pulsations of the self's own internal consciousness, we hear the gestation of this music, as deep in the singer's heart a song emerges, takes wing, and hurries to the beloved. And with the modified repetition of the first verse both we and the subject can actually hear this song, for it is nothing other than the song he has been singing since the start.[50] We should be clear that the text does not make this point explicit: this understanding is achieved by Schumann's decision to repeat the opening verse. The musical self-consciousness witnessed here is thus truly a *musical* self-consciousness, not achieved simply by textual signification but by the interaction of the words with the musical setting.

---

[50] 'Intermezzo' thus provides a stronger instance of the design of 'Stille Liebe', discussed in Chapter 4.

At the song's end, imitative entries of the vocal incipit twine around each other in a typically Schumannesque instrumental postlude (including some delicious false relations) – an explicit recognition and harmonising of both personas in the manner seen at the close of 'Lied der Suleika' earlier and which will be taken up in the second song of *Frauenliebe*. Augmented syncopations across the barline fittingly bring the song to rest.

'Intermezzo' forms the perfect exemplification of the path to musical self-consciousness, the objective that has been sought over the course of the last two chapters. It reveals the attainment of subjectivity in its deeper sense: not only the presence of self, but the knowledge of the presence of self, not only the reflection of the self in the other, but recognition of the self in the other. Through recognition of the other, the image of the beloved in his heart, the subject has become conscious of himself, of his own voice. In hearing himself singing, he reveals a coming to lyricism that is fully a coming to self-consciousness. And this has been realised not merely through verbal signification, but musically: it is Schumann's setting that realises this possibility. Momentarily at least, we seem to have found a successful movement to musical self-consciousness through the dialectic of self and other. For Schumann, such an accomplishment is hard-won; it will not always last.

*

In a famous *Märchen* or fairy tale interpolated into his unfinished novel, *Die Lehrlinge zu Sais*, Novalis tells of the youth Hyazinth, who leaves his home and childhood love Rosenblütchen in search of a mysterious goddess, the 'mother of all things', related to him by a travelling stranger. After years of wandering he at last comes to the dwelling place of Isis, where he dreams he lifts the veil of the divine woman – only to see his sweetheart Rosenblütchen, who falls into his arms. Their loving reunion is marked by the appearance of 'a distant music' – a quintessential Romantic symbol for the state of highest spiritual oneness, of being at home with the world. This ending distinctly mirrors a fragment left by Novalis that is thought to transmit the story's ending, in which it is told how one of the apprentices at Sais finally managed to lift the veil of the goddess. 'But what did he see?' asks Novalis. 'He saw – wonder of wonders – himself.'[51] In both instances the truth sought turns out to be the same: the self is the other and the other

---

[51] Novalis, *Die Lehrlinge zu Sais*, in *Gedichte; Die Lehrlinge zu Sais* (Stuttgart: Reclam, 1997), pp. 81, 99.

the self. The path to absolute knowledge is none other than the path to full self-understanding, and full self-understanding may be found through the union with the beloved.

But another, darker prospect lurks under such total identification of self with the other, as Romantic authors were only too well aware. In his satirical novella *Viel Lärmen um Nichts* (1832) – the original source of 'In der Fremde', the song preceding 'Intermezzo' in Schumann's Op. 39 *Liederkreis* – Eichendorff relates the following troubling dream of the protagonist, Prince Romano:

> He was standing once more on the beautiful hills overlooking the Neckar by Heidelberg. Summer was long gone, and night was falling. From over the mountains there came an old and beautiful song ['das alte, schöne Lied'] from his past; he followed its tones over the sleeping landscape, lying silent and pale in the shimmer of the moon, towards his childhood home. Stepping over the body of the doorkeeper slumped against the gate he entered the familiar garden. Statues of gods slumbered on their pedestals; a solitary swan, its head under its wing, described silent circles in the pond. In the fitful moonlight he thought he suddenly glimpsed the beguiling figure of his sweetheart among the trees; but she seemed to elude him as he approached, as if he was chasing his own shadow. But at last within the bushes he caught up with her and grasped her hand. And as she turned to meet his gaze he saw – to his horror – his own face looking back at him. 'Let me go', he cried, 'you don't exist, it is only a dream!' 'I am not and never was a dream' replied his horrifying mirror-image: 'only now are you awakening'.[52]

Not only is the beloved in fact absent, but the self has merely been doubled – that is to say, split yet again. Like Aristophanes' divided hermaphroditic halves, the lover ardently desires the beloved with whom he or she may become one again. The subject seeks an other in which it may find recognition and completion, a solution to its own internal contradictions, into whose image it projects its own desires – but this may turn out all along to be merely an image of the self.

Eichendorff's nightmarish, psychologically intriguing story offers a warning of how easily the search for the other might spill into narcissism. For Narcissus, the mythical figure who gives his name to both a common genus of hermaphroditic flower and condition of excessive self-love, so

---

[52] Eichendorff, *Viel Lärmen um Nichts*, in *Sämtliche Erzählungen* (Stuttgart: Reclam, 1990), pp. 211–12, given in summary here. The opening landscape would have been well known to the composer: both Eichendorff and Schumann – like Romano it appears – had been students at Heidelberg.

enamoured did the youth become of his own reflection that he fell into the water and drowned. Resonating with the themes of this chapter as it does with unhappy circumstances of the composer's own life, this points us forward to the concerns of future chapters, where the other, and even the self, may in fact prove to be absent.

PART III

Hearing Absence

6 | Absence of the Other

Voices Present – and Absent

As the exposition of the first movement of Schumann's Piano Trio No. 2 dies away over the murmur of gently reiterated tonic harmonies, we hear a new yet distantly familiar melody entering sweetly in the violin (b. 106, Ex. 6.1a). As unexpected in its emergence as it is softly appealing in its simplicity, this new theme forms an unanticipated turn in the course of events, appearing at a moment of formal uncertainty in the movement. The exposition had already reached its structural close some bars earlier at b. 85, fourteen post-cadential bars drawn from earlier material subsequently confirming C major as the secondary tonality. Following the cadence at b. 99 the music's energy had dissipated, rhythmic momentum and thematic content being liquidated into rocking quavers prolonging tonic harmony. It is perhaps unlikely by this stage that we would expect to hear an exposition repeat (a convention still present in the first movement of Schumann's D minor Piano Trio, written earlier that year of 1847): the momentum has been attenuated too smoothly to lurch back to the assertive opening chords that launch the work. But after eight static bars of pure C major harmony devoid of any meaningful thematic content the listener knows some change must happen soon; in phrasal terms, too, we have reached the end of two units in the four-bar hypermetre that had been re-established at b. 91. (Four bars of tonic prolongation might have already been enough for a composer more given to urgency; even bb. 103–6 flirt with overplaying things.) Everything in the music is indicating that something will occur at this point.

It is into this vacant space that the violin's new theme enters. Seemingly unrelated to any material previously heard in the movement, and more distinctive as a lyrical entity than the second subject given at b. 51, the idea seems to be already imbued with an unusual significance.[1] But crucially, the

---

[1] There is a possible similarity between the new theme and the second motive of the second subject (bb. 53–4) in the descending line from $\hat{5}$, though I suspect few listeners would pick this up.

Ex. 6.1a Schumann: Piano Trio No. 2 in F major, Op. 80, i, start of development, bb. 106–18

melody itself might be familiar to many who are acquainted with at least some of Schumann's music: it appears to reference the 'Intermezzo' from the Op. 39 *Liederkreis*, the melodic line that was associated with the words 'Dein Bildnis wunderselig' – the image of the beloved that softly sung its way in tones to her there. And there is something about the manner in which it materialises now in the Trio that, even without knowing the textual associations, might impart a similar romantic tone to this later appearance. One need not recognise the possible allusion to the Eichendorff song to intuit that this theme provokes a similar sensation of unexpected recognition, of hearing a once familiar voice, one resonating with the promise of the romantic other.[2]

---

[2] Whether this theme should be interpreted as the voice of the other – given that it is the song sung by the self in the context of 'Intermezzo' – is admittedly open to divergent interpretations. In the context of the Trio, I am hearing it very much as a different voice – the voice of the romantic other – though in the earlier song the phrase was the voice of the self that expressed the image of the other. It should also be noted that the status of the Trio's new theme as a conscious quotation

Treated soon to imitative dialogue between parts before giving way to earlier material and a fugato that continues the contrapuntal techniques in a central developmental core, the theme reappears later towards the end of the development section over a V/V pedal, preparing the retransition (b. 228). Already here, though, the tail phrase has become shortened and now hints at the opening fifth of the fugato subject which has been heard so insistently in the intervening bars; the vision is no longer of the same intensity. Absent from the recapitulation, which as so often in Schumann's chamber music symmetrically balances the exposition, the theme is expected once more at the analogous point at the start of the coda, being prepared by the corresponding attenuation of texture. But now in place of the gracefully descending conjunct melody, when the same moment arrives at b. 379 we hear just a sequence of empty falling intervals (an initial fifth, expanded into a sixth and seventh) presented between violin and cello, alluding to the 'Dein Bildnis' theme in no more than barest outline (Ex. 6.1b). These intervals are thematic – the fifths growing out of the continuation of the second subject (bb. 72ff), reused conspicuously in the fugato theme of the development, introduced as we saw surreptitiously into the tail of the recalled new theme (b. 232), and thence expanded in the retransition to link to the initial octave drop of the recapitulated first subject (b. 270) – but they had no evident relation to the opening phrase of the new development theme that

Ex. **6.1b** Schumann: Piano Trio No. 2, Op. 80, i, start of coda, bb. 379–86

of 'Intermezzo' is not certain, given first Schumann's predilection for reusing similar phrases across his oeuvre, and second, the inexact match for the respective continuation phrases. More important is that it evokes a similar romantic mood; one can easily imagine that it does refer to both the song and the idea of a (probably female) romantic partner. On these matters see the longer discussion in Chapter 8; for a brief and less sceptical account of this theme as a reference to Clara Schumann see also John Daverio, *Crossing Paths: Schubert, Schumann, and Brahms* (New York: Oxford University Press, 2002), pp. 139–42.

they now replace. Only at the close of the phrase (bb. 383–6) do we hear an echo of the end of that original theme (unrelated to the apparent source in Op. 39 No. 2, but likewise a favourite Schumannian turn of phrase).[3] But the memorable opening phrase is absent, and absent where it should most be felt present.

Yet the theme might still be sensed as hidden somewhere within these fifths. In fact, the two share the same harmonic template, and alternate notes in the texture pick out alternate notes of the 'Bildnis' theme (c–[b♭]–a–[g]–f♯–[a]–g), albeit split successively across the violin, cello, and piano in pointillistic fashion. In a curious way, the listener hears the notes of the absent melody resounding from within the broken texture; but the link between them – the thread that holds them together – needs to be provided by our memory. Finally, the opening phrase of the theme returns in b. 477 for the coda's closing stretto (*Nach und nach schneller*). Again, though, the recall is incomplete: now the original concluding phrase is missing, the opening descent being heard in imitation and inversion between piano and strings, reduced to its thematic substrate in the movement's final bars.

There is clearly a major motivic conceit going on in this piece, the composer showing how previously unrelated themes are actually relatable retrospectively and finally liquidating their separate identities in the coda. In this sense, from a structural or formalist perspective one could interpret Schumann's procedure as skilfully integrating the 'Bildnis' theme (the 'voice of the other', perhaps) into the motivic substance of the rest of the movement (the 'self'). Yet on an expressive level, this underplays the sense of loss attendant with the breaking down of the once complete melodic phrase into its separate constituents, the sense that this technical integration cannot but diminish the spontaneous charm that the theme initially possessed.

We might perceive something of this quality in the way in which this material is reworked in the later movements of the trio. The amorously blossoming opening theme of the slow movement – that duet between violin and cello already referred to in Chapter 5 – seems distantly related; though descending from $\hat{3}$ to $\hat{5}$, it possesses an unmistakable affinity in conjunct descending gesture and romantic ethos. Still, it is curious that this opening melody should give way to a clear reminiscence of the actual first-movement theme at b. 14

---

[3] Compare, for instance, with the opening number of *Der Rose Pilgerfahrt*, 'Die Frühlingslüfte bringen'.

darkened into the *minor* key. For some reason the recall of the theme heard, lost, and then partially regained in the earlier movement gives rise to a sense of melancholy that casts an unexpected shadow over the romantic murmurings of the violin and cello just prior to it. It is this sense of giving way to a more amorphous stream of musical memories that dominates the next bars, with an echo of another Schumannesque inter-opus *idée fixe* arising in b. 21 (most familiar perhaps from the 'Romanza' of the Symphony No. 4). And even though the latter reappears later in the movement, the 'Bildnis' theme is never heard again.

The third movement, meanwhile, provides a gently melancholic dwelling on the residue of this idea, the empty falling fifths and canonic imitation between parts forming a reverberation of the first-movement material (even the successive presentations on $\hat{5}$ and $\hat{6}$ form a logical consequence of the first movement's presentation of the theme on those scale degrees in the coda's stretto). Since the falling fifth gesture was heard in the coda of that opening movement as the distant outline of the missing 'Bildnis' theme, what we have in the third movement is an echo of an echo (itself echoed canonically between piano and strings); finally in the coda, its echo is missing, the phrase going unanswered. Thereafter the new theme does not return. But in the course of the finale we might become dimly aware that much of the material of the trio shares certain similarities: the opening tonic $^6_3$ and rising $\hat{5}$–$\sharp\hat{5}$–$\hat{6}$ inner voice recalling the opening gesture of the first movement, and the latter chromatic line being further present in the cello under the violin's romantic cantabile of the slow movement.

On one level, as we have said, the trio might be interpreted in terms of a narrative that reads the allusion to 'Intermezzo' (if that is indeed what it is) as being incorporated motivically into a larger multi-movement work, which itself proves to be thematically integrated at a deeper level beyond this. But there is nevertheless also a sense of expressive loss attendant with this narrative of technical control and sophistication. By the coda of the first movement, the theme has become objectified into motivic and contrapuntal working. Even within the tender opening duet of the slow movement the recollection of this earlier theme causes a break in proceedings – as if in the midst of this romantic dream of fulfilment the recalled image of the beloved momentarily shows that something has nevertheless been lost. The 'Bildnis' theme in its subsequent reworkings never again recaptures the unsullied presence of its radiant first appearance. The image of the other becomes part of the self, but in so doing she has been removed from living, external reality. In being incorporated into the fabric of the self, the other has lost its alterity; it has become, in short, little more than an extension of the subject.

Maybe it was never any more than this all along. After all, in hearing the voice singing 'Dein Bildnis wunderselig' in 'Intermezzo', the self was merely hearing itself singing. Perhaps the other never really existed.

Voices Distant – and Present

The theme heard in the development section of the F major Piano Trio may suggest the voice of a romantic other not merely owing to the possible associations with the Eichendorff song and the 'beauteous image' of the beloved spoken of there, or indeed because of the manner in which it emerges and its seemingly intrinsic lyrical, romantic qualities, but further – more controversially – since it is a variant of what Eric Sams has christened the 'Clara' theme: a conjunct figure typically consisting of five notes, sometimes featuring a chromatic turn.[4] There is no hard evidence that Schumann ever thought of this motive in this way or derived its notes cryptically in the fashion conjectured by Sams, but the idea has proved seemingly ineradicable in popular consciousness. In such cases as the F major Piano Trio, we might understand why the view can seem alluring: the phrase certainly seems to be imbued with a private, inward significance, aesthetic susceptibility triumphing over the evidentially dubious grounding. In the earlier *Novelletten*, Op. 21 (1838), however, we unquestionably *do* hear a 'Clara' theme. This is the famous 'Stimme aus der Ferne' that interposes itself within the eighth piece, the melody being taken by Schumann from the 'Notturno' of Clara Wieck's *Soirées musicales*, Op. 6 No. 2. Here again, though, it will become unclear as to who eventually is singing this voice, as distance – absent presence – appears to become replaced by presence by the end.

The sound of the distant voice of the beloved forms an effect that Schumann dwells upon in this concluding number of the collection, the composer delighting in the poetic qualities of what Berthold Hoeckner has aptly termed an aesthetic of Romantic distance.[5] Heard first at b. 198,

[4] See Sams, *The Songs of Robert Schumann*, pp. 22–5.
[5] Hoeckner, 'Schumann and Romantic Distance'.

presented at *piano* dynamic and in elongated note values with respect to Clara's original theme, the characteristic melodic descent and octave leap of this 'voice from afar' is returned to in successively transformed guises, first at b. 228, re-clad in nocturne-like figuration, and subsequently towards the end of the work at b. 446. The first two appearances of the theme occupy what appears to form a separate *Novellette* in D major (bb. 129–281) embedded within the larger final *Novellette* of the set (which indeed does reflect the compositional genesis of the piece).[6] The theme enters towards the end of an extended codetta section following a small-ternary main theme (bb. 129–57); by this stage the earlier thematic material has been substantially liquidated, so the soft entry of the 'Stimme aus der Ferne' already occupies an area marked as valedictory in tone, increasing the nostalgic resonance of the passage. With this allusion to the distant voice of Clara's piece the D major *Novellette* appears to have drawn to a close, but curiously, following a *Fortsetzung* passage offering a second transformation of Clara's theme (bb. 228–55) the earlier codetta material returns, finally bringing the entire interpolated *Novellette* to an end already heralded as imminent one hundred bars earlier. It is as if we are resuming the codetta before the mysterious emergence of the faraway voice, as if the latter had never effectively happened; the effect is to mark off the *Stimme* as a parenthetical interpolation that occupies no time in the course of the music. Parataxis breaks down into a series of hierarchical enfoldings. Not only does the *Stimme* seem to issue from a faraway place, but it seems to be located outside the normal passage of time.

More surprising still is the final recall of Clara's nocturne theme, as this occurs in the final section of Schumann's piece, an apparently new and unrelated *Novellette* (bb. 282–561). Even more now is this a distant voice, one issuing from the musical past, if no longer from an imaginary spatial distance. Yet it is here given for the first and only time at a fuller dynamic (*rfz*), and finally at the original pitch level of Clara's theme. For some commentators this fact has suggested a symbolic union of Robert with Clara: her voice is now sung back to her by her lover, separated physically in space but united in spirit despite her father's opposition.[7] Having first

---

[6] The present F sharp minor opening section was added to what were originally a pair of *Novelletten* in D and B flat major to make the Eighth *Novellette* of the final version. See Hans Joachim Köhler, 'Die Stichvorlagen zum Erstdruck von Opus 21 – Assoziationen zu Schumanns *Novelletten*', *Schumann Studien*, 3/4 (1994), 75–94.

[7] See, for instance, Todd, 'On Quotation in Schumann's Music', pp. 101–2; Hoeckner, 'Schumann and Romantic Distance', 131, who makes a neat analogy with what he terms the complementary 'voice exchange' in the Op. 17 *Fantasie*.

appeared as a quotation from without, the melody is finally assimilated into the fabric of Schumann's own work. On the other hand, this is to miss the way in which even at its first appearance, the theme is materially linked to the preceding music. And even on its final, apparently triumphant resounding, the theme is harmonically unstable and never attains closure in Clara's key of F major.

Rather than appearing ex machina and being only gradually incorporated into the *Novellette*, even at its first appearance the other's voice grows out of the thematic working of the preceding material. The codetta passage from b. 157 suggests a post-cadential function in liquidating the leaping arpeggio motive from the preceding section over a descending $\hat{8}$–$\hat{7}$–$\hat{6}$–$\hat{5}$ bassline, the latter being transferred into the treble from b. 174, continuing the descent in two repeated stages ($\hat{5}$–$\hat{4}$–$\hat{3}$, $\hat{3}$–$\hat{2}$–$\hat{1}$; see the highlighted notes in Ex. 6.2). The conjunct descent of Clara's theme ($\hat{3}$–$\hat{2}$–$\hat{1}$–$\hat{7}$–$\hat{6}$/$\hat{6}$–$\hat{5}$–$\hat{4}$) hence grows fairly naturally out of this existing thematic substance, one already shaded with the hues of passing and distancing. Even the characteristic $\sharp\hat{5}$–$\hat{6}$ inner voice that supports the initial movement to vi in the recollected theme could be related to the cadential $\flat\hat{6}$–$\hat{5}$ motion in the immediately preceding bars, B♭ being enharmonically reinterpreted as A♯.[8] This 'voice from the distance', in other words, arises unobtrusively from the existing material of Schumann's *Novellette* as it is already fading away into the distance. And while the final recall of Clara's theme at b. 446 is undeniably more forceful, crying out its immediacy and presence, it remains a fragment within the wider movement, one which is never able to obtain completion.

Set up again through a suggestion of motivic linkage some bars preceding (cf. bb. 424–8), when the voice rematerialises it is at the same pitch level as Clara's 'Nocturne', though paradoxically the harmonic context is quite different. While the D minor harmony towards which the opening of Clara's theme moves functions clearly as vi in an F major context, this same D minor chord in Schumann's reworking arises out of a lengthy passage that has insistently pointed to an A minor tonic. Rather than being heard as vi, the harmony here functions as a momentary tonicisation of iv: the chord is the same, but the function quite different. Only near the end of the phrase would we realise the melody is heading towards F major, with the

---

[8] This $\hat{5}$–$\sharp\hat{5}$–$\hat{6}$ motive, we might recall, is also found throughout the F major Piano Trio; indeed, the romantic duet of the slow movement features this harmonic pattern supporting a scalic descent from $\hat{3}$, not at all unlike the melody of Clara's 'Nocturne'.

Ex. 6.2 Schumann: *Novellette*, Op. 21 No. 8, Trio II with the *Stimme aus der Ferne*, bb. 157–229

Ex. 6.2 (cont.)

seemingly decisive $^6_4$ attained at b. 469. Once reached, however, this harmony does not resolve to a root position tonic but dissipates back to the preceding A minor music; eventually, working its way back to its starting point, this final *Novellette* will end in D major. The minor-mode context in which the greater part of the theme is heard casts a strangely sombre shadow over the passage, and the projected F major goal proves impermanent, if not illusory. If Clara's theme has been finally grasped by Schumann in this work, if it has finally been made present to himself, it nevertheless has never been securely held, and will be ultimately lost. To the end, it remains a romantic fragment.

What the case of the 'Voice from afar' in the eighth *Novellette* points to is the uncertain status of ownership of musical voices, owing as much as anything to the designative imprecision and consequent ambiguity of the musical subject. One may interpret the piece as tracing a synthetic trajectory, an overcoming of distance and separation between self and other, where the alterity of Clara's distant voice is gradually subsumed into Schumann's work; but one could equally point to the fact that even on its first appearance this supposedly 'other' voice arises out of the existing music (the 'self'). Looking beyond the dynamic amplification, it is no more integrated with the rest of the piece on its final rendition than it was at the start. A standard formal narrative of integration and the imposition of biographical factors so common in accounts of this composer supports the former reading, but the musical procedures afford both interpretations equally well.

In this instance, the verbal designation in the score, 'Stimme aus der Ferne', helps indicate the alterity of the voice, giving some clue as to who is singing. Likewise, in a song, the text set may in some cases provide the means for ascertaining the identity of the voice heard. But even here, as we saw, words can lie.

Imagined Presence: The Narcissistic Dialogue

A theme ubiquitous in Romantic poetry and song is the notion of voice (and by extension, breath or sound) as a medium of presence, even – especially – amidst the absence of the romantic other from the self, overcoming separation by space and time, replacing absence with presence. Unsurprisingly, numerous instances can be found throughout Schumann's song output; beyond the examples already discussed, we might think of 'Liebesbotschaft', the final song of the *Sechs Gedichter aus dem Liederbuch eines Malers*, Op. 36, or the opening song of the *Minnespiel*, Op. 101, 'Meine Töne still und heiter'. But in some cases the pseudo-presence generated by the voice of the other is suspicious. One such example is 'Ihre Stimme', Op. 96 No. 3 (1850), a song that foregrounds voice as the communicative means to subjectivity and assurance of the other's subjective presence. August von Platen's text speaks of the power of the beloved's voice and the hold it seems to have over the self. 'Let me read deep within you . . . what magic being speaks from your voice!' There is something about the other's voice that the subject believes allows access to his or her inner being (its 'Zauberwesen'): whereas 'so many words are spoken aimlessly and forgotten . . . your tones reach me even from afar'. (Here, we might note, it is clearly the sonorous quality of the voice, its uniqueness as a medium of the other's subjectivity, and not the semantic content of any words spoken, that is decisive.) 'My heart and your voice understand each other all too well!' the subject concludes.

Both in the words and in melody, the song recalls aspects of the 'Lied der Suleika' from *Myrthen*, discussed in the Chapter 5 as an example of recognition of the self in the other in which full self-consciousness may be attained. But here in Schumann's later setting there seems to be a curious absence. For Graham Johnson, picking up on this quality, the setting suggests 'a love song turned into elegy by absence and distance', as if the voice of the beloved is 'a distant memory, something the poet has lost'.[9] The vocal melody is suitably melodious and clear (in this, proving more reminiscent of Schumann's earlier

---

[9] Graham Johnson, *The Songs of Robert Schumann*, vol. 1, Hyperion CDJ33101 (1996), p. 30.

1840 manner than many other songs from 1849–50), yet there is nothing like such a close mirroring between the piano and the voice as found in 'Suleika'. Most of the notes of the vocal line are picked out at some stage in the piano's accompanimental arpeggios (see Ex. 6.3a), but this is almost invariably belatedly, often on the last note of four-semiquaver groupings, an echo submerged within the texture, and in some cases this is probably due simply to the limited range of harmonic tones possible within the accompaniment. (More prominent, indeed, is the construction of the outer voices from parallel tenths.) In a song infatuated with the sound of the other's voice, for the most part we only hear the sonorous presence of one voice, and that is the subject's. If the self can hear the other, it must be primarily in his imagination, or through misrecognising his own echo.

But not entirely. Notably, it is only after the text speaks of those many aimless words that are forgotten 'even before they have died away', but how 'your tones can reach / my ear even from afar', that we hear the clearest sense of an independent vocal line in the piano's treble register. For three lines (bb. 16–21, Ex. 6.3b) the piano's accompanimental figuration changes, from arch-shaped pairs or ascending arpeggios that place the highest pitch on the final semiquaver beat to downward or mixed patterns of motion, which allows the uppermost note in many places to ring forth simultaneously with the melodic line, doubling voice with piano. Schumann emphasises the newly emergent line with crotchet stems in b. 16, and indeed for the briefest of moments we hear a melodic voice in the piano (bb. 17–18) that is distinct from the vocal part, a diminution of the opening motive in quavers. Perhaps this is the voice of the beloved wafted by the distant breeze, 'a suggestion of faint-heard whispers in a wind'.[10]

Ex. 6.3a Schumann: 'Ihre Stimme' (von Platen), *Lieder und Gesänge* vol. IV, Op. 96 No. 3, opening

---

[10] Sams, *The Songs of Robert Schumann*, p. 244.

Ex. 6.3b Schumann: 'Ihre Stimme', Op. 96 No. 3, bb. 16–21

Yet even this might merely be the wishful dreaming of the subject; those faint-heard whispers appear to be a distant reverberation of the self's opening melodic line. The melody is indistinct even at this fleeting passage of its most explicit acoustic presence, and its identity, as with so much in this song, remains uncertain. Indeed, introducing biographical factors into the mix, we know that Platen's poem was written to a beloved (a man in this case) who spurned the poet's advances. Nothing in the text can determine the veracity or otherwise of the reciprocation sought – there is no criterion of truth within the literary world of the text that will tell us whether the beloved even exists – but the poem is nonetheless the product of wishful thinking. The distant tones of his or her voice may well not be there, or there only in the subject's imagination; and Schumann's setting, especially when set against comparable earlier examples from the composer, provides sufficient ambiguity as to suggest the possibility of either situation.

In Greek mythology, we remember, it was the youth Narcissus who was unable to distinguish his reflection from another; in love with himself, he drowns in the clear waters of a pool. In Ovid's retelling of the story, his fate is connected to that of the nymph Echo.[11] Punished by Hera for her

---

[11] Ovid, *Metamorphoses*, III: 339–58.

mischievous loquacity, Echo is fated merely to repeat the ends of other people's utterances. Seeing the beautiful Narcissus, she immediately falls in love and tries to communicate with him by responding to the words he speaks. But while Narcissus is puzzled by the echo of his voice, as soon as he sees the nymph he is repulsed (such is the degree of his self-love that only his own image will form the recipient of his affections), and their verbal exchange comes rapidly to grief, the youth not realising that what he hears spoken back are merely his own last words. As a consequence of this rejection, the scorned Echo withers away into nothing and becomes a disembodied sound, 'a pure voice of resonance without a body' that to this day haunts the mountains and valleys.[12] 'Echo's voice is, in fact, not her voice' Adriana Cavarero explains: 'it is a mere acoustic resonance, a voice that returns, foreign, to the one who emitted it.' The juxtaposition of Echo and Narcissus in Ovid's version is therefore perfect. 'The absolute ego of Narcissus, for whom the other is nothing but "another himself", corresponds to the reduction of the vocalic nymph to a mere sonorous reverberation of the other.'[13] In thinking he hears another, Narcissus is in fact only hearing himself, just as in thinking he sees another, he is only seeing himself reflected; the tale hinges around misrecognition and auto-affection. 'In the end, in his exemplary narcissism, Narcissus "dialogues" coherently only with himself, not with Echo. He dialogues with himself, he interprets himself, and he misunderstands himself.'[14]

This most resonant of myths clearly reverberates in the present case. In all three examples discussed, there is a question mark over whether the other voice heard really is other, or at what stage this may become a projection of the musical subject's own voice. What distinguishes the voice of the self from the voice of the other (Piano Trio No. 2), the voice of the other from the voice of the self singing back the other's phrases (*Novellette*), or the voice of the other from the voice of the self singing as if it were that of the other ('Ihre Stimme')? Given music's denotative imprecision, this task is inevitably hermeneutic to a greater or lesser degree; even the presence of a text, initially seen as a possible aid, proves to be at least as open to interpretative ambiguity, introducing the possibility of (self-) deception. Perhaps when the duet is too perfect, too identical (an identity without difference), when it echoes itself without allowing alterity, we might have reasons for supposing that the other heard is merely

---

[12] Adriana Cavarero, *For More Than One Voice: Toward a Philosophy of Vocal Expression*, trans. Paul A. Kottman (Stanford: Stanford University Press, 2005), p. 166.

[13] *Ibid.*, pp. 167–8.   [14] *Ibid.*, p. 167.

a double of the self. Or when the purported voice of the other is an unequal interlocutor, a shadow of the subject, clearly derivative, the other might be supposed to be a figment of the self's fantasy projection. In music written for more than one instrument or voice, with more than one human subject interacting in performance, it may be easier to ground the reading of plurality, but again there are no clear rules surrounding this (as we saw in earlier chapters, a standard line of interpretation reads the singer and accompanist of the solo Lied as suggesting the split consciousness of a single subject). The double bind, of course, is that to the extent the other is shown as distinct from the self, the act of self-recognition becomes more troublesome, and to the extent that the two approach the identical, it becomes more troubling to perceive the other as anything but the self misrecognising itself in the acoustic mirror. Speculative, hermeneutic, to be sure, but upon such matters rest the issue of what is a duet – the self recognising itself in the other – and what, conversely, is merely a narcissistic form of ventriloquism – the self fantasising a relation with an imaginary other constructed in the self's own image.

'Music', asserts Slavoj Žižek, 'at its most elementary, [is] an act of *supplication*: a call to a figure of the big Other (beloved Lady, King, God . . .) to *respond*, not as the symbolic big Other, but in the real of his or her being'. It is therefore 'an attempt to provoke the "answer of the Real"'.[15] Music's ability to suggest a sense of subjective presence that is as powerful and pervasive as it is unclear in identity can be a powerful tool; but the danger is that the medium is so potent in suggesting this sense of presence that what seems to be a call-and-response, a dialogue from the self expressing itself in music and being answered by the other (even the 'big Other') is in fact just ventriloquism. This, of course, applies at least as much to us as listeners encountering the audible body of sound as it does to the fictitious subjects that one might construe as acting in the piece. Beyond any hermeneutical hairsplitting over the identity of these fictional voices in the music and poetic text, when we relate to music, when we identify with aspects of it as a surrogate subject or extension of our selves, we are often on some level engaging in this narcissistic mollycoddling too. This point will be returned to in a later chapter – as indeed will the question of the identity of the voice and the problem of mistaking the self for an other.

---

[15] Žižek, 'Robert Schumann: The Romantic Anti-Humanist', p. 192. Compare with Cavarero: 'In the etymology of the Latin *vox*, the fist meaning of *vocare* is "to call", or "invoke" . . . .the voice is an invocation that is addressed to the other and that entrusts itself to an ear that receives it' (*For More Than One Voice*, p. 169).

Hearing Absence

All three of the preceding examples foreground the problem of distinguishing self and other, and the voice of the self from that of the other, in music. They also highlight the problem of musical absence. As is explicitly recognised by the protagonist of 'Ihre Stimme', the musical voice can conjure up the sense of the other's presence even when physically absented – when heard from afar, or in memory.[16] Such is music's aura of evoking presence that it can sometimes be read as if real (perhaps even the 'Real', in the Lacanian sense proposed by Žižek). But what of those cases where music's 'call to the other' goes unanswered, when the other does not respond and the subject recognises this as such, without delusion or resort to acts of musical ventriloquism? In this sometimes-deceptive medium of presence, how do we *hear* absence?

It might initially appear difficult to see how music, an art form which does not easily divide into a signifier and a signified, which does not appear to separate medium from message, can denote its own negation (this is one reason for its apparent immediacy and sense of presence). One obvious starting point would be in the sheer absence of sound, in the use of silence. Silence, after all, is part of the musical experience, and unsurprisingly may play a major part in evoking the absence of a musical subject. But still, on its own, silence forms a rather limited means of achieving this aim and thus normally needs to be set up contextually; silence must be heard as a pregnant silence, as an absence of sound when presence of sound was expected. It is more in the relation between sound and silence, in the interstices between sonic presence and non-presence, that the effect of absence is most tellingly situated.

Music is a medium that is always a presence that is passing away into absence. As has been well documented, Schumann loves dwelling on the sound of transience, the present absenting itself, the dying tone. His very first published compositions feature startlingly unusual and idiosyncratic manifestations of this peculiar aesthetic sensibility. Thus, the finale of the composer's Opus 1, the 'Abegg' Variations, features a curious quasi-cadenza (bb. 196–7, Ex. 6.4), where the notes of the piece's motto (the A–B♭–E–G–G that in German musical nomenclature spells out the name of the mysterious 'Countess Abegg') are successively detached from the blurred chord formed from the work's opening harmony (the initial A is

---

[16] We remember how it was the phonic substance of the other's voice, the pure quality of the sound, not the semantic valence of any words spoken, that was highlighted in Platen's text.

Ex. 6.4 Schumann: 'Abegg' Variations, Op. 1, finale, bb. 195–7

contained in the anacrusis). Famously – notoriously – the sustained notes are marked with impossible accents. Obviously, on one level the passage works as *Augenmusik*, the score intimating us into the existence of a hidden essence that no sonorous presentation could ever realise. But still, as we hear the wash of notes gradually being released and the sonorous mass clarifies itself onto successively fewer pitches, we become aware of absence negatively through the increasingly fragile resonant remainder. For Rosen, Schumann here 'invented the idea of playing a melody by *withdrawing* notes from a chord – a melody by absence'.[17] In this case, the none-too-cryptic cipher standing for the (probably imaginary) female dedicatee is expressed by the removal of sound from a harmonic plenitude to a single tone, from the immediacy of the motive's full presence as a simultaneity to its attenuation through temporal distention, its emptying out or *kenosis* into the transient course of time. Fittingly, the non-existent other is articulated by her motive's sonic negation.

The final number of *Papillons*, Op. 2, is, if anything, a more thorough compendium of musical techniques evoking Romantic distance, if less purely startling than Op. 1.[18] Inspired it seems by a passage from the end of Jean Paul's *Flegeljahre* speaking of the sound of Vult's flute becoming fainter as he passes into the distance, the piece is replete with the sounds and symbols of Romantic distance: horn calls and the blurred harmonies of distant reverberation (taking a cue from the opening movement of Beethoven's *Les Adieux*, 'L'absence'), recall of the work's own musical past, and the increasingly fragmentary appearance of the thematic material

---

[17] Rosen, *The Romantic Generation*, p. 25. 'There is no more Schumannesque effect than the single note that detaches itself from a cloud of sonority' Rosen later opines (p. 663).

[18] For a more detailed discussion of *Papillons* see Hoeckner, 'Schumann and Romantic Distance', 63–72. It is possible the effect in Op. 2 gave rise to the passage in Op. 1; the first edition of Op. 1 (published by Kistner in November 1831) featured the motto at this point articulated conventionally by attack rather than by release; a later revised imprint (of unknown date, but likely after early 1832 when *Papillons* was issued) transmits the version familiar to us today.

towards the end. This is not so much the sound of absence as the sound of increasing distance, or of presence gradually absenting itself. But most characteristic is the penultimate harmony (Ex. 6.5), a softly arpeggiated dominant seventh, whose notes are again successively released from below in an iridescent rainbow of sonic non-being, presence turning to absence. Even his Op. 3, the *Paganini Etudes*, includes a curious if not bizarre example of this latter conceit in the composer's preface, Schumann suggesting the performer practice releasing the notes of D^7 and A^7 harmonies in ascending and descending forms respectively (Ex. 6.6; there seems no relation to the piece here prefaced).[19]

In these three examples, the natural transience of the musical tone on the piano is utilised by Schumann to poetic effect. The sound of the decaying reverberation is the sound of the formerly present moment already fading into the past, a type of direct aesthetic similitude of what phenomenology

Ex. 6.5 Schumann: *Papillons*, Op. 2, finale, closing bars, bb. 195–8

Ex. 6.6 Schumann: *Etudes after Paganini's Caprices*, Op. 3, preface

[19] 'Folgende Uebungen gehören auch in's Adagio' Schumann writes to introduce the musical example the context of a discussion of his third *Etude* (*Andante*); there is no *Adagio* in his entire Op. 3 set, however, and neither does Paganini's original *Caprice* (Op. 1 No. 11 in the first Ricordi edition), used as model, contain this tempo direction. The potential function of these D^7 and A^7 harmonies in the C major piece is also unclear; the A^7 harmony would in fact be identical to that heard at the end of *Papillons*, except that in Op. 3 the sound sustained descends from treble to bass.

might call 'retentional' hearing. It can also mimic (as implied in the Jean Paulian subtext of Op. 2) the sound of distance. Both these categories imply absence as a distant presence: in one, the object was present in the past but is becoming absent in the present (temporal distance); in the other the tones are faint owing to the distance they have traversed (spatial distance, albeit likewise implicating some minimal temporal passage). In neither case is the original source of the sound present in the here and now.

As already prefigured in *Papillons*, though, music can also conjure up a sense of temporal absence through its capacity to stylise or evoke the memory of something actually gone. This can take several forms. In one of these, the music suggests a stylised memory: we hear something that both is and yet is not there, the aural image of memory being present to the mind but the original object no longer existing in the present. This may be simply the recall of an earlier passage in a location where this return is unexpected, or it may be musical recall that is altered somehow to intensify the sense that this is now a subjective memory and not objective repetition; or indeed it may be formed by music never before heard but yet marked in such a way as to imply its unreality or pastness. Thus, a range of techniques for suggesting memory exist for Romantic composers, including dynamic reduction, blurred or decontextualised harmonies, and timbral attenuation; for some reason, musical memories are frequently slower too. Often contextual factors – the way in which a passage is set up – play just as important a role.[20] Through such techniques the music heard is marked as unreal, as not truly present, and may hence be interpreted as denoting pastness (or for that matter distance; the musical phenomena are largely the same). In another, more concentrated, and perhaps purer form, however, the sounding elements of music once heard do not return where expected: we are met with silence where once there was sound, silence where at least we were led to expect sound, or the absence of a particular voice within a texture. We as listeners have to supply this missing music, by activating our own memory. Silence is heard as absence, or lack of voice qua lack.

A variety of such means have been witnessed in the pieces discussed earlier. Thus, the 'Stimme aus der Ferne' of the eighth *Novellette* stylises physical and perhaps also temporal distance through the presentation of Clara's nocturne theme at a soft dynamic in an area marked as 'after the end' in function; the final number of *Papillons* plays with a whole range of distancing techniques including thematic recall and sonic attenuation; and

---

[20] I discuss these factors in more detail in *The Melody of Time*, pp. 150–3.

the coda of the Op. 80 Piano Trio evokes our memory of what is missing by returning to the accompanimental texture of the movement's new development theme without the reappearance of the original melody. Other examples can readily be found throughout Schumann's oeuvre. The penultimate piece of the *Davidsbündlertänze*, marked 'Wie aus der Ferne' (Op. 6 No. 17), plays with the suggestion of physical distance through the use of echo effects within a resonant piano texture awash with pedal, and with the idea of temporal distance through the ensuing recall of the cycle's second piece for its latter half, an unexpected and somewhat melancholy return to the musical past.[21] The first of the *Nachtstücke*, Op. 23 No. 1, disintegrates at its end by missing out odd notes of the opening theme in the right hand, an effect decidedly more sinister than that in the Piano Trio.[22] Or take 'Des Sennen Abschied', Op. 79 No. 23 (1849), a song which provides a notable example of a voice cut short, of absence when we expect sonic presence. Schiller's text from *Wilhelm Tell* presents an exemplary case of parting, distance, and future absence set in the Swiss Alpine landscape traditionally linked with the idea of nostalgia. A herding boy bids a wistful farewell to summer and the upper mountain pastures alike, over repeated rustic drone effects conveying the reverberant wide spaces. But in the second verse the climactic repetition of 'im lieblichen Mai' is cut off on the final word, Schumann leaving the implied repetition of 'Mai' silent (Ex. 6.7). Whether the boy is choking back tears and cannot utter the word or the wind has carried off this final syllable we cannot tell,[23] but the effect is deeply expressive; the missing word is left hanging in the air, the implied perfect cadence to E major breaking off before completion, the preceding crescendo met only by the soft return of the rustic opening figure in the tonic C major, with a new sense of depth and solemnity imparted by the transferral of the bass drones into a lower octave.

What is particularly of interest for the current discussion, however, are those moments where musical absence points to the absence of another fictive musical subject – when it has significant implications for the notion of musical subjectivity. In more extreme cases such absence can point to death. And looking forward to the concerns of the next chapter, when the

---

[21] A longer account of this piece is again given by Hoeckner in 'Schumann and Romantic Distance', 95–109.

[22] The procedure is not unlike the close of the funeral march of Beethoven's *Eroica* Symphony; the original title of this piece was indeed 'Funeral Procession', and as Holly Watkins argues, the absence here might well connote death (Watkins, *Metaphors of Depth in German Musical Thought*, pp. 108–9).

[23] See, for instance, the interpretation offered by Sams, *The Songs of Robert Schumann*, p. 208.

Ex. 6.7 Schumann: 'Des Sennen Abschied' (Schiller), *Lieder-Album für die Jugend*, Op. 79 No. 23, bb. 36–43

existence of the other is under threat, sometimes even the sense of musical self may become imperilled.

Absent Voices

Many of the preceding instances of Romantic absence have been of distant voices – voices that are or were there but are yet felt as distanced from the perceiving subject in space or time, and hence absent from the here and now. More acute, however, are those situations where voices are not simply distanced, but absent altogether: voices that are not heard at all, even though they may be expected. One such case, continuing and intensifying some of the themes highlighted in the last example, is Schumann's 1850 setting of 'Die Sennin', Op. 90 No. 4, a song about absence and echo, about the living immediacy of voice and its eventual disappearance from the natural world with the death of the singer. Lenau's text revisits the mountains and valleys of Schiller's 'Des Sennin Abschied', here with a female protagonist, the 'schöne Sennin' of the opening line. Her characteristic *Ruf* or calling figure ($\hat{3}$–$\hat{2}$–$\hat{1}$–$\hat{5}$–) is heard in the vocal part throughout the first two verses, with accompanimental support from yodelling triplet undulations in the piano (Ex. 6.8a). As the speaker tells of the 'cheerful speech of the mountains' awakening to her clear call we hear the echo of the girl's *Ruf* figure in the accompaniment (bb. 10–12). Forming a link between the first two verses, these two bars are in some respects analogous to the song's introductory bars, but beside the slightly altered harmony what was initially missing was just this reverberation; the echo naturally occurs only after the voice's call.

This innocent state of nature will not last, however. The two final verses speak of the time when, whether through following the path of love or through her eventual death, the herding girl will leave these arcadian slopes

Ex. 6.8a Schumann: 'Die Sennin' (Lenau), *Sechs Gedichter von N. Lenau und Requiem*, Op. 90 No. 4, first verse

and her tones will no longer resound throughout them. In the piano interlude between the second and third verses the *Ruf* figure is modified to remain on dominant harmony, and the call is now absent from the vocal line that opens the third verse. Just one last allusion to it is heard in the voice at bb. 26–7, the characteristic triplet figure now altered as the possibility of love moves the girl on to pastures new, but at the corresponding phrase in bb. 28–9 the motive is missing as the text raises the eventuality of the girl's death and the ultimate disappearance of her voice. From this point on the call is never heard again from the singer's voice; instead of which, we hear merely its echo in the accompaniment. As the grey rocks stand reflecting sadly on her lost songs, the memory of her call reverberates in the piano – a response to a non-existent source, the sonic trace of an absence subject, an echo without body. Schumann's setting demonstrates how the echo of a voice that is itself no longer there can convey far more powerfully than silence the absence of the musical subject.

Just as tellingly, the song does not even find cadential completion but fades away on a dominant chord – and not even the dominant of the tonic, but on V of vi. This same D sharp major harmony had earlier been prolonged for five whole bars at the mention of the mountains standing sad and silent (bb. 33–7), the strange harmonic stasis underscoring the barren landscape devoid of animating voice.[24] Though the music had subsequently worked its way back to the song's B major tonic, the final echo of the *Ruf*-figure in the accompaniment at b. 41 turns once again to the relative minor, and the piece ends on the latter's dominant (Ex. 6.8b). A similar technique was famously used in 'Im wunderschönen Monat Mai', whose dominant-seventh harmony is yet more unstable, though in that song the duality between F sharp minor and A major was much more evenly balanced. Here in 'Die Sennin', there is a far more definite sense that the piece has ended on the dominant of the wrong key. The effect goes beyond the aesthetics of the Romantic fragment commonly imputed to *Dichterliebe* and suggests the irretrievable loss of the original condition: the girl will return no more to these mountain valleys, just as B major may no longer be regained. Instead of which, we are left on an unfinished penultimate harmony, the sense of closure permanently deferred. The object of desire – the sonorous presence of the other's voice – is now forever absent.

---

[24] In fact, the parallel mode, D sharp minor, had already been heard in the opening two verses as the unexpected goal of the initial melodic phrase (a point also noted in Finson, *Robert Schumann*, p. 205).

Ex. 6.8b Schumann: 'Die Sennin', Op. 90 No. 4, close, bb. 32–45

In the reading just proposed, it is the voice of another subject, separate and distinct from the self, that is heard as absent: yet here, as elsewhere, the identity of the subject has a potential to become blurred with that of the musical 'self'. Although the text is written in a second-person imperative tending towards a third-person perspective, it is notable how the vocal presence of the singer takes on something of the role of the herding girl, whose human voice is contrasted with the natural echoes of the surrounding landscape in the piano. (We might perceive something of this passing identification in the reuse of the calling figure for the phrase 'noch einmal'; the singer's voice provides 'once again' the sound, becoming one with the source, even while the words speak of it in the second person.) In other words, the identities of the textual and musical subject can be slippery. While the text narrates the protagonist in the second or third person, the voice can often take on something of that persona with a first-person immediacy. By implication then, not only the other may be absent here, but something of the self too.

A similar ambiguity between an absent other and the self's absence of voice can be observed in what is surely the most famous of all instances of the missing voice in Schumann *Lieder*, the final song of *Frauenliebe*. In the eighth number, 'Nun hast du mir den ersten Schmerz gethan', the female protagonist mourns the death of her husband, bringing the cycle to a subdued and bittersweet close. The newly widowed subject speaks of withdrawing back into her interior world, where she still has her husband and her happiness. From this point, the text (and consequently vocal part) falls silent, but Schumann provides a piano postlude that recalls almost literally the accompaniment to the cycle's opening song, 'Seit ich ihn gesehen'. This recall has commonly been understood as a process of interiorisation of the image of the dead partner through memory, as Schumann's music realises something that is only implicit in Chamisso's text. The returning music is able to bring this memory of what once was forth, with an expressive immediacy that would be hard for words to convey. The vocal part is missing, though, and therein lies the sense of loss.

The recall of the first verse of 'Seit ich ihn gesehen' in the piano is almost literal; and as we remember from Chapter 5, the piano not only doubled much of the vocal line there but the voice seemed if anything to grow out of the piano (just as the subject initially seemed to take her sense of identity from the image of the other), so for the initial stages the absence of the voice does not reduce the effective textural fullness of the repeated passage. But of course, the vocal part is still missing, and this is set to affect just that memorable moment when the voice seemed to soar free of the piano's support at b. 9 in the first song, having finally emerged as a subject in its own right. The absence of the melody now, at the most expressive part of the whole phrase, can be heartrending (more so since the initial two-bar statement that was doubled by the piano is still there at bb. 30–2, setting up the expectation for the matching phrase at b. 32); we as listeners want to hear it – and yet it is silent.

And yet not completely silent. As both Charles Rosen and, following him, Kristina Muxfeldt have observed, even on its first appearance the voice's melodic line can be found hidden within the right hand's accompanimental chords, albeit primarily in an inner alto voice. For Muxfeldt, 'the retreat into an inner voice mimics a physiological manifestation of self-absorption, taking the melody into the register in which the widow might hum it consolingly to herself: sounding from within the texture, an octave below the original sung register, it becomes an emblem of her interiority'.[25] In some performances the pianist may choose to bring out the notes of the missing vocal line here, ringing forth from within the texture, interiorised an octave lower into the depths of the self, even though this becomes more difficult in the subsequent bars which break up and rhythmically displace the implied voice (bb. 35–8).[26] On the other hand, overplaying this latent voice risks missing something of the peculiar pathos of this moment. The melody has gone, at least in the full vocal presence which it had originally possessed, just as the other is dead, and no memory is really going to substitute for him; to keep the 'missing' inner voice only latent within the sounding harmonies is to turn the expressive screw to a more acute pitch. 'In the end', observes Rosen, 'the unexpected void is more affecting than the original melody.'[27]

Thus, *Frauenliebe* ends on a note of loss that is barely mollified by the self's interiorisation of the other's image (the crucial missing passage being appropriately that which had accompanied the text 'schwebt sein Bild mir vor' in the opening song). Indeed, the very attempt to make the missing voice resound, ending as it does inevitably in failure, adds to the pain of the loss. With the loss of the other, part of the self has died too (that self which had, problematically, taken its original identity from the other); after all, it is the widow's voice which is silent.

The Presence of Absence

Other protagonists of Schumann's *Lieder* cycles seem, however, to believe more fully in the possibility of bringing back the spirit of the dead. Probably the most curious example of such musical necromancy is 'Auf das Trinkglas eines verstorbenen Freundes' ('To the Drinking Glass of a Dead Friend') from the Kerner *Liederreihe*, Op. 35 No. 6. At the midnight hour the solitary protagonist toasts the spirit of his dead friend from the latter's drinking glass (evidently a sacred relic, the holy grail of

---

[25] Muxfeldt, '*Frauenliebe und Leben* Now and Then', p. 113.

[26] I think especially of a live performance by Kathleen Ferrier and Bruno Walter from the Edinburgh Festival in 1947, where Walter brings out the hidden line so prominently as to suggest there has been no real loss but more a transmigration of subjective voice.

[27] Rosen, *The Romantic Generation*, p. 115.

their friendship); in doing so, he senses the mysterious presence of his departed spirit once again, the truth that nothing – not even death – can part one friend from another. Schumann's setting is suitably out of the ordinary. An opening two-bar phrase harmonised in simple four-part homophony is met with an austere monodic response, doubled in octaves in the piano. The opening suggests a communal song, a hymn, or perhaps a drinking song from a German student *Burschenschaft*, certainly something convivial, signifying the companionship of voices joined together; but the bare line that answers it is solitary, disembodied, denuded of harmonic support, and consequently somewhat ambiguous in tonal implication (Ex. 6.9). This alternation between textural fullness and emptiness sets up a powerful expressive paradigm running throughout the song: the responsorial nature of the verse's construction, structured as a series of discrete melodic phrases in a manner akin to a chorale, underscores how this opening call to collectiveness, to share in the presence of friends, is answered by an uncanny absence. The fact that the harmony of these awkward and sometimes tonally obscure unison lines is not there in actuality but only an absent potential aptly conveys this sense of non-being in the midst of the protagonist's own present experience. There is the sense of something continually missing which was once there – the body of the dead friend, his tangible, material presence.

The start of verse two shifts unexpectedly down to D flat major, the ambiguity of the preceding unharmonised line utilised by reinterpreting the concluding F of the opening verse (perhaps implying $\hat{5}$ of the dominant, B♭) as $\hat{3}$ of D♭, imparting a sense of warm interiority to the music at this point as the singer praises the qualities of the German wine with which he is filling the hallowed vessel. Now more than ever the full texture and harmonic language suggest a chorale, a mildly sacrilegious hymn to the vine, though the abrupt tonal shifts – D♭ subsequently moving up another common-tone third to F minor – maintain the sense of uncertainty. Rightly so it transpires, for the critical juncture of this eerie ritual is intimated now in verse 3. In a solemn, partly unison setting, the protagonist speaks of the mysterious, almost transcendent experience that is coming into being – albeit one whose full nature is not yet revealed. Again, monodic bareness is contrasted with harmonic fullness, but now emptiness is answered briefly by presence – the reverse of the opening procedure. Unison G♭s, heard initially as a Neapolitan to the preceding F minor, sink down to incomplete F^7 chords (the fifth is missing), a foreboding progression whose angularity is emphasised by the exposed tritones in the right hand, and the figure,

Ex. 6.9 Schumann: 'Auf das Trinkglas eines verstorbenen Freundes' (Kerner), *Zwölf Gedichte von Justinus Kerner*, Op. 35 No. 6

Ex. 6.9 (cont.)

Ex. 6.9 (cont.)

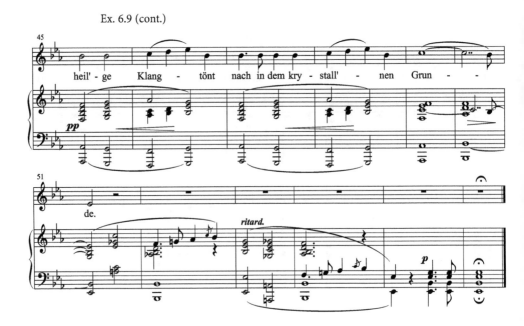

initially repeated in elaborated form on this pitch level, is then shifted down a fourth (with the interval of the tritone again disconcertingly prominent in the root motion from an F^7 chord to unison C♭s in b. 20).[28] From the concluding B♭^{7} harmony of this passage the music of the opening returns for verse 4: taking courage the protagonist raises the glass and drinks to his friend. But the most audacious line is saved to the end: the wine, it seems, has become blood (the dead friend's?). This somewhat macabre ceremony has become a sacrament to friendship, an act of communion that ensures the real bodily presence of the departed other through this unexpected process of transubstantiation. And it is verse 5 that finally reveals this mystical experience. The moon passes over the valley; the midnight bell solemnly tolls; the glass stands empty once more – but the sacred sound still resounds in its depths.

As the landscape is flooded with moonlight a mysterious passage of repeated seventh chords now offers a miraculous contrast with the preceding bare octaves (bb. 33–44). Connected by the principle of minimal outer-voice

[28] The bar numbering adopted for this song ignores the frequent partial bars of melodic anacrusis at the start of phrases. This same progression is echoed a few months later in the outer movements of the D minor Symphony for the portentous brass interjections that set off the development section.

movement, their harmonic progression ($B\flat^7$–C_2^4 –A^7–F_5^6) is essentially non-functional, serving in broad terms to lead from the $B\flat$ dominant to its own dominant at the end of the passage; the secret lies instead in the characteristic atmosphere these sonorities impart. Twelve bars they last, and we hear twelve sets of reverberations echoing between low and high registers: thus, we might think of the midnight chimes referred to in the text, and yet a strangely distended version, as if at this witching hour time itself is subject to a curious dilation. Taking up the incantatory repeated rhythms of the third verse, these chords form the full realisation of what was briefly glimpsed there as the isolated melodic line was met with the fullness of harmony – the intimation of the continued existence in some form of the spirit of the deceased friend. The air reverberates with the sonorous plenitude of these seventh chords, their warm pulsations enveloping the listener with the mystery of Being. This is not yet the emergence of lyricism, the indication of another conscious subject, but simply a more visceral sense of all-enveloping presence, something that can be felt, not cognised (especially after a glass or two of Swabian wine, incantation running naturally alongside decantation). The echoes of the midnight bell become transmuted into the otherworldly presence of the departed spirit.

'Leer steht das Glas! der heil'ge Klang tönt nach in dem krystall'nen Grunde' – it is unclear, however, which sounds the protagonist is referring to in the final line of the poem. On a mundane level Kerner's text might merely imply that the midnight bell still echoes on inside the empty glass (though this seems acoustically unlikely). More poetically, Kerner could be underscoring how despite the lack of material presence (the wine has gone; the body returned to dust) the spirit lives on (these enigmatic tones resound), playing with the established link between animating spirit and sound. This later reading is one that the medium of music is especially suited to convey, and seems to be brought out by Schumann's setting, whose final bars introduce two new distinctive melodic ideas into the song. First, underpinning the final lines of text (bb. 45–51), we hear a softly lyrical idea, whose repeated rising $\hat{5}$–$\hat{6}$–$\hat{7}$–$\hat{8}$–$\hat{5}$ contour possesses a distant affinity to those songlike themes that emerge at the conclusions of the Second Symphony and opening movement of the *Fantasie* in C. To see this as another potential allusion to *An die ferne Geliebte* would be rather far-fetched; but at the very least, we finally arrive at a undeniably lyrical melodic idea in the closing bars of the song, conveying something of the process that in earlier chapters was associated with the emergence of a subjective voice. Then in the piano's postlude, a further two-bar phrase materialises (bb. 51–3, repeated in the tenor voice in the following two bars); whether intentionally or not, this is a fairly close paraphrase of the concluding phrase of 'So wahr die Sonne scheinet', the final song of *Liebesfrühling* (see Ex. 5.5 in chapter 5).[29] There, the melodic line accompanied the mutual profession of romantic love: 'dich lieb' ich wie du mich'. The implied bonds of friendship as enduring beyond the grave would be touching in this interpretation (not to impose any stronger reading onto this passage).

There is a sense, then, that a subject has come to the fore by the end of this song in the emergence of lyricism by the end. But whether this is the spirit of the dead friend, and not rather the subjectivity of the protagonist who in this manner is able to come to terms with the loss of the other, is open to question. Unlike the duet in *Liebesfrühling*, two voices are not heard simultaneously here, mirroring each other: there is an intimation between the treble and tenor voices in the closing bars, but the former entry is unfinished, the descending $\hat{3}$–♭$\hat{3}$–$\hat{2}$ line in the treble clef trailing off, left registrally incomplete in b. 54 on the f^1. There is no sonic reflection of the living other here, but an echo, a memory of someone now dead, a conception that brings out how here, as in *Frauenliebe*, the other is constituted in memory, in the mind of the self.

This is not the last time that a Schumannian protagonist will attempt to summon the voice of the dead, however. In the incidental music to Byron's *Manfred*, Op. 115, the eponymous antihero seeks not only to see but also more crucially to hear the voice of his dead sister Astarte. In the spiritual netherworld to which he descends in Act II, summoning up her shade is the easy part; getting her to speak proves more intractable. And though he wishes to hear confirmation of the questions he puts to her, he desires even more desperately to hear the sound of her voice, 'the voice that was my music'.[30]

Manfred is already intriguing in this regard as Schumann's setting makes substantial use of melodrama, mixing outright vocal setting, instrumental numbers, and spoken dialogue with passages of text declaimed over an instrumental backdrop (melodrama as such). As Elizabeth Paley has argued, accounts from Schumann's lifetime reveal how melodrama was perceived as ideally suited for producing 'otherworldly' effects, given the

---

[29] This possible allusion is noted by Graham Johnson in his notes to *The Songs of Robert Schumann*, vol. 2, Hyperion CDJ33102 (1998), pp. 68–9.

[30] Byron, *Manfred: A Dramatic Poem*, II.iv.35, quotations taken from *The Poetical Works of Lord Byron* (London: Oxford University Press, 1909), p. 391. I am choosing to use the original English here rather than translating back Karl Adolf Suckow's 1839 German translation which Schumann used as the basis of his work.

mysterious provenance and uncertain diegetic status of the musical sounds within the aesthetic world set up by the genre (we don't see the characters singing but only speaking, yet music issues from somewhere), which leads her to conclude that melodramatic music was seen as peculiarly capable of bridging 'the gaps between the invisible and the visible, the silent and the spoken, and the living and the dead'.[31] After the well-known overture – one of the most powerfully developed of all Schumann's symphonic utterances – it is for this scene concluding the second part of his work (Byron's Act II Scene iv, set in the Hall of Arimanes) that Schumann contributed the most substantial amount of music.

Astarte's phantom is bidden to appear in a melodrama (No. 10, 'Beschwörung der Astarte', Ex. 6.10), the character of Nemesis declaiming over a soft passage in E flat minor for muted strings and wind. The meandering melodic line in first violins is repeated three times, each in varied form, over the most minimal harmonic support, forming an apt musical analogue for the wandering, disembodied spirit of the departed woman. Following the third iteration, the phantom of Astarte appears to *pianississimo* puffs of E flat major wind chords. 'Can this be death?' asks Manfred, such is the likeness of his sister – 'there's bloom upon her cheek'; yet closer inspection reveals 'it is no living hue'. 'Bid her speak!' he beseeches. But Astarte is mute.

This moment, where the request for acoustic presence is greeted merely by silence, by a sonic void, is the crux of the scene. More so, as the music trails off at this point on a Bb^7 harmony, the penultimate chord in a perfect cadence to the E flat minor tonic that is apparently withheld. For Paley, the missing E flat chord is paradoxically still 'heard' here, the perfect cadence completed in the listener's head in an example of 'unsung music', owing in part, she claims, to the expectation set up from previous versions of the phrase.[32] One might equally argue precisely the opposite: Schumann's decision to let the Bb^7 go answered lets absence eloquently speak through denying the most powerful sense of musical causality known to western music – resolving a dominant seventh to a tonic. But even this reading requires more careful analytical underpinning.

For a start, there is no unproblematic perfect cadence provided in any of the previous three iterations of the melodic phrase, so any straightforward expectation of a cadence here in the fourth statement must be partly

---

[31] Elizabeth Paley, '"The Voice Which Was My Music": Narrative and Nonnarrative Musical Discourse in Schumann's *Manfred*', *19th-Century Music*, 24 (2000), 4.
[32] *Ibid.*, 8.

Ex. 6.10 Schumann: *Manfred*, Op. 115, No. 10, 'Beschwörung der Astarte'

qualified. Each of these versions differs subtly from each other in phrase length, instrumentation, and harmonisation, though the first and third and second and fourth to some extent correspond. The first cycle (bb. 1–3) ends on the dominant, reached through an Italian sixth; the third (bb. 7–11) appears by melodic implication to reiterate tonic and dominant harmonies, ending with an IAC, though the accompaniment underneath stays fixed to the tonic throughout, thus undermining any sense of cadential movement. The closest model for the critical fourth phrase is the second (bb. 4–7), but the apparent cadence over bb. 6–7 is not, on closer inspection, a perfect cadence at all. Had the bass resolved from B♭ to E♭ in a timely manner on the downbeat of b. 7, it would have been, but by the time the cellos and bass complete the cadential root motion the melodic line has left the E♭, via a dissonant A♮, for B♭, already initiating a new melodic cycle. The attempted cadence dissolves through metric misalignment, consecutive melodic phrases being desynchronised from their supporting bass motion. Furthermore, while a perfect cadence is grammatically acceptable both here at bb. 6–7 and at bb. 14–15, the preceding music had lightly tonicised A flat minor just prior to this in a manner that slightly destabilises the cadential approach (having moved to the subdominant from the tonic seventh, we would expect at the very least an equivalent strengthening of the dominant through its own applied dominant here). It is slightly precipitous to cadence decisively back to E♭ now; indeed, given the propensity for chromatic slippage and deflected cadences in this work we might sooner expect an interrupted cadence to ♭VI harmony at this point (paralleling the progression heard repeatedly at the start of the overture (bb. 6–7, reiterated more forcefully in bb. 22–4)).

The point is not that a perfect cadence is unlikely here, but simply that the music has so far proved evasive to such clear tonal articulation.[33] Undoubtedly the listener expects a resolution to the pitch E♭ in the melodic line on the downbeat of what would be b. 15, but while a supporting E flat minor harmony is a likely option, it is not certain. In the event, though, the music breaks off, and we hear no resolution at all. Not only is no perfect cadence given, but no sound emerges either. And not even Arimanes is subsequently able to elicit an answer from the silent apparition of Astarte.[34]

---

[33] The new bassoon line added in bb. 13–14 in fact slightly strengthens the expectation of cadential closure in the fourth phrase, however, by adding the seventh to the dominant chord.

[34] Arimanes's command, solemnly scored for three trombones and tuba, finally provides what could be a perfect cadence, this time a tone higher in E major. As Paley notes, this progression could be thought of as presenting and reinterpreting the 'missing' E♭ as the D♯ leading note in the initial dominant harmony ('The Voice Which Was My Music', 14). I am more inclined to hear the initial B major chord as the enharmonic ♭VI (C♭) formed from an (interrupted) implied interrupted cadence at bb. 14–15 – the same progression that we noted was heard

Why does Manfred desire so strongly to hear his sister's voice? The answer, surely, is because voice is the exemplary differential between the dead and the living. 'Nothing without soul has voice' we recall from the sage of Stagira; and as Sigmund Freud is keen to remind us, the meaning of silence in psychoanalytical terms is clear: those pallid figures who in dreams are seen but cannot speak, who are strangely mute, invariably signify death.[35] The dead may be seen, but not heard. Even though Astarte can be seen again, until she speaks, until she emits a sound from the living breath of her voice, she does not really take on the semblance of life once more.

Both Nemesis and Arimanes fail to compel Astarte into speech. It is left to Manfred to accomplish this final act of sonic necromancy. And in Schumann's version, this is achieved with the help of music, in the extended melodrama of the eleventh number. Music occupies a curious position in Schumann's setting, a more complex one than in Byron's already highly musical conception: both the natural and supernatural world are given direct musical voice, but not the main figures – Manfred, Astarte, the Abbot, the Witch of the Alps, and so on, who are spoken roles. To a large extent, of course, this feature has a practical explanation, as this is fundamentally a spoken drama played by actors or declaimed by a speaker, not an opera.[36] Yet where does the supplicating music that finally elicits Astarte's voice come from? Can Manfred even hear it?[37] This is a question that cannot be answered fully here, but we might doubt whether the effect would be anything like as dramatically successful without the orphic eloquence of Schumann's moving musical backdrop. While Manfred implores through the spoken word, the orchestral music pleads on his behalf yet more eloquently. More than ever, music serves here as that 'supplication to the other', to respond even when from beyond the grave; and finally, it will in fact

---

repeatedly in the overture. Hence there is also a mild aural effect of I–IV rather than V–I to this progression at bb. 15–16.

[35] See, for instance, 'The Theme of the Three Caskets', in Sigmund Freud, *Art and Literature* (*Penguin Freud Library*, vol. XIV) (Harmondsworth: Penguin, 1990), pp. 239–41.

[36] Byron's 'dramatic poem' was already famously anti-theatrical in conception; on the question of the differing approaches adopted for productions of Schumann's work see Ardelle Striker, '*Manfred* in Concert: An American Premiere', *Bulletin of Research in the Humanities*, 85 (1982), 479–88, and Laura Tunbridge, 'Schumann's "Manfred" in the Mental Theatre', *Cambridge Opera Journal*, 15 (2003), 153–83.

[37] Similarly, Paley observes how 'Manfred's plea begins not with words, but with music. When he implores Astarte, "hear me, hear me" . . . it is not clear whether he is referring solely to the words he will soon utter or also to the plaintive music interspersed and interwoven with his dialogue' ('The Voice Which Was My Music', 14).

succeed in making the dead speak, as the shade of Astarte at long last utters a few desultory words before vanishing back into her native nothingness.

Music in this passage appears the essential supplement to language – superfluous, literally 'incidental' – and yet strangely crucial. And this attribute of Schumann's work furthermore bears out Manfred's own expressed desires. It has not gone unnoted how Manfred is concerned more with hearing the musical qualities of Astarte's voice than with the semantic content it imparts. 'I would hear yet once more before I perish / The voice which was my music, – Speak to me!'; 'Say on – I live but in the sound – it is thy voice!'[38] It is not that words really need to be spoken to impart information: 'She is silent, and in that silence I am more than answer'd' Manfred earlier observes, and even later when she does respond, Astarte conveys almost nothing in her cursory statements (totalling a mere seven words) – nothing at least that Manfred did not already know.[39] More than *logos*, he desires *phone*. As Cavarero has argued in this context, 'the voice is the equivalent of what the unique person has that is most hidden and most genuine.' What the voice communicates is 'precisely the true, vital, and perceptible uniqueness of the one who emits it.'[40]

But though Manfred wants to hear Astarte's voice more for its sound than for its semantics, for its musicality than for its meaning, and though it is arguably music that coaxes her to break her silence, at best she will only ever speak. Her 'music' is distinctly lacking lyricism. Astarte never sings – and neither does Manfred. Earlier we recall, he ardently sought to become music, that 'viewless spirit of a lovely sound, a living voice, a breathing harmony'.[41] Yet in Schumann's setting this troubled protagonist can never obtain musical voice, a state of lyricism, a sense of musical subjecthood. (If his is the music issuing from the orchestra, he evidently doesn't recognise it; this most self-absorbed of men cannot even hear his own voice.) Wishing to be musical sound, *phone*, he remains nonetheless a wielder of the word, *logos*.[42] He is but a broken man, a half torn from an incestuous hermaphroditic whole, where *phone* and *logos*, sound and sense, would be ideally united. And his lost other half,

---

[38] Byron, *Manfred*, II.iv.1 34–5; II.iv.150–1.   [39] *Ibid.*, II.iv.110–11.
[40] Cavarero, *For More Than One Voice*, pp. 4, 5.   [41] Byron, *Manfred*, I.ii.53–4.
[42] 'Manfred's expressly stated inability to sing makes him into a cipher for *logos*' asserts Daverio, a little loosely (*Robert Schumann*, p. 361).

Astarte – she who should be his music – a breath, sound, living presence – can provide no answer here.[43]

*

In Byron's drama, Manfred relates how Astarte is in so many ways a reflection of himself, both visually and vocally, yet his better half ('Mein guter Geist, mein bess'res ich!' he might have said, putting it in the lines of Rückert that Schumann dedicated to Clara in *Myrthen*):

> *She was like me in lineaments; her eyes,*
> *Her hair, her features, all, to the very tone*
> *Even of her voice, they said were like to mine;*
> *But soften'd all, and temper'd into beauty:*
> . . .
> *Her faults were mine – her virtues were her own –*
> *I loved her, and destroy'd her!*[44]

Such perfect mirroring, though, might once again sound suspiciously like narcissistic fantasy. The reflection is too exact, too idealised. As Paley observes, 'literary critics typically read the phantom of Astarte not as a remaining trace of her human incarnation but as a narcissistic reflection of Manfred's own mind, without any voice or identity of her own'. 'Astarte is (literally) dead and therefore devoid of any self-defining character of her own, frozen forever unchanged in Manfred's mind. [H]aving no independent existence of her own, she exists solely to complement her hero.'[45] After all, the first (and last) words she eventually utters are his name. And all she tells him – the only propositional content she ever imparts – is that he is to die the following day, the fulfilment of that wish for oblivion that he has sought since the start of the poem. In losing her he feels he has lost the better part of himself; having destroyed her he desires to destroy himself. In the moment of reflection of self-in-other, this example reminds us that the absence of the other can imperil the musical subject itself.

A point that the previous discussion has repeatedly circled back to is that of the reciprocity or mutually supportive relation between the other and the self; how removing one leaves the status of the other vulnerable. From the start, the distinction between the voice of the self and that of the other has proved on several occasions difficult to maintain. Thus, when the other

---

[43] This opposition between verbal speech and song is exacerbated in Schumann's setting, but even in Byron's original drama the 'music' which Manfred seeks throughout and especially locates in Astarte's voice is surely somewhat underwhelming.
[44] Byron, *Manfred*, II.ii.105–17.   [45] Paley, 'The Voice Which Was My Music', 6, 5.

appears to be missing, we may in fact be faced with a scenario where the subject is absent too. And in each of the last two sections the loss of the other's voice has appeared to cast doubts on the status of the musical subject, especially when the other may be little more than a wishful fantasy of the narcissistic self unable to recognise its own voice. If the subject only arrives at full selfhood, at self-consciousness, through its recognition by the other, when that other is no more, or never in fact existed outside the subject's imagination, the self may well become lost. The claims of this point can no longer be ignored. Thus, we now turn to those parallel and often complementary situations where not only the other but, more worryingly, the self may prove silent, vacant, or ultimately missing.

7 | Absence of the Self

The Abandoned Self: Attestation and the Absent Other

In 'Die Fensterscheibe' (Op. 107 No. 2) we encounter a variant of a familiar story. A servant girl is cleaning the windows when all of a sudden, *he* went by, proudly. 'He' is evidently a man of more exalted birth than actions, and clearly deports himself with some airs; Schumann gives him the little prancing fanfare that starts his setting of Ulrich's poem.[1] In her surprise, the girl claims, she thrusts her hand right through the windowpane. Her blood flows red over her hand, the pain burns; but at least he has noticed her. When he heard the sound of glass breaking, his eyes had been compelled to meet hers – something which had not happened for a long time. Had he but once glanced at her when he broke her heart, she laments.

Schumann's setting immediately places the female protagonist in a subsidiary position to the man who has abandoned her; while 'his' miniature fanfare demarcates tonic and dominant, her voice starts from a weakened tonic $^6_3$ as part of a cadential approach, the continuation of a phrase initiated by him (Ex. 7.1). It may initially seem artless, unconcerned even, the oscillation with the minor subdominant in bb. 5–6 idly prolonging the B minor tonic that is reached, but a sense of wayward chromaticism gradually infects her line as dotted rhythms herald the approach of her former lover. The cadence in an unexpected tonic major is immediately unsettled by the subsequent Neapolitan harmony in the piano's cadential echo. Each of the following two verses offers an increasing alienation from the B minor tonic, developing the subdominant tendencies and Neapolitan inflection of the opening verse by reinterpreting the opening melodic phrase in E minor. Each time, however, the music has to find its way even further back to the tonic

---

[1] It is tempting to think of him as a nobleman or the son of a nobleman, perhaps mounted on a horse in light of Schumann's initiating figure (Ulrich's text does not specify this, but note the song's close parallels with the following number in Op. 107, 'Der Gärtner' where, in a complementary situation, a lowly gardener is in love with a princess who rides by on a horse).

Ex. 7.1 Schumann: 'Die Fensterscheibe' (Lenau), *6 Gesänge*, Op. 107 No. 2

Ex. 7.1 (Cont.)

hast ei-nen Blick doch her - auf ge-schickt,   als laut das Glas ge-knickt.

Und in die Au-gen dir hab' ich ge - seh'n, Ach Gott, wie lang ist es   nicht ge-scheh'n!   Hast

mich ja nicht ein-mal an-ge-blickt,   als   leis' mein Herz ge - knickt!

by the end of the verse. The final bars are tonally unsettled, permeated by successive diminished harmonies and a curious rising chromatic bass that seems almost aimless despite its underlying linear basis.

Though the music is slowly infiltrated by chromaticism, the expression is muted, the pain numb (the musical depiction of the flow of blood in verse 2 is decidedly subdued, only the newly slurred syncopations suggesting a greater fluidity, Schumann eschewing any more explicit word-painting or expression of the pain that must be going through the girl). For the most part, this subject rarely attains flights of lyricism, just as she scarcely perceives her own bodily presence. Only for one brief passage in the second half of the third verse do we enter a warmer passage of fleeting lyricism (bb. 27–30), reflecting the moment when his gaze met hers ('hast einen Blick doch herauf geschickt / Als laut das Glas geknickt'). Not coincidentally, this also corresponds with the moment she moves from describing the man in the third person to addressing him directly in the second.

Here we meet a distinctly darker version of the theme already raised in Chapter 5: the subject's demand for recognition by the other. The forsaken girl desperately desires the man who has abandoned her to notice her: only by resorting to wounding herself does he cast his gaze at her. In this act of masochistic self-effacement, the injury is hardly noted: the abasement is such that physical pain (the sensation of oneself, one's own bodily presence) becomes less important to the subject than the recognition by the other – the demand for attestation by the lost love-object that the self still exists. Once again, the absence of the other causes a diminution of being in the self. Subjectivity, as noted earlier, is a relational quality, a subjectivity *for* someone, a mode of situating the self in the world vis-à-vis other subjects. When the self has been abandoned by the other, something of its full sense of selfhood has gone with it.

In this respect, 'Die Fensterscheibe', dating from 1851, offers a complement to the scenario already witnessed at the close of *Frauenliebe und Leben* over a decade earlier. This latter example has already been discussed in terms of the absence of the other, the image of the widow's dead husband being interiorised in her memory though the withdrawal of the singing voice for the piano postlude at the end of the eighth song; but it was also noted how ultimately it was the loss of the subject's own voice that was transmitted by this closing passage. The implications for the self were not spelled out there but warrant fuller consideration now.

It is worth underscoring how it is not the husband's voice that is missing (it was never heard in the cycle), but that of the widowed female protagonist – not the other, but the self.[2] And this is doubly significant, for as we saw in Chapter 5 there was the sense at the start of the cycle that the voice of the self arose out of the image of the other, the idea that the youthful protagonist initially takes much of her identity from the man she idealises as 'der Herrlichste von Allen'. (The fact that both the above examples transmit passive female subjects taking their identity from dominant male

---

[2] A more drastic critique would see the husband as already musically 'present' in the piano accompaniment at the start (as noted, it does appear to represent his image as seen by the female protagonist); thus, the cycle begins and ends with what is effectively the male voice, and the female subject is merely a derivation of his musical self. This might seem to offer some support to the famous criticism levelled by Ruth Solie that the female subject in this work is merely an other impersonated by a male self (Solie, 'Whose Life', p. 220).

others is admittedly problematic, but just as surely reflects a nineteenth-century social reality; there is no inherent reason why the relation should not be reversed.) Thus, the opening of 'Seit ich ihn gesehen' charted a musical coming to lyricism that mirrored the protagonist's path to realising her full subjecthood. Now at the end of the cycle, in losing the other, she has lost a fundamental part of that on which she had constructed her very sense of self. It is no surprise that the foremost musical sign of subjectivity, the singing voice, is now missing.

This complete withdrawal of subjective voice (in the literal sense, as the singer is mute for the last twenty bars of the work) is already prepared in the loss of lyricism suffered by the vocal line in the final song's opening twenty-three bars. In stark contrast to the preceding seven songs, the vocal part of 'Nun hast du den ersten Schmerz gethan' shuns songlike melody, replacing it by a recitative-like directness of expression. A bare falling fifth, numb repeated notes, a painfully slow climb back up the D minor penta-chord to the starting pitch where the whole process starts over again, the tonal estrangement through tenebrous flattened minor realms – such are the signs of the wounded, depleted subject, singularly lacking that sense of lyricism that marked the emergent subjectivity of the first song.

At the close of Schumann's cycle, the widow is silent; the piano may express her thoughts, a sense of interiority, but she no longer possesses voice. Rather than coming to lyricism, what we are faced with here is a withdrawal of lyricism, a retreat from subjectivity – that relational category through which the self negotiates and positions itself with the world – into a near solipsistic interiority. The veil falls, the curtains are drawn as the premature dusk descends; we on the outside can see no more into this private world. With the birth of the child in which, in the two preceding songs, she had seen her husband's image ('dein Bildniss!'), the patriarchal lineage may be perpetuated, but her own existence as an individuated and self-expressive subject is effectively over.[3]

The Absent Voice and the Failure to Attain Subjectivity

As we saw in Chapter 4, the emergence of a lyrical voice in a musical texture may sometimes serve to signify the emergence of subjectivity. The inverse, too, was shown to be present in *Frauenliebe*, where the subjective voice that

---

[3] Schumann particularly emphasises this point in the musical setting by echoing the music that at the end of No. 6 accompanied the words 'dein Bildniss!' in turn at the end of No. 7.

was tentatively built up at the opening of the cycle was ultimately with-drawn at the end, mirroring the sense that the self took something of its identity from the other, and correspondingly with the other's death lost a crucial part of its own being with it. In some even more extreme cases, however, there is simply no voice in the first place: the erstwhile subject or subjects have not attained a state of subjective self-awareness, if indeed they are there at all. Such is already indicated by the melodrama of *Manfred*, where neither the self-divided protagonist nor his lifeless sister (nor for that matter any of the principal characters) attain a state of lyricism – at least directly through vocal personification. Another conspicuous instance of this situation can be found in the three 'Ballads for Declamation' that Schumann wrote towards the end of his creative life (the first dates from late 1849, the latter two from 1851–3). In these settings of poems by Friedrich Hebbel and Percy Shelley, published as Op. 106 and Op. 122, a speaker declaims the poetic text over or interspersed with the musical accompaniment in the piano. This use of the melodramatic principle outside a larger dramatic context was apparently one of Schumann's aesthetic innovations (he, at least, thought it was new) and resulted in a curious, albeit little-known subgenre.

Obviously, Schumann's decision to write in this style cannot be merely attributed to a desire to reveal the loss of subjective voice in the musical protagonists, or indeed even more dubiously related to a perceived loss of personal voice in the later Schumann (incipient signs of mental illness leaving their mark, as biographers are all too wont to read). In part, it surely relates to his increasing interest in verbal declamation in the songs of the late 1840s and early 1850s, the move to a flexible arioso or recitative-like style of vocal writing which replaces quadratic phrase structures with something more akin to musical prose.[4] It also ties in with an increased interest in works for the stage and the dramatic or narrative forms devel-oped over the 1840s, which significantly extended the stylistic range and subjective ethos of the early piano works and solo songs. Ballads are customarily more detached narrative forms, where first-person subjective identification (the lyric 'I' of the Romantic Lied) is commonly replaced by third-person narration, and stylised melodic construction and mimetic word painting are more prevalent than the illusion of lyric immediacy. The difference in lyrical content between the still vocal setting of Schiller's 'Die Handschuh' (Op. 87) and the declaimed Hebbel ballad 'Schön Hedwig' (Op. 106), both dating from 1849, are only a matter of degree. Yet one

---

[4] This is a point which Jon Finson discusses at length in *Robert Schumann: The Book of Songs*.

further reason for resorting to the verbal recitation of text over musical backdrop might stem from the desire to convey the dramatic text at a reasonable speed (a principle akin to that governing recitative) – a feature probably most apparent in the Shelley setting 'Die Flüchtlinge' (The Fugitives), Op. 122 No. 2.

Nevertheless, in at least one of these examples the absence of the singing voice, underscored by the absence of lyricism more generally in the piano part, does seem to impart a telling aesthetic quality to the work. This is namely the 'Ballade vom Haideknaben' (Ballad of the Moorland Boy), Op. 122 No. 1. Hebbel's grisly and psychologically disturbing narrative tells of a youth who dreams he is murdered whilst crossing the moor on an errand for his master. Waking up in a cold sweat he finds his master shaking him awake and bidding him journey across the moor for him. The terrified boy cannot refuse but, encountering a shepherd's hut *en route*, seeks someone to accompany him to keep him safe. In a twist familiar from gothic horror, the attempt to avoid the fate foreseen only leads yet more certainly and cruelly to his very doom: in the face of the lanky lad – the shepherd's helper – who appears, the boy recognises the murderer from his dream, who insists on accompanying him despite his protestations. Unable to outrun him, the boy eventually submits to the inevitable. (In the most disturbing twist, the murderer insists on hearing the boy relate his dream first; he himself, it transpires, has had the same dream. We will return to this point in Chapter 9.) At least the gallows claim the murderer, we learn at the end.

There is a human voice in this piece, but this is merely a speaking one; it has not attained lyricism, falling short of ever reaching subjective expression. In this sense one may justly speak of the absence of voice. (It is worth underscoring that these ballads for declamation are not *songs*: indeed, neither Eric Sams nor Jon Finson considers them in their respective surveys of Schumann's song output.) The potential for the sonorous voice of the singer to provide a proxy subjective warmth to the narration (those cases, as witnessed in 'Die Sennin', in which the singing voice may sonorously embody the third-person with a first-person immediacy) is denied to the work. Unlike the melodrama that accompanied Manfred's pleas to Astarte to speak, however, there is scarcely any lyricism in the musical accompaniment either; only rarely does the listener have the sense that the music may be taking on the burden of expression for the mute characters (the boy's appeal to the shepherd being perhaps the sole occasion). In place of any subjective, cantabile quality Schumann provides motivic fragments serving as naturalistic scene-setting (the wind whining over the bleak heath) or the mimesis of physical movement (the frantic attempt of the boy to flee his pursuer). The means are not subtle: one may easily recognise here Sarah Hibberd's description of the melodramatic genre's 'clichéd vocabulary', involving the liberal use of tremolo, diminished sevenths and chords of the minor ninth, and 'swirling scalic runs to convey atmosphere'.[5] But such means are undeniably effective in conveying the nightmarish quality of the story, the compassionless chain of events set against the dreadful emptiness of the moorland landscape.

What is especially noteworthy here is how the piano's opening figure, a sinuous, chromatic descent from the fifth scale degree echoed in successively lower octaves, is almost identical to that which opened 'Aus den hebräischen Gesängen' (Op. 25 No. 15), in which, we recall, Byron's listless protagonist was suffering from a deep spiritual malaise (compare Ex. 7.2 with Ex. 4.4). In that earlier work, the soft emergence of a lyrical theme allowed a means for overcoming the earlier state of self-alienation, the music's coming to lyricism initiating a successful reattainment of selfhood in the perturbed king. But no such solace through the voice of music ever occurs here. The winding chromatic figure persists throughout much of the

Ex. 7.2 Schumann: 'Ballade vom Haideknaben' (Hebbel), *Ballads for Declamation*, Op. 122 No. 1, opening

Der Knabe träumt, man schicke ihn fort
mit dreissig Thalern zum Haideort, er
ward drum erschlagen am Wege
und war doch nicht langsam und träge.

[5] Sarah Hibberd (ed.), *Melodramatic Voices: Understanding Music Drama* (Farnham: Ashgate, 2011), 'Introduction', p. 1.

ballad, an omnipresent presence stalking the protagonist which no nascent lyricism ever threatens to shake off, which never blossoms into cantabile warmth.

This ballad is about the obliteration of a subject. It might seem indecent to convey such a gruesome tale through the quintessential mode of subjective expression; a human subject, after all, is murdered here. In such circumstances even singing may seem an outrage, clothing an inhuman act with the false garb of humanity.

The absence of subjective voice distinguishing Schumann's work corresponds aptly to the absence of subjectivity in Hebbel's story – the protagonist caught in a course of events that he foresees and yet which he appears powerless to change. Against the merciless machinery through which the plot unfolds the subject has no voice. (If only, like Arion, he could sing, he would perhaps have been saved.) But as was noted in qualifying this reading, the mere absence of a singing voice, lyricism, or some other characteristic marker of subjectivity in music should not necessarily be taken to be hermeneutically salient; there may be many reasons why a musical work would not manifest such qualities. Care, in other words, should be taken to distinguish the 'absent subject' from those cases – normally much more numerous – where one would not reasonably expect a musical 'self' to be present in the first place. Subjectivity seems to be a fixation in accounting for Romantic music, but not all music warrants the attribution of subjective qualities, and certainly not all of Schumann's music does either (we will return to this point in Chapter 8).

The Silent Voice, Withdrawn: *Humoreske*, Op. 20

For present purposes we are not concerned with music which simply does not seem to project some sense of subjectivity, but rather with those cases where aspects of the music, verbal text, or associated paratext may be taken to imply an aesthetic subject, yet where this putative subject is at the same time problematised, undermined, or silenced. To hear the subject as absent is not at all the same as not to hear a subject. The absent, self-divided, or internally conflicted subject, the subject that cannot come to full selfhood or realise itself, is still in a sense a subject. It is a subject that is lost to itself, or what, in psychoanalytical or poststructuralist terms would be called $\cancel{S}$ – the 'barred subject' or the subject 'under erasure'.

What Slavoj Žižek already singled out as the truth-telling function of Schumann's music was precisely this quality. 'The very formal structure of Schumann's music expresses the paradox of modern subjectivity' holds Žižek: 'the bar – the impossibility of "becoming oneself", of actualizing one's identity'.[6] The work he was specifically referring to in making this assertion was the last and for many commentators finest of Schumann's piano works of the 1830s, the *Humoreske*, Op. 20 (1838–9). *Humoreske* is a succession of six or seven smaller numbers which alternate passages of dreamy reverie with those of more vigorous assertiveness – Eusebius and Florestan as it were – in a particularly fluid structure.[7] Most celebrated, though, is the second section, with its famous 'innere Stimme' – a mysterious 'inner voice' written on a third stave between the piano's treble and bass, present on the page yet not to be played. This silent voice is in acoustic terms a missing voice and becomes a doubly missing voice later when the passage returns, the sounding substance unchanged but the inner stave missing.

Schumann's whimsical conceit clearly forms a continuation of his interest in the aesthetics of 'Romantic distance' already glimpsed in *Papillons*, in the 'Aus der Ferne' number from the *Davidsbündlertänze* and the 'Stimme aus der Ferne' of the eighth *Novellette*, with something of the enigmatic presence of the silent sphinxes of *Carnaval* thrown in for good measure. Humour is certainly also an explanation for this bizarrerie in a work named *Humoreske*, though, like his beloved Jean Paul, there is rather more seriousness to Schumann's humour than mere absurdity: after all, this was in his own words 'perhaps the most melancholy' of his works written to that date, a product of 'laughing and crying all at once'.[8]

The 'innere Stimme' appears at the start of the work's second section (bb. 251–74, Ex. 7.3a), a new textural idea in G minor that flirts with the B flat major of the work's opening (and in which key the section will

[6] Žižek, 'Robert Schumann', p. 205.

[7] The most comprehensive study of the work's structure and aesthetic background is given by Bernhard Appel, 'R. Schumanns Humoreske für Klavier op. 20: Zum musikalischen Humor in der ersten Hälfte des 19. Jahrhunderts unter besonderer Berücksichtigung des Formproblems', PhD diss. University of Saarbrücken, 1981.

[8] Letters to Ernst Adolph Becker, 7 August 1839, and Clara Wieck 11 March 1839 (*Briefe, Neue Folge*, p. 166; *SB* I.5:333 / *Briefwechsel*, 2:435). Appel provides a relevant background for Schumann's notion of 'Humor' (a combination of *das Gemütliche*, a great sensitivity and depth of feeling, and *das Witzige*, a sharp-witted irony) in Jean Paul's aesthetics ('Schumanns Humoreske', pp. 87–97, 165–94).

Ex. 7.3a Schumann: *Humoreske*, Op. 20, *Innere Stimme*, bb. 251–74

ultimately close). All the notes of the silent melodic line are present somewhere in the texture that is sounded, but rarely do the onsets of each coincide, and sometimes the pitches of the voice's melody are doubled only in another octave.[9] The melody both is, and is not, present. Charles Rosen's account of this passage is particularly fine. This melody 'is embodied in the upper and lower parts as a kind of after-resonance – out of phase, delicate, and shadowy. What one hears is the echo of an unperformed melody, an accompaniment of a song.'[10] We might be reminded at this point of something Schumann himself described a few years earlier, reviewing the first two volumes of Mendelssohn's *Lieder ohne Worte*:

Who has not once sat at the piano in the twilight . . . and in the midst of fantasising sung to himself a soft melody? If one can fortuitously connect the melody with the accompaniment in the hands alone, and primarily if one is a Mendelssohn, then the most beautiful songs without words will come into being.[11]

Schumann was not a Mendelssohn: the melody remains unsung in the piano. It is thus 'an inner voice that it never exteriorized. It has its being with the mind and its existence only through its echo.'[12]

It is worth noting that already Schumann's notation assures us of a paradox: in the reprise of the opening phrase at b. 267, the first bar of the inner melody is missing, though the music we hear is unchanged from b. 251 where this inner voice was notated. As Rosen puts it, 'for one bar a voice which was not present before is *not*, now, *not present*.' In fact, any notated rest in the silent line is somewhat absurd – a notated silence in a silent notated melody. Even earlier at b. 261 we have a comparable situation, as the entry of the initial d^1 is held over to the second half of the bar when it is no less not-present (or put more positively, equally shadowed in the sounding pitches) on the downbeat. To say this delayed entry was probably written for expressive effect might sound preposterous on a literal level, but there surely is this sense to it, if the melody is felt internally while performing or listening to it.

It is this contradiction between the presence of absence and the absence of absence that is highlighted when this passage returns near the end of the section. The second half of the passage (that following the double bar) is restated from b. 483 to b. 499; the outer staves transmit exactly the same notes as were performed the first time round, but the inner stave is now

---

[9] The stemming of pitches in the piano's treble suggests the inner voice is primarily conceived as the essential form of a melody that is belatedly echoed an octave higher in the piano, though some of the pitches are present in the same register (and even at times coincide metrically) in the left hand.

[10] Rosen, *The Romantic Generation*, pp. 8–9.

[11] Schumann's June 1835 review of Mendelssohn's *Lieder ohne Worte*, Op. 30 (1835), *GS*, I: 98.

[12] Rosen, *The Romantic Generation*, p. 9. For Appel, similarly 'The inner voice is, to speak with Hegel, the expression of a self-withdrawing interiority' ('Schumanns Humoreske', p. 269).

missing (Ex. 7.3b). The music that is actually heard is incontrovertibly identical to that which was heard earlier, and yet it is missing something, something that was silent and now is silenced. The practical explanation often given for Schumann's curious original notation is that the inner voice

Ex. 7.3b Schumann: *Humoreske*, Op. 20, bb. 447–89

helps the pianist bring out the right-hand melody that is stemmed in quavers above the semiquaver figuration – the upper echo of the 'innere Stimme'. As Clara Schumann related years later, the inner voice, she thought, was intended 'to give the pianist a support to the melody of the right hand.'[13] Yet these same notes are also stemmed in the reprise here, despite the fact that the silent melody is no longer there: according to the notation the performer should bring out the upper line just as before (the passage is marked 'wie vorher', though this is probably referring primarily to the tempo), but the inner voice – in the first instance 'to be sensed in a shadowy manner' – is now not to be sensed.[14]

The most audibly poetic moment is not, however, either of these passages, but rather the mysterious succession of chords that precedes the reprise of the theme's second part and in fact substitutes for the missing first half (bb. 447–82). In a curious way the listener hears the earlier passage with the inner voice resounding through these harmonies: the harmonic template is exactly the same as the first half of the theme, but everything has been augmented, the opening bar stretched into eight (subsequent ones being quadrupled), the rippling semiquaver texture flattened out into sustained harmonies, and presented softly following a diminuendo from *pianissimo*, as if heard from a great distance.[15] Rosen hears this later chordal version as 'only the remote resonance of the original appearance, an echo of an echo. It would be more precise to say here that the melody has disappeared and we are left only with the reduced echo of the harmonies.' Yet we might also perceive that another implicit melody has been picked out of the original sounding notes; not precisely the silent 'innere Stimme', but a new variant from the upper notes of the right-hand line (the ascending fourths d^2–g^2, c^2–f^2), with a more characteristic melodic descent to b♭ added at the cadence (d^2–c^2–b♭^{1}–c^2–d^2, bb. 475–82). The result is the sound of improvising an echo, 'an accompaniment to a melody which exists only in its reflection'.[16]

---

[13] Clara Schumann, letter to Georg Henschel, 14 May 1883, cited by Ernst Herttrich in the foreword to Robert Schumann, *Sämtliche Klavierwerke*, 6 vols. (Munich: Henle, 2010), vol. IV, p. viii. Clara confirms here that the inner voice is not to be played ('<u>Mitgespielt</u> wird aber die innere Stimme <u>nicht</u>').

[14] *Ibid.* ('in phantastischer Weise … ahnen lassen').

[15] The question of speed is interesting here: the tempo has increasingly picked up since the opening 'Hastig' – 'Nach und nach schneller', 'Nach und nach immer lebhafter und stärker' – although a *ritardando* is marked in the preceding bars. Thus, the chordal passage might still be going by at some speed, what looks static on the page being in effect rapidly moving, merely dilated to the eye's vision.

[16] Rosen, *The Romantic Generation*, p. 10.

Likewise noteworthy is the way in which this return is orchestrated, namely the long dominant pedal point that precedes it (bb. 423–46), whose reverberation of the pitch d^1 in an inner pedal persists for some twenty-four bars. This is the same pitch and register as the headnote of the 'innere Stimme', and its extraordinarily clangorous phenomenal resounding now appears to call attention to this soon-to-be-absent noumenal voice (its swansong, a final, uniquely perceptible protest before its silent presence is removed). The course of the larger section thus follows its own Romantic logic of aesthetic distance and loss. It is as if, following the drastic distancing of the theme in bb. 447–82, the 'innere Stimme' now becomes completely absent.

Subjectivity as Absence

The missing voice – the voice that was at first present and then later withdrawn – earlier suggested a reversal of the 'coming to lyricism' paradigm, where the subjective element was withdrawn from the musical texture, corresponding to what might be interpreted as a loss of self in the projected aesthetic subject. In the *Humoreske* the situation is more complex, since the voice that is missing was never there in the sonorous being of the music in the first place. This may still suggest the withdrawal of subjectivity but introduces a crucial and for our purposes far-reaching twist: that subjectivity, that even the subject itself, might be understood as being constituted by this lack, as 'always already' predicated upon an absence.

We might start with a more traditional line of interpretation. The fact that the original *Stimme* is not sonically realised, is not materially present in the sounding substance of the music, might serve to emphasise how the self in its most essential state is intangible, non-material entity (indeed the word 'soul' might equally be used here). From a solipsistically inclined perspective, it perhaps suggests that the most essential core of subjectivity (the lyrical melody) is the inward song of the soul which hears itself singing to itself; outward manifestations only approximate to it. We cannot hear it as listeners, but we can imagine or intuit it, feel it, or sing it inwardly to ourselves. To this extent, though, this very lack of literal voice enlists our selves as subjects to fill the void. Subjectivity, as we have insisted, is relational, and paradoxically never more so than here in the 'innere Stimme' of the *Humoreske*, where the being of the (fictional) musical subject is foregrounded as an aesthetic act of the (very real) listener.

When the passage returns, that subjectivity has gone. The second appearance is identical but different: it is missing that ineffable something, that which we cannot say (which is aptly silence). It is this remainder that constitutes the living self, that inscrutable mystery between a soulful and soulless being. As a result, Schumann's conceit aptly highlights the 'mysteries of animation', to use a phrase of Lawrence Kramer: what distinguishes a soulful, living performance (the first appearance of the passage) possessing that 'inner melody' from one without soul or life in it (the same notes as heard in the reprise)? How is it that some musical constructions of subjectivity can appear as false, artificial, 'a simulation or simulacrum' of genuine expression, while others are persuasive, appearing spontaneous, natural, 'real'?[17]

The sounding substance does not reveal the voice's presence; it is intimated only by the written score, as *Augenmusik*. There is an implicit confrontation here with a tenet of the poststructuralist credo, a challenge to an influential line of thought most famously formulated by Jacques Derrida in *Of Grammatology* and the other key works of 1967 that sees in mildly hyperbolic terms the entire history of Western metaphysics as based on the privileging of the living voice of spoken language over the dead letter of the written text.[18] Music, barely considered by Derrida, in many ways escapes the binaries of post-Saussurean linguistics to which his critique of this view of language and presence is indebted, but in this specific instance offers an unlikely alternative to the conventional metaphysical order Derrida opposes.[19] The challenge that Schumann's *Humoreske* presents is namely that the written score (lifeless inscription, *graphe*) conveys the existence of this immaterial, intangible being, this pure presence, which the living sound (*phone*) that is considered the essence of music does not. In the midst of the Romantic fixation on aurality – the privileging of sound over sight in conveying the living soul (corpses, we remember from Astarte, cannot generally speak) – we have a return to the metaphysics of the eye. Or as Adriana Cavarero would propose (offering a gentle correction to the binaries of

---

[17] Lawrence Kramer, 'The Mysteries of Animation', 166.

[18] See Jacques Derrida, *Of Grammatology*, trans. Gayatri Chakravorty Spivak (Baltimore: John Hopkins University Press, 1997); also *Writing and Difference*, trans. Alan Bass (Abingdon: Routledge, 2001), especially the chapter 'Freud and the Scene of Writing', pp. 246–91, and to a lesser extent *Voice and Phenomenon*.

[19] Music, Peter Dayan observes, was a topic with which Derrida had his most spectacular public failure ('"Sing Me a Song to Make Death Tolerable": Music in Mourning for Derrida', *Music Writing Literature: From Sand via Debussy to Derrida* (Aldershot: Ashgate, 2006), pp. 113–30).

Derrida), the reversal here is that a Platonic metaphysics, which in its strong form sees writing as the trace of the living presence of voice that is crucially *itself* inferior and subsidiary to the ideal mute language of the soul, is reconfigured so that now writing, the written text, may be seen as the more direct copy, trace, or (to face the opposite direction, augur) of the ultimate reality, the silent language of the soul conversing with itself, the pure realm of ideas, the noumenal, the Real.[20] The living sound has been written out (is 'under erasure'). Platonic the conception remains, however.

More radically, however, Schumann's missing voice need not be read as corresponding to the ineffability of the subject so much as the recognition that this subject was 'always already' built around an absence. Such a reading would fit with what are popularly assumed to be postmodern pronouncements on the dissolution of the subject, although one can, of course, find such notions distinctly voiced already in Romantic thought (indeed even in Idealism, following Kant's distinction between the empirical self and the transcendental conditions upon which that self must be grounded). Hence for Žižek, 'this disappearance, far from signalling the "death of the subject", signals its exact opposite, the emergence of the "barred" subject'.

In the traditional Romantic song, the subject is still defined by the substantial content of the inner wealth expressed by his voice, to which the piano provides the background fold; all that remains in Schumann is the fold itself, deprived of the melody, which is rejected as too 'substantial' to be able to express the void of subjectivity in an appropriate way. The only way to evoke the subject properly is to express it as a void around which the fold of 'variations without a theme' circulate.[21]

Moving in this manner from the Derridan to the Lacanian register, the musical voice without sound takes on the mantle of a subjectivity grounded on absence, on the subject's exclusion from the 'Real' (the noumenal, pre-individuated realm, roughly correlate to the Kantian *Ding an sich*) upon falling into the 'Symbolic' (the realm of language and culture, through which the subject only comes to consciousness of its status as a subject through the separation from an imagined original wholeness prior to this fall).[22] Thus, withdrawing the inner voice withdraws a subject that is already built around an absence, around an impossible desire for the

---

[20] See Cavarero, *For More Than One Voice*, esp. pp. 42–6 and 213–34.

[21] Žižek, 'Robert Schumann', p. 204.

[22] This is slightly simplifying along familiar generic lines; in Lacan, there are three registers or orders: the Real, the Imaginary, and the Symbolic.

fullness of self-presence that would be provided by the sound of 'hearing itself speaking' (to revert momentarily to the other Jacques). 'In short,' concludes Žižek, 'the subject is correlative to an "impossible" object whose existence is purely "virtual".'[23] And this 'impossible object' may easily take on the qualities of what is known in Lacanian circles as *objet petit autre* (or *petit a* for short) – the fetishised love object that, were we ever to obtain it, would appear to permit us direct access to this lost wholeness. 'Is not the "inner voice" as the paradox of a voice which cannot be materialised thus an exemplary case of the Lacanian *objet petit a*?' asks Žižek. We know the answer, of course.

These two series of notes somehow 'sound different', although they are exactly the same – is this not the very definition of *objet petit a*, in so far as *objet petit a* is the unfathomable X, the mysterious *je ne sais quoi* which is to be found nowhere in positive reality, yet whose presence or absence causes this positive reality to appear 'entirely different'?[24]

Less versed in Lacanese than Žižek, we are compelled again to agree. It may in fact be worth devoting a little more space to explicating these ideas here, unravelling Žižek's suggestive argument by bringing attention to another important and influential model of the modern subject hitherto mentioned only in passing, that of Jacques Lacan.

Music and the Illusion of the Real

In Part Two of this book, we explored ways in which the subject (above all that subject that knows and is known to Idealism) sought to transcend its divided state – the dilemma of being both subject and object to itself – through the dialectical movement of recognition in the other, a movement that had offered some hope but also one that courted the twin perils of narcissism and of self-loss when the other upon which the self is dependent had gone. Another approach, however, was to try to avoid the divided self through attaining a unity not *posterior* to the emergence of the subject, but rather, *prior* to it; this may not be a fully self-conscious subject, but it appears to be an undivided one. The 'absence of the self' foregrounded in this chapter may refer in a negative sense to a subject that was once present but is now lost; but it might also be used in a potentially more positive manner to characterise the attempt to reach back to a precognitive

---

[23] *Ibid.*, p. 204.   [24] *Ibid.*, p. 204.

immediacy in the subject prior to separation and individuation through language, to attain something close to that sense of undifferentiated being or pure self-presence that was illustrated at the opening of Chapter 4. In this understanding, the self as self-conscious subject has not yet fully emerged; it is still latent, rather than already lost.

Music may be particularly enticing in this context, as it is often associated with just such a precognitive immediacy of feeling, forming, in Julia Kristeva's words, a 'non-verbal signifying system' which, rather than being symbolic (as to a large part language is), is 'constructed exclusively on the basis of the semiotic'.[25] In Kristeva's development of Lacanian theory, music is closely linked with the *chora*, an idea Kristeva borrows from Plato's *Timeaus* and reworks 'to denote an essentially mobile and extremely provisional articulation constituted by movements and their ephemeral stases'.[26] The *chora* is an inchoate womb-like state of flux, bodily rhythms, and psychological drives, in which the nascent subject has partly differentiated itself from the mother, but prior to the subject's attainment of language and its complete articulation as an individuated self that comes with the entry into the symbolic order (as a consequence, it proves resistant to adequate articulation through such language). As Kristeva elucidates, 'the *chora* is a modality of significance in which the linguistic sign is not yet articulated as the absence of an object and as the distinction between real and symbolic . . . . the place where the subject is both generated and negated.'[27]

Music would therefore appear to be one of the most promising avenues to take in searching for this lost connexion prior to complete individuation, a mode of articulating a pre-symbolic realm resistant to language. Indeed, rather than trying to apply the dialectical movement of Idealist philosophical concepts onto the fictional subjects we have identified in music (with the continual possibility of straining hermeneutics to a conceptual vacuousness, a concern that has haunted much of the preceding discussion), what music does could be understood in a more direct way as 'appealing to the other' (or '(m)other') by invoking the maternal *chora*, the retroactive fantasy of a 'primary fusion prior to the imposition of a signifier and a lack'.[28]

---

[25] Julia Kristeva, *Revolution in Poetic Language*, p. 93. Kristeva juxtaposes here the two signifying systems of the semiotic and the symbolic; the former is broadly congruent with Lacan's Imaginary, the latter with the Symbolic.

[26] *Ibid.*, p. 93.   [27] *Ibid.*, pp. 94, 95.

[28] Mladen Dolar, *A Voice and Nothing More* (Cambridge MA: Massachusetts Institute of Technology Press, 2006), p. 41. A note may be appropriate on the agency attributed to music here: as Michael Klein argues, 'from this (Lacanian) subjective point of view, the agency of music is quite real'. Although we might think statements like music 'makes an appeal to the

Sadly, however, in Lacanian psychoanalytical thought the subject is simply unable ever to attain such a state. 'Lacan's model of the subject is not a pleasant one', explains Michael Klein. 'The subject is alienated and fractured: the site of a symptomatic structure delivered by the Symbolic. Any fantasy of wholeness is nostalgia for a moment that never was. Any future vision of wholeness is mere wishful thinking.'[29] The subject is constituted around a lack, around the desire to regain the lost unity with the mother (behind whom stands yet another, unreachable level, the Real). As for Freud, the mother becomes the originary love object, and the separation from her becomes a psychical 'castration', opening up a wound that will never heal but in fact constitutes subjectivity – an absence searching continually for an impossible presence. Seeking to fill this void, the subject fastens onto a substitute for the lost object that it believes will make it whole once more. But this search is ever in vain. Music, an artistic activity built upon the drive to replace the lost love object, does not for a moment escape from this diagnosis of the split subject, but indeed forms a particularly powerful symptom of it by offering another, fictitious semblance of unity in place of the Real (which we may never access, which in all likelihood does not exist).

The famous Lacanian term for this illusory object of desire is the *objet petit a*, whose 'two paramount embodiments' isolated by Lacan are the gaze and the voice.[30] Of these the gaze has received considerably more attention, both in Lacan's writings and in subsequent theory, but as Mladen Dolar has argued, the voice is arguably an even more striking and elementary instance, as before the infant reaches the mirror stage of visual self-recognition it can hear itself in the 'acoustic mirror' – an auto-affection that is not even reflection, as no external mediator is needed – while prior to the gaze the mother's voice becomes the primary link between her and the baby.[31] By placing such value on the voice qua bearer of presence, one is turning the voice into *objet a* or the 'object voice', asking it to fill the void left by the separation from the mother and loss of the presumed state of fusion with the fall into the symbolic order of language and culture. As Dolar argues,

Real' are metaphors, the work of art is organised 'by the same symbolic necessities that organise the subject'. Klein, *Music and the Crises of the Modern Subject*, p. 20; also see pp. 122–6.

[29] Klein, *Music and the Crises of the Modern Subject*, p. 154.

[30] Dolar, *A Voice and Nothing More*, p. 39.

[31] *Ibid.*, p. 39 (and more generally on this matter, pp. 35–42); the term 'acoustic mirror' is taken from Kaja Silverman, *The Acoustic Mirror: The Female Voice in Psychoanalysis and Cinema* (Bloomington: Indiana University Press, 1988). Lacan's predominantly visual perspective is set out in 'The Mirror Stage as Formative of the Function of the I', in Jacques Lacan, *Écrits: A Selection*, trans. Alan Sheridan (Abingdon: Routledge, 2001), pp. 1–8.

The voice as the bearer of a deeper sense, of some profound message, is a structural illusion, the core of a fantasy that the singing voice might cure the wound inflicted by culture, restore the loss that we suffered by the assumption of the symbolic order. This deceptive promise disavows the fact that the voice owes its fascination to this wound, and that its allegedly miraculous force stems from its being situated in this gap.[32]

According to this Lacanian viewpoint, then, the voice 'always already' denotes absence. Playing with the absence and presence of a musical voice is therefore setting up a simulacrum of a situation of where the search for voice may result in a successful outcome, an aesthetic similitude of an impossible state of affairs. It is a classic instance of art as wish-fulfilment, replacing a real absence with a surrogate and ultimately empty presence. Art, by 'dismantling the symbolic' through the semiotic, leads 'to the establishment of an object as a substitute for the symbolic order under attack'; and to the extent that it is a purely semiotic system (rather than a mixed mode of semiotic and symbolic signification like verbal language), music would seem the exemplary instance of this. 'In short, isn't art the fetish *par excellence*, one that badly camouflages its archaeology?' wonders Kristeva: 'the very practice of art necessitates reinvesting the maternal *chora* so that it transgresses the symbolic order'.[33]

Music merely sustains the illusion of re-attaining lost presence, playing with the gap between the subject's inherently divided nature and the fiction of obtaining access to the Real. In such a reading, even coming to lyricism is not in reality a coming to subjectivity, or at least not a full attainment of the impossible plenitude of selfhood. At best, coming to lyricism is a coming to subjectivity which is in fact never more than a split subjectivity (the barred subject, S). Schumann's conceit in *Humoreske* (as Žižek perhaps senses) reveals the emptiness of the illusion, its logical absurdity. For in the silent *innere Stimme*, the musical notation makes plain the hollow truth that this voice that is withdrawn, that this subjectivity that is vacated, was itself 'always already' pure absence.

The Phantasmagoria of Self-Presence: The Eichendorff *Liederkreis*, Op. 39

To speak of the subject based around an absence does not, as we have said, necessarily mean there is not a subject present (whether an actual person or

---

[32] Dolar, *A Voice and Nothing More*, p. 31.   [33] Kristeva, *Revolution in Poetic Language*, p. 115.

the aesthetic subject of language and music), paradoxical though this may sound. The subject that cannot come to full selfhood, the barred subject, is a subject grounded in an absence that constitutes its core. Oriented around an empty centre, it seeks a love object to fill its void and restore its presumed lost wholeness, but this search is seldom successful. Such a failing is common to many Romantic protagonists and a theme exemplified in numerous songs and song cycles from the nineteenth century; but there is one famous cycle of Schumann's that surely problematises the status of the Romantic subject beyond all others. This is, namely, the *Liederkreis* on poems by Joseph von Eichendorff, Op. 39, composed in May 1840. The whole cycle appears to circle around the search for a love object which is almost invariably absent, while the coherence and identity of the subject seeking it is subjected to serious question.[34] Such would appear to make it an ideal expression of the vacant modern subject.

Roland Barthes, writing of Schumann, described an idiosyncratic quality of the composer's music that could have been expressly written of Op. 39. His music

continuously refers to concrete things: seasons, times of the day, landscapes, festivals, professions. But this reality is threatened with disarticulation, dissociation, with movements ... ceaselessly 'mutant': nothing lasts long, each movement interrupts the next: this is the realm of the *intermezzo*, a rather dizzying notion that extends to all of his music.[35]

This view is akin to a distinctive trait of Eichendorff's own writing, which for want of a better word one might term 'phantasmagoric'.[36] Throughout Eichendorff's poetry and prose fiction one is struck by the recurring images, verbal formulae, situations, and even character names that return in ever new variations. Episodes appear almost interchangeable; one scene

---

[34] I am purposefully avoiding discussion here of whether there is a single protagonist across all twelve songs in the cycle – a much-disputed question foregrounded in my earlier study 'Absent Subjects and Empty Centers: Eichendorff's Romantic Phantasmagoria and Schumann's *Liederkreis* Op. 39', *19th-Century Music*, 40 (2017), 201–22. In a sense, if the subject is already understood as self-estranged at the level of the individual song it may seem distinctly futile to split hairs over whether all twelve songs refer to the same alienated subject or to twelve different ones, especially as there is no ultimate way of settling this matter. On the other hand, the curious motivic and harmonic links between songs, often noted by earlier commentators, might suggest on a hermeneutic level that at least some of them share a common subject, as argued earlier in relation to the phenomenology of the divided subject in Chapter 3.

[35] Roland Barthes, 'Loving Schumann', p. 295.

[36] This point, as with much of that discussed in the following two sections, is treated more extensively in 'Absent Subjects and Empty Centers', which provides a more detailed discussion of Eichendorff's style and literary output.

could often be transposed directly into another.[37] Often the very inter-changeability creates a deficit in narrative order, an episodic quality that is conspicuous in Eichendorff's two novels *Ahnung und Gegenwart* and *Dichter und ihre Gesellen*, and indeed a trait parodied by the author himself in his satirical novella, *Viel Lärmen um Nichts* – works that are the original locations for six of the poems in Schumann's cycle. Poetic immediacy of mood and sensation is often present at the expense of narrative coherence and action: Eichendorff's writing is rich in sensory evocations of atmosphere and feeling, dreamlike, fantastical, at once in motion but strangely static. Image follows image with little causal link in evidence. What narrative or action that there is appears elementary if not simply confusing.

The operative word here is *Verwirrung* – confusion, bewilderment. 'The word "wirr" is one of his favourites', observed Theodor Adorno in a pioneering account of Eichendorff from 1957. 'It proclaims the suspension of the ego, its disclosure to a chaotic urging.'[38] These recurring images, the episodic chain of events and unstable sense of identity, serve to articulate one of the poet's overriding themes: the uncertainty of the self and the world, the potential for deception to lurk under the beguiling surface, the constant threat to the subject of losing itself through romantic enticement and the beauties of nature. Through such means, Eichendorff creates a vision of the world as profoundly ambiguous and confusing, where stable notions of the self are constantly imperilled, and attempts to make narrative sense of the succession of external events and impose causal order on our lives often in doubt.

Schumann's second 'In der Fremde' setting (No. 8 of the cycle) may stand as a prototypical example of such phantasmagoric *Verwirrung* at the level of the individual song. Eichendorff's poem (one of the half-dozen in Op. 39 not originally drawn from a larger prose work) is a model of sensory blurring and confusion: in the recurring murmur of sounds (the onomatopoeic 'rauschen' – rustling, whispering, whirring, swishing – must be Eichendorff's other favourite word) and fantastical flicker of moonlight the protagonist knows neither where nor when he is. Alienated from

---

[37] See, for instance, Richard Alewyn, 'Eine Landschaft Eichendorffs' (1957), reprinted in *Probleme und Gestalten* (Frankfurt: Insel, 1974), pp. 205–6; also, Oskar Seidlin, *Versuche über Eichendorff* (Göttingen: Vandenhoeck & Ruprecht, 1965), pp. 259–60.

[38] Theodor Adorno, 'Zum Gedächtnis Eichendorffs', in *Noten zur Literatur I* (Frankfurt: Suhrkamp, 1958), p. 121('es meldet die Suspension des Ichs, seine Preisgabe an ein chaotisch Andrängendes an'). Adorno was clearly drawn to the poet from his love of Schumann's Op. 39 settings, as his selection of poems reveals.

reality, from the bearings of space around him and the time of the present, he becomes lost in his subjunctive mood of fantasy.

Ich hör' die Bächlein rauschen	*I hear the brooklets rushing*
Im Walde her und hin,	*In the woods fro and to,*
Im Walde in dem Rauschen,	*In the woods in the rustling,*
Ich weiß nicht, wo ich bin.	*I know not where I am.*
Die Nachtigallen schlagen	*The nightingales resound*
Hier in der Einsamkeit,	*Here in the solitude,*
Als wollten sie was sagen	*As if they wished to tell something*
Von der alten, schönen Zeit.	*Of the beautiful times of old.*
Die Mondesschimmer fliegen,	*The shimmering moonbeams fly,*
Als säh ich unter mir	*As if I saw below me*
Das Schloß im Tale liegen,	*The castle lying in the valley,*
Und ist doch so weit von hier!	*And yet it is so far from here!*
Als müßte in dem Garten	*As if in the garden*
Voll Rosen weiß und rot,	*Full of white and red roses,*
Meine Liebste auf mich	*My darling must be waiting for*
warten,	*me,*
Und ist doch [so] lange tot.[39]	*And yet she is [so] long dead.*

Schumann's setting responds to the poet's bewitching vision by circling round and round on itself in a dizzying ceaseless shimmer of semiquaver movement, tracing recurring harmonic cycles on multiple levels which forestall any larger sense of directed purpose (Ex. 7.4).

Schumann sets Eichendorff's four stanzas to two pairs of verses, with a brief coda that threatens to cycle back to the opening material, as if the music would repeat indefinitely. At a smaller scale, too, the song alternates at one-bar intervals throughout between a running legato figure in octaves in the accompaniment (suggestive perhaps of the bewitching murmuring of brooklets running confusedly 'fro and to' in the woods around us) and a quicksilver harmonic texture broken between the two hands that supports the detached vocal phrases. In the first and third stanzas the latter circles through a recurring $i-\frac{6}{3}-iv-V$ harmonic cadential pattern, which in turn oscillates between tonic and dominant; the alternating stanzas trace sequentially descending Phrygian progressions slipping away to the illusory region of the subdominant minor and relative major. Only in the very last bars does the music break free of this incessant

---

[39] Joseph von Eichendorff, *Sämtliche Gedichte* (Frankfurt: Insel, 2001), pp. 173–4; the word 'so' was added by Schumann.

Ex. 7.4 Schumann: 'In der Fremde' (II) (Eichendorff), *Liederkreis*, Op. 39 No. 8, verses 1 & 2

harmonic cycle, but even here, in a typically enigmatic moment of Schumannesque understatement, the realisation that his beloved is already dead seems barely to register on the protagonist. The phrase needs to be repeated twice before the flow of semiquavers disperses in a distinctly uneasy plagal close.

There is a temporal disconnect in the mind of the protagonist between the present and the past, and a spatial confusion too: time, and space, is 'out of joint' for the subject, and with it the emotional valence accorded to each. These are recursive themes throughout the cycle – both internal to the poems set, and effectively at a larger level in the obscure narrative order (if existent at all) traced by the cycle as a whole.[40] The clearest illustration of such dissociation of images, and the problematisation of the subject perceiving them, is given the eleventh song in the cycle, 'Im Walde':

A wedding procession passes by; the observer hears birds calling. A merry hunt flashes past, the riders sounding their horns.

The sounds have already died away. Night descends. The subject feels an unaccountable fear.

For all the apparent cheerfulness of the opening images (as so often in Eichendorff, both visual and sonic) there is a peculiarly disconcerting quality to the account. How are the external impressions connected, and what is the relation of the perceiver to them? One can barely speak of narrative here. The events related are episodic in nature, passing vignettes of outdoor life, whose temporal succession appears chronologically consistent but yet strangely dissociated: we might suppose some time has elapsed between the wedding and the hunt, and certainly before the onset of evening, but all is compressed into a few lines without any causal link being offered. A first-person subject position is given in Eichendorff's second line ('Ich hörte die Vögel schlagen'), but nothing is known of the perceiver beyond the perception he (or she) has.

A succession of external impressions without any logical link passes over the subject. Before we know it, all has vanished. What remains? Suddenly the emptiness in the centre becomes palpable: we feel afraid. Eichendorff's conception might serve as a paradigmatic expression of the nature of the modern self – the Humean 'bundle of perceptions', a series of sense impressions in constant flux with no causal link demonstrable between them, the vacant stage on which these phantas-magoric images glide in and out. If, as Hume holds, 'I never catch

---

[40] The latter is a complicated topic that I will again refrain from discussing here but is treated at length in 'Absent Subjects and Empty Centers'.

myself *without* a perception, and never observe anything *but* the perception,' how can we ever know our own self?[41] The answer suggested here lies in the fear that suddenly overtakes us, in *feeling* (*Gefühl*) – for the German Romantics the only way we can obtain unmediated access to our self.

The dissociation of scenes is already manifest in Eichendorff's poem, but Schumann's setting responds in kind through its continual harmonic slippage between harmonic centres and corresponding fragmentation of the musical-poetic discourse. In harmonic layout the song is formed from the large-scale composing-out of a $\hat{8}$–$\flat\hat{7}$–$\hat{6}$–$\sharp\hat{7}$–$\hat{8}$ schema (Ex. 7.5). Starting from the tonic A major, the successive images chart a large-scale movement down via tonicisations of $\flat\hat{7}$ (G major, leading plagally to D major), $\hat{6}$ (F sharp major), and back up to $\sharp\hat{7}$ (G sharp minor), prolonging the dominant E for several bars before a somewhat indecisive return to A at the end (probably still heard in a plagal relation to E). Although the opening music is as merry as could be wished (the $\frac{6}{8}$ time signature and bouncing rhythm recall a hunting topic), the curious, faltering ritardandi at the middle of vocal phrases, abrupt shifts between tonal centres, and constant ambiguity between tonic and dominant relations splinter any sense of continuity and association across the successive images. No one harmonic shift is the same as another: A major leads to G by abrupt shift down a tone (with cheerfully rustic parallels); D major to F sharp by single-voice semitonal shift followed by common-tone linkage; F sharp to G sharp minor by utilising the passing I→ii modulation already present in the original phrase; and the latter key leads to E via a *Leittonwechsel* shift. And apart from the large-scale dominant prolongation near the end (perhaps compensatory), what is conspicuous throughout is the complete absence at a medium level of conventional dominant-tonic tonal articulation. The successive episodes are held together merely by an abstract thread.

The Empty Centre

'Im Walde' is an exemplification of the 'punctual' modern subject of empiricism, a fragmentary and decentred entity posited behind the flux of phenomena it observes, but which proves strangely recalcitrant to self-apperception.[42] Knowing only what it can perceive, it remains largely

---

[41] Hume, *A Treatise of Human Nature*, p. 252.
[42] The term 'punctual self' is Charles Taylor's; see *Sources of the Self*, p. 49, and pp. 159–76.

Ex. 7.5 Schumann: 'Im Walde' (Eichendorff), *Liederkreis*, Op. 39 No. 11

Ex. 7.5 (Cont.)

unknown to itself. Op. 39 is not short of other examples of such self-alienation. Not only is the subject estranged from time and space (as seen in 'In der Fremde') and from itself (as here in 'Im Walde'), but it is exiled from its home and alienated from other subjects too. The former is explicitly thematised in the first 'In der Fremde' setting that opens the cycle.[43]

From the homeland behind the red lightning clouds are rolling in, but father and mother are long dead, and no one there knows the protagonist anymore. Schumann's setting seems to speak of an existential homelessness, mirrored in the manner in which the opening F sharp minor, initially so stable, becomes estranged for the subject over the course of the song. The opening bars, while suffused by a pervading melancholy, could not be more secure in their outlining of F sharp minor through repeated tonic and dominant harmonies and the highly circumscribed compass of the vocal line (Ex. 7.6). At the mention of the protagonist's parents, though, the tone darkens, slipping diminished harmonies offering the first departure from the extreme simplicity of the opening, and while the briefly disorientating chromatic progression soon elides with a cadence that returns to F sharp minor, the tonic is a touch more unsettled now. From the second stanza, however, the mood appears to brighten, with the B^7 chord at b. 10 marking the start of an apparent expanded cadential approach to the relative A major. The glimpse of the relative major held out here ultimately proves deceptive, though, and the music slips back through the tonic seventh to the subdominant, B minor (b. 16), coinciding with the thematic reprise of the opening melody, which thus emerges as the harmonic goal of the whole phrase.[44] There is something about this sense of return alongside the repose into the subdominant that deepens the effect of this passage, as if this recognition of the 'schöne Waldeinsamkeit' is the kernel of the whole song. In the subsequent bars F sharp minor tries to reassert itself, but its return is weakly grounded, and the Neapolitan inflections to the final bars give a strong Phrygian flavour to this harmony, as if the opening tonic has now been transformed into the dominant of its subdominant. As a consequence, the final F sharp minor is undermined as a stable resting point. By the end of the song, the tonic has been made unhomely, empty. The alienation from home is complete.

Or take 'Zwielicht' ('Twilight', No. 10), whose obscure voice, appearing out of the darkness, warns the subject of its betrayal by

---

[43] I am referring here to the second (1850) version familiar today, which replaced the opening 'Der frohe Wandersmann' of the 1842 edition with this F sharp minor 'In der Fremde' (likewise written in 1840 along with the other songs, but initially held back by the composer). See further on this point Jon W. Finson, 'The Intentional Tourist: Romantic Irony in the Eichendorff *Liederkreis* of Robert Schumann', in R. Larry Todd (ed.), *Schumann and His World* (Princeton: Princeton University Press, 1994), pp. 156–70.

[44] This crucial turn to B minor was in fact introduced by Schumann into the second version of the song; see David Ferris, *Schumann's Eichendorff Liederkreis and the Genre of the Romantic Cycle* (New York: Oxford University Press, 2000), pp. 109–16.

Ex. 7.6 Schumann: 'In der Fremde' (I) (Eichendorff), *Liederkreis*, Op. 39 No. 1

Ex. 7.6 (Cont.)

those closest to it: the self is alienated from those others it would call its friends. Possibly it is nothing less than a loss of the subject's own sense of identity that is at stake here, the 'self-alienation of the ego' as Adorno holds, an interpretation developed by Reinhold Brinkmann, who reads the song as a musical expression of separation, alienation, and loss of identity.[45] Not for nothing does this song recall the opening of 'Aus den hebräischen Gesängen', Op. 25 No. 15, which was associated with the loss of self there (see Chapter 4), while the distorted voice of the increasingly syncopated and metrically displaced bassline offers an even darker illustration of the metric dissonance observed in the final piece of *Kreisleriana*, offered in Chapter 3 as a prime expression of the split subject.

There are intimations of a spiritual homecoming glimpsed throughout the cycle, most famously 'Mondnacht' (No. 5), an exquisite moonlit vision of spiritual union, a fragile epiphany between man and nature, yet one that is given in an unreal subjective throughout, projecting an 'as if' quality, while the following 'Schöne Fremde' holds out the hope of 'future great happiness'.[46] But these brief glimpses of transcendence are more than counterbalanced by the more negative admonitory or illusionary songs, especially as the listener moves towards the latter part of the cycle. And even when in the final song, 'Frühlingsnacht', the subject appears to find fulfilment, there is nevertheless a strange absence at the very heart of the scene.

Über'n Garten durch die Lüfte	*Over the garden, through the air*
Hört' ich Wandervögel ziehn,	*I heard the birds come flying in,*
Das bedeutet Frühlingsdüfte,	*That means spring's fragrant scents*
Unten fängt's schon an zu blühn.	*Already below it starts to blossom.*
Jauchzen möcht' ich, möchte weinen,	*I want to rejoice, want to cry,*
Ist mir's doch, als könnt's nicht sein!	*It is to me yet as if it could not be!*
Alte Wunder wieder scheinen	*Old miracles appear once more*
Mit dem Mondesglanz herein.	*With the shimmering moon.*
Und der Mond, die Sterne sagen's,	*And the moon, the stars say it,*
Und im Traume rauscht's der Hain,	*And in dreams the grove murmurs it,*
Und die Nachtigallen schlagen's:	*And the nightingales sing it:*
Sie ist deine! Sie ist dein!	*She is yours! She is yours!*

The effect of the song – and there is no doubt that Schumann's setting is one of the most joyous outpourings in all Romantic *Lieder* – is certainly

---

[45] Adorno, 'Zum Gedächtnis Eichendorffs', p. 121; Reinhold Brinkmann, 'Das ungenaue Unisono: Sechs Kommentare zu Schumanns "Zwielicht"', in *Schumann und Eichendorff*, pp. 49–63.

[46] On the subjunctive quality of 'Mondnacht', see especially Brinkmann, 'Eichendorff, Schumann und der Conjunctivus irrealis', in *Schumann und Eichendorff*, pp. 12–48. The theme of returning home is also given a distinctly ironic resonance placed against the events related in the third song, 'Waldesgespräch', which shares the same key of E major and an almost identical vocal line and evaded cadential progression at the final point of arrival.

that of an exuberant conclusion to the cycle. For the listener as for the protagonist, the effect relies on the overwhelming power of subjective emotion: in a state of subjective ecstasy the subject is transported outside himself to a feeling of blissful union with nature, the world, and his beloved. Such is the sheer euphoria, however, that we might overlook a rather crucial absence: the beloved is not there.

Love scenes generally involve two people: here the ecstatic swelling of subjective emotion is in danger of overshadowing the identity of the woman who the moon and the stars and the dreaming woods tell the protagonist is his. But she never speaks. Barely concealed in this song is a tendency towards Romantic solipsism, a fantasising imagination that perceives inanimate objects speaking to oneself, corroborating the love of a woman who is conspicuously never actually present. 'Ist mir's doch, als könnt's nicht sein!': 'It is to me yet as if it could not be!' – and perhaps it isn't. Like so many of the other songs across the cycle, a lot resides in that telling subjunctive. What we are left with is a subject alone outside at night: the same situation as given at the end of the preceding song, 'Im Walde', where the protagonist had unaccountably shuddered in the depths of his heart, as expressed in the alienation of 'Zwielicht', as with 'In der Fremde', in fact, how the cycle had all started out in the very first song. The other is absent.

In the context of Eichendorff's literary practice, something is highly suspicious about the situation. One of the author's *idées fixes* is of the dangers of enticement and self-loss through sensual love, symbolised repeatedly throughout his oeuvre by the motive of the blossoming spring night, and personified in the pagan goddess Venus, who often appears to unwary male protagonists as a phantasmagoric presence at night. In the clear light of day, it becomes apparent that the alluring woman never existed outside the deluded mind of the subject, seduced by his desire and the natural beauty of the earth's season of fertility (a classic example is found in the novella *Das Marmorbild*, 1819, widely read in Schumann's day). Romantic love, in fact, seldom solves much for Eichendorff: some stories do have a happy end, but many do not, and when they do it is never with a lover alone in a garden at night.[47]

---

[47] Times of day are immensely important for Eichendorff: almost invariably, he prefers mornings for the concluding point of a story. In fact, the only story by Eichendorff that ends with romantic fulfilment at night is *Aus dem Leben eines Taugenichts* (1826); the protagonist is not alone, however, but amidst a happy group of friends. This novella is significantly the source for 'Der frohe Wandersmann', originally used by Schumann as the opening song of Op. 39, which appears virtually at the start.

In fact, simply taken within the terms of Schumann's cycle, the events of the preceding eleven songs may likewise give us cause for concern here. So often within this work the beloved turns out to be dead, absent, or there is something wrong gnawing at the heart of the scene. Given the history throughout the cycle of undercutting such moments of apparent fulfilment, can we fully believe she is really his now (especially as the preceding songs show no reason for any upturn in circumstances – in fact, suggest a disturbing loss of self)? On the miraculous day of 18 May 1840, Schumann not only wrote 'Frühlingsnacht' and the setting of 'Wehmut', but also composed the second 'In der Fremde'. In the spring garden of one song, the beloved is strangely absent; in the other, the figure waiting amongst the garden of red and white roses turned out to have died a long time ago.

The *Liederkreis* has an absence at its very centre – a double absence, as the subject often appears distracted or missing. It is filled with Romantic sounds and images of moonlight, nightingales, ruined castles, rustling woods and babbling streams, glimmering statues of gods, the rose-garden. But it is shot through with uneasy visions of loss, passing, absence, and phantasmagoric illusion. Figures are often missing, or the joy can quickly turn to emptiness. Only on one solitary occasion in all these songs does the object of the protagonist's desire actually seem to be present; for this one moment we even appear to hear her voice. This is of course in No. 3, 'Waldesgespräch'. And here she turns out to be the 'Hexe Lorelei' – the famous beguiling siren of German folklore – and the subject is doomed.[48] Approaching the *objet a* is a perilous undertaking; it will never bring the satisfaction it promised and may even lead to death.

This *Liederkreis* – literally a circle of songs – spirals round the search for a replacement love-object to make the wandering, self-estranged subject whole, but even at the end the protagonist never in actuality attains this. 'In Lacanian theory', explains Kenneth Smith, 'the human drive mechanism aims for the object *a* but always realizes that, in actual fact, its real goal was to orbit it perpetually.'[49] Reworking the generic formulation that the term

---

[48] This song might anyway be interpreted as one in which the 'persona' is speaking in role, retelling a ballad (as the original appearance in chapter 15 of *Ahnung and Gegenwart* implies).

[49] Kenneth M. Smith, 'The Tonic Chord and Lacan's Object *a* in Selected Songs by Charles Ives', *Journal of the Royal Musical Association*, 136 (2011), 372. As noted in ch. 3, this description would also fit the ever-absent but ever-projected F sharp minor tonic of *Dichterliebe*'s 'Im wunderschönen Monat Mai' – a cycle started directly after Op. 39 in that same wondrous month of 1840.

'*Kreis* suggests the presence of a thematic centre from which the poems radiate,' we might propose that Schumann's *Liederkreis* orients itself around an absent centre, an empty space which constitutes the subjectivity of a protagonist based around an absence – a void it would fill with the other, the love object, who likewise never appears.[50] In the ecstatic close of 'Frühlingsnacht' that absence is no less present, albeit resounding in Schumann's music with an elation that might help us momentarily forget that this promise of 'future great happiness' may well be merely an illusion.

*

In chapter 23 of Eichendorff's *Dichter und ihre Gesellen* (1834), we re-encounter the all-too-impressionable young poet Otto, now slipping inexorably towards madness and an early death. Visiting the garden of an unknown villa by night, in the bewitching moonlight and surrounded by lilac blossoms and nightingales Otto comes to believe that a beautiful woman living in the residence is enamoured of him. The episode restages the scene of 'Frühlingsnacht' almost to the letter. Sadly, it is all a delusion. The residence is deserted, and no woman lives there. It is a fantasy of Otto's overactive imagination. Sometime later, recovering from a high fever brought on by his mental overexcitement, he returns to the villa at dusk to find to his surprise a woman singing in the garden: it is all a practical joke played by the mischievous actress Kordelchen (a vivacious Philine-like figure in Eichendorff's novel). But Otto never recovers; separating fact from fantasy proves too much for his overdeveloped Romantic sensibilities. At the end of the chapter, in a strangely moving scene, the poet finds himself led by an orphaned child (perhaps a vision of himself) back home, to the quietude of the forest loneliness; a sleep from which this weary traveller never wakes again. The resonance with other songs in Schumann's cycle – the return 'nach Hause' of 'Mondnacht', the 'stille Zeit' and 'Waldeinsamkeit' of the opening 'In der Fremde', the characterisation of the protagonist as a 'Wandersmann' – is unmistakable.

An orphan, bereft of mother and father, Otto stands as a sympathetic cipher for the Romantic artist, for the alluring but ultimately sick dreams of Romanticism – the 'inconsolable desolation of young souls, that homesickness without home, that labyrinthine self-torment'.[51] Yet his fate is not shared by all. As the plural of Eichendorff's title indicates, Otto is not the

---

[50] The characterisation is Wilhelm Müller's, as expressed by Barbara Turchin ('Robert Schumann's Song-Cycles in the Context of the Early Nineteenth-Century *Liederkreis*', Ph.D. diss., Columbia University, 1981, pp. 276–7).

[51] Joseph von Eichendorff, *Dichter und ihre Gesellen* (Stuttgart: Reclam, 1987), p. 32 (ch. 4).

only poet treated in this novel. There is the mysterious Count Victor, for instance, who keeps his Romanticism in check through an aristocratic cynicism, at first a shadowy presence hiding under a pseudonym but by the end a dominant figure; and then there is probably the book's central character, the sanguine, even-keeled Fortunato, who sings the poem we know from Schumann's 'Schöne Fremde', and after many tribulations (the path of true love never being smooth, especially in Romantic novels) ends up with his beloved. The narrative contains multiple protagonists. It might indeed be no less profitable to conceive of how Schumann's Op. 39 could be viewed from multiple subject positions, as a poetic vision of life in its diverse forms and varieties.

Likewise, we might turn consideration now to those instances where it is the voices and subjectivity of others that can be heard. The 'absence of the self' in music need not imply that the subject is barred from realising itself but may simply indicate that the music is not speaking in a first-person singular voice at all, so much as in the plural – as several voices – or in the third person. A subject need not be directly expressed as a self but it may be represented as an other, or others. In the following chapter we look to such cases.

PART IV

Hearing Others

8 | Hearing Another's Voice

Clara's Voice?

Despite its personal quality, Schumann's music often appears to speak in a voice that is not exactly that of the musical self – that is to say, in the voice or voices of others. Most prominent of all such voices are surely the so-called 'Clara Themes' that thread their way throughout his oeuvre. We saw an example earlier in the first movement of the Piano Trio Op. 80, but perhaps an even better instance is found in the Cello Concerto, Op. 129 (1850). At the conclusion of the first movement, the final tutti (b. 264) that had until now broadly corresponded with that closing the exposition breaks off over a series of chromatically slipping seventh harmonies, and there now enters one of Schumann's most moving ideas in the solo cello (b. 282, Ex. 8.1). It is as if the phrase enters from a different world, one of a hitherto undisclosed interiority, a memory of something or someone of the utmost value to the subject. After all the bluster of the preceding tutti, this brief interjection forms a decisive turning point, linking to the gentle *Langsam* movement that follows on directly.

Or take the second of the scenes Schumann set from Part I of Goethe's *Faust*, composed the year previously – the portrayal of Gretchen standing before the image of the Mater dolorosa, tormented by guilt. Again, the previously fraught musical rhetoric accompanying Gretchen's heartbroken weeping suddenly gives way to an unexpected stillness, and the same little phrase heard in the Cello Concerto appears in the violins, its graceful contour picked out by delicate flecks of colour in flute and oboe (Ex. 8.2, the commonality underscored by the mutual key of F major). The effect is magical, though the reference in the text directly following this point – a reference to the flowers, wet with her tears, that Gretchen picked early that morning – would scarcely prepare us for this musical response.

In fact, the very same theme turns up rather earlier in the finale of the G minor Piano Sonata, Op. 22 (a movement written in 1838 to replace that in the original version of the sonata, composed between 1833 and 1835).

Ex. 8.1 Schumann: Cello Concerto in A minor, Op. 129, i, link into slow movement, bb. 280–5

Ex. 8.2 Schumann: *Szenen aus Goethes Faust*, Part I, No. 2, 'Gretchen vor dem Bild der Mater dolorosa', bb. 38–44

Ex. 8.3 Schumann: Piano Sonata in G minor, Op. 22, finale (1838 version), secondary theme, bb. 27–63

Following the close of the agitated G minor opening theme, the familiar phrase emerges in the relative major (b. 29, Ex. 8.3). Attention is drawn to it not only due to the sudden drop in tempo (marked 'Etwas langsamer') and dynamic, but also owing to the unusually static, reiterative quality of the theme. Three times the phrase enters, outlining a half-cadential approach from subdominant to dominant harmony, but only at the last does this cadence to the tonic, and this in turn overlaps with the introduction of a new variant, before the whole passage cycles back to the opening version, trailing off without reaching cadential completion. The highly static treatment emphasises the theme's 'otherness', its removal from the driving momentum of the surrounding music, and suggests the idea possesses some special, though undisclosed, private resonance.

Though the instrumental voices that utter it are diverse – in the second scene from *Faust* it appears in the orchestra, in the Cello Concerto it is actually the soloist that voices it – this phrase is readily heard as to some extent 'other': as a different voice, entering the music from another realm, of deeply private import. And for at least two generations of writers, this particular melodic idea is popularly supposed to be of just such significance: this is none other than the celebrated 'Clara theme'. As Eric Sams has proposed, Schumann, who had a documented fondness for musical ciphers, is supposed to have encoded the name of his beloved in musical notes, resulting in a series of conjunct, five-note motives that are found across many of his compositions.[1]

There are numerous weak spots in Sams's theory, not least of which is the fact that there is simply no evidence that Schumann ever constructed musical ciphers in this way or ever thought of this specific musical idea as symbolising Clara.[2] Even its use in Schumann's music often has little or no evident connexion with her. For all the fact of this theme's permeation throughout the D minor Symphony (which Schumann once claimed to his new bride as being his 'Clara' Symphony), the use in the examples above scarcely bears out such associations. Take the scenes from *Faust*, for instance: it is hardly obvious why Clara should be associated with Gretchen, and even less apparent why this same theme should then recur later in the opening scene of Part II ('Ariel, Sonnenaufgang'), preceding Faust's awakening to the dawn – the point of his spiritual rebirth and forgetting of Gretchen alongside the whole sorry affair of Part I. The only possible connexion between the two passages is the common theme of the fresh arrival of day in Goethe's text, but this has no discernible link to Schumann's wife.

Few if any serious scholars accept Sams's hypothesis now. But it has proved difficult to eradicate in popular conceptions of Schumann, in part because the idea seems not only to confirm a Romanticised image of the

---

[1] Sams developed the idea of the 'Clara' theme in a series of short articles in *The Musical Times* from the late 1960s, and it became disseminated widely in his influential survey *The Songs of Robert Schumann*, pp. 22–5.

[2] The most detailed critique of Sams will be found in Daverio, *Crossing Paths*, ch. 3 and 4.

composer, encoding his life and love into his art, but often so apt for explaining the particular quality of the music at these points. In such moments it is easy to understand the popularity of this phrase's designation as the 'Clara theme', since the music takes on a quality of inwardness, tenderness, and deep personal import, for which the romantic association serves as a perfect explanation. The important thing, I would argue, is not the music's questionable association with Clara, then, but the very fact of its appearing to hold some deeper signification. Schumann's music possesses this peculiar cryptic quality, as if some private meaning is so often borne within it – even when one is quite possibly not actually there. (Such passages 'may contain a secret,' observes Charles Rosen, 'but they do not hide one: on the contrary, they insist openly on the presence of a secret'.[3]) To bring out this quality, the music must be performed as if it did indeed possess some veiled message. In scholarly terms, the belief in a 'Clara theme' is almost certainly unfounded, but in aesthetic terms it is not so far wide of the mark.

Such familiar turns of phrase are, in fact, extremely common through-out Schumann's oeuvre. Each of us can probably compile a list of appar-ent Schumannesque self-borrowings: part of the enchantment of the *Adagio and Allegro*, Op. 70, for instance, surely results from how the primary phrase of the *Adagio* harks back to numerous other Schumannesque sources, most notably the 'Lied der Suleika' (which as noted earlier, itself seems echoed in 'Ihre Stimme'). The result of these inter-opus resonances is to create a richly allusive tapestry of recurring themes running across Schumann's output, inadvertently adding to a sense of his music as forming 'confessions from a poetic life', even without the need for identifying a specific Clara theme. And yet, while such intertextual themes might well convey a broader sense of a single overriding subjectivity (the composer 'Schumann') at work across his compositional output, there is nevertheless often a sense of otherness to their appearance. In hearing a voice that is both part of the work and yet marked as extraneous, we are effectively hearing the voice of another. This is perhaps why the idea of the 'Clara' theme works so well, despite its evident factual limitations. And it is not only Schumann's self-borrowings that can be marked by alterity. Even more obviously, we may hear the voices of others in Schumann's allusions to and quotations of other composers' music.

---

[3] Rosen, *The Romantic Generation*, p. 10.

Whose Voice?

Real 'Clara themes' can of course be found permeating Schumann's music, in the numerous references to Clara's Wieck's compositions in the piano works of the 1830s, discussed in Chapter 5. Such intertextuality is not limited to her music, though. Two celebrated examples of works in which the voice of another composer is heard amidst Schumann's own were also discussed earlier: the first movement of the *Fantasie* in C, Op. 17, and the finale of the Symphony No. 2, in which what appears to be a deliberate allusion to Beethoven's *An die ferne Geliebte* forms a crucial turning point near the end of the respective movements. Only mildly less prominent are other Beethovenian resonances in Schumann's work: the opening of the *Faust* Overture, for instance, which reworks the iconic dissonant B flat over D minor $^6_4$ harmony of the Ninth Symphony's finale; the homage to that symphony's slow movement in the String Quartet Op. 41 No. 1; or the allusion to Beethoven's Op. 31 No. 3 in the third quartet of that set. The manner of other composers is famously called up in the 'Paganini' and 'Chopin' numbers of *Carnaval*. Then, of course, we get to other types of overt reference: the *Marseillaise* makes a cheeky appearance in *Faschingsschwank aus Wien*, and crops up again in 'Die beiden Grenadiere' (Op. 49 No. 1) and the *Hermann und Dorothea* Overture. This is not even touching on the innumerable instances, as in any composer's work, in which the influence of another composer is felt, or a host of affinities that may or may not be deliberate. The question of what constitutes a quotation or allusion, whether this was intended by the composer, and if this is even an important consideration, is vexed. What does seem incontestable, however, is the fact that Schumann's music seems to play with allusion to other works, both by himself and others, in a manner that (as Rosen discerns) frequently marks such reference out as an important aesthetic part of the music's meaning.[4]

Such apparent references to other composers' 'voices' might nonetheless have important repercussions for the type of voice in which Schumann's music is heard to speak. A more traditional view of musical influence, for instance, might suggest that the voice of another composer is something that should be 'worked through' in order to arrive at one's own

---

[4] A much more extensive account of Schumann's borrowings and some of the problems in their identification can be found in Todd, 'On Quotation in Schumann's Music', who rightly cautions that 'in searching for these references, we may be satisfying our need to discover a meaning, to read, reread, and interpret Schumann's musical text, more than elucidating Schumann's need to indulge in allusions' (p. 95).

individuality (a paradigm that has been given theoretical weight in recent decades by applications of Harold Bloom's notion of the 'anxiety of influence' to music). Thus Mark Evan Bonds can read the Fourth Symphony in general terms as Schumann's attempt to assert his independence from Beethoven's imposing symphonic precedent through deliberate 'misreading' of this tradition.[5] Along such lines might also seem to run Michael Steinberg's more specific reading of the inner movements in Schumann's Symphony No. 2, in which Schumann attains his own sense of subjective identity by asserting his difference from his friend and implicit symphonic rival Mendelssohn. Yet in Steinberg's view, this pursuit of a personal voice (if such it is) does not end successfully: 'Schumann does not seem to develop a coherent subjective voice that is allegorised in music.'[6]

For Steinberg, the symphony's second-movement scherzo is 'clearly and brilliantly a Mendelssohnian movement, and no less so for the layer of melancholy that underlies its jocularity', the author drawing on Anthony Newcomb's influential reading of the work to suggest that the movement is in fact 'not quite what it pretends to be'. In contrast, the 'exquisite *Adagio espressivo*' that follows 'unfolds in a confessional, first-person mode'.

It is the music that says 'I'; the investment in the musical first person of Robert Schumann is certain but not readily decipherable. The overall posture of the movement seems to impart the thought – part confession, part defense, part self-assertion – 'I am not Mendelssohn.' In a way the movement turns away from – unwrites – the work of the Scherzo.

So far all conforms to a Bloomian reading of the 'strong artist' struggling to attain his own authentic voice. Yet for Steinberg, 'the *Adagio*'s first-person utterance offers a consistent melancholic mood but does not progress in a unified voice. Multivocality is made clear by varied orchestration and use of solo instruments', not to mention what Steinberg perceives as references to other styles and composers, such as characteristic baroque *Affektenlehre* figures (sighing diminished fourths) and Bachian counterpoint, 'invocations of Mozartian as well as Schubertian gestures', and more widely 'figured in the work's tendency to quote Beethoven'. By the end of the movement, then, 'nothing is worked through'.[7] And while the finale 'reclaims an extroverted, public voice', 'it does so not by transcending the private, interior melancholy of the *Adagio*' – which Steinberg reads as

[5] Mark Evan Bonds, *After Beethoven: Imperatives of Originality in the Symphony* (Cambridge, MA: Harvard University Press, 1996).
[6] Steinberg, 'Schumann's Homelessness', p. 54.   [7] *Ibid.*, p. 75.

Schumann's 'authentic' voice – but rather by 'somewhat glibly' suppressing it.[8]

Steinberg's account is a little fuzzy on details (the scherzo may be broadly considered 'Mendelssohnian' in tone, but the link is not that clear, certainly nowhere near as direct as that, say, between the scherzo in Schumann's Op. 41 No. 1 and Mendelssohn's own quartet Op. 44 No. 3), and orchestral music is invariably going to be 'multivocal' in the sense offered here: a more precise definition is perhaps needed. Yet Steinberg is bringing into relief a feature that is true of the symphony as a whole and characteristic of the larger trajectory it traces (which might also be read in more positive terms than he allows). This is the sheer weight of possible intertextual references that make up its fabric, and an expressive journey that finds a solution to the dramatic impasse in the finale's development section through turning to the lyrical *An die ferne Geliebte* theme. If the aim of this music is to attain an authentic subjective voice, then as Steinberg perceives, Schumann's symphony hardly succeeds in working free of other musical influences, given that the finale leads to an apparent quotation from Beethoven followed by the return of the first movement's introductory material along with its purported reference to the opening of Haydn's final symphony.

The peculiarity of this situation was raised in Chapter 4 but left unanswered there. Why is it in a work that forms one of the primary examples of the 'coming to lyricism' paradigm, a 'coming to self-consciousness' in which the musical subject purportedly attains a deeper awareness of itself, Schumann's music appears to reach its heightened state of selfhood by singing to another's tune? Somehow two of Schumann's most iconic, 'personal' works – the *Fantasie* in C and Second Symphony – actually appear to revolve around actualising another's voice. Of course, one could argue that the apparent Beethoven citation is not actually a reference at all (after all, Schumann never mentioned it, and no one seems to have spotted it for half a century after his death); or point to the fact that the theme in the *Fantasie* is made to sound as if it all along belongs to the work, forming a natural part of Schumann's own language (as Rosen claims).[9] But still the 'multivocality' of these works – indeed of so much of Schumann's music – cannot easily be dismissed.

One way of thinking this through would be to approach the idea of inter-textuality not as an exception but as a constitutive feature, not only of Schumann's language, but of musical language in general. More recently, scholars have sought to nuance the understanding of influence and allusion,

---

[8] *Ibid.*, pp. 75–6.   [9] Rosen, *The Romantic Generation*, p. 103.

for instance, by proposing intertextuality as a normal condition of music. The work of Christopher Reynolds in particular has explored the apparent web of references and seemingly deliberate allusions between the music of nineteenth-century composers such as Robert and Clara Schumann, Fanny and Felix Mendelssohn, Johannes Brahms, and their predecessors such as Bach, Beethoven, and Schubert.[10] But we might extend this further to the sense of subjectivity conveyed by the music. While it is habitual to think of original artists as creating their own language and mode of utterance, this is true neither of verbal language nor of music, where language is pre-given and necessarily shared, marked through and through by the qualities of intertextuality and 'heteroglossia'.[11] So too with questions of subjectivity. The apparent subjectivity of the implied author 'Schumann' heard in his music is in fact negotiated with that of other compositional voices by means of a shared musical language. In a more extreme form familiar from some poststructuralist critics in the wake of Barthes, it could even be claimed that the 'subject' is merely a construction from a public language which is 'always already' there.[12] Thus 'the subject', as Derrida puts it, 'is inscribed in language, is a "function" of language, becomes a speaking subject only by making its speech conform – even in so-called "creation", or in so-called "transgression" – to the system of the rules of language'.[13]

We have insisted throughout this book that subjectivity is not a hermetic, solipsistic quality but rather a means of negotiating between self and world, subject and society. And this is unavoidable, since the very language, be it musical or verbal, in which the subject expresses itself is already present before the subject can constitute itself – indeed the medium through which the subject is constituted. The apparent irony of the Beethoven references in Schumann's works merely calls attention to how

---

[10] Christopher Reynolds, *Motives for Allusion: Context and Content in Nineteenth-Century Music* (Cambridge, MA: Harvard University Press, 2003).

[11] To use the famous term of Mikhail Bakhtin; see 'Discourse in the Novel', in *The Dialogic Imagination: Four Essays by M. M. Bakhtin*, trans. Caryl Emerson and Michael Holquist (Austin: University of Texas Press, 1981), pp. 259–422.

[12] The classic formulation is Roland Barthes, 'The Death of the Author', in *Image, Music, Text* (London: Fontana, 1977), pp. 142–8. This viewpoint is especially typical of the earlier Michel Foucault: see 'What Is an Author?', in *Language, Counter-Memory, Practice: Selected Interviews and Essays*, ed. D. Bouchard (Oxford: Blackwell, 1977), pp. 113–38; also, the later account 'The Subject and Power', in *Beyond Structuralism and Hermeneutics*, ed. H. Dreyfus and P. Rabinow (Chicago: University of Chicago Press, 1983), pp. 208–26.

[13] Jacques Derrida, 'Différance', in *Margins of Philosophy*, trans. Alan Bass (Chicago: Chicago University Press, 1982), p. 15. Owing to its basis in the notion of *différance* and its associated Saussurean linguistic framework, it should be noted that Derrida's argument has little hold on music.

even one of music history's most 'subjective' compositional voices is not averse to expressing itself in borrowed phrases.[14]

Staging (Other) Subjects

Such considerations suggest that the idea music can give us an unmediated, direct expression of subjectivity is a chimera, for the very medium in which this subjectivity is conveyed is not transparent but rather shot through with the echoes of earlier voices and styles. The subject is mediated through the language of others. Moreover, by participating in this shared language, it is representing itself *for* others. That subjectivity is to some extent 'performative', a staging of the self for another subject, is in itself unexceptional as a proposition; but in music this fact can often go unobserved, especially under Romantic aesthetics which prize music for its apparent immediacy and authenticity. Since the pioneering musical representations of the self in opera and the madrigal at the turn of the seventeenth century, if not earlier, the fact that subjectivity is a 'performance' – quite literally 'staged' in the case of opera – has been readily apparent. 'From the late sixteenth-century Italian madrigal to musical Expressionism in the early twentieth century,' writes Julian Johnson, 'music concerns itself with the inner life of individual feeling, while at the same time placing this music in the public sphere.'

> In the modern age, composers were expected to find public expression for private experience because music was valued precisely for its performative staging of the modern idea of private identity . . .. [H]owever theoretically unsustainable it may be, the idea of an authentic expression formed the basis of the contract which music makes with its listeners in the modern age. Music presents itself as *if it* were the disclosure of something private, and the listener experiences it *as if* it spoke for himself or herself.[15]

Michael Spitzer similarly observes that 'at the deepest level, one might argue that musical emotion was social through and through, since to externalize feeling (*Entäusserung*) entails mediating it through intersubjective convention, like language'.[16] Yet it is only in recent years that

---

[14] Tragically, however, in his final years in Endenich Schumann suffered delusional voices accusing him of having not composed his own music but having stolen it from others. The line between acknowledging the inevitable intertextuality of the subject's voice and misrecognising it as that of another (a theme that is foregrounded in the following chapter) is a fine one.

[15] Julian Johnson, *Out of Time: Music and the Making of Modernity* (New York: Oxford University Press, 2015), pp. 220–1.

[16] Spitzer, *A History of Emotion in Western Music*, p. 316.

scholars have turned attention to this same type of 'staging' of subjectivity that is articulated in the supposedly private genres of the nineteenth-century piano piece or Lied.[17] In part this is due to the emphasis on lyrical expression in these genres, the overriding adoption of the lyrical mode over the dramatic or epic, in which the self is expressed with such directness and immediacy that the mediating mechanism is commonly overlooked and becomes all but invisible.

 Much of Schumann's earlier music – the piano pieces of the 1830s and Lieder of 1840 – works well under a lyrical mode which presents the illusion of a direct, unmediated expression of the self. However, over the 1840s Schumann appears ever more interested in openly mediated representations of subjects – in quasi-dramatic stagings or epic narrations – a predilection which runs alongside his turning to larger, public genres such as the secular oratorio, choral ballad, and opera. Reinhard Kapp indeed sees this move as deliberate on Schumann's part, the composer consciously abandoning the notion of a direct, unmediated expression of the self and the associated lyric mode in favour of the aesthetic of *Erzählung* (narration, storytelling) and epic distance, which comes to dominate his later music.[18] We might see something of this shift in three of Schumann's song collections dealing with the lives of female protagonists. The earlier *Frauenliebe und Leben* works very successfully as the apparently direct expression of the self. (Schumann cuts Chamisso's final poem 'Traum der eignen Tage', in which the widow speaks in the present to her granddaughter, thereby projecting an epic distance back over the preceding eight poems which in Schumann's setting have been given a lyric immediacy.) Hence too, the feminist controversy over the appropriation of the female subject's voice by the male creative artist in this work. In later cycles like the *Sieben Lieder von Elisabeth Kulmann zur Erinnerung an die Dichterin*, Op. 104 (1851), for which Schumann contributed a linking narration explaining the songs and their relation to the life of the poetess, and the *Gedichte der Königin Maria Stuart*, Op. 135 (1852), there is a much greater sense of narrative distance, the lives of the suffering protagonists being overtly 'staged' by the composer. In part, the fact that these are real historical

---

[17] See, for instance, Jennifer Ronyak, *Intimacy, Performance, and the Lied in the Early Nineteenth Century* (Bloomington: Indiana University Press, 2018).

[18] Reinhard Kapp, *Studien zum Spätwerk Robert Schumanns* (Tutzing: Hans Schneider, 1984), p. 130. This reading of a larger movement from lyric to epic across Schumann's oeuvre was proposed earlier by Adolf Schubring as part of his schematic view of history: see 'Schumanniana No. 4: The Present Musical Epoch and Robert Schumann's Position in Music History (1861)', trans. John Michael Cooper, in R. Larry Todd (ed.), *Schumann and His World* (Princeton: Princeton University Press, 1994), pp. 370–1.

persons purportedly speaking in their own words helps, as does the fact that few critics have ever liked these songs and few audiences ever heard them; but no controversy over impersonation has ever dogged these pieces.[19] This is, I would propose, partly because their staging of the respective subjects is so open that no illusion of unmediated subjective identification ever arises. We do not experience these subjects from a first-person perspective, identifying with them as if part of ourselves, but as *other* subjects, from a third-person perspective as it were. The 'I' of these songs is heard as uttered in another's voice, or even more, as the staging of another voice – not as a surrogate or extension for our own.

The same might be said for the song collections that present scenes from a renowned work of literature – the Op. 98a *Wilhelm Meister* songs in particular – in which Schumann represents fictional subjects from larger narratives that are already well known to the audience (and in the case of *Wilhelm Meister*, in which a degree of theatricality is already strongly pronounced). Or consider the later *Liederspiele* that give opportunity for convivial presentation by a small group of singers – the *Spanisches Liederspiel*, Op. 74, *Spanische Liebeslieder*, Op. 138, or the *Minnespiel*, Op. 101, all dating from 1849. Schumann had devised song collections before that had presented a latent narrative progression from the perspective of multiple protagonists, such as in *Liebesfrühling*, Op. 37 (1841), but the sense of performative role playing in the later cycles – the sense that the subjects portrayed are dramatic personas 'put on' – is quite distinct. Indeed, the *Minnespiel*, whose text is drawn again from Rückert's *Liebesfrühling* collection, contains new settings of 'Schön ist das Fest des Lebens' and 'So wahr die Sonne scheinet', but the two duets from Op. 37 are rewritten as vocal quartets in Op. 101. The Rückert poems which had earlier elicited a setting in which the loving couple were able to reflect themselves in each other is replaced by a more theatrical or stylised *Minne-Spiel* between four singers; the solitary or enamoured pair of subjects in the earlier Schumann makes room for a multiplicity of distinct characters (*not* split subjects) in 1849. It is when Schumann is single that he composes for the solitary subject of the solo piano piece and Lied, and with marriage – and, in time, children and growing civic

---

[19] On the *Stuart* poems (and their dubious authenticity) see Jon W. Finson, 'At the Interstice between "Popular" and "Classical": Schumann's *Poems of Queen Mary Stuart* and European Sentimentality at Midcentury', in Roe-Min Kok and Laura Tunbridge (eds.), *Rethinking Schumann* (New York: Oxford University Press, 2011), pp. 69–87. Some of these issues in Opp. 104 and 135 are also discussed by Laura Tunbridge in 'Robert Schumann's *Frauenleben*', in Emmanouil Perrakis (ed.), *Life as an Aesthetic Idea of Music* (Vienna: Universal Edition, 2019), pp. 45–62.

responsibility – he turns to larger forces and the presentation of a plurality of subjects.[20] What contributes to the performative element of the subjectivity constructed here is also, of course, the very nature of their rendering – the fact that this is music to be performed by a group of musical friends, each of whom 'plays their part' for the duration.

Another related factor is Schumann's interest in telling stories through his music – or more precisely evoking the world of storytelling through the interaction between virtual characters – what could be called his *Märchenhaft* or *Erzählung* aesthetic. In an instrumental context, this interest in representing the play of different 'third-person' subjective voices finds an expression in such pieces as the *Märchenbilder*, Op. 113 (1851), or the *Märchenerzählungen*, Op. 132 (1853). In the first piece of the latter set, for instance, the play of different virtual subjects is conveyed perfectly by the interaction between the three highly profiled instrumental characters (viola, clarinet, piano), who share the cheery opening theme around in turn as if characters from a children's story having a good-natured discussion about what to do next (Ex. 8.4). This is a tendency which seems always to have been strong in Schumann (witness the *Kinderszenen*, Op. 15, or playful 'narrative' titles like *Novelletten*, Op. 21), but is often somehow qualitatively different in the later music. One important distinction between the masked subjects of *Carnaval*, say, and the diminutive virtual protagonists of the *Märchenerzählungen* is that the former are conjured up by a single virtuoso performer, whereas the latter are actually voiced by three separate performers. As with the *Liederspiele* from these later years, the multiplicity of the music's subjects is in part actualised through the very performing conditions, and to this extent such subjectivity more obviously shown as a representation, mediated through human performance, 'staged'.

Multiple Voices, Multiple Subjects: The Phenomenology of Musical Plurality

The Op. 132 *Märchenerzählungen* illustrate an intriguing albeit somewhat specialised question concerning the nature of the subjectivity music can be

---

[20] Even Schumann's first set of duets – the four published as Op. 34 – emerged in the latter months of 1840 (the exact date of composition is unknown), and with the ensuing *Liebesfrühling* collection seem to mirror his newly coupled status. Daverio remarks in this context upon the transformation of the 'lyric-epic "I"' into a lyric-epic "we"' in the four books of *Romanze und Balladen* issued as part-songs after 1849 (Opp. 67, 75, 145, and 146; the earlier four books, Opp. 45, 49, 53, and 64, had been for solo voice and piano); *Robert Schumann*, p. 399.

Ex. 8.4 Schumann: *Märchenerzählungen*, Op. 132, No. 1, *Lebhaft, nicht zu schnell*, opening

heard to project, namely, the question of plurality. How can we distinguish a single virtual musical subject from several, the one from the many? One might instinctively think the answer is easy: multiple voices imply multiple subjects; but as we have seen, the idea that the subject, though singular, is split into diverse elements, is commonplace in accounts of the musical persona ever since Edward T. Cone. So, what, if anything, distinguishes the divided subject from multiple subjects? Reworking Steinberg's query 'What does it mean to recognize a first-person voice in music?', what does music sound like when it speaks in the first-person plural?[21] And how is this distinguishable from a divided single subject?

The short answer is: with extreme difficulty. The shadow of hermeneutic overload hangs over us once again, the attempt to define musical subjectivity in danger of being taken, *ad absurdum*, to the limits of sensible discussion. Yet still, I think there are some cases where the reading of the music possessing multiple virtual subjects seems persuasive, and others in which there might be reasons for us to interpret it as reflecting a divided subjectivity; and it is not out of place to inquire quite why, and especially how.

Musical features are the trickiest to codify and delimit. Tonal music possesses the ability to present multiple elements that can be attributed proto-subjective qualities of volition, and discussions of musical subjectivity or agency readily interpret the musical textures encountered in nineteenth-century music as consisting of a host of different actants and agents. How this relates to the question of deciding between a larger single subject or multiple subjects is, however, less well defined, as much as anything because prominent theorists such as Cone and, most recently, Robert Hatten ultimately reduce all such potential subjects to a 'single overriding subjectivity'.[22] To do this, however, is to deny or overlook music's well-documented capacity to be heard to speak in the voices of multiple subjects, to speak as a 'we'; and this is simply not borne out by common musical experience. Eighteenth-century aesthetics of sociability and the familiar adage of the string quartet as a 'conversation between four rational people' depends on just such a capacity to be heard as multiple subjects, while recent accounts of nineteenth-century nationalism have emphasised how powerful music's ability to project a first-person plural voice, a communal 'we are the people', can be.[23] Nevertheless, in practice some features seem potentially more significant than others in distinguishing between the multiple elements of a single subject on the one hand, and the multiple voices of a plurality of subjects on the other.

---

[21] Steinberg, 'Schumann's Homelessness', p. 47.

[22] Hatten, *A Theory of Virtual Agency for Western Art Music*.

[23] Recent revisionist scholarship on the conversation model in late eighteenth-century music includes Sutcliffe, *Instrumental Music in an Age of Sociability*, and with particular attention to performance, Klorman, *Mozart's Music of Friends*. On the collective voice of the people, see Steinberg, 'The Voice of the People at the Moment of the Nation', in *Listening to Reason*, pp. 163–92, and more recently Katherine Hambridge, 'Staging Singing in the Theater of War (Berlin, 1805)', *Journal of the American Musicological Society*, 68 (2015), 39–98, who usefully makes the distinction between music which seeks to unify a country under 'one voice' (such as patriotic songs sung to a single line), and that expressing a polyphony of separate voices and views.

Two of the most important musical factors – often interrelated – are timbral differentiation and the realisation by multiple performers.

As in the example of the *Märchenerzählungen*, the timbral distinctiveness of different voices can be a contributing cause: the distinctive timbres of clarinet, viola, and piano in this work more readily lend themselves to suggesting three distinct voices or protagonists, rather than a single (divided) subject. It helps, of course, that the music is played by three different performers too. Still, there are elements that in other circumstances might suggest the subjectivity of the whole is of a single subject divided into multiple elements. Already in the opening piece the imitative sharing of material between parts proceeds with a regularity that might suggest these voices form parts of a larger composite organism rather than independent actors, and this quality is prominent again in the third piece, in which the intimate melodic exchanges between clarinet and viola are woven together over the murmuring figuration in the piano, which soon adds contrapuntal interest of its own to the texture (Ex. 8.5). Though the differentiated timbres of the three instruments probably maintain the sense of distinct personalities, in another situation the voices might be heard to blend into the blurred internal rhythms of a dreaming solitary subject.[24]

On the other hand, the subjectivity of a solo piano piece is more obviously attributable to a single overriding subject, given the greater timbral uniformity and the fact that all is realised by one performer, even if tonal or textural elements might create a sense of internal division to this subject. But most other combinations of more than one instrument create a hermeneutic leeway that makes determining the number of subjects evoked rather a matter of ad hoc interpretation, more or less plausible in any argument put forward, rather than watertight. The string quartet, for instance, has famously been understood as a conversation between four different individuals, and yet its sound can blend extremely homogenously, to this extent being potentially understood as voicing one overriding subject. Again, other musical factors, such as the tonal duality seen in Schumann's Op. 41 No. 1, might subsequently suggest something of a split in the singular subject. Chamber music that mixes timbres, such as that combining piano with strings, is trickier to determine in the abstract case and can be more fluid in moving between different implied subjective voices. We saw in the discussion of the Piano Quartet how the slow movement's opening clearly projects a romantic duet between violin and cello, with the piano and viola offering 'neutral' support, a sonic backdrop

---

[24] John Daverio, for example, attributes this number to 'Eusebius' (*Robert Schumann*, p. 479).

Ex. 8.5 Schumann: *Märchenerzählungen*, Op. 132, No. 3, *Ruhiges Tempo, mit zartem Ausdruck*, opening

for the amorous subjects. But as the movement progresses the sense of two distinct voices dissipates, and by the central G flat section a homophonic and largely homorhythmic passage for all four instruments blends into a single enveloping subjectivity.

As with the solo piano piece, the accompanied solo song is one of the most iconic Romantic carriers of subjectivity and is customarily interpreted as the expression of a single subject, but the differentiation between voice and piano gives ample room for exploring the multiple sides of a single, perhaps divided subject, besides numerous other ambiguities in subject position. Again, different subjective voices can be set off by tonal or other means (as in the otherworldly G major of the flowers answering the protagonist's B major in 'Ich wandelte unter den Bäumen'), or the piano can evoke other, often non-human voices (such as the sounds of nature). But it is probably more unusual in a solo song for the music to be heard speaking as a 'we'. Finally, with the full orchestra we come to the most complex textural and timbral interaction of all, one which can suggest a single subject, a divided subject, multiple subjects, a collective subject, objectivity – and pretty much anything in between. In the concerto, for instance, the orchestra often takes on a collective voice, of the 'they', against which the subjective voice of the soloist is set into relief. Yet despite the potential variety of voices on offer, it is probably easier (and in practice, more common) for an orchestra to be heard to blend into some form of single subject than it is for a small ensemble of highly differentiated voices.

Schumann's *Konzertstück* for Four Horns and Orchestra, Op. 86, seems a pertinent exemplification of some of the issues raised here. Though one could hear the work as speaking in a single voice of the imagined composer 'Schumann', it would nonetheless be most likely, I would submit, to hear the subjectivity of the work as plural, created from the four 'subjects' plus the backing orchestral forces. Although timbral differentiation is minimal to non-existent, the four players performing it, and the type of give and take created between their parts, overrides the unitary voice with multiplicity. So, too, the practicalities of its performance alongside the work's over-ridingly cheerful, sociable tone supersedes any sense of a divided, fractured subject with the conviviality of a group of subjects.

At least as important, however, if not more so in coming to determine how music can be heard to speak in plural voices are non-musical factors – verbal indicators in scores and the interpretative contexts provided by reception history. Given how much less precise musical designations of subjectivity are than verbal ones, it should hardly come as a surprise that verbal indicators may play probably the most substantial part in conveying the specific type or number of subjects purported to be present.

Piano music, as stated, will generally convey a single subject, though this may be a divided one. But differentiating between different voices of the same subject, and different subjects, is more or less impossible from the music without the aid of words. Take *Carnaval*, which offers a series of 'masks' for different personas, some of which are to be taken for sides of Schumann's own psyche (as in the *Davidsbündlertänze*), some of whom are stylised personas of other real people, some of which are generic fictional characters of the *commedia dell'arte*. Only the verbal clues in the score would surely be able to alert us to the difference between pieces expressing two sides of the same subject (Florestan, Eusebius) and other personas adopted (Chiarina, Estrella, Paganini, Chopin, Pierrot, Arlequin, etc.). In the former case, the music purportedly represents two sides of a divided subject, in the latter multiple stylised other subjects. The final 'March of the Davidsbündler' presumably accompanies a plurality of subjects, a 'we', though as a march they are not heard 'speaking' as such, and without the title there would be no way of telling whether one subject or many were marching. In *Kreisleriana* the intercutting of different types of music may suggest a split personality, Johannes Kreisler torn between the ideal world of his art and the reality of the artist in the world, but could equally reflect the interlocking narrative technique of *Kater Murr* – the passionate voice of Kreisler alternating with the self-contented purrs and harmonious caterwauling of Murr as it were – and without more precise verbal indication by Schumann as to the work's relation with Hoffmann's writings, commentators have been unable to agree on which.

Allied with this is the importance of reception history. It is arguable that the propensity to read different subjects in Schumann's music stems from project-ing a popular view of him as someone almost fixated with his own subjectivity and creative alter egos, which overspills from his playful attributions of author-ship to Florestan and Eusebius in a few scores of the 1830s to cover his entire output. So much so, that even the operatic representation of multiple subjects, in which several distinct characters are explicitly portrayed on stage, is not spared. Such is exemplified by Nikolaus Harnoncourt's interpretation of *Genoveva*, which proposes that the opera's different characters can be imagined 'as different facets of a single complex character'. Though he offers justification for this reading in Schumann's use of common leitmotivs, it is hard to think that Harnoncourt would have been so receptive to what is, on the face of it, a distinctly counterintuitive reading, had Schumann not been famous for dividing his personality into alter egos, were he not already celebrated for being one of the most subject-centred of all composers.[25]

---

[25] 'Schumann's leitmotifs are not attached to individual characters', holds Harnoncourt; they suggest, rather, 'the infinite range of possibilities contained within any one character.' 'I can well imagine all the characters as different facets of a single complex character.' Monika Mertl, 'Reinventing Opera: Nikolaus Harnoncourt and his view of *Genoveva*', liner notes to Teldec CD 0630–13144-2 (1997), 19–20. The reading is, however, consistent with the attempts of Cone and Hatten to reduce all potential musical subjects to a single controlling one.

Ultimately the whole question posed here is inescapably hermeneutic, and the pursuit of strong rules for determining a phenomenology of musical subjectivity desperately imprecise without the aid of language. But more often than not, words are not lacking. And imprecision is anyway not the same as being meaningless. It may even be fruitful – as when the listener can move at once between rejection, empathy, identification, or participation; with musical subjects that may appear to be other, similar, or one's own; and singular, plural, or even something in between, which common-sense language, quite reasonably, fails to grasp . . .

Objectivity, Intersubjectivity, or the loss of Subjectivity

Notwithstanding Harnoncourt's views on *Genoveva*, a work written in the years 1847–8, there has been a longstanding belief that Schumann's music over the 1840s shows a general trend away from the 'subjective' to what is, predictably, termed the 'objective'. Franz Brendel, a critic on friendly terms with Schumann in this period (albeit differing in aesthetic values), crystallised this perspective even while was occurring in his 1845 essay, 'Robert Schumann with Reference to Mendelssohn-Bartholdy and the Development of Modern Music in General', written soon after he had taken up editorship of Schumann's *Neue Zeitschrift für Musik*. For Brendel, as a composer Schumann had begun with the 'most decisive inwardness', following 'the urge of his inner self'.[26] His earlier pieces

reveal a subject focussed entire on itself, one that lives and breathes exclusively in its own inwardness and only moves outward from this centre into the external . . . It is an individuality that expresses only itself and its personal emotional states, but it depicts the world only as far as the Self has been touched by it.[27]

Schumann's piano and song collections do not contain 'objective portrayals' but instead form lyrical interconnected cycles of emotional states.[28] In more recent years, however (Brendel names the symphonies, string quartets, piano quartet and quintet, and *Das Paradies und die Peri*), the composer 'emerges from his inwardness; he moves away from the fantastic humour and indulgence in fantasy of his earlier works and comes closer to an objective style and expression'.[29]

---

[26] Franz Brendel, 'Robert Schumann', p. 333.   [27] *Ibid.*, p. 324.   [28] *Ibid.*, p. 321.
[29] *Ibid.*, p. 328.

Brendel, confirmed Hegelian as he was, characteristically seeks to map Schumann's 'evolution' onto a stage in a logical progression that seeks to reconcile the subjective with the objective, reflecting a deeper historical process. Yet Brendel cannot help find some loss along with the 'advancements and expansions' in the move to greater objectivity he identifies in Schumann's later music. Even in the earlier music, Schumann was less successful in 'older forms' (like the sonata) than with the 'free outpourings of his inner self', and so it appears that his expression is also not entirely successful in some of these later works'.

> It seems as though the composer, from his subjective standpoint, is not entirely at home in the objective world and thus occasionally passes into lack of clarity, even dryness . . . .The fountain of Schumann's creativity is his subjectivity, and at the present time he loses unity of style and character when he ventures into the epic realm.[30]

In this, Brendel was pre-empting much subsequent criticism, which devalued Schumann's music after 1840 and sought to find the essence of Schumann in the early piano works and songs, in the youthful, 'subjective' poetic voice rather than the 'objective' later one. Yet it is clear that Schumann also perceived a change in his compositional aesthetic, and conversely valued it quite differently – as showing greater technical resource, an advance in scale, breadth of output, and capability. (It is also clear that, at least later in life, Schumann had little time for such sweeping abstractions popular in aesthetic discussion of the time, for the crude separation of art and artists into 'objective' and 'subjective' camps.[31])

We may well question the judgement that relegates Schumann's symphonies, chamber works, and choral pieces to secondary status, while what Brendel means by 'subjectivity' is also not necessarily identical with all later uses of the term. It would nonetheless be flying in the face of reception history to treat all of Schumann's compositional output as conveying the same type of subjective ethos familiar from his earlier music, and hence the

---

[30] *Ibid.*, p. 331.

[31] In 1854 Schumann would upbraid the critic Richard Pohl for the blanket application of such ready-made philosophic terms to his oeuvre (and that of other composers): 'are there really two kinds of creativity, one objective and the other subjective?' he asks. 'Was Beethoven an objective [composer]?' On the contrary, 'such miserable words' cannot convey the secret of music: 'A fool with a free, inward soul understood more of music than did the shrewdly thoughtful Kant!' Schumann, letter of 6 February 1854, published in the appendix to Richard Pohl, 'Reminiscences of Robert Schumann (1878)', trans. John Michael Cooper, in R. Larry Todd (ed.), *Schumann and His World* (Princeton: Princeton University Press, 1994), p. 261 (German original in *SB* II.5:409–12).

notion of subjectivity may well be limited in its range of application.[32] 'Subjectivity', at least in the sense understood from the earlier piano music and song cycles of 1840, may still be applicable in some measure but is unlikely to provide the most pertinent category for seeking to understand *The Paradise and the Peri* or the *Scenes from Goethe's Faust*, a key for unlocking the *Album für die Jugend* or *Requiem für Mignon*.

The causes for this change are no doubt manifold – generic, personal, social-historical. In part, this perceived shift in emphasis owes to the genres chosen by Schumann, his turning to larger-scale pieces and more public genres (symphony, cantata, choral ballad, opera) over the course of the 1840s that are less readily understood as 'subjective', alongside the increasing interest in music for domestic, social, and pedagogical use. In terms of compositional style this may be due in part to Schumann's increased interest in contrapuntal technique and intricate motivic working, in the 'new manner of composing' that he claimed to have adopted in the mid-1840s.[33] An increasing respect for 'classical' forms and genres is apparent from the early 1840s, buoyed on by his newly attained capacity to write in them, the supportive environment of Leipzig, and friendship with Mendelssohn. (Though some of Schumann's earlier comments on the natural decline of the old genres are still trotted out by adherents of the old-fashioned view that sees his best work as over by 1840, there is no doubt that he recognised how his compositional abilities had developed enormously in the following years; there is an unmistakable element of cutting one's vision of historical necessity to fit one's own aptitude, and Schumann, for one, overcame this.) In addition, the greater involvement in social music making, and not least his own experience as father to a growing brood of offspring led Schumann to turn increasingly to the production of music for amateur, communal music making. As Anthony Newcomb contends with the later piano music, this movement towards *Hausmusik* may be a reflection of economic factors – the fact that Schumann is writing for the marketplace – but this is also a contributing reason for the change in subjective voice at this time.[34]

---

[32] Alexander Stefaniak has called into question the extent to which the notion of subjective interiority even covers Schumann's earlier aesthetics, focusing instead on ideas of virtuosity and transcendence in Schumann's criticism; see *Schumann's Virtuosity: Criticism, Composition, and Performance in Nineteenth-Century Germany* (Bloomington: Indiana University Press, 2016).

[33] 'eine ganz andere Art zu componiren zu entwickeln begonnen': the famous statement is contained in an undated diary entry from 1846 (*Tagebücher*, vol. II, p. 402).

[34] Newcomb, 'Schumann and the Marketplace'.

The notion of the self and its relation to society is also not historically invariant (society itself is clearly not), and not only might the idea of subjectivity mean slightly different things for different critics over the last two centuries but may possibly have been something on which Schumann's own views shifted over the course of his life. Schumann's early views and aesthetics often align with earlier Romantic notions of subjectivity gleaned from Jean Paul and Hoffmann, which in the 1830s were already several decades old. Though it seems he remained close to these authors to the end of his life (witness the compilation of *Dichtergarten* in his last active months), it is nevertheless the case that his own relation with the world around him changed quite dramatically over the 1840s, as he went from a moderately successful journalist and lesser-known composer of eccentric piano music to a public figure, a composer of symphonies and the hugely successful *Paradies*, conductor of a *Liedertafel* and a civic orchestral society. Schumann's own experiences as a subject moving within a larger society evolved in this period; the idea of subjectivity across Schumann's life also changed culturally and politically, especially in the German states in the years leading up to the failed revolutions of 1848–9, in which the aesthetic of emotional inwardness was increasingly 'tainted by the suspicion of political irresponsibility'.[35]

I would naturally not propose to drop the idea of subjectivity altogether from consideration of Schumann's music dating from the 1840s onwards. But it is certainly advisable to remain aware of the range of meanings and different manifestations that the subjective can take in this repertoire. A work like the popular 'Rhenish' Symphony, Op. 97 (1850), engages with the communal, civic institution of the symphony and speaks in tones that range from the subjective (the intimate third movement), the collective (the second-movement *Ländler*), the austere baroque objectivity of the *Feierlich* fourth movement, and a compositional voice that merges the 'I' with a larger, universalising thrust familiar from the Beethovenian symphonic covenant (the buoyant surge of the outer movements, still infused with a 'subjective' lyricism as in the reworking of the *An die ferne Geliebte* theme in the finale, and culminating in a celebratory cyclic round-up of the work's themes).[36]

---

[35] Spitzer, *A History of Emotion in Western Music*, p. 316. This is a point that Laura Tunbridge tentatively proposes may have influenced the change in Schumann's outlook; see *Schumann's Late Style* (Cambridge: Cambridge University Press, 2007), p. 106.

[36] The communal aspect of this symphony is especially brought out by Gerd Nauhaus, 'Schumann's Symphonic Finales', trans. Susan Gillespie, in R. Larry Todd (ed.), *Schumann and His World* (Princeton: Princeton University Press, 1994), pp. 124–5, who refers in turn to

Or, rather than a binary opposition between the extremes of a private, Romantic subjectivity and a public, Classical objectivity, we might consider the notion of 'intersubjectivity'. Such a relational understanding of the subject is prominent in the eighteenth century, especially in the moral philosophy of Enlightenment thinkers like Hume and Adam Smith. Developing the point that subjectivity is relational, a more recent figure like Jürgen Habermas would insist that we shift from a Cartesian 'monological' subjectivity to a discursive 'intersubjectivity' for explaining the socially constituted relation between the individual and others.[37] Just as the concerto is commonly interpreted as a stylised negotiation of the self with its surrounding society, so several of Schumann's larger choral works articulate this dynamic. *Der Rose Pilgerfahrt*, Op. 112 (1851), for instance, revolves around a subject (predictably female), at odds with her surrounding society, sacrificing herself out of love for another; in *Faust* and *Manfred*, conversely, it is a male subject at odds with society and the world, who is pointedly unwilling to compromise. It is not that subjectivity is irrelevant for the music; simply that this is not the private, lyrical, self-absorbed subject of the 1830s, that 'amorous and imprisoned soul that speaks to itself', but rather a social individual openly coming into conflict and negotiating its relationship – sometimes successfully, sometimes not – with those others around it.[38] And for various musical reasons, the subject portrayed may be more often heard in later years as an external dramatic protagonist, rather than experienced with the lyric immediacy of first-person identification, as was more frequent in the earlier music.

One problem which may nevertheless arise is how the expectation of subjective interiority, based on a selective corpus of Schumann's earlier piano works and songs and combined with the Romanticised interweaving of his music with his life, has affected the criteria used to assess his later music. Though such 'objective' qualities are hardly absent even in the 1830s, in the later Schumann one more frequently encounters a situation where the music seems to propose no particular subject position, a detached 'third-person' perspective, or an inconsistent one. Few listeners expect a baroque fugue to exude qualities of Romantic subjectivity, yet for

Peter Gülke, 'Zur "Rheinischen Sinfonie"', in Hans-Klaus Metzger and Rainer Riehn (eds.), *Musik-Konzepte: Robert Schumann II* (Munich: text+kritik, 1982), pp. 251–3.

[37] Such ideas are present throughout most of Habermas's work; on the intersubjective basis of communication see especially his *Theory of Communicative Action*, vol. I, *Reason and the Rationalization of Society*, trans. Thomas A. McCarthy (Cambridge: Polity Press, 1984), while the critique of a self-constituting subjectivity is notably pursued in *The Philosophical Discourse of Modernity*, trans. Frederick G. Lawrence (Cambridge: Polity Press, 1985).

[38] Roland Barthes, 'Loving Schumann', p. 293.

a Schumann character piece this seems a more or less normative demand. When it is not so apparent, it is too easy to find the result disconcerting, an aesthetic flaw, our failure to find the subjective becoming Schumann's failure to express the subjective, which in some cases even leads to the biographical imposition that he was already losing his own sense of self.

A pertinent case which both illustrates and partially problematises this point might be provided by the *Gesänge der Frühe*, Op. 133, a collection of five short piano pieces written in the autumn of 1853. Schumann described them in a letter of early 1854 as 'musical pieces that portray [*schildern*] the feelings at the approach and growth of morning, but more as expressions of feeling than painting', thus implying the adoption of some subjective position.[39] But one would be hard pressed to identify any familiar 'subject-ive' quality – at least as recognisable in many of Schumann's earlier piano pieces of the 1830s – throughout much of this opus. This is compounded by the decision to label them *Gesänge* – songs – which as Laura Tunbridge observes 'seems an odd choice given that they are not for voice' or 'particu-larly lyrical' either.[40] Only the last one has a distinctively songlike charac-ter, and this is in the collective mode of the chorale. If anything, one would be tempted to claim that the aesthetic subject seems to have withdrawn from the music (a formulation that reveals the debt to Adorno's reading of late Beethoven in positing another composer's 'late style').[41] In the opening piece, for instance, austere octaves announce a theme in fifths, whose continuation is harmonised in a chorale-like manner (Ex. 8.6). The con-ception is akin to 'Auf das Trinkglas eines verstorbenen Freundes' from Op. 35 (see Ex. 6.9), though here in Op. 133 the solitary line is met with the collective. There is an impersonal quality to the material (the opening might easily serve as a commonplace baroque fugal subject), which the communal voicing does little to dispel. There is a 'subject' certainly, in the technical sense that a fugue has a subject, but yet the figurative aesthetic subject seems missing, or hardened into some unyielding objective form, as if turned to stone.

This theme winds its way throughout the piece, entering in successive keys, as if a cross between a baroque invention and a chorale prelude, the

---

[39] Schumann, letter to his publisher F. W. Arnold, 24 February 1854 (*SB* III.5:125); the formulation clearly echoes Beethoven's famous comment on the 'Pastoral' Symphony. There are also associations Schumann draws between this opus and the work of Hölderlin, though to my mind they confuse rather than clarify interpretation.

[40] Tunbridge, *Schumann's Late Style*, p. 203.

[41] See the discussion of this piece by Scott Burnham, 'Late Styles', in Roe-Min Kok and Laura Tunbridge (eds.), *Rethinking Schumann* (New York: Oxford University Press, 2011), pp. 423–6.

Ex. 8.6 Schumann: *Gesänge der Frühe*, Op. 133, No. 1, *Im Ruhigen Tempo*

phrase modified each time it is heard. (It also re-emerges, reconstituted, in the second piece of the set.) Despite the calmness of its processional tread there is a mildly unsettling quality to the music. Scott Burnham has called attention to the prevalence of dissonance in the piece, mostly diatonic in the form of clashing seconds arising from the part writing, and curious rhythmic suspensions offset the regularity of the metric design.[42] Such is the effect of impersonal, objective architecture that Daverio is led to hear the piece as if issuing from the same solemn spaces as the 'Rhenish' Symphony's imposing Cologne Cathedral movement: 'the bass and inner voices become curiously dislodged from the melody, as if to imitate the overlapping and clashing of sonorities in a great reverberatory space'.[43] Subjectivity seems to have abdicated itself, leaving a vacant subject position behind.

This example holds up to us the problems encountered in trying to access the meaning of Schumann's later music. For the apparent absence of a subject forms an expressive dissonance with the purported connotations of this work divulged by the composer.[44] It seems that Schumann's language, his musical mode of speaking, has become altered in his later music through the adoption and internalisation of contrapuntal techniques and a sometimes dense motivic working, whereby the 'expression of feeling' can proceed in a language which seems, on the face of it, far removed from the clichés of Romantic subjectivity. It is worth remembering that for Schumann, Bach's fugues were 'character pieces of the highest sort'.[45] We might ask if we are simply listening for the wrong type of subjectivity, for the wrong expressive rhetoric. Or perhaps subjectivity is here sublimated into something greater.

' . . . for in this immensity my thoughts are drowned'

The passing of the subjective voice over into apparent objectivity, witnessed here in the first of the *Gesänge der Frühe*, is not a unique occurrence in Schumann's later music. Yet rather than denoting the suppression of subjectivity per se, it could instead imply the idea of the dissolution of the subject into a greater, all-encompassing objectivity, the merging of self with world. As Gerald Izenberg has argued, one of the characteristic tendencies

[42] *Ibid.*, p. 425.   [43] Daverio, *Robert Schumann*, p. 481.
[44] Rosen, *The Romantic Generation*, p. 689.
[45] Schumann, 'Etuden für Pianoforte' (1838), *Gesammelte Schriften*, vol. I, p. 354.

of Romantic subjectivity is the desire to surrender the self to the whole, to lose the I in the not-I, dissolving the fragile ego in the immensity of the cosmos – which forms the other side of the Fichtean longing for self-assertion, the self-constituting, world-making subject, in which the other exists merely through being posited by the self.[46] A defining image of Romanticism is of the self reaching out over the far horizon towards the infinite, overcoming the finitude of its bounded condition by the sublime thought of its own tiny position within the boundless ocean of space and time. The sense of subjective detachment heard in some of Schumann's later music might convey not so much the absence of the subject as its longing for transcendence.

'Abendlied', Op. 107 No. 6 (1851), realises something of this quality (Ex. 8.7). The poem by Gottfried Kinkel (no mere Romantic dreamer but a convicted revolutionary who had just escaped from a Prussian prison) takes up the theme of stillness and the immersion of the subject in the wider natural world, escaping from the self and its troubles in the immensity of the evening sky opening up above. All is still; so hushed is the evening that you hear everywhere the feet of passing angels. Indeed, it is almost as if time is stilled; and yet the stars will run their steady course through the encircling heavens. Rocking triplets and a pronounced tendency towards subdominant regions create a reassuring, almost cradling quality to the piano accompaniment, played una corda throughout, while the almost constant disparity between the triplets in the accompaniment and duple values in the vocal line impart a gentle cross-rhythmic effect, which hovers between a state that would dissolve clear temporal articulation and perhaps just a touch of unease, the sense of the subject still being at odds with the world. The strophic repetition of the music for the second verse is likewise blurred through phrasal overlap, the cadential dominant in b. 18 elided into the retuning music by holding the seventh over as a suspension that becomes the opening phrase's subdominant harmony in the second half of the following bar. This dissolution of such potential moments of articulation, aided by the ambiguity over the opening melody's anacrusis (the piano seems to pre-empt the vocal line by half a bar here), contributes to the sense of floating torpor, in which the subject's identity is already half dissolved into the world around it. The final line, 'cast away what ails you, heart, and your anxiety', is a typical Schumannian plea for healing at the close of a song collection (the Op. 35

---

[46] Gerald Izenberg, *Impossible Individuality: Romanticism, Revolution, and the Origins of Modern Selfhood, 1787–1802* (Princeton: Princeton University Press, 1992).

Ex. 8.7 Schumann: 'Abendlied' (Kinkel), *6 Gesänge*, Op. 107 No. 6, bb. 1–20

Kerner cycle provides an earlier example), but here sought through submission of the individual subject to the greater, objective majesty of the universe.

In 'Nachtlied', Op. 96 No. 1 (1850), night draws on, and the peace of death is more clearly the implication of Goethe's celebrated text ('Über allen Gipfeln ist Ruh"). Schumann responds with a setting that reflects the stillness and grandeur of the surrounding world, from the nearby branches to the distant horizon, yet in which an almost indefinable disquiet animates the subject's intimate self-counsel (Ex. 8.8).[47] Circling chords in the lower-middle register of the piano and predominantly diatonic harmonic language create an atmosphere of hushed solemnity and gravity. The tempo is markedly slow (*Sehr langsam*), and with the frequent unanticipated elongations in vocal line as well as accompaniment imparts a virtual pulselessness to proceedings: not quite 'timelessness', but a loosening of the bonds of temporal measure, plunging the subject back towards a more undifferentiated state behind individualisation in space and time.[48] The chordal spacing and C major tonality might suggest an affinity with the 'Arietta' of Beethoven's Op. 111, but Schumann's world is more troubled than his predecessor's calm radiance.

Graham Johnson makes the point that despite the stillness and monumental spacing of the chords, something in Schumann's setting is slightly awkward: 'the effect is rapt, even serene, but not comfortable'.[49] The harmonic rhythm and phrasing often seems to be slightly out of skew. Schumann's prosody, bringing out the resonating rhymes within Goethe's enjambment, avoids any sense of regular metre, but the accompaniment is also a key factor here.[50] This is despite the sense of putative regularity in the piano's solemn harmonic cycles, whose bass line repeatedly circles up from the tonic to F and down again to the tonic, but almost every time in a different form. The first phrase would appear to present a complete four-bar unit, but the penultimate passing V_3^4 (b. 3^3) is extended past its expected minim duration, tied over the bar, only resolving on the second half of b. 4. This concluding tonic is then elided with the start of a new cycle, but now in an instance of further compression the harmony

[47] An insightful account of the poem and four of its other settings is provided by Scott Burnham in 'The Stillness of Time, the Fullness of Space: Four Settings of Goethe's "Wandrers Nachtlied"', *19th-Century Music*, 40 (2017), 189–200.

[48] Jon Finson, in a sympathetic account of the song concentrating on the composer's prosody, likewise calls attention to how Schumann 'effaces meter almost entirely and with it our sense of passing time' (*Robert Schumann: The Book of Songs*, p. 237).

[49] Graham Johnson, notes to *The Songs of Robert Schumann*, vol. 1, p. 31.

[50] On the text setting see Finson, *Robert Schumann: The Book of Songs*, p. 237.

Ex. 8.8 Schumann: 'Nachtlied' (Goethe), *Lieder und Gesänge* vol. IV, Op. 96 No. 1

above the F in in on the downbeat of b. 5 – what would be the second stage of
the new cycle – elides with the fourth stage of the initial progression (b. 2^4).
With the penultimate second-inversion dominant in b. 6^3 reduced to
a minim, what might have been eight bars – a pair of four-bar phrases – is

compressed irregularly into six bars, which elide in turn with the resumption of the opening harmonic cycle at b. 7, forming a one-bar overlap between vocal and accompanimental phrases. Voice and accompaniment – like self and world – co-exist but are not yet one. From b. 11 the grip of the opening chord progression loosens as the music modulates via the introduction of accidentals for the first time in the piece, but the circling progression returns, varied again, at the conclusion of the poem. Even at the close, though, the upper line remains on $\hat{5}$, linking up with the opening sonority of the piece as if the progression could repeat indefinitely. There is both stillness and solidity in these cycles, and yet imperfection and incompletion.

Goethe, then in his early thirties, inscribed the words of the poem on the wall of a mountain hut near Ilmeneu, to return half a century later in 1831, when, deeply moved, he re-encountered the trace of his younger self. The story is well known; it is highly likely Schumann would have been familiar with it.[51] The subject comes face to face with another that is in fact his younger self, and after so many years cannot help musing on that which endures and what is transitory ('das Dauernde, das Verschwundene', as Goethe puts it).[52] Can a musical setting hope to convey this facet of reception history, which has attached itself almost inseparably to this famous poem? It is possible; Schumann had earlier devised a comparable reflection on the continuity of human life amidst the passing of time in the duet 'Familien-Gemälde', Op. 34 No. 4 (1840), which treats the simultaneity of life's different stages glimpsed across generations. The listener to Schumann's setting may be struck by a moment almost at the end of the song – the little melodic phrase in the piano arching up to the tonic (a^1–d^2–c^2–c^2–g^1, bb. 29–30), which, entering after the voice has trailed off from its heart-stopping rise of a seventh on 'auch!', brings the seemingly eternal procession of the accompanimental chords at last to a cadential close. It may appear rather familiar, as something almost identical occurs in the first movement of the C major *Fantasie* Op. 17 – an expressive melodic fragment, marked *Adagio*, that twice causes the music to break off on a diminished seventh that remains unresolved (bb. 79–81 and 271–3; see Ex 2.4). Is this the older Schumann remembering his younger self, and, revisiting one of his favourite achievements from his early years, gently

---

[51] Goethe related the circumstances in a letter to Carl Friedrich Zelter of 4 September 1831, which was made public in 1834 with the posthumous publication of their correspondence (the letter in question is No. 813 of the *Briefwechsel zwischen Goethe und Zelter in den Jahren 1796 bis 1832*, 6 vols. (Berlin: Dunker und Humblot, 1834), vol. IV, p. 280). The wooden cabin on Kickelhahn had become famous as the 'Goethehäuschen' by the end of the decade.

[52] *Ibid.*, p. 280.

guiding the earlier phrase to its proper resting place? Perhaps. On the other hand, given his music's rich intertextual quality, its many apparent allusions, this is more likely a case of the interpreter being enticed into the seemingly self-referential, cryptic musical world spun by Schumann, desiring to make meanings where probably there are none.[53] Rather than Schumann recognising his earlier self, we might be misrecognising both.

*

Both 'Abendlied' and 'Nachtlied' seek solace for the troubled, finite human subject in the submission to the immensity of nature, lying still and expectant around us. Willingly drowning the subjective in the objective, the self in the all, appears balm for troubled souls. Yet for those who know a little of Schumann's life, the idea of hearing the sound of angels and the coming on of night might form an uncanny and disturbing parallel to events that within a few years would drive the composer to losing his self more literally, in the rather more unwelcome of guise of insanity or *Umnachtung*, and barely two years afterwards, death. As the following chapter explores, the idea of losing one's sense of self is also, more troublingly, associated with mental disturbance, manifested through the inability to recognise oneself, commonly exemplified in a musical context by misrecognising the voice of the self as that of another. Yet as it will also reveal, mysterious angelic voices can be heard cropping up throughout Schumann's earlier music too; even in the manner of his psychological breakdown, life was apparently following art.

Perhaps the temptation to link the two can be carried too far, however. For in discerning the traits of encroaching insanity in Schumann's music, earlier commentators have almost invariably gone beyond what can reasonably be demonstrated; the subjectivity of the music simply cannot be identified with that of the composer. The implications for our own activities as interpreting subjects are, at the very least, cautionary.

---

[53] The phrase is clearly a contraction of the triplet figure heard earlier at bb. 19 and 21, which doesn't militate against it being an intertextual allusion (the *Fantasie*'s own purported Beethoven quotation emerges likewise as the outcome of earlier thematic working) but does provide an internal 'logic' to explain its presence here.

9 | Hearing Oneself as Another

Troubled Beauty

In Chapter 4 we examined the feeling of subjective plenitude in the *Larghetto* of the 'Spring' Symphony, the sense of unmediated self-presence that can be created through music. Over a decade later, we encounter a similar mood at the start of the slow movement of Schumann's Violin Concerto: an expressive melodic line of swaying quavers given to half the cellos, projected against a warm sonority of lower strings and bassoons and horns (Ex. 9.1). Yet there is something wrong here. To the innocent ear it seems as if the accompaniment is displaced with respect to the cello melody; a largely unobtrusive lagging that only on occasions jars. The effect is akin to the syncopated pulsations of the symphony's slow movement, imparting a hazy, floating quality; but nonetheless what is different in the concerto is that only the cello part conforms to the metre it projects. All the other instruments are out of synchrony with it; and while the cello is the first voice heard, initially suggesting that its metric structure corresponds to the notated downbeat, in fact it is this melodic line that is misaligned against the notated metre followed by the accompaniment (as becomes evident at the end of the phrase, when the cello line has to be held over by a semiquaver to coincide with the cadence articulated by the rest of the orchestra). The effect is dreamy, even a little nostalgic; but nonetheless the serenity of the music's lyricism is slightly troubled.

Even more curiously, this beautiful opening phrase is ignored by the solo violin, entering with a quite new melody in bar 5, an expressive, almost hymn-like idea constructed from essentially a series of descending thirds. It is unusual enough for a concerto's slow movement to open with a passage that sounds like another instrument has taken over the starting role (Brahms no doubt was remembering Schumann's conception when he came to write the *Andante* of his B flat major Piano Concerto), but even more noteworthy

Ex. 9.1 Schumann: Violin Concerto in D minor (1853), ii, opening

when the soloist simply ignores this rival opening theme.[1] Regardless of their eloquence, in Schumann's movement the two themes seem almost to be talking at cross-purposes.

Initially, the cellos' opening theme might be considered simply a prefatory phrase, subordinate to the soloist's principal theme. But as the movement progresses, the relationship between the two ideas becomes more complex, even a little perplexing. The new idea given to the soloist is strangely unfocussed for a main theme, proving markedly loose-knit in construction and tonally mobile. Following the sequential restatement of its initial two-bar idea a third higher it becomes transitional in function, moving towards the secondary tonality of F major after only six bars, as well as increasingly thematically digressive, incorporating reminiscences of the second subject of the preceding movement (bb. 11–12) followed by a lapse into this opening cello melody (bb. 13–14). The latter had twice briefly resurfaced in the accompanimental voices in the preceding bars (bb. 6 & 8), forming a type of metrically dissonant counterpoint that seems to rub against more than integrate with the violin's theme, and here it is given in a thematically vacant spot in the exposition, heard over a sustained dominant pedal that briefly defers the cadential attainment of the secondary tonality.[2] The eventual cadence to F major in b. 19 is marked by the return in the orchestra of the violin's opening phrase, used effectively as a closing theme in lieu of any secondary thematic material; but within three bars the music slips back to the tonic and the soloist resumes the cello's opening melody, marking the onset of a brief development section that will be dominated by this theme and clouded by the minor for the first time in this movement.

---

[1] The slow movements of Beethoven's last two piano concertos provide probably the closest precedents: in No. 4, the orchestra and soloist are famously opposed almost the entire way throughout; in No. 5 the soloist enters with new, meditative material, though by the reprise the first theme returns in the piano and the soloist fully integrated with the orchestra – pointedly unlike what happens in the present work. More typical would be either to start directly with the soloist (as with Schumann's two previous concertos) or to give the soloist a restatement of the theme heard in the orchestra, often as if forming the consequent to the orchestra's antecedent phrase. Even later in Brahms's Violin Concerto, the extended opening thematic statement given to the solo oboe is answered with a restatement of the theme by the soloist.

[2] It is possible to see the reuse of the cello figure as an example of the type of motivic combination increasingly favoured by Schumann in his later music; John Daverio's brief and characteristically positive reading interprets the movement along such lines, as concerned with thematic versatility (*Robert Schumann*, p. 17). The integration in this movement is fitful at best, however, and doesn't explain the latter stages of the form. Indeed, the lapse back into the cello melody here in b. 13 may appear somewhat parenthetical; the immediate transitional function has already been completed, and the music could continue from b. 12 into b. 16 easily enough, bypassing the recalled theme.

This cello theme forms the only real thematic contrast with the violin melody and initiates all the movement's major structural divisions, being given at the start of the exposition and development and returning subsequently to instigate the recapitulation (b. 32) and coda (b. 50). The soloist's single long, digressive phrase has served as a primary theme, transition, and secondary/closing theme, but is framed by the cellos' opening idea that articulates the movement's largest formal course. Thus, while fragments of the cello theme are incorporated into its texture and melodic line, the music given to the soloist manifests a strangely oblique, even subordinate status to this opening passage. And when the violin theme returns in the reprise (b. 36), it is darkened to the minor mode. Tonally estranged in G minor, the relative of the home key of B flat major, the ostensible expositional material of the movement is now alienated from the tonic in, of all places, the recapitulation. Whereas this theme in the exposition had led after 14 bars to the cadence in the secondary tonal area, no such confirmation is attained now. With the return of the cello phrase at b. 50, the music just slips from the dominant of G minor where the soloist has become stranded back to B flat and accelerates into the finale. Though a neat piece of motivic linkage connects the figure derived from the first movement into the prominent anacrusis of the ensuing polonaise, there is little sense that the preceding tonal split is resolved.

Despite its wistful beauty, the violin's opening idea has become alienated over the course of the movement; its greatest assuredness was when given in the orchestra in the dominant key at the end of the exposition, but this vision is lost, and the theme never returns with such strength or in the major after this point. In contrast, the finale twice briefly reworks the cello figure in the accompaniment (bb. 137 and 143), though again the thematic recall is not really integrated. If anything, the returning material momentarily darkens the music, appearing in F sharp minor and B minor now, without having any lasting effect on the finale.[3]

Without trying to impose too great a hermeneutic specificity, there seems something slightly odd about the musical subjects heard in this movement. Ostensibly a solo concerto with the violin providing the primary subject (or 'self') against the collective body of the orchestra (or 'other'), the soloist's lyricism proves anything but stable over the

---

[3] Joseph Kerman finds the allusion to the earlier movement 'positively uncanny' ('The Concertos', p. 185). In Laura Tunbridge's view, similarly, this theme's return 'seems to unnerve the soloist'. 'Its effect is to disturb; it is, perhaps, the voice that cannot be silenced.' *Schumann's Late Style*, pp. 126, 127.

course of the movement, while the opening cello theme takes on, in its own right, something of the sense of self-possession characteristic of musical subjectivity. Unlike the material given to the violin, the latter is tight-knit and tonally closed as a melodic entity and serves to articulate the principal stages of the movement's form, drawing the music back from G minor at the close after the soloist has wandered and lost its way. Yet this theme is itself troubled, being riven by an inherent metric disturbance that persists to the end. There are two potential musical 'selves' conveyed by this music, neither of which is completely at ease with itself, and whose relationship with each other remains problematic. Such uneasiness haunts much of Schumann's music – arguably increasingly towards the end of his career.

'Birds whistle, man alone sings . . . '

'Vogel als Prophet' (Bird as Prophet) from the *Waldszenen*, Op. 82, is a distinctly curious creation, a 'bizarre and enigmatic piece' as Eric Jensen puts it, 'often regarded as one of Schumann's most inexplicable works'.[4] Composed after the other eight *Waldszenen* were completed, almost as if an afterthought, it is probably the most well-known number of a collection that is itself the only piano work from Schumann's later years to have entered the concert repertoire. The two materials that make up the piece's ternary form are strikingly disjunct: first the whimsical, flighty outer section in G minor, and secondly the brief chorale-like central passage in G major. Both strongly characterised in topical content, it is not hard to associate the outer sections with the bird of the title and the central section with the prophetic capacity attributed to it, but how (and why) they should relate to the same creature is rather more mysterious.

The enigmatic quality is partly a result of a curious mixing of representational modes. Rather than signalling the bird through stylised evocation of birdsong, the outer section seems designed more as mimesis of its physical movement, with its treble tessitura, quick fluttering gestures, sporadic rhythmic motion, and runs of semiquavers conveying a nimble lightness, though the grace notes and trills might equally suggest a slight element of sonic emulation too (Ex. 9.2a). The emphasis is, however, on the

---

[4] Eric Frederick Jensen, 'A New Manuscript of Robert Schumann's *Waldszenen* Op. 82', *Journal of Musicology*, 3 (1984), 80, 83. John Daverio similarly describes it as 'the most enigmatic miniature in the set' (*Robert Schumann*, p. 411).

Ex. 9.2a Schumann: 'Vogel als Prophet', *Waldszenen*, Op. 82 No. 7, opening

Ex. 9.2b Schumann: 'Vogel als Prophet', central chorale, bb. 18–25

external appearance of the bird, its movements translated into established musical metaphors for visual qualities.

   This contrasts markedly with the interior section, for here we hear something unmistakably aural in essence – the sound of singing (Ex. 9.2b). Yet even more curiously, this is the sound, not of birdsong, but of humans ('Birds whistle, man alone sings', we remember Rousseau had claimed).[5] Schumann appears not unduly concerned with imitating birdsong in the outer section, but he could have certainly done a better job of suggesting it than choosing a chorale-like melody and texture in this central passage. This is obviously the

---

[5] Rousseau, *Essay on the Origin of Languages*, p. 326.

prophetic message that the bird is trying to convey. Strangely, the melody is not dissimilar from the soloist's theme in the slow movement of the Violin Concerto a few years later; though not identical (the tune here starts on the tonic scale degree rather than the third), the melodic profile, metric displacement, and much of the rhythmic structure make it at least a close relative.

There results a type of split between perceptual domains: we see, as it were, merely a bird, fluttering in the forest; but at some point, switching senses from the visual to aural, we become able to perceive something much stranger: we hear the bird speaking, and not in its own accustomed sounds but in human tongues, a mysterious communication from somewhere beyond. Indeed, given the religious connotations of the material, the song of the bird might even appear to be that of an angel, a heavenly envoy sent to man from God. Yet if this is the case, the chorale remains unfinished, the message incomplete; having modulated after four bars to the dominant, the opening phrase returns (b. 22), but its repetition is unexpectedly shifted to the flat submediant E♭ then falters, trailing off softly before switching back via a German sixth to the return of the opening section. The bird resumes flitting about as if nothing had happened. A very curious bird this, which acts like a normal avian inhabitant of the forest and yet sings in human tones; and equally curious, perhaps, are those that are able to hear its song.

In the autograph score, Schumann included an epigram at the end – 'Hüte dich, sei wach u[nd] munter' (be on guard: be wakeful and alert) – taken from Eichendorff's 'Zwielicht', previously set as the tenth song of the *Liederkreis*, Op. 39. Many commentators have sought to connect this enigmatic warning to the rest of the piece, though it seems to relate most clearly to the original ending that directly preceded it in the manuscript – one and a half bars of alternating dominant and tonic chords in resolute dotted rhythms – which Schumann discarded for publication along with the epigram. By cutting this ending and keeping the final bars open, Schumann creates a far more uncertain effect. The perfect cadence at b. 40 would make a perfectly satisfactory close to the piece, but instead, as at the end of the opening section, Schumann returns to the two-bar segment that opens the theme. These bars' alternation between tonic and predominant harmony, however, provides no cadential confirmation, and the melodic line ends questioningly on $\hat{5}$; the piece trails off as if unfinished. The dark saying of the prophecy is left obscure. Is it somehow foretelling the deeper, yet more troubled lyricism of the Violin Concerto some four years later? Did the bird really sing a chorale?

This piece's opening motive, indeed, possesses an odd connexion with a cadential figure heard at the close of the fourth piece of the collection, 'Verrufene Stelle' (Infamous Place). This is the one piece for which Schumann kept an epigram in the published score, and very dark it is too. The poetic text, from Friedrich Hebbel, speaks of a solitary flower that grows amidst its deathly pale companions; its vivid dark red results not from the sun but from drinking human blood. This is no celestial *blaue Blume*. Life feeds on death; beauty grows from corpses. (Maybe like Siegfried, those – like the red flower – who taste the blood can also understand the bird's speech.) This veiled meaning encapsulates perfectly the ambiguities of Schumann's cycle: danger as well as innocence is present within this forest. As the suppressed epigram from 'Zwielicht' warned us, nothing is quite what it seems. Be on guard . . .

In its ambiguous, equivocal message and subdued tone, 'Vogel als Prophet', written in the opening days of 1849, points to features that might be considered typical of 'late Schumann' – a questionable category in many ways, in that its primary use has been in a qualitative sense to separate Schumann's more popular earlier compositions from the 'problematic' later ones (behind which lurks the spectre of his eventual mental illness). Yet lateness often appears less a chronological descriptor than an aesthetic type, even admission of preference; many of its associated features can be heard in pieces from Schumann's earlier years (while conversely, music that is chronologically 'late' may seem not at all 'late' in style, as arguably found with the 'Rhenish' Symphony of 1850). A case in point is the Kerner *Liederreihe*, Op. 35, written in the closing months of 1840 and considered by some older commentators as already marking a falling off from the exuberance of Schumann's earlier creations from that year of song. In fact, the same curious conjunction of the avian and angelic, of birds singing in chorale-like strains, can be found at the close of the Kerner set, along with a similar sense of disquiet and potential cross purposes. For the final two songs, No. 11, 'Wer machte dich so krank?' (Who made you so ill?), and No. 12, 'Alte Laute' (Old sounds), Schumann reuses the same melody, marked just to be played slower and more softly, with only tiny alterations the second time round. Unlike the musical pairing in *Liebesfrühling*, there is no intrinsic link between the poems conjoined; they come indeed from different parts of Kerner's published collection, and Schumann had to cut one of the verses from 'Wer machte dich' to make the two poems correspond in length; the link, in other words, is fashioned entirely by him.[6] The repetition of the same music, only slower and more withdrawn the second time, provides an

---

[6] See Graham Johnson, notes to *The Songs of Robert Schumann*, vol. 2, p. 78.

unexpectedly subdued end to a collection that has started out with the hearty 'Lust der Sturmnacht'.

Despite the musical commonality, the two songs are in some ways at cross purposes with each other. The first, 'Wer machte dich so krank?', blames humankind for the illness that afflicts the protagonist and seeks the restorative powers of nature for healing the 'Todeswunden' (mortal wounds) dealt by man. Yet by the second, even nature seems powerless to help; neither the bird singing nor the blossoming tree, nor even the herbs of the meadow, restore the damaged heart; only an angel can wake the subject from his fearful dream. The illness here seems more psychological and emotional, one of deep depression that cannot be overcome by any natural cure (indeed in which the beauties of nature only exacerbate the sense of alienation, bringing up melancholic memories of the time when the subject was young and still believed in the world and its joys). This is not the only disparity, however; despite the repeated appeals to 'listen' in the second song, it is not clear whether we as listeners, or the protagonist himself, can actually hear what he is describing – whether it is actually audibly there, or if what is heard is being misrecognised.

'Hörst du den Vogel singen?' (Do you hear the bird singing?) the protagonist asks at the start of 'Alte Laute'. But if he hears something, the listener cannot; no new sound is added to the texture here (Ex. 9.3). Perhaps the soft

Ex. 9.3 Schumann: 'Alte Laute' (Kerner), *Zwölf Gedichte von Justinus Kerner*, Op. 35 No. 12, opening verse

descending line in the piano's treble is a type of transfigured birdsong – more chorale-like than twittering, though to this extent like the heavenly envoy from 'Vogel als Prophet' eight years later – but it was already there before in the previous song.[7] The possibility arises that we have all along been hearing the bird singing, but only now at the start of the second song is this fact recognised, in such as way the two songs show a process of growing sonic awareness (that the sound is in the accompaniment rather than the voice suggests this is less a case of hearing oneself singing – of coming to self-consciousness – than of recognising ambient sounds in the background). Still, the birdlike quality of the music is questionable, and the interrogative form the query takes – do *you* hear the bird singing? – might cast some doubt on whether the subject is really sure there is a bird singing at this moment.

If anything, matters become more uncertain in the following stanza. 'Was hör' ich? alte Laute' – 'What do I hear? old sounds', he responds – 'from the time I believed in the world and its joys.' These 'old sounds' are what gives the poem its title, but Schumann's decision to repeat the music of 'Wer machte dich so krank' for this final song means that literally the old sounds listeners hear are those of the music of the previous number. It seems unlikely that this immediately preceding song, in which the protagonist is already suffering from some illness, corresponds to this youthful time of hope; even the potentially self-reflexive step (as with *Dichterliebe*) of referring by 'alte Laute' to the entirety of the preceding cycle is doubtful (a sense of loss or alienation already runs through the *Liederreihe*, albeit not as pronounced as here at the close). Only in the last lines is a clue given as to the actual identity of the sounds: 'and from this fearful dream only an angel can awaken me'. For perhaps it is not the sound of a bird at all, but that of an angel, that has been accompanying the singer throughout. The soft melody in the treble is high, but apart from that not very fluttery and birdlike, and much closer to a chorale in its simple conjunct line and harmonisation; with the plagal cadence heard at the end of No. 11 and its prominent 'Amen' suspension, the angelic reading seems to fall into place as rather more plausible.[8] The voice heard in the piano is the blurred echo of the angel in the final line, the only thing that might awaken the protagonist from his fearful dream.

---

[7] In another reading, Dieter Conrad proposes that the two-bar linking figure at the start – a conventional 'menschlich-melancholisch' vocal gesture – constitutes a deliberate negation of birdsong, pointing to the absence of any healing for the protagonist. See Conrad, 'Schumanns Liedkomposition – von Schubert her gesehen', *Die Musikforschung*, 24/2 (1971), 160 n. 99.

[8] It might nevertheless seem curious that the plagal cadence and Amen suspension from the end of song 11 are missing at the end of song 12 given the explicit mention of the angel here. Then again, by closing directly with the perfect cadence on the words 'Engel nur', Schumann's setting imparts a simplicity and beseeching quality that would otherwise be smothered by too evident a religiosity.

Yet the protagonist seems not to be aware of this. Wrapped up in his own melancholia, he remains unaware that the bird he hears is possibly an angelic voice, and the old sounds are none other than his own music. The situation is effectively the inverse of that witnessed in the earlier songs from Op. 35 discussed in Chapter 4, 'Sehnsucht nach dem Waldgegend' and 'Stille Liebe', where the protagonist gradually became aware of his own voice, of the emergence of lyricism that marked a coming to self-consciousness through the ability to hear himself signing.[9] Here at the end of the cycle, he is unsure who or what is singing, and the set ends on a note of vulnerability and spiritual unease. Here we seem to see already present the seeds of the later, withdrawn, and emotionally enigmatic Schumann.[10]

Mirrors, Reflections, and *Doppelgänger*

Birds also feature in another poem set by Schumann, though sadly no angels are there to save the protagonist. The gruesome tale of Friedrich Hebbel's 'Ballad vom Haideknaben' that Schumann set as a 'Ballad for Declamation', Op. 122 No. 1, was encountered earlier in Chapter 7. Schumann's melodrama, written in September of 1853 just before embarking on the Violin Concerto, can be interpreted as the elimination of subjective voice, corresponding to the remorseless fate that awaits the youth who dreams his own death, murdered whilst crossing the moor. But a yet darker reading remains unplumbed in the depths of Hebbel's psychologically disturbing narrative, arising from two questions which were not addressed in Chapter 7. How does the youth's murderer come to have exactly the same dream as his victim; and why does he insist on his victim confirming the details of the dream before he kills him? 'Come … tell me your horrible dream', he demands: 'I dreamed too – God damn me if it doesn't match with yours!'

'Now speak, you dreamed' – "there came a man" –
'was I him? Look more closely at me,

---

[9] Indeed, throughout the two final songs, the vocal line is (at least initially) subsidiary to the melodic idea in the piano, fitted in quasi-*parlante* around the accompanimental construction, though the voice gradually takes on more equal melodic quality in the second verse and final bars.

[10] For Johnson, the final song is thus 'both an epitaph for the glorious epoch which was now at an end, and a disturbing signpost pointing to an uncertain future.' *The Songs of Robert Schumann*, vol. 2, p. 80. An autobiographical reading would no doubt suggest that Schumann identified with the protagonist of Kerner's poems and saw Clara as that angel – admittedly not an implausible idea, given the need Schumann expresses in his poems of 1838 for Clara to rescue him as a kind of *angela ex machina*.

I think it was me you saw!
Now continue, how did it happen?'
"he drew a knife!" – 'was it like this one?'–
"ah yes, ah yes!" – 'He drew it?' – "and thrust" –
'He thrust it into your throat?
But how does it help to torture you?'

It is as if he needs this confirmation in order to commit his atrocity. (The final line above should be taken seriously: the murderer could otherwise just be a sadist, but he expressly does not want to torment the victim and prolong the ritual once he has confirmed its validity.) Perversely, the murderer seems to require attestation by his victim, his recognition by the other as an existing subject in his own right and not just as a figment of his dream, before he can do the grisly deed – a dark reworking of the reflection of self in other explored in Chapter 5.

The fact that the youth dreams of his death and then finds reality horrifically corresponding to his nightmare could simply be considered a trait of the gothic horror genre, as is the attempt to escape his doom that unwittingly brings him all the closer to it. But why have both the youth and murderer dreamt exactly the same dream? This aspect of the story seems inexplicable, unless the answer lies in the fact that they share the same consciousness: the two figures are perhaps just two sides of the same divided ego. All might make more sense if we realise that the two figures are – like Jekyll and Hyde, or Cardillac in Hoffmann's *Mademoiselle de Scudéri* (1819) – merely two sides of a pathologically split subject. In demanding his recognition as an existing subject, the murderous side effectively takes over the entire personality, and innocence is destroyed. Intriguingly, it is not explicitly stated that the youth is finally murdered: the outcome of the scene is told obliquely through its two witnesses, a dove and a raven. We learn from the former merely that the youth wept and prayed, while from the latter that the evil doer's own throat eventually meets the hangman's noose. The two characters might thus be embodied in the same physical person; the youth's weeping is therefore for his effective death, the final destruction of his personality by his dark alter ego.

That this piece is in some sense about the loss of self is further suggested by the musical setting, specifically Schumann's use of a melodic figure that is virtually identical, as mentioned earlier, to one in 'Aus den hebräischen Gesängen', Op. 25 No. 15 (Ex 4.4), which spoke of an initial loss of self that was there overcome by the subject's coming to lyricism. The similarity might just be fortuitous (as discussed in Chapter 8, Schumann commonly has recourse to a stock of familiar figures throughout his oeuvre), but the further use of a closely related idea in 'Zwielicht' (Op. 39 No. 10), interpreted similarly by commentators such as Adorno and Brinkmann as a song about the 'self-alienation of the ego', does suggest a common interpretative association on the part of the composer.[11] Here, however, in the declaimed ballad of Op. 122, there is no possibility of the subject hearing himself singing, but instead the total absence of any lyricism whatsoever. Even the prominent use of this melodic figure in canonic imitation at the start of the work (see Ex. 7.2) – the doubling of the musical subject – might suggest an apt musical expression for the self-divided psychological subject. Indeed, for the crucial passage of recognition, as the murderer proposes that his dream corresponds with that of the youth, the figure emerges mirrored between two voices an octave apart (bb. 63–4), reconstituted from a sequence based on its fragmentation into its first three notes, before in turn being liquidated into generic arpeggios (Ex. 9.4). By the end of the work the motive has completely disappeared; the subject is now destroyed.

Hebbel's ballad shows how the demand for recognition may extend even to situations when the subject is self-divided into self and other. The dire

Ex. 9.4 Schumann: 'Ballade vom Haideknaben' (Hebbel), *Ballads for Declamation*, Op. 122 No. 1, bb. 59–66

---

[11] Adorno, 'Zum Gedächtnis Eichendorffs', p. 121; see the discussion in Chapter 7. There is also a general resemblance to an accompanimental figure in 'Muttertraum', Op. 40 No. 2 (Andersen), however, which speaks of a raven prophesying the death of the mother's son on the gallows – almost as if a preparation for the story related in the 'Haidenknaben'.

consequences of such a split when the subject is unable to recognise that the image it sees is indeed the darkened reflection of itself was foregrounded a few years earlier in Schumann's only opera, *Genoveva* (1847–8), likewise based on a source by Hebbel (Schumann compiled the libretto primarily from Hebbel's 1843 psychological drama, with some elements taken from Tieck's earlier 1799 version of the story, assisted in part by his friend, the poet Robert Reinick). In Act III, based closely on Act IV scene 6 of Hebbel's play, the sorceress Magaretha entices Count Siegfried to look into her magic mirror, her accomplice Golo having implanted seeds of doubt in his mind over the conduct of his wife, the virtuous Genoveva, while he was away fighting the Moors. This *Zauberspiegel* supposedly allows Siegfried to look back at the past, in which he may see for himself the behaviour of his wife during his absence. A strange mirror indeed; but while the *Zauberspiegel* possesses remarkable qualities, time travel is beyond it. In fact, it really is a type of mirror – a psychological mirror, reflecting the observer's own fears and insecurities. As Nikolaus Harnoncourt puts it, 'the magic mirror reveals the blackest depths of the human soul, where doubt and distrust take root', the unpleasant depths of the imagination, the side of ourselves that we would rather not face.[12] In looking into Magaretha's mirror, Siegfried merely sees his own worst fears reflected: the imagined infidelity of Genoveva, suggested to him by the lies of the scheming pair.

Siegfried is initially doubtful over the genuineness of this rather unlikely device: 'Do you believe in such a mirror?' he asks Golo. 'I don't much, yet I'm compelled to consult it,' he concludes, as mistrust quickly gets the better of reason. A beguiling chorus of offstage women's voices and liquid undulations in the clarinets accompanies the mirror's first image of Genoveva in the grounds outside Siegfried's castle at early dusk, a picture of pastoral innocence. Here and in the second tableau, her interaction with their servant Drago does not immediately cause Siegfried alarm, but led on by Golo doubt is increasingly gnawing away at him, and he becomes impatient to see the third and final picture, which confirms his worst fears: Genoveva welcoming Drago into her bedchamber at night. The text for the chorus here, speaking of mankind's first fall in the Garden of Eden, ostensibly suggests that the two are enjoying the fruits of a forbidden pleasure. The ironic implication, however, is that without Siegfried's own temptation to eat from the tree of knowledge – without succumbing to looking in the duplicitous *Zauberspiegel* – there would be no downfall, no sin, no sullying of Genoveva (whose name even echoes that of her first

---

[12] Mertl, 'Reinventing Opera', 21.

ancestor). Siegfried angrily smashes the mirror and hurries away to avenge himself upon his innocent wife. Here the inability of Siegfried to recognise that he is only seeing effectively himself – that the other figure in the mirror, Genoveva, is only the projection of his own insecurity and suspicion – nearly causes disaster. Once more, a subject is unable to recognise that the image of another can sometimes be nothing more than a reflection of its own darker side.

Mirrors and *Doppelgänger* are familiar devices in Romantic literature, especially prominent in the works of Jean Paul and Hoffmann that Schumann loved so much. In several cases these authors point to how a breakdown in recognition of the self can have a damaging, even fatal effect on their characters. One could think of the figure of Schoppe in Jean Paul's *Titan*, with his fear of mirrors, of seeing his self, his absolute 'I', which in his exaggerated Fichtean idealism he believes posits him and can thus destroy his very existence. The increasingly unstable Schoppe expires near the end of the novel when coming face to face with his real-life spitting image, his friend Siebenkäs, whom he misrecognises as his self.[13] Or there is Johannes Kreisler, Hoffmann's fictional Kapellmeister, who encounters alter egos and reflected doubles both in *Kreisleriana* and in the broken narrative of *Kater Murr*. On first encountering Kreisler in the latter novel, for instance, Princess Hedwiga is troubled by his presence, as something of him reminds her of the court painter, Leonhard Ettlinger, who went mad and tried to kill her as a child. Kreisler is deeply shaken on being told this, for he had always been preoccupied with the idea that madness might lie in wait for him Hoffmann tells us.[14] Alone, Kreisler falls into a stupor by the side of a lake as an ominous dusk descends. Waking from his reverie, he sees his reflection in the water and recognising it as Ettlinger, addresses his dark double sarcastically. Then on leaving the scene he is seized with horror to see 'his likeness, his own Self, walking beside him', and flees into Meister Abraham's neighbouring cottage.[15] The latter mystery is immediately undercut, however: the trick, Meister Abraham shows him, is achieved through the apt use of a concealed concave mirror, and Kreisler feels vexed at his mistake. ('Dreadful terrors please a man more than their natural

---

[13] Jean Paul, *Titan*, Thirty-Fourth Jubilee, Cycle 139. Schoppe, it turns out, is none other than the figure of Leibgeber from Jean Paul's earlier novel *Siebenkäs*, who saves his visually indistinguishable friend from a broken marriage by pretending to be his corpse (literally 'giving his body').

[14] E. T. A. Hoffmann, *The Life and Opinions of the Tomcat Murr*, trans. Anthea Bell (Harmondsworth: Penguin, 1999), p. 117.

[15] *Ibid.*, p. 124.

explanation,' Hoffmann comments laconically.)[16] In rejecting his supposed doppelgänger's behaviour, Kreisler at least shows himself a consciously distinct and independent persona – though his apparent misrecognition of his own reflection is concerning.[17]

Ettlinger was a painter, not a musician like Kreisler, and in the above examples, as in *Genoveva* before, there is a sense of a breakdown of recognition from the visual reflection of the self, of seeing the reflected self as another. But what of aural reflection, of a specifically musical instantiation of this theme, in which the musical subject doesn't recognise its own voice, can hear itself singing, but misrecognises this as someone else? Some possible approaches to this question have been given at the start of this chapter with the examples of the Violin Concerto, 'Vogel als Prophet', and the closing songs of the Kerner cycle, where a troubling split in potential subjects is accompanied by a sense of misrecognition; but in none of these cases is it clear that both voices relate to the self. This may arguably be the case in the Violin Concerto, but the hermeneutic imprecision of designating subjects as selves there warns against offering too specific an interpretation. A comparable issue accompanies a work of Schumann's that might be thought particularly apposite here – his own piano cycle *Kreisleriana*, Op. 16 (1838), that was explored in Chapter 3. There is certainly a recurring sense of doubling over the eight pieces – the oft-noted tonal pairing, the similar thematic constructions of much of the gentler B flat major music, the return of the sinister G minor of No. 3 at the end of the cycle reworked into No. 8. It would nonetheless be hard to show that these doublings should be taken to convey the misrecognition between Kreisler and his doppelgänger Ettlinger (a minor figure in *Kater Murr*), any more than reflecting the Kapellmeister's alternations between moments of bliss and despair, or indeed the formal interleaving of his story and that of Murr. To support such a reading we would need rather greater hermeneutic specificity to be given by the composer. Commentators can hardly agree on which Kreisler-related work of Hoffmann's – if either – Schumann's work relates to; attempting to demonstrate specific significations of its music to characters is hence unlikely to be a fully persuasive strategy, even if the general idea of

---

[16] *Ibid.*, p. 125.

[17] It is not clear to what extent Kreisler is joking in addressing his own watery reflection as an other – i.e. an example of his eccentric humour rather than a sign of psychological instability; certainly his ensuing fear on seeing his doppelgänger walking alongside him is more explicable if we assume Kreisler knows that the reflection in the lake is really of himself.

doublings and dark mirrorings might be resonant with the structure and ethos of Schumann's cycle.[18]

What exactly constitutes insanity was – and still is – disputed, as Hoffmann himself knew well enough in his legal capacity as judge.[19] But being unable to recognise oneself is a circumstance that often has calamitous implications for the mental health of the subject involved. It is far from clear that Kreisler is actually insane: eccentric, certainly, and fears going mad, but this is hardly equivalent. For Kreisler in *Kater Murr*, the parallels he sees between his and Ettlinger's earlier situation (driven to insanity through love for a woman far above him, Hedwiga's mother, Princess Maria) are used by him as a warning to himself, as a means to keep a check on his emotions and wild tendencies. Such behaviour is clearly lucid and rational, resulting from Kreisler's ability to distinguish himself as subject from his double and a capacity for self-control (or what Hoffmann elsewhere praises as *Besonnenheit*, found strongly in the supposedly 'eccentric' music of Beethoven). In *Kreisleriana*, admittedly, Kreisler signs himself off as 'Kapellmeister and mad musician *par excellence*', and his earlier threat in that work to stab himself to death in the nearest forest with an augmented fifth is hardly sane behaviour, but these seem playful affectations: 'verrückter Musikus' might perhaps better be translated 'crazy' or 'madcap musician', and anyway, by the end of this work the persona of 'Kreisler' is clearly identified as the alter ego of the editor, 'E. T. A. Hoffmann', who we know was not mad.[20] But there are other characters portrayed by Schumann who are rather more gravely afflicted by psychological disturbance arising from an inability to recognise the self. One can see this especially clearly when, unlike the situation found in *Kreisleriana*, verbal clues help to designate a subject – in songs that foreground mental breakdown in their protagonists, music which 'stages' states of insanity.

---

[18] As John MacAuslan comments, 'in *Kreisleriana*, the texture of poetic and musical thought is dense. It does not invite a listener to superimpose a literary narrative or programme', but rather 'creates its own musical patterns' from some of Hoffmann's symbols and themes. MacAuslan, *Schumann's Music and E. T. A. Hoffmann's Fiction*, p. 171.

[19] Indeed, Theodore Ziolkowski points to Hoffmann's sensitive and nuanced treatment of insanity, as understood at the time, in his rulings on legal cases (*German Romanticism and Its Institutions* (Princeton: Princeton University Press, 1990), pp. 214–17).

[20] Hoffmann, *Kreisleriana*, II.2, 'Letter from Kapellmeister Kreisler to Baron Wallborn', translation by Martyn Clarke, from *E. T. A. Hoffmann's Musical Writings*, ed. David Charlton (Cambridge: Cambridge University Press, 1989), p. 131. The comment on stabbing himself with a musical interval is from the preface to the second part of *Kreisleriana*.

Staging Insanity

In his setting of Hans Christian Andersen's 'Der Spielmann' (The Fiddler), Op. 40 No. 4, Schumann bequeathed one of his most fascinating and troubling portrayals of a figure on the brink of madness. A wedding is being held, but the bride is as pale as death: she is apparently getting married to the wrong man. She cannot forget another who is actually there at the celebrations, the fiddler of the title, who is playing gaily enough, the narrator tells us. But his playing becomes wilder and wilder, as does the narration. It becomes apparent over the course of the song that the fiddler is none other than the narrator himself. At the close he begs, 'let none of us go mad; I am myself a poor musician'.

Schumann composed 'Der Spielmann' in July 1840 at a time he was still impatiently waiting to marry Clara Wieck in the face of her father's concerted opposition, and commentators have not been slow to point to this song as reflecting his evident psychological fear of losing her (especially given that a similar theme is treated in *Dichterliebe*'s 'Das ist ein Flöten und Geigen', composed barely two months earlier). More troublingly, the auto-biographical parallels have often been extended to the portrayal of the 'armer Musikant' slipping towards madness; though we know that at one stage in the early 1830s Schumann had feared losing his reason, it is questionable how illuminating it is to link the events of 1854 with a song written fourteen years earlier.[21] Setting such concerns aside for present purposes, 'Der Spielmann' is undeniably a 'masterful projection' of the dissociative state of mind expressed in Andersen's poem, in which the third-person narration of mental turmoil blurs into first-person identification.[22]

From the very beginning, Schumann's setting is marked by a tonal instability that aptly conveys the dissociated subject positions of the poem. The key signature is one flat, and the wrenching opening progression (a $\sharp iv^{o7} - {}^{6}_{4} - V - i$ cadential sequence) points unambiguously to D minor, but the singer's first verse simply starts from the subdominant chord of G minor, which becomes recast as the tonic through sheer fiat (Ex. 9.5a). The first verse establishes G minor by composing out a large-scale i–III–V–i progression, though, since the opening accompanimental progression returns to punctuate the singer's verses, the initial tonal disjunction simply recurs, the second verse lurching in turn into C minor, the

---

[21] Relating to events in 1833, as reported by Robert in a letter to Clara, 11 February 1838, *SB* I.4:222 / *Briefwechsel*, I: 95.

[22] The phrase is Daverio's; *Robert Schumann*, p. 208.

Ex. 9.5a Schumann: 'Der Spielmann' (H. C. Andersen), *5 Lieder*, Op. 40 No. 4, opening

subdominant of G. And while D minor is finally heard for the central third verse, the music returns to G minor for the fourth and will end in G major – or on a $\frac{6}{4}$ of G major at least, that retains something of the quality of the song's nominal tonic D. In other words, a split between two possible tonics is established from the outset, and the song never truly resolves the conflict. Even at the end G major remains unstable.

The music of the first four verses is, as Daverio puts it, 'conceived as a kind of mad dance, in which the left hand of the piano thumps out a waltz rhythm' while the right hand and vocal line imitate the fiddler's drunken turns.[23] The material – a simple arch motive spanning a third up from the tonic – is a close relation of that heard in 'Im Walde' from the Op. 39 *Liederkreis*, as is the procedure of echoing it immediately in the piano (here expanding the setting of a single poetic line from four bars into six) and its subsequent use in sequence. Though this echo may be purely coincidental – the Eichendorff song was written shortly before the Andersen – several commentators have pointed to the common theme of a wedding celebration in the two songs' opening lines.[24] In fact, the musical similarity with

---

[23] *Ibid.*, p. 208. Jon Finson similarly calls it a 'demented waltz' (*Robert Schumann: The Book of Songs*, p. 101).

[24] E.g. Sams, *The Songs of Robert Schumann*, p. 147; Dietrich Fischer-Dieskau, *Robert Schumann: Wort und Musik: Das Vokalwerk* (Stuttgart: Deutsche Verlags-Anstalt, 1981), p. 94.

'Im Walde' might point to a deeper affinity in meaning, since that song, as we saw in Chapter 7, was a notable expression of the distracted modern subject: the 'I' that forms the vacant stage for perceiving the world and yet, unable to perceive itself, is dissociated from itself. Given that the narrator is trying to dissociate himself from the fiddler – detaching himself into the third person – the resonance is undoubtedly apt. Yet the pretence will not last.

At the start of the song, the sound of the fiddle seems to be conveyed in the right hand's turn figure (b. 9). It is present, too, in the vocal line just before (b. 7), though there is no reason to connect the narrator with the fiddler at this stage; the latter is not indeed mentioned until the end of the second verse. The order of the appearance, though – the echoing of the narrator by the fiddler, and not the other way around – is from a hermeneutic perspective already a noteworthy feature. It may just arise from reasons of musical construction, but even so, in the context of the poem's dissociated subject it might be a tiny indication that the relation between narrator and fiddler is not as detached as might at first be assumed.

In Andersen's poem it is only at the start of the fifth and final verse that the identity of the narrator as that of the musician is obviously given away: 'who told you to point a finger at me?' the narrator asks. But in Schumann's setting this fact is becoming clear as early as the third verse – the one in which the narrator's account of the fiddler becomes increasingly demented, as his hair turns grey in front of everyone's eyes and he presses his shrill instrument to his heart, 'heedless of whether it shatters into a thousand pieces'. Breaking the model of the first two verses, the preceding piano interjection (bb. 60–4) slips chromatically from its projected cadence in C minor to A minor, and the third verse emerges in the latter's subdomin-ant, D minor (Ex. 9.5b).

For the first time in the song a verse is presented in the purported tonic, and with the music reaching a *fortissimo* dynamic it seems as if the true situation will finally be revealed now. Moreover, what adds to the sense of decisive arrival is the fact that the melodic phrase is normalised. Unlike the other verses, verse three is tonally stable, remaining in D minor throughout rather than being subject to third shifts for each melodic segment. And now the piano no longer echoes the vocal part but plays simultaneously alongside it. The result is both a reduction of internal phrase lengths from six bars to four, with an ensuing acceleration of the verbal delivery, but more significantly the sonic identification of the narrator's voice with that of the fiddle. As Graham Johnson puts it, 'suddenly the singer and the accompaniment begin to fuse into a single

Ex. 9.5b Schumann: 'Der Spielmann', Op. 40 No. 4, verse 3

Er strei - chet die Gei-ge, sein Haar er - graut, es schwin - gen die Sai - ten gel - lend und laut, er drückt sie an's Herz und ach - tet es nicht, ob auch sie in tau-send Stü - cken zer - bricht.

personification . . . . this fiddle music has begun to inhabit the narrator'.[25] No longer the echo of one another, the two are coincident, the narrator and fiddler one and the same figure. Indeed, the fiddle motive is heard near obsessively; repeated not just once as before but stated six times in short succession.

This moment of musical identification is the extreme point of the setting: thereafter the turn figure reduces into a more generic descending third with the music returning to G minor. The final verse of the song comes as a plea for deliverance from the possibility of madness, played softly and more slowly in G major. Of the song's two possible tonics, the ostensible D minor has eventually proven subordinate to G. As in

---

[25] Graham Johnson, notes to *The Songs of Robert Schumann*, vol. 6, Hyperion CDJ33106 (2002), p. 53.

Kreisleriana, the harmonic duality between tonal centres is an effective representation of the split subject: D minor perhaps relates more directly to the fiddler, the ostensible subject of the poem foregrounded in the song's key signature and described in detail in the third verse, but the narration starts and ends in G, which is hence more readily associated with the narrator's subject position. As the music starts in D minor but ends unstably in G, there is a sense that over the course of the song the narrator becomes the principal subject, upstaging the musician, who is seen as a persona adopted and then discarded. At the point of musical identification in verse 3, the narrator adopts the fiddler's key and music, but the pretence over, D minor is discarded for good.

Both Andersen and Schumann leave us in no doubt that the narrator is none other than the demented fiddler he describes, but it is unclear at the end whether the narrator himself recognises that this is the case. He seems aware that his audience might take him for the musician (is this just paranoia?), but he never explicitly acknowledges he *is*. On one hand, if we assume the narrator's final verse to form a self-acknowledgement that he is indeed the fiddler, this suggests he retains a crucial element of lucidity to the end. In this reading, it is arguable that the *Spielmann*, while fearing insanity, is again not mad. There may be something crazed about his performance but there is still a core of self-recognition. The text hence speaks of a distraught subject trying to distance himself from the painful situation in which he finds himself – in itself what might be considered a perfectly sane strategy for coping with great distress.[26] He fails, though: the pain is such that his self-identification with his third-person self is ultimately unavoidable. On the other hand, distancing strategies continue to the end, suggesting the narrator acknowledges parallels but crucially no sense of identity between himself and the fiddler: 'I am myself a poor musician' – but not *that* poor musician. Coincidentally or otherwise, in Schumann's setting the crucially revealing line of rhetorical denial – why point your finger at me? – outlines Neapolitan harmony in G minor, namely A flat major, the tritonal pole of the fiddler's D minor, effectively the strongest denial of that key. It would appear, then, that recognition has broken down: the narrator refuses to countenance that he is indeed the fiddler. The subject is divided from himself and doesn't even know it.

---

[26] As Louis A. Sass points out, the same sense of disconnection or uncoupling of the self's relationship to itself that is found, for instance, in schizophrenics, forms a pointed correspondence with the value given to disengagement and reflexivity in modernity since Descartes, seen as thoroughly rational traits (*Madness and Modernism: Insanity in the Light of Modern Art, Literature, and Thought* (Cambridge MA: Harvard University Press, 1994), pp. 90–1).

In hearing the fiddler play he has from the very beginning been hearing merely his own echo – and yet cannot recognise himself.

Not being able to recognise one's voice as one's own is a problem that was encountered earlier in Chapter 6, where it corresponded with the tendency to narcissism: the belief that the beloved is speaking to the subject, when all along the latter is merely imagining it. This potential 'narcissistic dialogue' was identified in 'Ihre Stimme', Op. 96 No. 3, whose protagonist may simply be fantasising about an amorous relationship which does not exist, choosing to hear the echo of his own voice as the voice of the Romantic other. A similar situation is encountered in another song from 1850, 'Geisternähe' ('Near in Spirit'), Op. 77 No. 3, in which the subject imagines that his distant beloved is thinking of him, far in space but near in spirit: in the breeze that plays around his cheeks he feels her thoughts; in the harp-like sounds that swirl around his mind and senses he hears her voice murmuring his name.[27] A musical setting of such a poem gives full rein for the realisation of such sonic fantasy, and as so often in Schumann, there is a sense of the partial emergence of the vocal line doubled in the piano accompaniment across the verses. Harp-like arpeggios accompany the 'Harfen klänge', and the doubled voice retreats into an inner line at mention of the softness of its murmuring and then exultantly resounds in the upper voice at 'deinen Lippen irrt' (escapes from your lips).

It is unclear from the song taken on its own whether the beloved really is thinking of the protagonist or whether such desire is just imagined, but placed in the context of Friedrich Halm's *Hochzeitlieder*, a cycle of eight poems of which 'Geisternähe' is the last, it transpires that the woman has – in a repetition of a now familiar theme – gone and married another, and is almost certainly not giving a thought to the speaker, let alone longingly whispering his name.[28] The protagonist of 'Geisternähe' may be merely a fantasist, whereas that of 'Der Spielmann' is mentally unhinged, but both are deluded. Neither is able to recognise themselves.

If we understand the subject's sense of a coherent self as to an important degree constituted by the process of self-consciousness, and the latter, in turn, as being formed by the recognition *of* the self *by* the self *as* the self,

---

[27] 'Und was wie Harfen klänge / Um meine Sinne schwirrt': 'Sinne' could mean 'senses' or 'mind' here.

[28] The *Hochzeitlieder* were published in Halm's *Gedichte* of 1850, from which volume Schumann must have taken this text. We learn from the second stanza of the first poem that the 'schönes Fräulein' is going to marry another that very day, and moreover seems never to have considered the protagonist as a potential partner. Though there is a distinct element of flippancy throughout, the protagonist is evidently rather an obsessive and fantasist; this final poem is total self-delusion.

then in musical terms hearing oneself as another marks the breakdown of this process. Rather than completing the circular movement of self-consciousness, the self as a subject is dissociated from its representation as an object to itself. Such misrecognition can, in more serious cases, be the sign of an incipient breakdown in the self. For many thinkers in the nineteenth century such breakdown constitutes nothing less than madness.[29]

Und nur ein Engel . . .

It would be an understatement to claim that madness is a troubled subject applied to Schumann. So far, the accounts of madness or psychological disturbance have been applied merely to the musical and poetic subjects heard in Schumann's music and in the poems he set, but of course they have an unfortunate resonance with the life of the composer, whose last two years were spent in a mental asylum following his breakdown and suicide attempt in February 1854. The exact type of his mental illness – schizophrenia, bipolar disorder – and its causes – mental exhaustion, syphilis, hereditary factors – have been disputed since Schumann's own day and the debate shows little possibility of conclusive resolution, in part because insanity is not a topic that is fully understood even now.[30] But that Schumann did suffer from a serious mental illness in the last two years of his life no one denies.

The spectre of madness thus haunts the music of Schumann's later years (indeed, to read some commentators, it would appear to haunt Schumann's entire oeuvre). It is arguable that in nearly all cases, however, this is the result of retrospectively imposing an understanding of the composer's later biographical circumstances on to music written before such symptoms became fully manifest – the temptation of 'reading Schumann's life backwards' as Beate Perrey puts it.[31] Despite Schumann's flirting throughout his life with subjects linked to

---

[29] See, for instance, Hegel's *Philosophy of Mind*, §408, p. 117: in the deranged subject 'the *duality* into which he splits up is not brought to *unity*. Consequently, though the deranged individual is *in himself* one and the same subject, yet, as an object for himself, he is not an internally undivided subject, concordant with itself, but a subject diverging into *two different personalities*.' Hegel's argument, which is more complex than can be summarised here, takes some of its support from the earlier work of the pioneering French clinical psychiatrist Philippe Pinel.

[30] A good summary of the changing views and diagnoses of Schumann's condition in the last hundred and fifty years is given by Yael Braunschweig, 'Robert Schumann and Retrospective Psychiatric Diagnosis', in 'Biographical Listening: Intimacy, Madness and the Music of Robert Schumann', PhD diss., University of California, Berkeley (2013), pp. 69–118.

[31] Perrey, 'Schumann's lives, and afterlives', p. 5. This topic has been well covered in scholarly literature from the last two decades: it is explicitly the starting point of John Worthen's revisionist biography, *Robert Schumann: Life and Death of a Musician*.

some sense of mental disorder – works like *Kreisleriana* and the 'Spielmann' setting just discussed spring to mind – it is not his earlier music that has really suffered, however eccentric some of it may be, but that from the latter part of his career, the period leading up to his final breakdown. This is especially apparent in relation to the Violin Concerto, that much maligned product of Schumann's Indian Summer, which, written in the midst of a period of happy creativity in late September 1853, was subsequently held by its intended soloist Joseph Joachim to show signs of incipient madness (or 'mental exhaustion') – though pointedly only following Schumann's breakdown – and for nearly a century kept from the public.[32] There are personal reasons why those close to the composer might have allowed their views on his later work to have become retrospectively tainted by his mental illness, but no convincing musical ones. No claim has been made in the foregoing account that the possible states of psychological disorder interpreted in the music's virtual subjects has any direct connexion with the psychological state of the composer who wrote them. Neither will it be made now, as the link is not just dubious, but as we will see, can seem to be expressly contradicted by the music.[33]

One piece stands out in this context – both for how it supports the contemporary intuition of self-misrecognition as tantamount to madness, and yet shows how problematic it remains to link the composer's psychology with that of any hypothetical musical subject. This is Schumann's final completed work, the *Theme with Variations* in E flat major, WoO 24, known as the *Geistervariationen* for reasons that will become apparent. This is the only piece of Schumann's that, in terms of genesis, might justify being linked with the insanity of its composer, since it was actually written during his final breakdown. The biographical details can be given briefly: on the evening of 10 February 1854 Schumann became afflicted with the sound of ringing in his ears in the form of musical pitches, aural hallucinations that grew more pronounced in the following days, by which time he was hearing whole pieces in his head in 'magnificent harmonisations'. During the night of 17/18 February he got up and wrote down a theme

---

[32] Joachim explained his reasons long after the fact in a letter of 5 August 1898; see *Briefe von und an Joseph Joachim*, ed. Andreas Moser (Berlin: Bard, 1911), pp. 486–7.

[33] Referring to Schumann's playing with the idea of insanity, his 'wonderful effects of logical incoherence and schizophrenia' in his earlier piano music, Charles Rosen justly admonishes that 'Whatever Schumann's personal disposition, these elements are clearly stylistic rather than autobiographical. We have no warrant for taking them even as superficial reflections of Schumann's private life. In the rare case that we find an interesting correspondence between Schumann's art and his life, we must remember that the desire of the Romantic artist to express his personality through his work is no stronger than the effort to make his private character conform visibly to the stylistic personality of the work itself.' *The Romantic Generation*, p. 648.

he claimed was dictated by angels (in various accounts he is said to have ascribed it to the spirits of Schubert or Schubert and Mendelssohn).[34] The next morning, though, matters took a significant turn for the worse when the angelic voices turned into the hideous music of demons who threatened to cast him into hell. As the hallucinations continued, over the next week (probably around 22 and 23 February) he managed to complete a set of variations on the theme he had written down, activity which seems to have provided some respite from his suffering. Then on 27 February, in the midst of writing out a fair copy of the variations, he left his home half-dressed and attempted to drown himself in the freezing waters of the Rhine; rescued by fishermen, he was taken back home, and completed the score the following day. A few days later, on 4 March, at his request he was taken to the asylum in Endenich outside Bonn, where he would end his life a little over two years later. What little music he wrote down in those final two years – and it appears to have been largely contrapuntal exercises rather than original composition – has not come down to us. The variations are thus in effect Schumann's final composition, and the only surviving piece dating from his mental breakdown.

Schumann misrecognised himself. As is well known, the theme he notated in E flat major, supposedly dictated by the spirits of Schubert and Mendelssohn, starts as a variant of the melody he had given to the soloist in the slow movement of the Violin Concerto five months earlier. Indeed, similar ideas wind their way across Schumann's oeuvre: the opening phrase is almost identical to that of 'Frühlings Ankunft' from the *Lieder-Album für die Jugend* (Op. 79 No. 19), as well as a more distant relation to the central chorale in 'Vogel als Prophet'. In thinking he heard Schubert and Mendelssohn, Schumann was misremembering his own voice.[35] A clearer

---

[34] Rupert Becker mentioned just Schubert (see Georg Eismann, *Robert Schumann: Ein Quellenwerk über sein Leben und Schaffen*, 2 vols. (Leipzig: Breitkopf & Härtel, 1956), vol. 1, pp. 190–1); both composers are listed by Wasielewski, *Robert Schumann*, p. 288 / *Life of Robert Schumann*, p. 185.

[35] There is also a similarity with the opening of Norbert Burgmüller's (unfinished) Second Symphony, the scherzo of which Schumann had orchestrated two years before. In other circumstances, though, the attribution of the theme to Schubert and Mendelssohn would not be entirely unreasonable. There is something in Schumann's theme of the hymnic, benedictory tone sometimes found in late Schubert, of which *Winterreise*'s 'Das Wirtshaus' would form an apt parallel. It is also worth pointing out that while the theme's opening four-bar phrase is lifted virtually directly from the concerto (bb. 5–6), the continuation in bb. 5–8 is new to the variations. This phrase – a familiar contrapuntal schema in parallel tenths and sixths which grows out of the parallel sixths of the opening – is hardly unknown in Schumann's work ('Wehmut' from the Eichendorff *Liederkreis* offers a variant), but it is especially characteristic of Mendelssohn (e.g. the lovers' theme of the *Midsummer Night's Dream* Overture, or the start of his first published song, 'Minnelied', Op. 8 No. 1). If one were to attribute this phrase to another

Ex. 9.6 Schumann: *Thema mit Variationen*, WoO 24 (1854), theme

instance of the link between self-misrecognition – hearing oneself as another – and the breakdown of the subject could not be wished.[36] And yet, despite this, it is well-nigh impossible to point to any sense of supposed 'insanity' in the work he produced.

The opening theme, marked *Leise, innig*, is a model of simplicity, formed as a rounded binary structure characteristic of variation sets (Ex. 9.6). As with its earlier manifestation in the concerto, the theme

composer, then, Mendelssohn would not be a bad choice. The hallucinatory Schumann may have not recognised his own music, but he still dimly remembered that of some of his favourite predecessors.

[36] As noted in Chapter 8, the following years Schumann would also suffer aural hallucinations from voices telling him that the music published under his own name had in fact been borrowed from others – claims which he angrily denied. See Worthen, *Robert Schumann*, p. 375.

starts placidly over a prolonged tonic pedal, but by b. 5 the parallel sixths with which the tenor had doubled the melody migrate into the bassline for a new continuation, which forms the contrasting idea in an eight-bar antecedent; a modulating consequent phrase then leads to the double bar. The brief B section (bb. 17–24) continues the outer-voice structure of parallel tenths and descending melodic motion over a dominant pedal, being followed by a curtailed 4-bar reprise of the opening idea. All this is utterly typical for a variation theme. Neither are the variations that follow notable for any striking peculiarity, following a typical tendency of generally accelerating note values: the original quavers heard against quaver triplets in variation 1, different types of canonic imitation in variation 2 (at half-, two-, and one-bar intervals), semiquaver triplets with the theme in the bass in variation 3. Only in the fourth, as the theme appears solemnly in the minor – not the typical parallel or relative of the standard *minore* variation but rather the mediant, G minor – does Schumann introduce something a little unusual, and this in fact dimly echoes the curious recapitulation of the Violin Concerto's slow movement, where the theme also returned in this key. The fifth variation, back in the tonic E flat, dissolves the theme into a double neighbour-note chromatic oscillation of demisemi-quavers, whose brief passing discords, arising from the linear part-writing, would hardly be worthy of note in Schumann's piano writing two decades earlier. And here the piece ends.

I have not tried to impute subjects to the music, as it is not clear the music really supports such a reading – at least one that would go beyond generic commonalities of the theme-and-variations genre and bring out something distinctive about this piece. But one would be hard pressed to read insanity into this work – whatever this would be supposed to sound like. The E flat Variations may serve as an exemplary case of how the psychological qualities read into music and its virtual subjects may have no obvious connexion with the actual psychological state of the creator. This is the one piece indisputably written during the composer's mental break-down: if any piece of Schumann should show 'madness', it should be this. But in truth, the *Geistervariationen* are little more than a set of straightfor-ward variations on a simple and appealing theme, possibly one professing a modest affinity to the ethos of Beethoven's late variation sets. Even the reuse of a melodic phrase from one of his earlier works is not, in itself, unusual for Schumann; as we have seen, he does this all the time. It is hard to remove a sense of pathos on hearing this piece, as we know the sad circumstances that surround it, while from a biographical perspective it is concerning that Schumann was unable to recognise the similarity with the *Langsam* of the Violin Concerto; but nothing in the Variations points to insanity. In contrast, the concerto's slow movement forms rather a better example of a troubled musical subjectivity, with the serenity of the opening cello theme disturbed by its metric uncoupling from the accompaniment, the apparent discrepancy between this material and the soloist's theme over the course of the movement, and the alienation of the latter in the reprise – and this was written months before Schumann's breakdown, at a time when he was perfectly lucid.[37]

This is perhaps unsurprising. Just as Friedrich Hölderlin's later poems written after his *Umnachtung* are quite simple, a far cry from the complexity of the great hymns and odes of the years leading up to 1805, it is questionable whether madness has ever resulted in remarkable art, or at the very least, art that is remarkable for its ostensibly 'mad' qualities. There is a popular and longstanding myth that insanity might provide insight into higher realms of consciousness otherwise inaccessible to thought, and madness and artistic depth were indeed often linked in the early nineteenth century, a period in which mental illness became seen to be seen in a more sympathetic and modern light, as an affliction potentially capable of treatment.[38] Romantic thinkers were also well aware of the irrationality at the heart of the Enlightenment project, the impossibility of providing a first principle or ultimate ground for philosophical knowledge, and thus realms of thought that escaped the constraints of rationality were thought potentially disclosive of truths unarticulable within the limits of conventional forms of communication (from which tendency instrumental music also benefited).[39] 'Since Aristotle it is even customary to say of people that nothing great can be accomplished without a touch of madness,' writes

[37] Dagmar Hoffmann-Axthelm makes a similar point in his reading of the concerto, underscoring the rational self-command a composer would have needed to create the music's apparently troubled psychological state (*Robert Schumann: 'Glücklichsein und tiefe Einsamkeit'* (Stuttgart: Reclaim, 1994), pp. 167–73).

[38] The literature on the perceived link between madness and genius in this period is legion. On the developing understanding of mental illness in early 19th-century Germany, see especially Ziolkowski, 'The Madhouse: Asylum of the Spirit', in *German Romanticism and Its Institutions*, pp. 138–217.

[39] Even in the early work of Michel Foucault there persists a view of madness as possibly offering access to an 'inaccessible primitive purity' (original preface to *Folie et Déraison: Histoire de la folie à l'âge classique* (Paris: Librarie Plon, 1961), p. xxxiii, a line famously suppressed in later editions; see Foucault, *History of Madness*, trans. Jonathan Murphy and Jean Khalfa (London: Routledge, 2006), p. xi). This viewpoint is criticised by the psychologist Louis Sass, who observes that the Romanticised 'wildman' view of insanity as providing access to fundamental, primitive truths is scarcely supported by clinical cases (*Madness and Modernism*, cf. esp. p. 246).

Schelling in 1815, who has just designated music as an exemplary instance of such 'inner madness'. 'In place of this, we would like to say: nothing great can be accomplished without a constant solicitation of madness, which should always be overcome, but should never be utterly lacking.'[40] But Schelling, the onetime roommate of Hölderlin in Tübingen, pointedly stops short of advocating surrender to unreason. The more extreme Romantic notion of insanity as providing access to deeper, interior soul states, is questionable. At any rate, madness was of no benefit to Robert Schumann or his creativity, and the Romanticisation of madness has done little to help his later music's posthumous reputation.[41] It seems, rather, to have obscured the often-exquisite qualities of his final orchestral work, and to have weighed down his final surviving composition with an aura of heavy portent that is in danger of drowning this fragile and strangely moving little piece.

✳✳✳

When the prophetic seer was asked whether the boy would live to a ripe old age, he replied: 'Yes, if he does not come to know himself.' For a long time this pronouncement seemed to be nothing but empty words: however, it was justified by the outcome of events: the strange madness which afflicted the boy and the nature of his death proved its truth.[42]

So Ovid relates the story of Narcissus. In this poet's telling, the youth, unable to grasp his own reflection in the water, wastes away from frustrated self-love and becomes a yellow aquatic flower; but we could easily imagine a less elaborate scenario where Narcissus simply drowns in attempting to embrace his own reflection. Ovid's version pointedly abjures the Delphic injunction 'know thyself'. Better, it would seem, is not to know oneself at all. Yet Narcissus, in seeing himself, misrecognises himself, perceiving his own reflection as that of another, just as through Echo he misrecognises his own words as those of another. The prophetic utterance is, as usual, enigmatic: he comes to see himself, but even then, does he really come to know himself?

---

[40] F. W. J. Schelling, *The Ages of the World*, trans. Jason M. Worth (Albany, NY: State University of New York Press, 2000), p. 103.

[41] In recent years, however, quite a creative industry has grown up around compositional *hommages* to Schumann's late style, its 'troubling' qualities seen now in a positive light, including the work of Wolfgang Rihm, Heinz Holliger, and Aribert Reimann. Reimann's *Sieben Fragmente für Orchester in memoriam Robert Schumann* (1988) is a particularly problematic case in point, which effectively restages Schumann's mental breakdown by sonically reimagining the *Geistervariationen* in the context of the composer's aural hallucinations.

[42] Ovid, *Metamorphoses*, III, trans. Mary M. Innes (Harmondsworth: Penguin, 1955), p. 83.

In this chapter we have seen how misrecognition of the self as another can have dangerous consequences for the subject; in extreme cases it may even suggest madness. Yet it is a mistake to identify the music's subjectivity with that of the biographical subject – ironically, perhaps, given the interweaving of life and art which Schumann's own aesthetics often seem to support. As the Violin Concerto and E flat Variations show in their different ways, a direct link between the composer's mental state and the projected subjectivity of the music is often questionable. However hermeneutically tempting it may be, the danger is that in reading the composer's subjectivity into the subjectivity of the music we are simply projecting our own assumptions onto it. In thinking we hear another voice, that of the psychologically stricken Schumann, we are merely making our own, most often unwarranted, imposition onto the music's subjectivity. Ironically in the context of this chapter, in the magical mirror of Schumann's music we are liable to misrecognise ourselves.

But ultimately, isn't this also an important part of the subjectivity of music? Subjectivity, as so often claimed in these preceding pages, is a relational category; as was set out in Chapter 1, too, there are different types of subjectivity in play when understanding music's subjective quality. One is the composer's subjectivity; another is that of the music 'itself', its construction of a virtual persona; and it is these two that have often been mixed and sometimes confused in accounting for Schumann's music, problematically when it comes to his later works and his mental illness. But there is, of course, another subjectivity, no less important, and often overlooked: our own, as performers or listeners. It is this latter type of subjectivity, and how it relates to the others, that we address now in this book's final chapter.

Epilogue

So he is in love, but he knows not with whom; he does not understand his own condition and cannot explain it; he sees himself in his lover as in a mirror, but is not conscious of the fact.

Plato, *Phaedrus*, 255d

10 | Hearing Ourselves

Recalling the Subject

The preceding eight chapters have traced, as it were, the journey of the musical subject – an account specifically of the sense of subjectivity heard in Schumann's music – and the problems encountered over its course. As foreshadowed in Chapter 1, the overall path of the narrative seems to describe a spiral, or a series of circular movements around common concerns. Repeatedly, attempts to define or ground the subject's identity have led to new challenges, in which the dialectical play with the notion of the other or not-self has emerged as a crucial element in the attempt to overcome problems seemingly inherent in the subject. Despite the importance given within to the notion of recognition, too, the question of *mis*recognition has loomed ever larger.

We started with the broad notion of subjectivity to be heard in Schumann's earlier music, refining this idea into a handful of characteristic traits such as idiosyncrasy, interiority, allusiveness, and a certain fantasy quality in its alternation of mood. More precisely, though, the subject presented here often appeared to be fragmentary or self-divided, a topic explored in Chapter 2, which looked at Schumann's playful adoption of alter egos and the ways in which this specific sense of a split subjectivity may be manifested in music. The tension, latent in these two chapters, between the whole that does not yet know itself qua subject, and the subject's attempt to know itself that results almost inevitably in division, returned more explicitly in the second part of the study. Here the sense of self-presence, of immediacy of feeling, contrasts with the difficulty of coming to self-consciousness without introducing a split in the subject. The idea of 'coming to lyricism' suggested a possible emergence of subjective voice in music, but to show that this virtual consciousness could be said to constitute a musical analogue of self-consciousness apparently necessitated once again some separation of the self into subject and object.

It was here that the introduction of the 'other' as another subject in which the self can see itself reflected appeared to offer an attractive solution, tracing a movement familiar from German idealist and Romantic thought. By the mutual recognition of self and other, attained in most pointed form in the hermaphroditic fusion of lover and beloved, the dilemma between the subject that is whole but does not fully know itself and that which can perceive itself but only by pain of splitting into an object for itself seems to be resolved. Yet in turn, there lurked the difficulty of distinguishing between what was really the voice of the other, and what was narcissistic fantasy or self-projection – a situation in which the subject is not only divided once more but, even worse, no longer cognisant of this fact. This was not merely a consequence of the metaphorical nature of musical subjectivity, its seemingly inherent lack of precision in denoting subjective identity; but it is a worry that finds verbal expression in the texts of several Lieder set by Schumann. Words may lie just as much as music may deceive. In Part III, the actual absence of the other in these circumstances led as if inexorably to an even greater concern – the absence of the self: the loss of subjective voice and the emptiness at the heart of the subject, in which Schumann's musical procedures resonated with more recent theories associated with psychoanalysis and poststructuralism that see the subject as 'always already' built around an absence that in fact constitutes its very nature.

Attempting to sidestep this apparent aporia, the following chapter attended to others and the voices of others, seeking more positively to escape from the fixation on the troubled Romantic ego through notions of intersubjectivity, objectivity, and the merging of the subject with the greater whole. In this context, the loss of a particular type of subjective voice might point to a more social and intersubjective model of subjectivity, or simply point to the limits of this concept for understanding the music of even this supposedly most subjective of composers. To look for subjective qualities in all of Schumann's musical output is in many instances to look for the wrong thing. But in one final reversal, self-estrangement re-emerges within the voice of alterity, in those cases where the voice of the self is misrecognised as belonging to another. Chapter 9 effectively circled back over the question of mishearing the self, raised earlier with respect to the 'narcissistic dialogue' to explore the breakdown of self-awareness of the borders between self and other, subject and world, a situation which in contemporary thought was often associated with the ultimate symbol of self-loss: losing one's mind. Perhaps it didn't need to end like this; but in the case of Schumann himself – the biographical subject – it actually did. Still, what emerges from this chapter is how musical representations of a self-estranged subject have no automatic association with the psychological state of the composer who wrote them. In a chapter that hinges on misrecognition, the final irony is one of critical misrecognition. The question that remained open at the end concerned our own role as interpreting subjects of music's subjectivity. For with this positing, we move from the virtual subjects of music and the biographical subject that composed it to foreground the agency of those subjects that hear and interpret it.

Recognising Ourselves

That we end up with ourselves may not be entirely a surprise. The idea that the subjectivity of music is a product of our own interpretative agency – that the only real consciousness we directly encounter in the musical experience is our own – and the implication that can be drawn from this, that music may consequently be important for articulating elements of our own subjectivity, is an insight recognised by several earlier writers and has been present in this account, implicitly or explicitly, since the opening chapter.[1] Thus we have come, in a sense, full circle, back to our initial theoretical conjectures and starting points. Only now, of course, we have fleshed out the topic, obtaining a far fuller and richer picture of the ways in which subjectivity can be manifested in Schumann's music, alongside a greater awareness of the many critical problems attendant with the enterprise. With this, too, we have progressed from the largely descriptive impulse of the book's first three chapters – from the relatively impartial outlining of the various ways in which the idea of musical subjectivity has been used – to establish more prescriptive or normative criteria for how the term might better be applied. And finally, not the least of the features we are now in a position to see are the more than incidental parallels between the path of the musical subject and that of ourselves interpreting it. In true

---

[1] This is a position proposed by both Naomi Cumming and Lawrence Kramer, for instance, as explicated earlier in my opening chapter. For Cumming, we recall, the subjective qualities of music invite 'the listener's engagement in a manner that transforms his or her own subjectivity' ('The Subjectivities of "Erbarme dich"', 17), while for Kramer, similarly, 'Music meant to be listened to with a degree of focused attention addresses itself to an actual or virtual subject position that the listening subject ventures to fill. The subjectivity of the listener qua listener arises in a process of dialogue in which music acts as the ideal or authoritative subject in whose place I, the listener, come to be, whose subjective character I reproduce as my own' ('The Mysteries of Animation', 157).

Idealistic fashion, recapitulating the course of the past is in some form a coming to self-consciousness.

It was noted in the opening chapter that subjectivity may be understood as a journey of self-understanding and self-definition, a process rather than a thing, and one that is relational between subjects and between self and others. It is also one that implicates a first-person involvement. Music's capacity to elicit at times our own subjective engagement with it as a quasi or virtual subject – our feelings of empathy, sympathy, identification, or sometimes indeed rejection – thus implicates our own subjectivity as self-interpretative, meaning-making subjects. Ultimately, then, this points to the insight that the subjectivity of music is not simply 'in' the work, but in our relation to it; in other words, the virtual aesthetic subject (what in Chapter 1 was given as the third possible identity of the subjectivity in music) is not only supported by the listening subject (the fourth and final candidate), but contributes to the latter's self-formation as well. In this, the encounter with the virtual musical subject is part of our own work of subjectivity, our work as meaning-making subjects. And thus, in a further reflexive step, this whole book, as a reflection on this, is itself, as it were, an instantiation of subjectivity.

The reflection of self in other, offered in Chapter 5 at the immanent level of the fictional musical subject's attempt to come to self-consciousness, is instantiated at a higher level in our encounter with the virtual other that is the subjectivity heard in music. Art offers a path to deeper knowledge of ourselves. This is, of course, a familiar tenet of Idealist and Romantic aesthetics – it is prominent in both Schelling's and Hegel's philosophies of art – but it is characteristic of a much wider range of aesthetic thought stretching up to the late twentieth century, if not beyond. In his foundational text of modern philosophical hermeneutics, *Truth and Method*, Hans-Georg Gadamer will make the comparable claim that the work of art offers just such a path to self-knowledge. 'Our experience of the aesthetic', writes Gadamer, 'is a mode of self-understanding'; 'we learn to understand ourselves in and through' the work of art.[2] Indeed, 'the work of art has its true being in the fact that it becomes an experience that changes the person who experiences it.'[3] This relation is not passive but implicates the interpretative actions of the reader or spectator (or listener). Thus, by

---

[2] Hans-Georg Gadamer, *Truth and Method* (1960), trans. Joel Weinsheimer and Donald G. Marshall (London: Continuum, 2006), p. 83; Gadamer, in fact, explicitly acknowledges the influence of Hegel on this point. Cumming also bases her argument partly on Gadamer's reflections on hermeneutic method (see 'The Subjectivities of "Erbarme dich"', 6–7).

[3] *Ibid.*, p. 103.

our interpretative actions, by the practice of our hermeneutic engagement, we particulate in the meaning of the work (a position anticipated by Friedrich Schlegel long before in his conception of Romantic criticism).[4]

Gadamer has little to say specifically or usefully about music; his focus is on literary works (and indeed he later attempts to reduce the meaning of non-verbal arts to the verbal forms of articulation that concern him).[5] But as we explored in the opening chapter, in a different way from and arguably to a greater or more immediate degree than other arts, music inspires a type of subjective relation that can move from empathy to partial or even total identification; akin in some significant respects to a subject, it is other than the self and yet can be felt at times as an extension of one's own self. 'I feel then as though I and the music I have heard are as one,' Hoffmann's Kreisler exclaims – 'it is as though at the point of greatest intensity only one psychical entity is in motion'.[6] And yet, however close the identification may be, the musical work is external to oneself. It has an element of otherness, a certain intractability of interpretation: a familiar point in hermeneutics is that it is not just that art's subject must be understood as really different from our own, but that it makes its own demands on understanding, sets its own limits on how it can be interpreted.[7] In hearing the subjective voice in music we are opening ourselves to another, powerful voice of great immediacy, one that we attempt to make our own.[8]

The subjectivity experienced in music is thus both self and other, '*simultaneously* a taking and a being taken' in Maurice Merleau-Ponty's apt phrase, possessing that power 'to implant subjective states in the listener that are paradoxically both native and alien, impossible either to own or disown'.[9] Music's quality of alterity alongside our capacity for self-identification with it

---

[4] *Ibid.*, p. 124. The latter is a point underscored especially by Philippe Lacoue-Labarthe and Jean-Luc Nancy in *The Literary Absolute: The Theory of Literature in German Romanticism*, trans. Philip Barnard and Cheryl Lester (Albany, NY: State University of New York Press, 1988), ch. 4, 'Criticism: The Formation of Character', pp. 101–19.

[5] Gadamer, *Truth and Method*, pp. 390–2, 400.

[6] Hoffmann, 'The Music-Hater', *Kreisleriana*, II/5, *E. T. A. Hoffmann's Musical Writings*, p. 149. We noted a similar tendency in the lines from Byron's *Manfred* cited at the start of this book.

[7] 'Self-understanding always occurs through understanding something other than the self, and includes the unity and integrity of the other,' avers Gadamer. 'The subject of the experience of art, that which remains and endures, is not the subjectivity of the person who experiences it but the work itself' (*Truth and Method*, pp. 83, 103).

[8] This position is already implicit in Edward T. Cone's equivocation that to 'listen to music is to yield our inner voice to the composer's domination. Or better: it is to make the composer's voice our own' (*The Composer's Voice*, p. 157).

[9] Maurice Merleau-Ponty (speaking specifically of his notion of 'chiasm', discussed again below), *The Visible and the Invisible*, ed. Claude Lefort, trans. Alphonso Lingis (Evanston, IL: Northwestern University Press, 1968), p. 266; Kramer, 'The Mysteries of Animation', 159.

might thereby offer a means to complete this movement of self-recognition, forming an ideal example of what Gadamer would call 'ecstasis' – a standing-outside-oneself in order to see oneself – that plays a crucial part in aesthetic subjectivity.[10] In fact, on such occasions, music can suggest an overcoming of distinctions between self and other, inhabiting the boundary or meeting point between the two. 'We situate ourselves in ourselves and in the things, in ourselves and in the other, at the point where, by a sort of chiasm, we become the others and we become world,' muses Merleau-Ponty in his late reflections on the paradoxical nature of subjectivity. Music in this way becomes akin to how Merleau-Ponty conceives of philosophy, 'the point where the passage from the self into the world and into the other is effected, at the crossing of avenues.'[11] Only, of course, music can achieve this non-conceptually, with an apparent power and immediacy distinct from other, verbal forms of articulation.

Misrecognising Others

But still, is there not something all too reassuring about this? After all, with the last chapter we ended up not with recognition but with *mis*recognition – the confusion by us, the listening and interpreting subjects, of the music's sense of subjectivity with that of the biographical subject. To end here is to break off retracing the course of our narrative at the seemingly triumphant close of Chapter 5, but there immediately followed reversals that questioned the very existence of the other apparently heard in the music, leading to an even more worrying absence located at the heart of the self in Chapter 7. Just as we saw the subject seeking to come to deeper self-knowledge through its reflection and recognition in the other, so we also witnessed the continued possibility of self-deception, of the other as merely the narcissistic fantasy of the self, built in its own image, but like Manfred's Astarte, strangely mute. The other in the 'narcissistic dialogue' is not actually another subject but a wishful construction of the self. Isn't the same true, but *really* true, of the other subjectivity we wish to hear in music? Throughout this study we were haunted by the difficulties of distinguishing the identities of the subjective voices projected in music: the fear of falling into the solitary monologue of solipsism (the concertos discussed in

---

[10] Gadamer, *Truth and Method*, p. 122. This notion of *Ekstasis* clearly draws on the discussion by Gadamer's teacher Heidegger of authentic temporality in *Sein und Zeit*; Gadamer relates this sense of being-outside-oneself in aesthetic experience back to Plato's discussion of poetic inspiration as 'divine madness' in his *Phaedrus* (244–5).

[11] Merleau-Ponty, *The Visible and the Invisible*, p. 160.

Chapter 1), the imaginary dialogue with the romantic other (Chapter 6), the breakdown of self-recognition that in extreme cases signalled insanity (Chapter 9). But the same problems arise in more pointed form when applied at a higher level to our own engagement with musical subjectivity.

While music can be used 'to recover stable and reassuring ideas of selfhood' as Kevin Korsyn puts it, this can easily risk turning into what I earlier styled 'narcissistic mollycoddling'.[12] Such a viewpoint would be supported by the broadly Lacanian psychoanalytical perspectives discussed in Chapter 7, whereby the 'big Other' invoked by music is simply a symptom of our own fantasy projection. Even the seemingly more comforting elements of Kristeva's theories of the subject – music's association with the maternal *chora*, its occupying of a pre-symbolic realm prior to full individuation – fail to reassure the vigilant observer that this art is not in truth the fetish object *par excellence*, sustaining the illusion of obtaining an impossible access to the Real.[13] All these concerns might merely point to the crushing conclusion that, of course, such problems arise, as there is in reality no other subject at all in music, and to think otherwise ironically lets us fall prey to the same trap observed in our fictional musical subject's supplication for a response from the other.

The work of art 'evokes a world which can be ascribed only to a subjectivity', claims the phenomenologist Mikel Dufrenne. 'The aesthetic object places us on the plane of the I and thou without opposing one to the other. Far from the other's usurping my world, he opens his world to me without compelling me, and I open myself to it.'[14] Yet this relation is very much an uneven one. While not identical to our own self, the alterity of the musical subject is distinctly limited and occupies a very different level of being.[15] Music may be 'other' than ourselves, but its own subjective agency is slight, and fundamentally posited by us (evoking the spectre of solipsism once more). We might think we recognise aspects of ourselves, how we could or would like to be, in the virtual musical subject, but the relation is non-reciprocal: there can be no recognition of us by the other, no self-attestation. Even Hegel's slave has a higher hold over his master.[16] Moreover, if the musical subject cannot recognise us, neither

---

[12] Korsyn, *Decentering Music*, p. 44, as cited earlier in Chapter 1; Korsyn, needless to say, is critical of this idea.

[13] Kristeva, *Revolution in Poetic Language*, p. 115.

[14] Mikel Dufrenne, *The Phenomenology of Aesthetic Experience* (1953), trans. Edward S. Casey (Evanston, IL: Northwestern University Press, 1973), pp. 102, 113.

[15] In referring to 'levels of being' here I am partly influenced by Kris McDaniel, *The Fragmentation of Being* (New York: Oxford University Press, 2017).

[16] Referring of course to the famous dialectic of Master and Slave in *The Phenomenology of Spirit*.

can it answer back: it is incapable of challenging us or contradicting the identity we impose on it. In this, it is redolent of Plato's argument against the written word in *Phaedrus*: unlike writing, music is not silent, but it cannot answer the questions we put to it or come to its own defence.[17]

In short, our relation with the musical subject lacks the all-important element of vulnerability. There is no real adventure in this encounter with the other, as Emmanuel Lévinas would put it, little possibility of radical confrontation or questioning of who we are.[18] This essentially ethical failing of a non-relational subjectivity is, in fact, a topic that particularly preoccupied Lévinas. Throughout his writings he insists on the absolute alterity of the other and our own openness to and responsibility for it; 'the subjectivity of a subject', in his view, 'is vulnerability, exposure to affection, sensibility'.[19]

One of Lévinas's favourite illustrations of the opposing position, the egocentric, non-reciprocal relation with the other, is the myth of Gyges and his ring. In Plato's version of the story, related by Glaucon in book two of the *Republic*, Gyges, a Lydian shepherd, discovered a magic ring which enabled him to become invisible. Using this ring, Gyges seduced the queen and killed the king, Candaules, taking over the throne himself.[20] Plato's Glaucon offers this story to make a pessimistic point about human nature: that almost everyone would have no compunction in committing numerous crimes if they knew they would get away with them. For Lévinas, this myth serves as a warning of the dangers of a self-relating subjectivity that does not hold itself responsible for the other. 'The myth of Gyges is the very myth of the I and interiority, which exist non-recognized', writes Lévinas, 'the subject that sees without being seen, without exposing himself, the secret of the inward subject.'[21] This is essentially solipsism: to see but not to participate, not to open oneself up to vulnerability, ultimately not to allow

---

[17] For Plato's Socrates, the written word preserves its silence. It cannot speak or respond to the questions we might put to it, or defend itself (*Phaedrus*, 275d).

[18] See Emmanuel Lévinas, *Otherwise Than Being or Beyond Essence*, trans. Alphonso Lingis (Dordecht: Kluwer, 1974), p. 99 ('this adventure is no adventure', speaking of the Idealist self).

[19] *Ibid.*, p. 50.

[20] Plato, *The Republic*, II, 359a–360d. Plato's version departs from the earlier account transmitted in Herodotus, *The Histories*, I, 8–12, in which Gyges was the favourite servant of King Candaules, who at his master's bidding, reluctantly observes the queen naked. But Gyges is not invisible: he is seen by the queen as he tries to slip out and given the choice by her between killing her husband and taking his place or being killed. He chooses the former. Herodotus' version intriguingly reframes the notion of recognition and attestation in relation to the sacred or innermost private realm raised in earlier chapters. Fittingly, in the year of Schumann's death an even more destructive outcome is devised by an author who has appeared several times throughout this book. In Friedrich Hebbel's 1856 play *Gyges und sein Ring*, Gyges reluctantly defeats the king only to have Queen Rhodope in turn kill herself.

[21] Lévinas, *Totality and Infinity*, p. 61, *Otherwise Than Being*, p. 145.

oneself to be recognised by the other. 'Gyges plays a double game, a presence to the others and an absence, speaking to "others" and evading speech; Gyges is the very condition of man, the possibility of injustice and radical egoism, the possibility of accepting the rules of the game, but cheating.'[22]

There is surely something here of our own relation with the musical subject: the egoistic fantasy that it speaks to us and in our voice of our innermost selves, that it tells us what we want to hear without demanding anything back, the omnipotent conceit that we are invisible and pull all the strings. Music, 'dealt with prosopopoeiacally', as Carolyn Abbate puts it, is 'made a ventriloquist's dummy, who can be made to speak any interpretation'.[23] This is exemplified in the imposition of insanity in the subjective voice of Schumann's music, in which critical preconceptions about the biographical subject are reinforced by the subjective agency of critics as listeners to overpower the more fragile and contingent subjectivity of the work.

Of course, we should not exaggerate music's muteness, its susceptibility to hermeneutic abuse. The alterity of music is partial but real and does impose some limits on its interpretation. Indeed, I have been able to dispute the readings of madness in Schumann's music by virtue of the fact that the music, in my view, affords the interpretation badly. In theory (if not always in practice), the excesses of musical hermeneutics can be revised and refined through intersubjective debate and agreement. Furthermore, music's resistance, its sense of agency, can be more apparent when our relation to music is more active or creative, when we engage with music in performance, for instance, or perhaps even more through composition.[24] But still, I think, it is necessary here to acknowledge the limitations of subjectivity as a model. This is where the primarily aesthetic questions I have been posing take on a larger ethical import.

The Limits of Subjectivity

Subjectivity may be limited in other ways, too. I have spoken earlier in this book of the historical emergence of subjectivity, though significantly not of its decline. But hasn't the appeal of subjectivity actually faded somewhat by now? Does the idea of subjectivity as a discursive framework for

---

[22] Lévinas, *Totality and Infinity*, p. 173.   [23] Abbate, *Unsung Voices*, p. 18.
[24] Nevertheless, one should be aware of similar potential for deception here; without a doubt there can be a sense of the music demanding something of us, in some (rare) cases springing as if of its own accord, spontaneously, into life. But my sceptical self tells me this is an illusion of the same order as those described above, only one that fools its composer.

understanding Western classical music still hold up in the context of contemporary cultural theory, or might the models of subjectivity associated with Schumann and his world appear a little outdated in our post-humanist, post-postmodern age? To put it bluntly, how can an account of subjectivity in Schumann's music, however nuanced and critical it may endeavour to be, have significance for us in the twenty-first century?

Such misgivings would be understandable in the current scholarly climate, but are nevertheless unwarranted I think, at least if applied to the world existing outside the confines of the academy. The notion of subjectivity may have arguably lost some of its lustre in theoretical circles – with the notable exception, that is, of the more suspicious, poststructuralist approaches explored in Chapters 6 and 7 (revealingly, Lacanian takes on the topic have been flavour of the decade in recent musicological writing) – but its hold on ordinary attitudes to music has far from been relinquished. A 'decline of subjectivity' may well be traceable in modernist and postmodernist aesthetics and in some modernist music over the twentieth century. Yet the very fact that Romantic music still makes up such a major part of the Western classical repertory today – alongside the far greater reach of popular and middlebrow art music over that of the avant-garde – points to the continued relevance of this broad conception of subjectivity for a much larger sway of the population. This is not, of course, to claim that popularity should be the most crucial factor in deciding what is worthy of scholarly consideration, nor that this apparent survival is unconditionally a good thing: challenges to these ideas may be healthy and necessary, and I have offered several in these pages. But a scholarship that seeks to relate to what people actually believe and practice ill affords to ignore the world that lies around it by being wrapped up in its own internal monologue.

This, in summary, is why an investigation into musical subjectivity is important now. Despite many changes and modifications in our conception of subjectivity in the interim and the challenges it has continually faced, the persistence of Schumann's music and the subjective ethos which it sustains and which partly sustains it forms a correlative to the persistence of many of the underlying beliefs about ourselves as subjects and what music can offer. As we saw at the start of this study, even to this day performers and audiences hold fast to the idea that in hearing Schumann's music we are given access to his inner self, eavesdropping on the composer's 'own deeply private world', being made privy to 'the sorts of truths one often hides even from oneself'.[25] Rightly or wrongly, many of the

---

[25] Isserlis, 'In defence of Schumann', Biss, 'From fact to fantasie'.

aesthetic assumptions and beliefs that were around in Schumann's time still permeate the general public understanding of art and of selfhood today. Non-specialist music lovers may not necessarily think in terms of an aesthetic subject in music (in my experience the idea comes as a surprise to many), but the vicarious emotional journey and curious sense of identification with the music they love points to the same features that the concept of subjectivity attempts, more rigorously, to explain.

Still, looking back on the picture that has emerged over the course of this book, I am aware of a possible tension between the seemingly ineradicable but, crucially, diffuse and inchoate way in which many people still relate to music's subjective qualities, and the critical precision and consistency that my account has sought to bring to the subject. In offering a critique of musical subjectivity, I have been seeking in these pages to refine the use of this concept, to find grounds as to how, and how far, we might justify its continued use. But the more precise the application, the more strained I have often felt the discussion becomes. How does one point to self-consciousness in music (Chapter 4)? By what means does the divided subject manifest itself (Chapter 3), and what distinguishes the divided subject from multiple subjects (Chapter 8)? Such discussion may be simply taking a seemingly legitimate idea to its logical conclusion, but the hermeneutic hair-splitting and interpretative overkill that results (what I have referred to as 'silly hermeneutics') leaves me uneasy.

It would appear that subjectivity is most prevalent and powerful as an explanatory metaphor when kept somewhat fuzzy. Amorphous, inconsistent, and intermittent – this is in many ways the cause of music's potency as an expression of subjectivity, what I earlier called its productive indeterminacy, its permitting of fluid movement between impossible subject positions and sense of emotional expression. Yet this would seem to imply that maintaining a degree of imprecision when using this term may in fact be a virtue; and one of the primary motivations for this project was a sense of dissatisfaction at the lack of clarity and logical foundation in the recourse to subjectivity in much musicological writing, its openness to hermeneutic abuse. One may justly respect the ancient adage not to demand more precision than a given subject allows, but how can we distinguish in this case between justified fuzziness and unfounded nonsense? Once again, only even more exasperatingly now, we run up against internal limits to the sensible discussion of musical subjectivity.

This final chapter has had in effect three ends: a comforting (and comfortable) aesthetic one; a more questioning ethical one; and finally, an unresolved, self-reflective one, which does not so much supplant the previous two as keep them both in play. How might it be possible to resolve the ethical and critical concerns of the proceeding discussion, or if not resolve them, at least offer some reconciliation, a way forward out of the unwelcome uncertainty and apparent obscurantism that appears to result?

The only answer I can offer is that the topic calls for a continual process of reflection and mediation. Both the unsupportedly vague and excessively exacting application of subjectivity to music may court meaninglessness, for instance, but there should be some sensible interpretive middle ground between the two. And such interpretations may further be refined through informed criticism and development of the viewpoints and arguments offered. As with the movement traced in Chapter 8, the course of the argument expands out to encompass a wider public realm, in which subjectivity is negotiated through intersubjective dialogue, thus leading to another reflexive level of subjectivity, of interpretative practice.[26] At the start of this book I contended that subjectivity 'is not a pre-given entity but a dynamic process that requires our own active participation for its interpretation' – and even at the end of the intervening account we can see how, more than ever, this process is one that has no fixed terminus (outside, I suppose, the death of the subject).

Subjectivity, as Kierkegaard argues, is a task – indeed the highest task given to us.[27] Crucially, it is as much an ethical as an aesthetic task, and one that calls for continued critical vigilance. We need not deny the value of music in being able to create a potent sense of aesthetic subjectivity, its role in the construction of a sense of self, to give rise to the experience of empathy and facilitate intersubjective communication. In this lies its potential value within the realm of ethics. Music's ability to instil a powerful feeling of subjective presence alongside the indeterminacy of its identity and fluidity of its forms of suggestion allows us to inhabit and move fluidly between multiple, sometimes impossible, subject positions in a way which appears inaccessible to other more precise modes of significa-tion, to experience from a privileged first-person perspective the subjectiv-ity of virtual others. Schumann, more than most, presents us with a particularly rich picture of the complex, multiple, often divided or paradoxical sense of subjecthood many listeners have felt to be true to

---

[26] This may, however, be hoping for too much: in light of the critical understanding and care often evidenced in contemporary musicology I fear this might, like the ensuing course of Chapter 9, merely foreground the problem of misrecognition once again.

[27] See Søren Kierkegaard (writing as 'Johannes Climacus'), 'Becoming Subjective', *Concluding Unscientific Postscript to Philosophical Fragments*, trans. Howard V. and Edna H. Hong, 2 vols. (Princeton: Princeton University Press, 1992), vol. I, pp. 129–88.

life. But just as his life and music calls for empathetic understanding, so within it is also a warning not to start believing that what stems from us really comes from others.

And this is as good a point as any to take leave of this account of musical subjectivity, this narrative of our own, ongoing encounter with music, with ourselves, and with others.

Bibliography

Abbate, Carolyn: *Unsung Voices: Opera and Musical Narrative in the Nineteenth Century* (Princeton: Princeton University Press, 1991).

Abert, Hermann: *Robert Schumann* (Berlin: Harmonie Verlagsgesellschaft für Literatur und Kunst, 1910).

Abrams, Meyer H.: *Natural Supernaturalism: Tradition and Revolution in Romantic Literature* (New York: Norton, 1971).

Abrams, Meyer H.: *The Mirror and the Lamp: Romantic Theory and the Critical Tradition* (Oxford: Oxford University Press, 1953).

Addis, Laird: *Of Mind and Music* (Ithaca, NY: Cornell University Press, 1999).

Adorno, Theodor W.: 'Zum Gedächtnis Eichendorffs', in *Noten zur Literatur I* (Frankfurt: Suhrkamp, 1958), pp. 105–43.

Agawu, Kofi: 'Structural "Highpoints" in Schumann's *Dichterliebe*', *Music Analysis*, 3 (1984), 159–80.

Alewyn, Richard: 'Eine Landschaft Eichendorffs' (1957), reprinted in *Probleme und Gestalten* (Frankfurt: Insel, 1974), pp. 203–31.

Appel, Bernhard: 'R. Schumanns Humoreske für Klavier op. 20: Zum musikalischen Humor in der ersten Hälfte des 19. Jahrhunderts unter besonderer Berücksichtigung des Formproblems', PhD diss., University of Saarbrücken, 1981.

Aristotle: *The Complete Works of Aristotle*, ed. Jonathan Barnes, 2 vols. (Princeton: Princeton University Press, 1984).

Atkins, Kim (ed.): *Self and Subjectivity* (Oxford: Wiley Blackwell, 2005).

Bailey, Robert: 'An Analytical Study of the Sketches and Drafts', in *Richard Wagner: Prelude and Transfiguration from 'Tristan und Isolde' (Norton Critical Score)*, ed. Robert Bailey (New York: W. W. Norton, 1985), pp. 113–46.

Bakhtin, Mikhail: 'Discourse in the Novel', in *The Dialogic Imagination: Four Essays by M. M. Bakhtin*, trans. Caryl Emerson and Michael Holquist (Austin: University of Texas Press, 1981), pp. 259–422.

Barresi, John and Martin, Raymond: 'History as Prologue: Western Theories of the Self', in Shaun Gallagher (ed.), *The Oxford Handbook of the Self* (Oxford: Oxford University Press, 2011), pp. 33–55.

Barresi, John and Martin, Raymond: *The Rise and Fall of Soul and Self: an Intellectual History of Personal Identity* (New York: Columbia University Press, 2006).

Barthes, Roland: *Elements of Semiology*, trans. A. Lavers and C. Smith (New York: Hill and Wang, 1968).

Barthes, Roland: 'Loving Schumann', in *The Responsibility of Forms: Critical Essays on Music, Art, and Representation*, trans. Richard Howard (Oxford: Blackwell, 1985), pp. 293–8.

Barthes, Roland: 'Rasch', in *The Responsibility of Forms: Critical Essays on Music, Art, and Representation*, trans. Richard Howard (Oxford: Blackwell, 1985), pp. 299–312.

Barthes, Roland: 'The Death of the Author', in *Image, Music, Text* (London: Fontana, 1977), pp. 142–8.

Beecham, Sir Thomas: *A Mingled Chime: Leaves from an Autobiography* (London: Hutchinson and Co., 1944).

Béguin, Albert: *L'Âme romantique et le rêve: Essai sur le romantisme allemand et la poésie française* (Marseille: Cahiers du Sud, 1937).

Benjamin, William: 'Hypermetric Dissonance in the Later Works of Robert Schumann', in Roe-Min Kok and Laura Tunbridge (eds.), *Rethinking Schumann* (New York: Oxford University Press, 2011), pp. 206–34.

Bent, Ian (ed.): *Music Analysis in the Nineteenth Century*, 2 vols. (Cambridge: Cambridge University Press, 1994).

Berlin, Isaiah: *The Roots of Romanticism*, ed. Henry Hardy (London: Chatto & Windus, 1999).

Biss, Jonathan: 'From fact to fantasie: discovering the real Schumann', *The Guardian*, 18 May 2013.

Bizzaro, Patrick: 'The Symbol of the Androgyne in Blake's *The Four Zoas* and Shelley's *Prometheus Unbound*: Marital Status among the Romantic Poets', in JoAnna Stephens Mink and Janet Doubler Ward (eds.), *Joinings and Disjoinings: the Significance of Marital Status in Literature* (Bowling Green, OH: Bowling Green University Press, 1991), pp. 36–51.

Bonds, Mark Evan: *After Beethoven: Imperatives of Originality in the Symphony* (Cambridge, MA: Harvard University Press, 1996).

Bonds, Mark Evan: *The Beethoven Syndrome: Hearing Music as Autobiography* (New York: Oxford University Press, 2020).

Booth, Wayne C.: *The Rhetoric of Fiction* (Chicago: University of Chicago Press, 1961).

Botstein, Leon: 'History, Rhetoric, and the Self: Robert Schumann and Music Making in German-Speaking Europe, 1800–1860', in R. Larry Todd (ed.), *Schumann and His World* (Princeton: Princeton University Press, 1994), pp. 3–46.

Bowie, Andrew: *Aesthetics and Subjectivity: from Kant to Nietzsche* (Manchester: Manchester University Press, 2003).

Bowie, Andrew: *Music, Philosophy, and Modernity* (Cambridge: Cambridge University Press, 2007).

Boyd, Melinda: 'Gendered Voices: the "Liebesfrühling" Lieder of Robert and Clara Schumann', *19th-Century Music*, 23 (1999), 145–62,

Braunschweig, Yael: 'Biographical Listening: Intimacy, Madness and the Music of Robert Schumann', PhD diss., University of California, Berkeley, 2013.

Brendel, Franz: 'Robert Schumann with Reference to Mendelssohn-Bartholdy and the Development of Modern Music in General (1845)', trans. Jürgen Thym, in R. Larry Todd (ed.), *Schumann and His World* (Princeton: Princeton University Press, 1994), pp. 317–37.

Brinkmann, Reinhold: *Schumann und Eichendorff: Studien zum Liederkreis Opus 39* (Munich: edition text+kritik, 1997).

Brown, Julie Hedges: '"A Higher Echo of the Past": Schumann's 1842 Chamber Music and the Rethinking of Classical Form', PhD diss., Yale University, 2000.

Brown, Marshall: 'Mozart and After: the Revolution in Musical Consciousness', *Critical Inquiry*, 7 (1981), 689–706.

Burnham, Scott: *Beethoven Hero* (Princeton: Princeton University Press, 1995).

Burnham, Scott: 'Late Styles', in Roe-Min Kok and Laura Tunbridge (eds.), *Rethinking Schumann* (New York: Oxford University Press, 2011), pp. 411–30.

Burnham, Scott: 'The Stillness of Time, the Fullness of Space: Four Settings of Goethe's "Wandrers Nachtlied"', *19th-Century Music*, 40 (2017), 189–200.

Burton, Anna: 'Robert Schumann and Clara Wieck: a Creative Partnership', *Music & Letters*, 69 (1988), 211–28.

Busst, Alan J. L.: 'The Image of the Androgyne in the Nineteenth Century', in Ian Fletcher (ed.), *Romantic Mythologies* (London: Routledge and Kegan Paul, 1967), pp. 1–95.

Butt, John: 'Bach's Passions and the Construction of Early Modern Subjectivities', in *Bach's Dialogue with Modernity: Perspectives on the Passions* (Cambridge: Cambridge University Press, 2010), pp. 36–96.

Butt, John: 'Do Musical Works Contain an Implied Listener? Towards a Theory of Musical Listening', *Journal of the Royal Musical Association*, 135 (2010), 5–18.

Byron, George Gordon, Lord: *The Poetical Works of Lord Byron* (London: Oxford University Press, 1909).

Calcagno, Mauro: *From Madrigal to Opera: Monteverdi's Staging of the Self* (Berkeley: University of California Press, 2012).

Cavarero, Adriana: *Relating Narratives: Storytelling and Selfhood*, trans. Paul Kottman (London and New York: Routledge, 2000).

Cavarero, Adriana: *For More Than One Voice: Toward a Philosophy of Vocal Expression*, trans. Paul A. Kottman (Stanford: Stanford University Press, 2005).

Chua, Daniel K. L.: *Absolute Music and the Construction of Meaning* (Cambridge: Cambridge University Press, 1999).

Clarke, David and Clarke, Eric (eds.): *Music and Consciousness: Philosophical, Psychological, and Cultural Perspectives* (Oxford: Oxford University Press, 2011).

Clarke, Eric: 'Lost and Found in Music: Music, Consciousness and Subjectivity', *Musicae Scientiae*, 18 (2014), 354–68.

Clarke, Eric: *Ways of Listening: An Ecological Approach to the Perception of Musical Meaning* (New York: Oxford University Press, 2005).

Cone, Edward T.: 'Poet's Love or Composer's Love?', in Steven Paul Scher (ed.), *Music and Text: Critical Inquiries* (Cambridge: Cambridge University Press, 1992), pp. 177–92.

Cone, Edward. T.: *The Composer's Voice* (Berkeley: University of California Press, 1974).

Conrad, Dieter: 'Schumanns Liedkomposition – von Schubert her gesehen', *Die Musikforschung*, 24/2 (1971), 135–67.

Cumming, Naomi: 'The Subjectivities of "Erbarme dich"', *Music Analysis*, 16 (1997), 5–44.

Cumming, Naomi: *The Sonic Self: Musical Subjectivity and Signification* (Bloomington: Indiana University Press, 2000).

Dahlhaus, Carl: *Ludwig van Beethoven: Approaches to his Music*, trans. Mary Whittall (Oxford: Oxford University Press, 1991).

Damasio, Antonio: *The Feeling of What Happens: Body, Emotion and the Making of Consciousness* (London: Heinemann, 1999).

Daverio, John: 'Schumann's Systems of Musical Fragments and *Witz*', in *Nineteenth-Century Music and the German Romantic Ideology* (New York: Schirmer, 1993), pp. 49–88.

Daverio, John: *Crossing Paths: Schubert, Schumann, and Brahms* (New York: Oxford University Press, 2002).

Daverio, John: *Robert Schumann: Herald of a 'New Poetic Age'* (New York: Oxford University Press, 1997).

Davies, Stephen: 'Contra the Hypothetical Persona in Music', in *Themes in the Philosophy of Music* (Oxford: Oxford University Press, 2003), pp. 152–68.

Dayan, Peter: '"Sing Me a Song to Make Death Tolerable": Music in Mourning for Derrida', in *Music Writing Literature: From Sand via Debussy to Derrida* (Aldershot: Ashgate, 2006), pp. 113–30.

de Man, Paul: 'The Rhetoric of Blindness: Jacques Derrida's Reading of Rousseau', in *Blindness and Insight: Essays in the Rhetoric of Contemporary Criticism* (Minneapolis: University of Minnesota Press, 1983), pp. 102–41.

Dennett, Daniel: *Consciousness Explained* (Harmondsworth: Penguin Books, 1991).

Dennett, Daniel: 'The Self as a Center of Narrative Gravity', in Frank S. Kessel, Pamela M. Cole, and Dale L. Johnson (eds.), *Self and Consciousness: Multiple Perspectives* (Hillsdale, NJ: Lawrence Erlbaum, 1992), pp. 103–15.

Derrida, Jacques: *Of Grammatology*, trans. Gayatri Chakravorty Spivak (Baltimore: John Hopkins University Press, 1997).

Derrida, Jacques: *Voice and Phenomenon: Introduction to the Problem of the Sign in Husserl's Phenomenology*, trans. Leonard Lawlor (Chicago: Northwestern University Press, 2010).

Derrida, Jacques: *Writing and Difference*, trans. Alan Bass (London: Routledge, 2001).

Derrida, Jacques: *Margins of Philosophy*, trans. Alan Bass (Chicago: Chicago University Press, 1982).

Desmond, Astra: *Schumann Songs* (London: BBC, 1972).

Dolar, Mladen: *A Voice and Nothing More* (Cambridge, MA: MIT Press, 2006).

Dufrenne, Mikel: *The Phenomenology of Aesthetic Experience* (1953), trans. Edward S. Casey (Evanston, IL: Northwestern University Press, 1973).

Eichendorff, Joseph von: *Dichter und ihre Gesellen* (Stuttgart: Reclam, 1987).

Eichendorff, Joseph von: *Sämtliche Gedichte* (Frankfurt: Insel, 2001).

Eichendorff, Joseph von: *Sämtliche Erzählungen* (Stuttgart: Reclam, 1990).

Eismann, Georg: *Robert Schumann: Ein Quellenwerk über sein Leben und Schaffen*, 2 vols. (Leipzig: Brietkopf und Härtel, 1956).

Eliot, T. S.: *Collected Poems 1909–1962* (London: Faber, 1974).

Ferris, David: *Schumann's Eichendorff Liederkreis and the Genre of the Romantic Cycle* (New York: Oxford University Press, 2000).

Fichte, Johann G.: *Science of Knowledge*, trans. Peter Heath and John Lachs (Cambridge: Cambridge University Press, 1982).

Finson, Jon W.: 'At the Interstice between "Popular" and "Classical": Schumann's *Poems of Queen Mary Stuart* and European Sentimentality at Midcentury', in Roe-Min Kok and Laura Tunbridge (eds.), *Rethinking Schumann* (New York: Oxford University Press, 2011), pp. 69–87.

Finson, Jon W.: 'The Intentional Tourist: Romantic Irony in the Eichendorff *Liederkreis* of Robert Schumann', in R. Larry Todd (ed.), *Schumann and His World* (Princeton: Princeton University Press, 1994), pp. 156–70.

Finson, Jon: *Robert Schumann: The Book of Songs* (Cambridge, MA: Harvard University Press, 2007).

Fischer-Dieskau, Dietrich: *Robert Schumann: Wort und Musik: Das Vokalwerk* (Stuttgart: Deutsche Verlags-Anstalt, 1981).

Foucault, Michel: 'The Subject and Power', in *Beyond Structuralism and Hermeneutics*, ed. H. Dreyfus and P. Rabinow (Chicago: University of Chicago Press, 1983), pp. 208–26.

Foucault, Michel: 'What Is an Author?', in *Language, Counter-Memory, Practice: Selected Interviews and Essays*, ed. D. Bouchard (Oxford: Blackwell, 1977), pp. 113–38.

Foucault, Michel: *Folie et Déraison: Histoire de la folie à l'âge classique* (Paris: Librarie Plon, 1961), trans. Jonathan Murphy and Jean Khalfa as *History of Madness* (London: Routledge, 2006).

Freud, Sigmund: *Art and Literature (Penguin Freud Library*, vol. XIV) (Harmondsworth: Penguin, 1990).

Friedrichsmeyer, Sara: *The Androgyne in Early German Romanticism: Friedrich Schlegel, Novalis, and the Metaphysics of Love* (Bern: Peter Lang, 1983).

Gadamer, Hans-Georg: *Truth and Method*, trans. Joel Weinsheimer and Donald G. Marshall (London: Continuum, 2006).

Gallagher, Shaun: *The Inordinance of Time* (Evanston, IL: Northwestern University Press, 1998).

Goethe, Johann Wolfgang von: *Poetische Werke: Vollständige Ausgabe*, 10 vols. (Phaidon Verlag: Essen, 1999).

Goethe, Johann Wolfgang von, and Zelter, Carl Friedrich: *Briefwechsel zwischen Goethe und Zelter in den Jahren 1796 bis 1832*, 6 vols. (Berlin: Dunker und Humblot, 1834).

Gülke, Peter: 'Zur "Rheinischen Sinfonie"', in Hans-Klaus Metzger and Rainer Riehn (eds.), *Musik-Konzepte: Robert Schumann II* (Munich: text+kritik, 1982), pp. 237–53.

Guralnick, Elissa S.: '"Ah Clara, I Am Not Worthy of Your Love": Rereading "Frauenliebe und Leben", the Poetry and the Music', *Music & Letters*, 87 (2006), 580–605.

Habermas, Jürgen: *The Philosophical Discourse of Modernity*, trans. Frederick G. Lawrence (Cambridge: Polity Press, 1985).

Habermas, Jürgen: *Theory of Communicative Action, vol. I, Reason and the Rationalization of Society*, trans. Thomas A. McCarthy (Cambridge: Polity Press, 1984).

Hadow, William Henry: *Studies in Modern Music: Hector Berlioz, Robert Schumann, Richard Wagner* (London: Seeley and Company, 1893).

Hallmark, Rufus: 'The Rückert Lieder of Robert and Clara Schumann', *19th-Century Music*, 14 (1990), 4–13.

Hallmark, Rufus: 'The Sketches for "Dichterliebe"', *19th-Century Music*, 1 (1977), 110–36.

Hallmark, Rufus: *Frauenliebe und Leben: Chamisso's Poems and Schumann's Songs* (Cambridge: Cambridge University Press, 2014).

Hambridge, Katherine: 'Staging Singing in the Theater of War (Berlin, 1805)', *Journal of the American Musicological Society*, 68 (2015), 39–98.

Hanslick, Eduard: *Sämtliche Schriften: Historisch-kritische Ausgabe*, ed. Dietmar Strauß (Vienna: Böhlau, 1993–), vol. I (*Aufsätze und Rezensionen 1844–48*).

Hatten, Robert: *A Theory of Virtual Agency for Western Art Music* (Bloomington: Indiana University Press, 2018).

Heero, Aigi: *Robert Schumanns Jugendlyrik* (Sinzig: Studio Verlag, 2003).

Hegel, Georg Wilhelm Friedrich: *Aesthetics: Lectures on Fine Art*, trans. T. M. Knox, 2 vols. (Oxford: Clarendon Press, 1975).

Hegel, Georg Wilhelm Friedrich: *Philosophy of Mind*, trans. W. Wallace and A. V. Miller (Oxford: Clarendon Press, 2007).

Hepokoski, James and Darcy, Warren: *Elements of Sonata Theory: Norms, Types, and Deformations in the Late-Eighteenth-Century Sonata* (New York: Oxford University Press, 2006).

Herbert, Ruth, Clarke, David, and Clarke, Eric (eds.): *Music and Consciousness 2: Worlds, Practices, Modalities* (Oxford: Oxford University Press, 2019).

Herodotus: *The Histories*, trans. Aubrey De Selincourt (Harmondsworth: Penguin, 2003).

Hibberd, Sarah (ed.): *Melodramatic Voices: Understanding Music Drama* (Farnham: Ashgate, 2011).

Hoeckner, Berthold: 'Poet's Love and Composer's Love', *Music Theory Online*, 7/5 (2001).

Hoeckner, Berthold: 'Schumann and Romantic Distance', *Journal of the American Musicological Society*, 50 (1997), 55–132.

Hoffmann, E. T. A.: *E. T. A. Hoffmann's Musical Writings*, trans. Martyn Clarke, ed. David Charlton (Cambridge: Cambridge University Press, 1989).

Hoffmann, E. T. A.: *The Life and Opinions of the Tomcat Murr*, trans. Anthea Bell (Harmondsworth: Penguin, 1999).

Hoffmann-Axthelm, Dagmar: *Robert Schumann: 'Glücklichsein und tiefe Einsamkeit'* (Stuttgart: Reclaim, 1994).

Hofstadter, Douglas R. and Dennett, Daniel C. (eds.): *The Mind's I: Fantasies and Reflections on Self and Soul* (New York: Basic Books, 1981).

Horton, Julian: *Brahms' Piano Concerto No. 2, Op. 83: Analytical and Contextual Studies* (Leuven: Peeters, 2017).

Hoy-Draheim, Susanne: 'Robert Schumann und E. T. A. Hoffmann', in Matthias Wendt (ed.), *Schumann und seine Dichter* (Mainz: Schott, 1993), 61–70.

Hume, David: *A Treatise of Human Nature*, ed. L. A. Selby-Bigge (Oxford: Clarendon Press, 1951).

Husserl, Edmund: *The Phenomenology of Internal Time Consciousness*, trans. James Churchill (The Hague: Martinus Nijhoff, 1964).

Isserlis, Steven: 'In defence of Schumann', *The Guardian*, 1 July 2010.

Izenberg, Gerald: *Impossible Individuality: Romanticism, Revolution, and the Origins of Modern Selfhood, 1787–1802* (Princeton: Princeton University Press, 1992).

Jacques, Claudine: 'Gender Transitivity in Three Dramatic Works by Robert Schumann: the *Szenen aus Goethes* Faust (WoO 3), *Genoveva* Op. 81, *Das Paradies und die Peri* Op. 50', PhD diss., McGill University, 2011.

Jean Paul [Richter, Jean Paul Friedrich]: *Werke*, ed. Norbert Miller and Gustav Lohmann, 6 vols. (Munich: Carl Hanser Verlag, 1959–63).

Jensen, Eric Frederick: 'Explicating Jean Paul: Robert Schumann's Program for *Papillons*, op. 2', *19th-Century Music*, 22 (1998), 127–43.

Jensen, Eric Frederick: *Schumann (The Master Musicians)* (Oxford: Oxford University Press, 2012).

Jensen, Eric Frederick: 'A New Manuscript of Robert Schumann's *Waldszenen* Op. 82', *Journal of Musicology*, 3 (1984), 69–89.

Johnson, Graham: notes to *The Songs of Robert Schumann*, vol. 1, Hyperion CDJ33101 (1996).

Johnson, Graham: notes to *The Songs of Robert Schumann*, vol. 2, Hyperion CDJ33102 (1998).

Johnson, Graham: notes to *The Songs of Robert Schumann*, vol. 4, Hyperion CDJ33104 (2000).

Johnson, Graham: notes to *The Songs of Robert Schumann*, vol. 6, Hyperion CDJ33106 (2002).

Johnson, Graham: notes to *The Songs of Robert Schumann*, vol. 7, Hyperion CDJ33107 (2002).

Johnson, Julian: 'Narrative Strategies in Hoffmann and Schumann', in Rudinger Görner (ed.), *Resounding Concerns* (Munich: Iudicium, 2003), pp. 55–70.

Johnson, Julian: 'The Status of the Subject in Mahler's Ninth Symphony', *19th-Century Music*, 18 (1994), 108–20.

Johnson, Julian: 'The Subjects of Music: A Theoretical and Analytical Enquiry into the Construction of Subjectivity in the Musical Structuring of Time', DPhil diss., University of Sussex (1994).

Johnson, Julian: *Mahler's Voices: Expression and Irony in the Songs and Symphonies* (New York: Oxford University Press, 2009).

Johnson, Julian: *Out of Time: Music and the Making of Modernity* (New York: Oxford University Press, 2015).

Kallberg, Jeffery: *Chopin at the Boundaries: Sex, History, and Musical Genre* (Cambridge, MA: Harvard University Press, 1996).

Kaminsky, Peter: 'Principles of Formal Structure in Schumann's Early Piano Cycles', *Music Theory Spectrum*, 11 (1989), 211–16.

Kant, Immanuel: *Werke*, 12 vols. (Frankfurt: Suhrkamp, 1977).

Kapp, Reinhard: *Studien zum Spätwerk Robert Schumanns* (Tutzing: Hans Schneider, 1984).

Keller, Hans: 'The Classical Romantics: Schumann and Mendelssohn', in H. H. Schönzeler (ed.), *Of German Music: A Symposium* (London: Oswald Wolff, 1976), pp. 179–218.

Kerman, Joseph: 'Mozart's Piano Concertos and Their Audience', in *Write All These Down: Essays on Music* (Berkeley: University of California Press, 1994), pp. 322–34.

Kerman, Joseph: 'The Concertos', in Beate Perrey (ed.), *The Cambridge Companion to Schumann* (Cambridge: Cambridge University Press, 2007), pp. 173–94.

Kierkegaard, Søren (writing as 'Johannes Climacus'): *Concluding Unscientific Postscript to Philosophical Fragments*, trans. Howard V. and Edna H. Hong, 2 vols. (Princeton: Princeton University Press, 1992).

Kinderman, William and Krebs, Harald (eds.): *The Second Practice of Nineteenth-Century Tonality* (Lincoln, NE: University of Nebraska Press, 1996).

Klein, Michael: *Music and the Crises of the Modern Subject* (Bloomington: Indiana University Press, 2015).

Klorman, Edward: *Mozart's Music of Friends: Social Interplay in the Chamber Works* (Cambridge: Cambridge University Press, 2016).

Köhler, Hans Joachim: 'Die Stichvorlagen zum Erstdruck von Opus 21 – Assoziationen zu Schumanns *Novelletten*', *Schumann Studien*, 3/4 (1994), 75–94.

Köhler, Hans Joachim: 'Schumann, der Autodiktat: Zum genetischen Zusammenhang von variativem Prinzip und poetischer Idee', in Gerd Nauhaus (ed.), *Schumann-Studien*, 3–4 (Cologne: Studio, 1994), pp. 188–98.

Kopp, David: 'Intermediate States of Key in Schumann', in Roe-Min Kok and Laura Tunbridge (eds.), *Rethinking Schumann* (New York: Oxford University Press, 2011), pp. 300–25.

Korsyn, Kevin: *Decentering Music: A Critique of Contemporary Musical Research* (Oxford: Oxford University Press, 2003).

Koßmaly, Carl: 'On Robert Schumann's Piano Compositions (1844)', trans. Susan Gillespie, in Ralph Larry Todd (ed.), *Schumann and His World* (Princeton: Princeton University Press, 1994), pp. 303–16.

Kramer, Lawrence: 'Rethinking Schumann's *Carnaval*: Identity, Meaning, and the Social Order', in *Musical Meaning: Toward a Critical History* (Berkeley and Los Angeles: University of California Press, 2002), 100–32.

Kramer, Lawrence: 'Subjectivity Unbound: Music, Language, Culture', in Martin Clayton, Trevor Herbert, and Richard Middleton (eds.), *The Cultural Study of Music: A Critical Introduction* (Oxford: Routledge, 2012), pp. 395–406.

Kramer, Lawrence: 'Subjectivity', in *Interpreting Music* (Berkeley and Los Angeles: University of California Press, 2011), pp. 46–62.

Kramer, Lawrence: 'The Mysteries of Animation: History, Analysis and Musical Subjectivity', *Music Analysis*, 20 (2001), 153–78.

Kramer, Lawrence: *Classical Music and Postmodern Knowledge* (Berkeley and Los Angeles: University of California Press, 1995).

Kramer, Lawrence: *Franz Schubert: Sexuality, Subjectivity, Song* (Cambridge: Cambridge University Press, 1998).

Kramer, Lawrence: *Music and Poetry: The Nineteenth Century and After* (Berkeley and Los Angeles: University of California Press, 1984).

Krebs, Harald: 'Meter and Expression in Robert Schumann's Op. 90', in Roe-Min Kok and Laura Tunbridge (eds.), *Rethinking Schumann* (New York: Oxford University Press, 2011), pp. 183–205.

Krebs, Harald: 'The Expressive Role of Rhythm and Meter in Schumann's Late Lieder', *Gamut*, 2 (2009), 267–98.

Krebs, Harald: *Fantasy Pieces: Metrical Dissonance in the Music of Robert Schumann* (New York: Oxford University Press, 1999).

Kristeva, Julia: *Revolution in Poetic Language*, in *The Kristeva Reader*, trans. Toril Moi (Oxford: Blackwell, 1986).

Lacan, Jacques: *Écrits: A Selection*, trans. Alan Sheridan (Abingdon: Routledge, 2001).

Lacoue-Labarthe, Philippe and Nancy, Jean-Luc: *The Literary Absolute: The Theory of Literature in German Romanticism*, trans. Philip Barnard and Cheryl Lester (Albany, NY: State University of New York Press, 1988).

Larson, Steve: *Musical Forces: Motion, Metaphor, and Meaning in Music* (Bloomington: Indiana University Press, 2012).

Lévinas, Emmanuel: *Otherwise Than Being or Beyond Essence*, trans. Alphonso Lingis (Dordecht: Kluwer, 1974).

Lévinas, Emmanuel: *Totality and Infinity: An Essay on Exteriority*, trans. Alphonso Lingis (The Hague: Martinus Nijhoff, 1969).

Levinson, Jerrold: 'Hope in the *Hebrides*', in *Music, Art, and Metaphysics* (Ithaca, NY: Cornell University Press, 1990), pp. 336–75.

Lindeman, Stephan D.: *Structural Novelty and Tradition in the Early Romantic Piano Concerto* (Stuyvesant, NY: Pendragon Press, 1999).

Litzmann, Berthold: *Clara Schumann: Ein Künstlerleben nach Tagebüchern und Briefen*, 3 vols. (Leipzig Breitkopf & Härtel, 1902).

Locke, John: *An Essay Concerning Human Understanding*, ed. Peter Nidditch (Oxford: Clarendon Press, 1975).

MacAuslan, John: *Schumann's Music and E. T. A. Hoffmann's Fiction* (Cambridge: Cambridge University Press, 2016).

Macdonald, Claudia: *Robert Schumann and the Piano Concerto* (New York: Routledge, 2005).

MacLeod, Catriona: *Embodying Ambiguity: Androgyny and Aesthetics from Winckelmann to Keller* (Detroit: Wayne State University Press, 1998).

Malin, Yonatan: 'Schumann: Doubling and Reverberation', in *Songs in Motion: Rhythm and Meter in the German Lied* (New York: Oxford University Press, 2010).

Marston, Nicholas: 'Schumann's Heroes: Schubert, Beethoven, Bach', in Beate Perrey (ed.), *The Cambridge Companion to Schumann* (Cambridge: Cambridge University Press, 2007), pp. 48–62.

Marston, Nicholas: 'Voicing Beethoven's Distant Beloved', in Scott Burnham and Michael Steinberg (eds.), *Beethoven and His World* (Princeton: Princeton University Press, 2000), pp. 124–47.

Marston, Nicholas: *Schumann: Fantasie, Op. 17* (Cambridge: Cambridge University Press, 1992).

Martin, Nathan John: 'Schumann's Fragment', *Indiana Theory Review*, 28 (2010), 85–109.

Maus, Fred Everett: 'Agency in Instrumental Music and Song', *College Music Symposium*, 29 (1989), 31–43.

Maus, Fred Everett: 'Edward T. Cone's *The Composer's Voice*: Elaborations and Departures', *College Music Symposium*, 29 (1989), 1–80, with contributions by Marion A. Guck, Charles Fisk, Fred Everett Maus, James Webster, Alicyn Warren, and a response by Edward T. Cone.

Maus, Fred Everett: 'Music as Drama', *Music Theory Spectrum*, 10 (1988), 56–73.

McClary, Susan: 'A Musical Dialectic from the Enlightenment: Mozart's *Piano Concerto in G major, K. 453, Movement 2*', *Cultural Critique*, 4 (1986), 129–69.

McClary, Susan: 'Constructions of Subjectivity in Schubert's Music', in Philip Brett, Elizabeth Wood, and Gary C. Thomas, *Queering the Pitch: The New Gay and Lesbian Musicology* (New York: Routledge, 1994), pp. 205–33.

McClary, Susan: 'The Blasphemy of Talking Politics during a Bach Year', in Susan McClary and Richard Leppert (eds.), *Music and Society: The Politics of Composition, Performance, and Reception* (Cambridge: Cambridge University Press, 1987), pp. 13–62.

McClary, Susan: *Desire and Pleasure in Seventeenth-Century Music* (Berkeley: University of California Press, 2012).

McClary, Susan: *Modal Subjectivities: Self-Fashioning in the Italian Madrigal* (Berkeley: University of California Press, 2004).

McDaniel, Kris: *The Fragmentation of Being* (New York: Oxford University Press, 2017).

Merleau-Ponty, Maurice: *The Visible and the Invisible*, ed. Claude Lefort, trans. Alphonso Lingis (Evanston IL: Northwestern University Press, 1968).

Mertl, Monika: 'Reinventing Opera: Nikolaus Harnoncourt and his view of *Genoveva*', liner notes to Teldec CD 0630–13144-2 (1997).

Monahan, Seth: 'Action and Agency Revisited', *Journal of Music Theory*, 57 (2013), 321–71.

Moreno, Jairo: *Musical Representations, Subjects, and Objects: The Construction of Musical Thought in Zarlino, Descartes, Rameau, and Weber* (Bloomington: Indiana University Press, 2004).

Moser, Andreas (ed.): *Briefe von und an Joseph Joachim*, (Berlin: Bard, 1911).

Muxfeldt, Kristina: *Vanishing Sensibilities: Essays in Reception and Historical Restoration – Schubert, Beethoven, Schumann* (New York: Oxford University Press, 2011).

Nagel, Thomas: *The View from Nowhere* (New York: Oxford University Press, 1986).

Nagel, Thomas: 'What Is It Like to Be a Bat?', *The Philosophical Review*, 83 (1974), 435–50.

Nattiez, Jean-Jacques: *Wagner Androgyne*, trans. Stewart Spencer (Princeton: Princeton University Press, 1993).

Nauhaus, Gerd: 'Schumann's Symphonic Finales', trans. Susan Gillespie, in Ralph Larry Todd (ed.), *Schumann and His World* (Princeton: Princeton University Press, 1994), pp. 113–28.

Neumeyer, David: 'Organic Structure and the Song Cycle: Another Look at Schumann's *Dichterliebe*', *Music Theory Spectrum*, 4 (1982), 92–105.

Newcomb, Anthony: 'Action and Agency in Mahler's Ninth Symphony, Second Movement', in Jenefer Robinson (ed.), *Music and Meaning* (Ithaca, NY: Cornell University Press, 1997), pp. 131–53.

Newcomb, Anthony: 'Once More "Between Absolute and Programme Music": Schumann's Second Symphony', *19th-Century Music*, 7 (1984), 233–50.

Newcomb, Anthony: 'Schumann's Music and the Marketplace: From Butterflies to *Hausmusik*', in Ralph Larry Todd (ed.), *Nineteenth-Century Piano Music* (New York: Schirmer, 1990), pp. 258–315.

Nietzsche, Friedrich: *Sämtliche Werke*, ed. Giorgio Colli and Mazzino Montinari, 15 vols. (Berlin and New York: de Gruyter, 1980).

Nietzsche, Friedrich: *The Will to Power*, trans. Walter Kaufmann and Reginald John Hollingdale (New York: Vintage, 1967).

Novalis: *Fichte Studies*, ed. and trans. Jane Kneller (Cambridge: Cambridge University Press, 2003).

Novalis: *Gedichte; Die Lehrlinge zu Sais* (Stuttgart: Reclam, 1997).

Nussbaum, Charles: *Musical Representation: Meaning, Ontology, and Emotion* (Cambridge, MA: Massachusetts Institute of Technology Press, 2007).

Ostwald, Peter: *Schumann: The Inner Voices of a Musical Genius*, revised edition (Boston: Northeastern University Press, 2010).

Ovid: *Metamorphoses*, trans. Mary M. Innes (Harmondsworth: Penguin, 1955).

Paley, Elizabeth: '"The Voice Which Was My Music": Narrative and Nonnarrative Musical Discourse in Schumann's *Manfred*', *19th-Century Music*, 24 (2000), 3–20.

Parry, Charles Hubert H. : *Studies of Great Composers* (London: George Routledge & Sons, 1887).

Peraino, Judith: *Giving Voice to Love: Song and Self-Expression from the Troubadours to Guillaume de Machaut* (Oxford: Oxford University Press, 2011).

Perrey, Beate: 'Schumann's lives, and afterlives: an introduction', in Beate Perrey (ed.), *The Cambridge Companion to Schumann* (Cambridge: Cambridge University Press, 2007), pp. 1–37.

Perrey, Beate: *Schumann's Dichterliebe and Early Romantic Poetics: Fragmentation of Desire* (Cambridge: Cambridge University Press, 2002).

Pippin, Robert B.: *The Persistence of Subjectivity: On the Kantian Aftermath* (Cambridge: Cambridge University Press, 2001).

Plato: *The Collected Dialogues of Plato*, ed. Edith Hamilton and Huntington Cairns (Princeton: Princeton University Press, 1961).

Pohl, Richard: 'Reminiscences of Robert Schumann (1878)', trans. John Michael Cooper, in Ralph Larry Todd (ed.), *Schumann and His World* (Princeton: Princeton University Press, 1994), pp. 233–67.

Reich, Nancy B.: *Clara Schumann: The Artist and the Woman* (Ithaca, NY: Cornell University Press, 1985).

Reid, Thomas: *Essays on the Intellectual Powers of Man* (1785) (Cambridge: John Bartlett, 1850).

Reiman, Erika: *Schumann's Piano Cycles and the Novels of Jean Paul* (Rochester, NY: University of Rochester Press, 2004).

Reissmann, August: *Robert Schumann: Sein Leben und Seine Werke* (Berlin: Guttentag, 1865).

Réti, Rudolf: 'Schumann's *Kinderszenen*: A "Theme with Variations"', in *The Thematic Process in Music* (New York: Macmillan, 1951), pp. 31–55.

Reynolds, Christopher: *Motives for Allusion: Context and Content in Nineteenth-Century Music* (Cambridge, MA: Harvard University Press, 2003).

Ricoeur, Paul: *Oneself as Another*, trans. Kathleen Blamey (Chicago: University of Chicago Press, 1992).

Ridley, Aaron: '*Persona* Sometimes *Grata*: On the Appreciation of Expressive Music', in Kathleen Stock (ed.), *Philosophers on Music: Experience, Meaning, and Work* (Oxford: Oxford University Press, 2007), pp. 130–46.

Robinson, Jenefer: *Deeper than Reason: Emotion and Its Role in Literature, Music and Art* (Oxford: Oxford University Press, 2005).

Rodgers, Stephen: '"This Body That Beats": Roland Barthes and Robert Schumann's *Kreisleriana*', *Indiana Theory Review*, 18 (1997), 75–91.

Roesner, Linda Correll: 'The Chamber Music', in Beate Perrey (ed.), *The Cambridge Companion to Schumann* (Cambridge: Cambridge University Press, 2007), pp. 123–47.

Ronyak, Jennifer: *Intimacy, Performance, and the Lied in the Early Nineteenth Century* (Bloomington: Indiana University Press, 2018).

Rosen, Charles: *The Romantic Generation* (London: HarperCollins, 1996).

Rousseau, Jean-Jacques: *Essay on the Origin of Languages, in which Melody and Musical Imitation Are Treated*, trans. John T. Scott, in *The Collected Writings of Rousseau*, vol. vii. (Hanover, NH: University Press of New England, 1998).

Ryle, Gilbert: *The Concept of Mind* (1949) (Harmondsworth: Penguin, 1990).

Sams, Eric: *The Songs of Robert Schumann* (London: Faber and Faber, 1993).

Sass, Louis A.: *Madness and Modernism: Insanity in the Light of Modern Art, Literature, and Thought* (Cambridge MA: Harvard University Press, 1994).

Schelling, Friedrich Wilhelm Joseph: *Philosophy of Art*, trans. Douglas W. Stott (Minneapolis: University of Minnesota Press, 1989).

Schelling, Friedrich Wilhelm Joseph: *System of Transcendental Idealism*, trans. Peter Heath (Charlottesville: University Press of Virginia, 1978).

Schelling, Friedrich Wilhelm Joseph: *The Ages of the World*, trans. Jason M. Worth (Albany, NY: State University of New York Press, 2000).

Schenker, Heinrich: *Harmony*, ed. Oswald Jonas, trans. Elizabeth Mann Borges (Chicago: University of Chicago Press, 1954).

Schiller, Friedrich: *On the Aesthetic Education of Man in a Series of Letters*, trans. Elizabeth M. Wilkinson and Leonard A. Willoughby (Oxford: Clarendon Press, 1967).

Schnebel, Dieter: 'Rückungen–Ver-rückungen: Psychoanalytische und musikanalytische Betrachtungen zu Schumanns Leben und Werk', in Heinz-Klaus Metzger and Rainer Riehn (eds.), *Musik-Konzepte: Robert Schumann I* (Munich: edition text+kritik, 1981), pp. 4–89.

Schubring, Adolf: 'Schumann und der Großvater', *Neue Zeitschrift für Musik*, 53/4 (20 July 1860), 29–30.

Schubring, Adolf: 'Schumanniana No. 4: The Present Musical Epoch and Robert Schumann's Position in Music History (1861)', trans. John Michael Cooper, in R. Larry Todd (ed.), *Schumann and His World* (Princeton: Princeton University Press, 1994), pp. 362–74.

Schumann, Clara and Robert: *Schumann Briefedition* [SB], ed. Michael Heinemann, Thomas Synofzik, et al., 50 vols. (Cologne: Dohr, 2008–[25]).

Schumann, Robert and Clara: *Briefwechsel: Kritische Gesamtausgabe*, ed. Eva Weissweiler, 3 vols. (Basel and Frankfurt: Stroemfeld/Roter Stern, 1984–2001).

Schumann, Robert: *Briefe: Neue Folge*, ed. Gustav Jansen, 2nd ed. (Leipzig: Breitkopf & Härtel, 1904).

Schumann, Robert: *Gesammelte Schriften über Musik und Musiker* [GS], ed. Martin Kreisig, 2 vols. (Leipzig: Breitkopf & Härtel, 1949).

Schumann, Robert: *Sämtliche Klavierwerke*, 6 vols. (Munich: Henle, 2010).

Schumann, Robert: *Tagebücher*, ed. Georg Eismann and Gerd Nauhaus, 3 vols. (Leipzig: Deutscher Verlag für Musik, 1971–82).

Scruton, Roger: *The Aesthetics of Music* (Oxford: Clarendon Press, 1997).

Seidlin, Oskar: *Versuche über Eichendorff* (Göttingen: Vandenhoeck & Ruprecht, 1965).

Seigel, Jerrold: *The Idea of the Self: Thought and Experience in Western Europe Since the Seventeenth Century* (Cambridge: Cambridge University Press, 2005).

Silverman, Kaja: *The Acoustic Mirror: The Female Voice in Psychoanalysis and Cinema* (Bloomington: Indiana University Press, 1988).

Sisman, Elaine: 'Memory and Invention at the Threshold of Beethoven's Late Style', in Scott Burnham and Michael Steinberg (eds.), *Beethoven and His World* (Princeton: Princeton University Press, 2000), pp. 51–87.

Smith, Kenneth M.: 'The Tonic Chord and Lacan's Object *a* in Selected Songs by Charles Ives', *Journal of the Royal Musical Association*, 136 (2011), 553–98.

Smith, Peter H.: 'Associative Harmony, Tonal Pairing, and Middleground Structure in Schumann's Sonata Expositions: The Role of the Mediant in the First Movements of the Piano Quintet, Piano Quartet, and *Rhenish* Symphony', in Roe-Min Kok and Laura Tunbridge (eds.), *Rethinking Schumann* (New York: Oxford University Press, 2011), pp. 235–64.

Smith, Peter H.: 'Harmonies Heard from Afar: Tonal Pairing, Formal Design, and Cyclical Integration in Schumann's A minor Violin Sonata, op. 105', *Theory and Practice*, 34 (2009), 47–86.

Smith, Peter H.: 'Schumann's A-minor Mood: Late-Style Dialectics in the First Movement of the Cello Concerto', *Journal of Music Theory*, 60 (2016), 51–88.

Smith, Peter H.: 'Schumann's Continuous Expositions and the Classical Tradition', *Journal of Music Theory*, 58 (2014), 25–56.

Smith, Peter H.: 'Tonal Pairing and Monotonality in Instrumental Forms of Beethoven, Schubert, Schumann, and Brahms', *Music Theory Spectrum*, 35 (2013), 77–102.

Solie, Ruth: 'Whose Life? The Gendered Self in Schumann's *Frauenliebe* Songs', in *Music and Text: Critical Inquiries*, ed. Steven Paul Scher (Cambridge: Cambridge University Press, 1992), pp. 219–40.

Solomon, Robert C.: 'Subjectivity', in Ted Honderich (ed.), *The Oxford Companion to Philosophy* (Oxford: Oxford University Press, 1995).

Spitzer, Michael: *Metaphor and Musical Thought* (Chicago: University of Chicago Press, 2004).

Spitzer, Michael: *A History of Emotion in Western Music* (New York: Oxford University Press, 2020).

Stefaniak, Alexander: *Schumann's Virtuosity: Criticism, Composition, and Performance in Nineteenth-Century Germany* (Bloomington: Indiana University Press, 2016).

Steinberg, Michael P.: *Listening to Reason: Culture, Subjectivity, and Nineteenth-Century Music* (Princeton: Princeton University Press, 2004).

Steinberg, Michael P.: 'Schumann's Homelessness', in R. Larry Todd (ed.), *Schumann and His World* (Princeton: Princeton University Press, 1994), pp. 47–79.

Strand, Mary R.: *I/You: Paradoxical Constructions of Self and Other in Early German Romanticism* (New York: Peter Lang, 1998).

Strawson, Galen (ed.): *The Self?* (Oxford: Blackwell, 2005).

Striker, Ardelle: '*Manfred* in Concert: An American Premiere', *Bulletin of Research in the Humanities*, 85 (1982), 479–88.

Sutcliffe, William Dean: *Instrumental Music in an Age of Sociability: Haydn, Mozart, and Friends* (Cambridge: Cambridge University Press, 2019).

Tarasti, Eero: *A Theory of Musical Semiotics* (Bloomington: Indiana University Press, 1994).

Taylor, Benedict: 'Musical History and Self-Consciousness in Mendelssohn's Octet, Op. 20', *19th-Century Music*, 32 (2008), 131–59.

Taylor, Benedict: *Mendelssohn, Time and Memory: The Romantic Conception of Cyclic Form* (Cambridge: Cambridge University Press, 2011).

Taylor, Benedict: 'Schubert and the Construction of Memory: The Quartet in A minor, D. 804 ('Rosamunde')', *Journal of the Royal Musical Association*, 139 (2014), 41–88.

Taylor, Benedict: *The Melody of Time: Music and Temporality in the Romantic Era* (New York: Oxford University Press, 2016).

Taylor, Benedict: 'Absent Subjects and Empty Centers: Eichendorff's Romantic Phantasmagoria and Schumann's *Liederkreis* Op. 39', *19th-Century Music*, 40 (2017), 201–22.

Taylor, Benedict: 'Clara Wieck's A minor Piano Concerto: Formal Innovation and the Problem of Parametric Disconnect in early Romantic Music', *Music Theory and Analysis*, 8/2 (2021), 1–28.

Taylor, Charles: *Sources of the Self: The Making of the Modern Identity* (Cambridge, MA: Harvard University Press, 1989).

Thumpston, Rebecca: 'The Embodiment of Yearning: Towards a Tripartite Theory of Musical Agency', in Costantino Maeder and Mark Reybrouck (eds.), *Music, Analysis, Experience* (Leuven: Leuven University Press, 2015), pp. 331–48.

Todd, R. Larry: 'On Quotation in Schumann's Music', in R. Larry Todd (ed.), *Schumann and His World* (Princeton: Princeton University Press, 1994), pp. 80–112.

Tunbridge, Laura: 'Robert Schumann's *Frauenleben*', in Emmanouil Perrakis (ed.), *Life as an Aesthetic Idea of Music* (Vienna: Universal Edition, 2019), pp. 45–62.

Tunbridge, Laura: 'Schumann's "Manfred" in the Mental Theatre', *Cambridge Opera Journal*, 15 (2003), 153–83.

Tunbridge, Laura: *Schumann's Late Style* (Cambridge: Cambridge University Press, 2007).

Turchin, Barbara: 'Robert Schumann's Song-Cycles in the Context of the Early Nineteenth-Century *Liederkreis*', PhD diss., Columbia University, 1981.

Turchin, Barbara: 'Schumann's Song Cycles: The Cycle within the Song', *19th-Century Music*, 8 (1985), 231–44.

Vermazen, Bruce: 'Expression as Expression', *Pacific Philosophical Quarterly*, 67 (1986), 196–223.

Wadsworth, Benjamin K.: 'Directional Tonality in Schumann's Early Works', *Music Theory Online*, 18/4 (2012).

Walsh, Stephen: *The Lieder of Schumann* (London: Cassell, 1971).

Wasielewski, Wilhelm Joseph von: *Robert Schumann: Eine Biographie* (1858; revised fourth edition, Leipzig: Breitkopf & Härtel, 1906), English trans. *Life of Robert Schumann*, trans. A. L. Alger (Boston: Oliver Ditson, 1871).

Watkins, Holly: *Metaphors of Depth in German Musical Thought: From E. T. A. Hoffmann to Arnold Schoenberg* (Cambridge: Cambridge University Press, 2011).

Watkins, Holly: *Musical Vitalities: Ventures in a Biotic Aesthetics of Music* (Chicago: Chicago University Press, 2018).

Weber, Carl Maria von: *Writings on Music*, trans. Martin Cooper, ed. John Warrack (Cambridge: Cambridge University Press, 1981).

Wendt, Matthias (ed.): *Schumann und seine Dichter* (Mainz: Schott, 1993).

Williams, Alastair: 'Swaying with Schumann: Subjectivity and Tradition in Wolfgang Rihm's "Fremde Szenen" I–III and Related Scores', *Music & Letters*, 87 (2006), 379–97.

Wölfel, Kurt: 'Schumanns Jean-Paul-Periode', in Matthias Wendt (ed.), *Schumann und seine Dichter* (Mainz: Schott, 1993), pp. 25–32.

Worthen, John: *Robert Schumann: Life and Death of a Musician* (New Haven: Yale University Press, 2007).

Zahavi, Dan: *Self-Awareness and Alterity: A Phenomenological Investigation* (Evanston, IL: Northwestern University Press, 1999).

Ziolkowski, Theodore: *German Romanticism and Its Institutions* (Princeton: Princeton University Press, 1990).

Žižek, Slavoj: 'Robert Schumann: The Romantic Anti-Humanist', in *The Plague of Fantasies* (London: Verso, 1997), pp. 192–212.

Index